Get a FREE eBook

To register this book, scan the code or go to
www.manning.com/freebook/gorshkova

By registering you get

- **FREE eBook copy**
  download in PDF and ePub

- **FREE online access**
  to Manning's liveBook platform

- **FREE audio**
  read and listen online in liveBook

- **FREE AI Assistant**
  it knows the book and what you are reading when it answers

- **FREE in-book testing**
  fun tests to lock in your knowledge

In Manning's liveBook platform you can share discussions and comments with other
readers, add your own bookmarks and highlights, insert personal notes anywhere
on the page, see color versions of all the book's graphics, download source code and
other resources, and more!
To register, scan the code or go to www.manning.com/freebook/gorshkova

---

MANNING

Kafka for Architects

EVENT-DRIVEN ARCHITECTURE, LOGS,
MICROSERVICES, REAL-TIME EVENT PROCESSING

KATYA GORSHKOVA

FOREWORD BY VIKTOR GAMOV

MANNING
SHELTER ISLAND

For online information and ordering of this and other Manning books, please visit www.manning.com. The publisher offers discounts on this book when ordered in quantity.

For more information, please contact

    Special Sales Department
    Manning Publications Co.
    20 Baldwin Road
    PO Box 761
    Shelter Island, NY 11964
    Email: orders@manning.com

Manning Publications Co.
20 Baldwin Road
PO Box 761
Shelter Island, NY 11964

Development editor:	Frances Lefkowitz
Technical editor:	Simeon Leyzerzon
Review editor:	Radmila Ercegovac
Production editor:	Kathy Rossland
Copy editor:	Andy Carroll
Proofreader:	Olga Milanko
Typesetter:	Tamara Švelić Sabljić
Cover designer:	Marija Tudor

ISBN 9781633436411

contents

2 Kafka cluster data architecture   24

3 Kafka clients and message production   54

6 Defining data contracts   146

7 Kafka interaction patterns   185

foreword

Even skilled software architects and development teams face challenges, such as scaling, updating data, and maintaining system stability. Kafka can help solve these complex problems, but it can feel like a powerful tool without enough instructions, so empathy and practical advice are essential. This is where Katya Gorshkova's book *Kafka for Architects* stands out.

With twenty years of experience as a software engineer and architect, and a gift for teaching even during tough times, Katya makes Kafka easy to understand and learn. She focuses on what architects care about most: big ideas, hard choices, and useful advice. The book takes you from the basics of EDA in chapter 1 through to real-world enterprise challenges, helping you feel confident using Kafka.

Katya is open about what Kafka is really like, talking about both its strengths and its delays and challenges, so readers feel understood. Chapters on data and practical patterns help teams avoid expensive mistakes. Other chapters give clear advice on governance and scaling, and her look at AI-powered streams helps readers feel confident about Kafka's future.

Many Kafka books focus on the step-by-step technical details. This book is different because it helps you see the big picture and make smart architectural choices. It stands out by guiding leaders to support EDA with a realistic approach, using real stories and showing both the pros and cons. After reading this book, you'll feel ready to build not just systems, but ecosystems that can grow and last.

Event-driven design shapes modern architecture. With Katya's guidance, Kafka becomes more than just a tool. It's a strategic foundation for the future!

—Viktor Gamov, Principal Developer Advocate, Confluent, coauthor of *Kafka in Action*

preface

One day, my team leader came to me with a simple question: "Hey, there's a new messaging system out there. Can you check if it could be useful for us?" That was how my journey with Apache Kafka began.

At first glance, Kafka's architecture felt clean and elegant. But implementing that first project was anything but seamless. It was too distributed, too low-level, and it lacked the tooling we take for granted today. I quickly learned that while Kafka had immense potential, it also demanded a deeper understanding than most systems I had worked with before.

The next chapter in my relationship with Kafka began when I was asked to create a course explaining its concepts. Teaching forced me to find clear ways to communicate the ideas behind event-driven architecture—not just how Kafka works, but how to think about it. And I discovered that most people weren't as interested in the implementation details as they were in the bigger question: *How can we incorporate Kafka into our project?*

The Kafka community has done a great job of building documentation, but most tutorials stop at "how to get Kafka running." Very few address the harder questions: *Should we even use Kafka for this project? How can we fit it into our existing architecture? What patterns will help us design Kafka systems that stand the test of time?* When I started, answers to these questions were scattered, incomplete, or hard-won through trial and error.

I kept encountering the same challenges over and over again—how to model events effectively, how to evolve schemas safely, how to balance throughput, ordering guarantees, and fault tolerance without overengineering, and, when something went wrong, how to trace responsibility and find the root cause.

Kafka for Architects grew out of those experiences. Its goal is to explore the questions that are often left untouched—the ones that sit between "Kafka is installed" and "Kafka is delivering real business value." It's about design decisions, trade-offs, and the mental models that guide successful implementations.

If you're holding this book, you've probably already decided that Kafka could play a role in your systems. My hope is that the following pages will help you not only make it work, but make it work well—for your architecture, your team, and the years ahead.

acknowledgments

I never intended to write a book—it happened all of a sudden. I set out on this journey without any idea of what lay ahead. It turned out to be a much longer road than it first appeared, and I am deeply grateful to my family and colleagues who supported me throughout.

I would like to thank all the contributors to the Apache Kafka project for creating such powerful tools and making them open source. *Kafka for Architects* wouldn't exist without your work.

Many thanks to the participants of my training sessions. You often stopped me from explaining what could be easily found in the documentation and instead asked how things really work. Your questions shaped this book—it is, in many ways, a collection of answers to your curiosity. You all deserve co-author credit.

I am deeply grateful to my family for their patience and love during this journey. I especially thank Stanislav for his continuous encouragement, Anna for helping me with the graphics, and my dog Artie for calmly waiting until I finished writing before taking him for a walk.

I am also thankful to my dear friends and colleagues for our endless discussions. I especially want to thank Peter Vašek, my earliest reviewer, for tirelessly reading and commenting on the manuscript again and again (and again). My special thanks go to Daniel Buchta, whose help in transforming my documentation-style drafts into readable content made this book accessible to a much wider audience.

I want to express my deep gratitude to Professor Boris Novikov from the University of Saint Petersburg, who believed in me from the very beginning. His early support and guidance played a significant role in shaping me into the professional I am today.

Thank you to my editors: development editor Frances Lefkowitz, for persistently challenging me to explain complex ideas clearly, and technical editor Simeon Leyzerzon, whose contributions to the content were invaluable. Simeon is a seasoned IT professional with over three decades of experience in software development and architecture. He excels in seamlessly integrating Kafka and other middleware solutions to develop high-performing, scalable enterprise applications, addressing complex technical challenges with creativity and precision.

Finally, to all the reviewers—Amarjit Bhandal, Afzal Mazhar, Alessandro Campeis, Bassam Ismail, Christoph Kappel, Danica Fine, Dinesh Reddy Chittibala, Erin Colvin, Francisco Lopez-Sancho Abraham, George Haines, Giuseppe Catalano, Israel Ekpo, James Black, Jeff Patterson, Karol Skorek, Krishna Kumaar, Mandar Kulkarni, Michael Williams, Mohammad Shahnawaz Akhter, Monika Rathor, Nathan B. Crocker, Nuwan Dias, Oscar Caraballo, Paul Grebenc, Pradeep Kumar Goudagunta, Rajiv Moghe, Ralph M. Debusmann, Richard Jepps, Sachin Handiekar, Sandhya Vinjam, Shay Elkin, Srinath Chandramohan, Sunil Murali, Swapneelkumar Deshpande, and Vlad Bezden—your suggestions helped make this a better book.

about this book

An architect's role involves choosing how systems communicate, and one proven method for coordinating distributed work is through events. Several technologies exist, each with trade-offs in reliability, flexibility, and integration complexity. Apache Kafka is a widely adopted, open source event-streaming platform that started as a messaging system and has grown into an ecosystem for real-time processing, backed by durable event storage. But while Kafka is powerful, its adoption isn't straightforward. Most tutorials and books focus on code and configuration, neglecting architectural and design questions crucial for success. This book fills that gap by focusing on architectural choices—fit, event design, patterns, and governance—ensuring deliberate Kafka adoption.

Who should read this book

Kafka for Architects is for software architects, technical leads, and developers who need to understand Kafka at a system level—how it operates and how to fit it into broader architectures. You do not need to know any specific programming language or technology stack to benefit from this book, but a basic grasp of distributed systems concepts, general architecture principles, and some experience delivering enterprise projects will be helpful.

My goal is to equip you with the insight to evaluate Kafka's role in your architecture, make informed trade-offs, and design solutions that last, regardless of the tools or languages you use.

How this book is organized: A road map

This book begins by introducing the main concepts and ideas that underpin Apache Kafka, and it's divided into three parts.

Part 1 (chapters 1–4) provides a foundational understanding: the key architectural principles, the organization of a Kafka cluster, and a detailed exploration of how producing and consuming messages work. These chapters also cover how Kafka fits into the broader ecosystem, giving you the context needed to reason about it as part of a larger system.

With this groundwork in place, part 2 (chapters 5–8) moves into applied architecture. Here, we'll explore real-world use cases, strategies for defining and managing data contracts, and architectural patterns (and anti-patterns) for integrating Kafka into diverse environments.

After exploring how Kafka is applied across various architectures, chapter 8 shifts focus to one of its most impactful uses—processing data in real time. This chapter discusses data transformation with Kafka Streams and other technologies designed to handle information in motion.

Part 3 (chapters 9–12) starts with the organizational and operational aspects of running Kafka and concludes with a look at emerging trends and the future of the platform. Chapter 9 discusses how to integrate Kafka into the enterprise infrastructure, chapter 10 covers organizing and managing Kafka projects, and chapter 11 dives into day-to-day operations, maintenance, and monitoring. Chapter 12 concludes the book by exploring emerging trends, upcoming features, and possible directions for Kafka's future.

liveBook discussion forum

Purchase of *Kafka for Architects* includes free access to liveBook, Manning's online reading platform. Using liveBook's exclusive discussion features, you can attach comments to the book globally or to specific sections or paragraphs. It's a snap to make notes for yourself, ask and answer technical questions, and receive help from the author and other users. To access the forum, go to https://livebook.manning.com/book/kafka-for-architects/discussion.

Manning's commitment to our readers is to provide a venue where a meaningful dialogue between individual readers and between readers and the author can take place. It is not a commitment to any specific amount of participation on the part of the author, whose contribution to the forum remains voluntary (and unpaid). We suggest you try asking the author some challenging questions lest her interest stray! The forum and the archives of previous discussions will be accessible from the publisher's website as long as the book is in print.

about the author

EKATERINA GORSHKOVA graduated from the University of Saint Petersburg with a degree in Applied Mathematics but shifted her focus to software engineering early in her career. Starting as a Junior Software Engineer, she specialized in the Java stack and data-intensive applications. She later pursued a PhD in Computer Science and moved to the Czech Republic.

Katya has extensive experience in the FinTech sector, serving as both a Software Engineer and a Solution Architect. About seven years ago, she developed a proof-of-concept project using Apache Kafka, sparking a deep passion for the technology. This led her to become a Kafka engineer, providing consultancy services for messaging systems architecture and developing applications for real-time data processing.

about the cover illustration

The figure on the cover of *Kafka for Architects* is "Il Galantariaro," or "a petty trader," taken from *Usi e Costumi di Napoli e Contorni Descritti e Dipinti* by Francesco de Bourcard, published in 1853. Each illustration is finely drawn and colored by hand.

In those days, it was easy to identify where people lived and what their trade or station in life was just by their dress. Manning celebrates the inventiveness and initiative of the computer business with book covers based on the rich diversity of regional culture centuries ago, brought back to life by pictures from collections such as this one.

Part 1

Exploring Kafka building blocks

Kafka's architecture is the outcome of intentional design decisions that balance scalability, reliability, and simplicity. In this part of the book, we'll uncover how Kafka really works and why those choices matter for architects.

In chapter 1, we'll discuss Kafka from a high-level architectural perspective, looking at its design principles, ecosystem components, and how it shapes enterprise architecture. Chapter 2 dives into the internals of the Kafka cluster, examining its structure and the role of topics and partitions and showing how configuration settings influence system behavior. We'll then turn to Kafka clients: chapter 3 explores producers, with strategies for partitioning, acknowledgments, and batching, while chapter 4 focuses on consumers, highlighting how they subscribe, manage offsets, and rebalance to ensure reliable processing at scale.

Getting to know Kafka
as an architect

This chapter covers

- Principles of event-driven architecture
- Overview of the Kafka ecosystem
- Utilizing Kafka in enterprise environments

Apache Kafka has grown from a high-throughput messaging system into a critical component of modern data architectures. The Kafka ecosystem now powers event-driven systems, large-scale data pipelines, and real-time analytics. It is a widely adopted, open-source streaming platform and its capabilities are impressive. But making the most of Kafka requires more than just getting it to run—it demands thoughtful architectural design.

Kafka plays a crucial role because it bridges the gap between event and action: producers publish once, and many consumers react, with Kafka providing low latency. That decoupling enables business systems to respond to events quickly and without brittle point-to-point integrations. Consider real-time order processing in e-commerce, for instance, where one event, a customer placing an order, gets published to a service, and many independent consumers—such as inventory, payment, shipping, and analytics—react in real time without any direct integrations. Kafka's strength lies in enabling real-time event processing, which has become a business imperative across industries, especially in critical functions where delays mean lost value—like fraud detection, personalized recommendations, and predictive maintenance.

To decide if Kafka is right for a project, and then to make the most of it, architects, engineers, tech leads, and even managers need to know how Kafka works, why it behaves the way it does, and how they can design systems that take full advantage of its strengths. That is what we'll examine in this book. We'll address the architectural questions that determine whether Kafka will bring long-term value, exploring its advantages and risks, as well as patterns and anti-patterns observed in real-world systems. You will find discussions on event modeling, schema evolution, integration strategies, and the trade-offs between performance, ordering, and fault tolerance. What you won't find is a lot of code showing you how to write Kafka applications or exploring client APIs in detail. Here, we are focused on the big-picture decisions that influence the design, architecture, and sustainability of distributed systems.

1.1 How an architect sees Kafka

In the past, when a new business requirement for systems integration arose, teams would typically create a new service. The architects had to decide how this service would talk to other services. Typically, communication was synchronous, and each service handled a specific business task.

For instance, a microservice dedicated to processing orders placed through the website might need the customer's shipping address, which was provided by another service. The typical approach for services was to communicate directly and synchronously via HTTP. In this setup, each time an order was placed, the OrderService would send a request to the CustomerService with the customer identifier, and it would receive the address in the response. This process is illustrated in figure 1.1.

Whenever an order is placed, the OrderService
requests the customer's address by providing
the customer identifier.

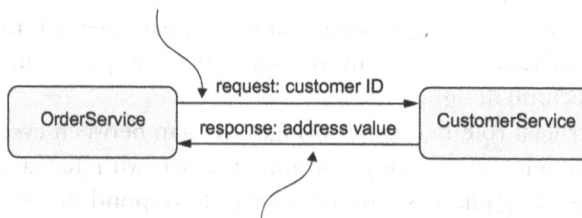

request: customer ID

OrderService   CustomerService

response: address value

CustomerService processes the request and
returns the address value in the response.

Figure 1.1
Request-response
design pattern

These architectural styles—with *Representational State Transfer* (REST) being the most popular—are straightforward, well-documented, and supported by a variety of tools.

However, for many scenarios, REST no longer meets business requirements. Using multiple synchronous calls to implement workflows can lead to potential difficulties with coordination, consistency, and resilience—especially in REST, where chained dependencies increase fragility and the risk of cascading failures. Project requirements now call for more flexible system interactions that allow each component to respond to events independently, thereby enhancing autonomy.

Event-driven architecture (EDA) reduces this coupling but does not eliminate consistency concerns; they shift toward managing eventual consistency, idempotency, and out-of-order events. Let's explore the concepts behind EDA and how they can be implemented with the assistance of Kafka.

1.1.1 Event-driven architecture

Nowadays, more companies are embracing EDA. Instead of using the traditional request-response approach, we now rely on events to let us know when something happens in the system. When an event of interest occurs, the system sends a notification message to an intermediary channel. Later, another system consumes the message from this channel and processes it independently.

EDA is a design pattern in which the production, detection, consumption, and reaction to events play a central role in the architecture. Kafka is a distributed streaming platform ideally suited for implementing EDA.

Following on from our example in figure 1.1, we no longer make direct calls to `CustomerService`. Instead, our `OrderService` listens to notifications. Whenever the address changes, it receives an event and stores the data locally on its side. This style of communication is shown in figure 1.2.

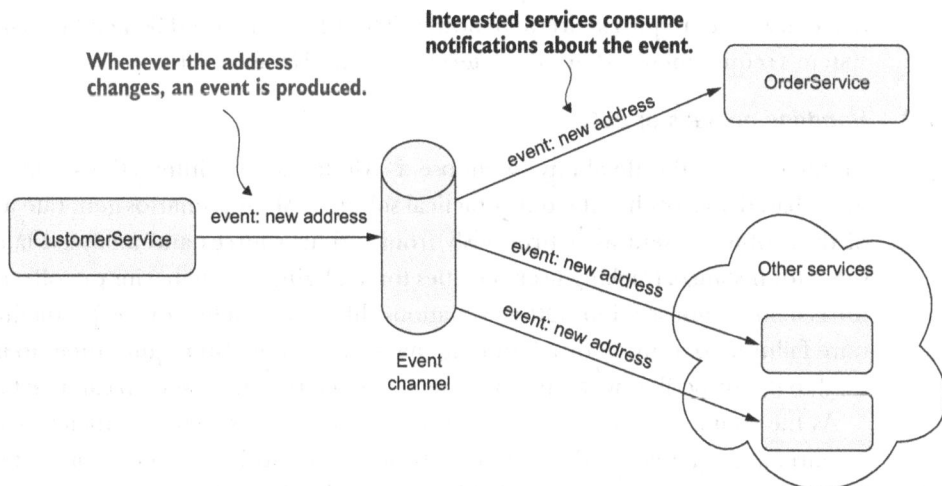

Figure 1.2 The EDA style of communication: systems communicate by publishing events that describe changes, allowing others to react asynchronously.

In EDA, multiple services often express interest in a particular event. The event containing the new address data can be broadcasted to every service that wishes to be informed about this change. These subscribed services can dynamically appear or disappear, and the system can readily adapt to these fluctuations.

One advantage of the event-driven style is its ability to accommodate systems that may not always be up and running. To ensure robust communication, messages are sent asynchronously, assuming that the recipient might not be online at the time. This asynchronous communication must be reliable, ensuring that messages are not lost and can be processed later. Consequently, the senders and receivers are entirely decoupled, allowing them to function independently without being aware of each other. This decoupling enhances system flexibility, scalability, and resilience, as each component can evolve or scale without impacting others.

For instance, if the `OrderService` is temporarily unavailable, it will receive the address notification from the channel once it is back online. On the other hand, if the `CustomerService` experiences downtime, it won't impact the `OrderService`, because the latter has copies of the data stored locally.

But what about data consistency? When systems communicate through events, there's a delay between when the address is updated and when the new address is received by the `OrderService`. This delay introduces the concept of *eventual consistency*, meaning that different parts of the system may temporarily be in different states until all events are fully processed. This leads to further questions: Could the order be sent to the old address? Can we ensure that events arrive in the correct order on our event channel? Could the same message be processed multiple times?

The EDA style comes with its own set of trade-offs, which the architect must carefully consider. Latency and higher operational overhead are common challenges, and eventual consistency requires careful handling. These factors should be weighed against the system's requirements when you determine if EDA is the right fit.

1.1.2   *Handling myriads of data*

Architects have the flexibility to choose a style for service interactions, but often an event-based approach is the only practical solution. Many scenarios generate a volume of data, which is sent asynchronously from various sources and analyzed later. Consider, for instance, tracking user activities for analyzing user behavior or collecting logs for system administration. Other situations, like fraud detection or predicting hardware failure, not only involve handling many events but also require them to be delivered to the subscriber with minimal latency so that the target system can react in time.

As the volume of data grows, event processing systems excel at efficiently utilizing resources, guaranteeing the required throughput and low latency. For an architect, Kafka represents a robust and reliable solution that helps them organize communications between services in an event-driven manner and handle high-rate message communications efficiently.

1.2 *Field notes: Journey of an event-driven project*

Throughout this book, we'll follow a fictional company called Northwind Insurance, a mid-sized insurer operating across several regions. Over the years, its internal systems have become increasingly fragmented—policy management, claims processing, and customer service each run on separate, aging platforms. The company's leadership has noticed growing inefficiencies: delays in claim updates, inconsistent customer data, and difficulties integrating new digital services. These "Field notes" sidebars capture moments from Northwind's internal discussions as the engineering team works to modernize their systems and address these challenges by creating a new *operational data store* (ODS)

The stage is set for a paradigm shift as the team contemplates the potential of an event-driven architecture, with Kafka at its core, for their transformative ODS. The journey into a new era of data processing begins.

Field Notes: Creating a new ODS from scratch

Max Sellington, the account manager, enters the meeting room, greeting Rob Routine, the lead architect, and Eva Catalyst, the senior data engineer.

Rob: What news do you have for us, Max?

Max: Got a bunch of change requests for the warehouse.

Rob: Let me guess. Pipeline performance, reconciliations of complex queries, and so on. I'm tired of this routine.

Max: Then, you're on the same page as them, Rob. They insist that with all the upgrades, the warehouse should perform at least as fast as it did a couple of years ago.

Rob: But we've done everything right. Automation, monitoring, the warehouse methodology—all up to date. They agreed to all of it. It's the best data processing platform I've ever seen.

Max: They argue that 14 hours for the overnight batch is too much. I understand their frustration—the aggregated results arrive in the afternoon, making the data appear outdated or inconsistent.

Rob: But how can we speed it up when the data volume has increased by more than five times in the last couple of years? And the data quality in the source systems is abysmal. Do you agree, Eva?

Eva starts to respond, but Max interrupts.

Max: Anyway, that's not the big news. They also want something new—an operational data store called the Customer 360 project. Customer 360 aims to provide a comprehensive view of each customer by consolidating data from various touchpoints and interactions. They want insights into customer profiles and their relationship with the company. Business and marketing are fully on board. The expectations are sky-high.

(continued)

Rob: That will only add to the complexity. They'll need new hardware.

Max: They want to go cloud-based, Rob. And we need this project. I'll send you the RFP.

Eva (finally getting a word in): I have some thoughts on all this but let me switch to presentation mode.

She clicks a button, and an article appears on their screens, starting with, "If you're tired of dealing with the complexity and inflexibility of traditional request-response architectures, it might be time to consider event-driven architecture."

Max reads the first paragraph but remains skeptical.

Max: Sounds like a lot of buzzwords. How exactly is it faster than the warehouse. What do we gain?

Eva: Think events first. Kafka gives us low-latency fan-out and a durable event log. Customer 360 subscribes to the stream and builds whatever projections it needs. I'm wondering how Customer 360 could look with Kafka. I'd like to prepare something. Can I present it at our next meeting?

Rob: Oh, come on, Eva . . .

Max: Please, Rob. We need to pivot. Eva, if it brings us the project, and the estimates are at least on par with the traditional approach, I'm willing to consider it. Let's at least try it out.

1.3 Key players in the Kafka ecosystem

Sometimes the best solution to multiple problems (as in the "Field notes" sidebar) is not to address each problem individually, but to introduce a whole new system. A radical decision like this comes with costs, of course, so it's important to understand as much about the new system as possible—*before* you implement it.

Let's look first at Kafka's components from a high-level perspective. Currently, Kafka positions itself as a distributed platform for processing real-time events. Throughout this book, we'll explore various ways to work with Kafka. However, it's essential to keep Kafka's roots as a message broker in mind—regardless of its various applications, the core function of transporting messages lies at the heart of all Kafka's use cases.

1.3.1 Brokers and clients

The central component of the Kafka platform is a cluster of message *brokers*. When systems communicate through messages, they don't interact directly but instead exchange information through an intermediary point. Applications that interact with brokers are called *clients*. A client can either send messages to Kafka as a producer or receive them as a consumer. The key components of the Kafka ecosystem—producers, brokers, and consumers—are depicted in figure 1.3.

Message brokers operate within a cluster, distributing messages from producers to consumers.

Kafka cluster

Producer app — Kafka broker — Kafka broker — Consumer app

Producer app — Kafka broker — Consumer app

Producers are responsible for sending messages to the brokers.

Consumers are responsible for reading messages from the brokers.

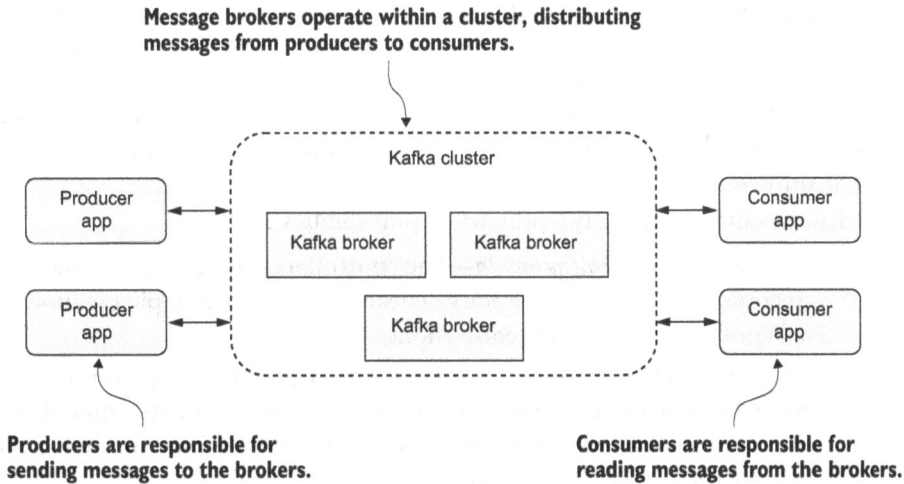

Figure 1.3 The key components in the Kafka ecosystem are producers, brokers, and consumers.

Producers are applications responsible for sending (pushing) messages to the message brokers. The *message brokers* play a key role in message processing and persistence. Their primary responsibilities include notifying the producer when a message has been successfully delivered, ensuring the message's reliable storage, and making it available for consumers. Message brokers operate in a fault-tolerant cluster, distributing workloads and ensuring cluster health through regular heartbeat reports. Finally, the *consumers* read messages from the brokers. Kafka operates on a pull-based model, which means that consumers need to actively subscribe to specific topics and request messages. It's important to note that an application can act as both a producer and a consumer, allowing it to send and receive messages within the same system.

In Kafka, messages are always persistent and are initially stored on durable local storage. It is also possible to use tiered storage, so that older data can be offloaded to slower, cost-effective storage tiers, while recent data remains on faster, local storage.

1.3.2 Controllers: Managing cluster metadata

To ensure high availability, we need to have a cluster of brokers with a control plane that maintains the cluster structure. We need, for instance, a way to detect if one of the brokers has failed and become unavailable.

In Kafka, a controller within the cluster manages metadata and coordinates broker operations. Servers, within a Kafka cluster, can play two roles: they can act as brokers (as we've discussed) interacting with clients and handling tasks such as message processing, storage, and replication, or they can act as *controllers*, coordinating cluster activities, monitoring broker health, and managing cluster metadata. A server can even take on both roles, depending on the cluster's specific configuration and requirements.

Kafka controllers are often called *KRaft controllers* because they implement the KRaft protocol—a specialized protocol for managing metadata and coordinating activities within the Kafka cluster. Among the controllers, one is designated as the active controller, while the others remain in a hot standby state, ready to take over if the active controller fails. In the event of a failure, a new active controller is elected from the pool of healthy controllers.

KRaft controllers have two primary responsibilities:

- *Storing and replicating metadata*—The controllers manage the metadata log, which records all changes to the Kafka cluster state, such as topic creation, partition assignments, and broker registrations.
- *Detecting broker failures*—Each broker in the cluster regularly sends heartbeat messages to the active controller to indicate it is healthy and operational. If a broker does not send a heartbeat within a defined timeout, it is considered failed and may be removed from the cluster.

An example Kafka cluster setup is shown in figure 1.4.

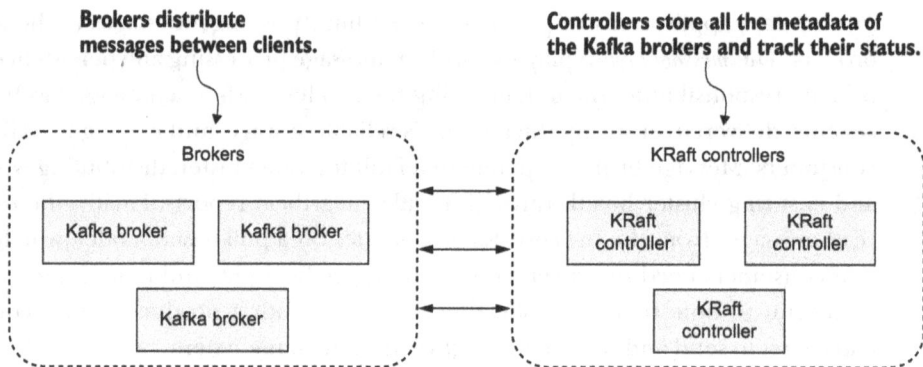

Figure 1.4   Structure of a Kafka cluster: brokers handle client traffic; KRaft controllers manage metadata and coordination.

1.4   *Applying Kafka's architectural principles*

When designing enterprise systems around events, messaging platforms often provide the backbone for communication. Over the decades, many such systems have emerged—each offering its own balance of scalability, reliability, and fault tolerance.

In this book, our focus is on building architectures with Apache Kafka. Kafka is more than just another messaging system—it introduces a unique set of design principles that shape how systems communicate, store, and react to data.

Let's explore the principles that make Kafka Kafka—the ideas that define its architecture and influence how it's applied in real-world enterprise solutions.

1.4.1 The publish-subscribe pattern

Kafka implements a publish-subscribe pattern. Producers, also known as *publishers*, send messages in a "fire-and-forget" manner, optionally receiving acknowledgment about delivery, and they are typically unaware of the consumers, who are referred to as *subscribers*. Each message can be received by several consumers, each processing it independently.

Returning to our example from section 1.1, when a customer changes their address, `CustomerService` stores the new address value in the database and sends a notification about the change. In this case, the microservice acts as a producer, and all applications interested in receiving this notification must subscribe to this type of event. For example, a `BillingService`, which handles payments, an `AnalyticalService`, which creates various reports, and an `OrderService`, which needs accurate delivery information could all subscribe to the events published by `CustomerService`, and each would receive the messages with the new address. This scenario is illustrated in figure 1.5.

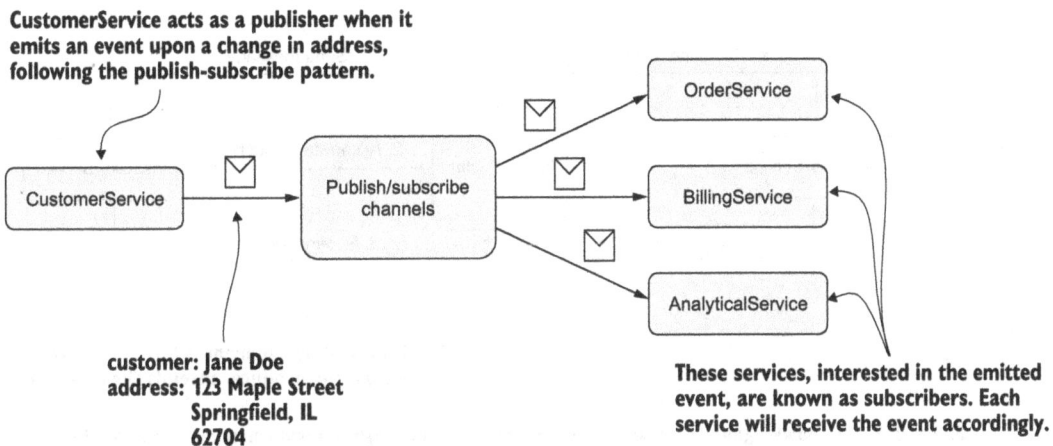

Figure 1.5 Publish-subscribe example: `CustomerService` publishes a "customer updated" event to a channel; all subscribers receive it independently.

If producers and consumers are unaware of each other, how does the producer know which events are of interest to other services? Usually, within a corporate setting, producers don't indiscriminately broadcast events; instead, they respond to explicit business requirements that dictate which notifications a consumer needs, thereby informing the producer what to emit. The potential consumers of an event are known. However, since the producer owns the data, it is responsible for the event structure, and it strives to make these notifications reusable.

Questions regarding data governance—specifically, where all these event pipelines are stored—are crucial, and we'll explore them in chapter 6.

1.4.2   *Reliable delivery*

The fundamental feature of Kafka is the reliable delivery of messages. To ensure this reliability, Kafka needs a cluster of servers, meaning that several message brokers will cooperate. Messages are replicated between the brokers so that there are always multiple copies of the messages, allowing the cluster to survive a server failure.

To ensure reliable message delivery, the Kafka cluster works closely with clients (both producers and consumers) to prevent message loss between the producer and the broker, to preserve messages, even in the event of broker failures, and to ensure message delivery to consumers, even if they experience temporary disconnections.

When a producer sends a message to Kafka, it awaits acknowledgment from the broker confirming successful message delivery. If the acknowledgment is not received, the producer retransmits the message. This process is depicted in figure 1.6.

The producer sends a message and waits for an acknowledgment from the cluster.

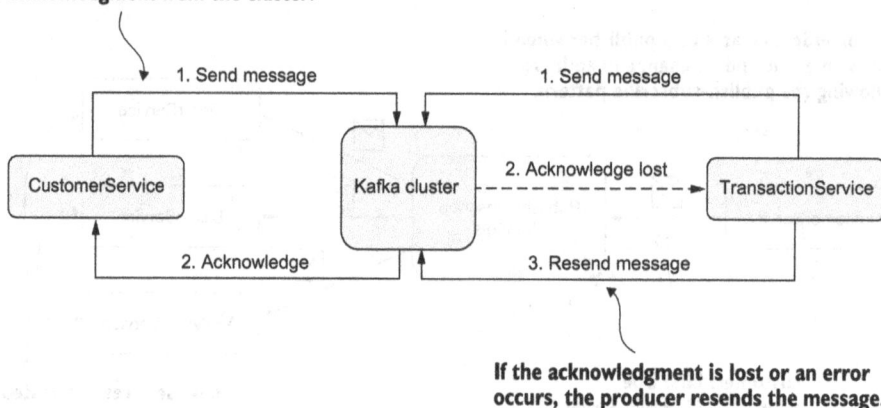

Figure 1.6   Acknowledgments: once the cluster accepts a message, it sends an acknowledgment to the service. If no acknowledgment arrives within the timeout, the service treats the send as failed and retries.

> **NOTE** In chapters 3 and 4, we'll look at various configuration settings on the client side and explore how to strike a balance between performance and reliability. We'll also cover some of the tricky aspects of working with producers and consumers, delving into best practices and potential pitfalls.

In Kafka, messages are persistent, which means they are stored on the brokers in the cluster. Kafka replicates messages between brokers, ensuring fault tolerance even if a node goes down. In the case of a broker failure, other brokers in the cluster take responsibility for the messages stored on the failed instance.

In cases of consumer failure, it is crucial that they receive all messages, including those sent while they were disconnected. Kafka tracks the messages that have been read and acknowledged by consumers. When a consumer reconnects after a failure, it resumes processing undelivered messages. Additionally, Kafka implements a feature often referred to as "replaying," where consumers can re-read stored messages from Kafka and reprocess them as needed—either after a failure or by design. The messages are stored for a specified retention period.

1.4.3 The commit log

One of Kafka's most powerful architectural concepts is the *commit log*. It's a familiar idea in the database world, where systems record every change before applying it to tables, ensuring durability and traceability. Kafka applies this same principle to messaging.

> **NOTE** In a database, a "commit" finalizes a transaction—changes are saved and become visible. In Kafka, the term "commit" usually means either that the cluster is confirming it has safely stored the messages you sent, or that a consumer has processed those messages and moved past them.

When a message arrives at a broker, it is appended to the end of a log file. This arrangement ensures that messages are recorded in the order they arrive, preserving their sequence. To go back to our example of updating addresses, each notification of a new address is appended in sequence, forming a log of changes. Consumers can replay this log to reconstruct the current state.

Kafka messages are immutable—they cannot be changed or removed individually. Instead, messages remain available for a period defined by the system's retention settings. If a service sends incorrect data, it cannot delete or overwrite the message; the only way to correct it is to send a new one.

1.5 Designing and managing data flows

Kafka is well-suited as a backbone for microservice communication. But in event-driven architectures, the focus often shifts from services to the data itself. Instead of calling APIs, we emit and react to data as messages whose structure and meaning act as a contract between systems. This shift requires us to treat data as a first-class citizen—something that must be modeled, validated, versioned, and understood across service boundaries.

This leads to deeper questions:

- What guarantees do we make about the structure of the messages?
- How do producers and consumers stay in sync as messages evolve?
- Can we use Kafka not just to emit events, but to replicate data between systems at scale?
- When a message needs to be transformed, where should that transformation happen?

These questions go beyond simple messaging. They touch on integration, schema governance, and stream processing—all of which are crucial for building robust Kafka-based systems.

That's where Schema Registry, Kafka Connect, and streaming frameworks come into play. Together, they form a supporting trio that helps you define data structures, move data between systems, and transform it as it flows through your architecture. We'll look at each briefly here and explore them in more depth in later chapters.

1.5.1 Schema Registry: Handling data contracts

Kafka's ability to efficiently handle high volumes of messages stems from a key architectural choice: Kafka brokers don't look inside messages. They treat each one as an opaque array of bytes—storing it as-is and passing it along to consumers without deserialization or interpretation.

This design keeps Kafka fast and flexible, but it also means that Kafka itself doesn't enforce structure. If producers and consumers need to agree on what a message contains—a common need in distributed systems—that structure must be defined and managed elsewhere.

That's where the schema registry comes in. A *schema registry* is a companion service in the Kafka ecosystem, designed to store and manage data schemas—formal definitions of what particular message types look like. It acts as a central source of truth for producers and consumers who want to share structured data without hard dependencies. While there are several implementations of schema registries, this book primarily refers to the Confluent Schema Registry, as it is the most widely used and best integrated with Kafka. Figure 1.7 shows how it works.

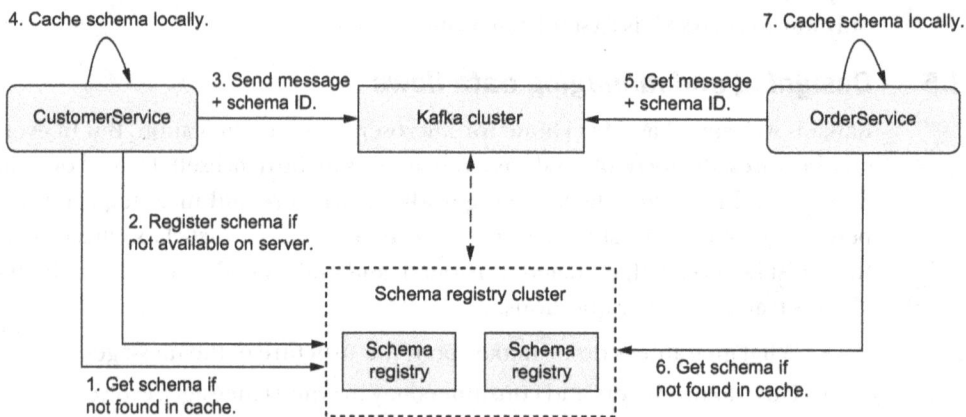

Figure 1.7 Working with Schema Registry: schemas are managed by a separate Schema Registry cluster; messages carry only a schema ID, which clients use to fetch (and cache) the writer schema.

As you can see, when a producer sends a message, it checks to see if the schema is already registered. If it's new, the schema is uploaded to the registry and is assigned a unique identifier. That identifier is embedded in the message. The consumer then uses the ID to retrieve the schema from the registry and deserializes the message accurately.

Because schemas are immutable, they can be safely cached and reused. When changes are needed, a new version must be registered—Kafka's schema registry supports versioning and compatibility checks to ensure that evolving data models don't break existing consumers.

We'll explore schema design, versioning strategies, and compatibility rules in detail in chapter 6, but throughout the book, we'll also return to key questions architects must ask:

- Who owns the definition of each message?
- How granular should events be?
- What happens when contracts evolve?
- How do teams stay aligned as schemas change?

Schema Registry helps answer these questions—but using it effectively requires thinking about data contracts not just as implementation details, but also as architectural building blocks.

While Schema Registry focuses on ensuring that messages have predictable structures, Kafka Connect addresses another critical challenge in event-driven systems: moving large volumes of data between Kafka and external systems.

1.5.2 Kafka Connect: Data replication without code

When teams first explore Kafka, they often begin with a simple proof of concept: a producer sends notifications when local database data changes, and a consumer picks up those messages and writes them to its own store. As more services follow this pattern, custom logic tends to grow, and so does the complexity.

But do these notifications always need to be coded into each application? Take our earlier example. If CustomerService stores addresses in a database, and OrderService needs to consume updates, do we really have to build a producer and consumer just to keep the two in sync? Or is there a more automated way to move data from one system to another?

That's where Kafka Connect comes in. As shown in figure 1.8, it represents a powerful architectural option: integrating systems through configuration, not code. *Kafka Connect* is a framework for replicating data between Kafka and external systems—such as databases, data warehouses, or cloud storage—without writing custom code. It runs as a separate cluster and uses connector plugins (Java libraries specific to external systems), from which connectors (instances with specific configurations) are created. These plugins act as adapters, enabling Kafka to either pull data from a source system or push data to a target system.

A wide selection of plugins—both open source and commercial—are available on the Confluent Hub (www.confluent.io/hub). Once a plugin is installed, you can create and configure one or more connectors, each representing a specific data pipeline between Kafka and an external source or *sink*.

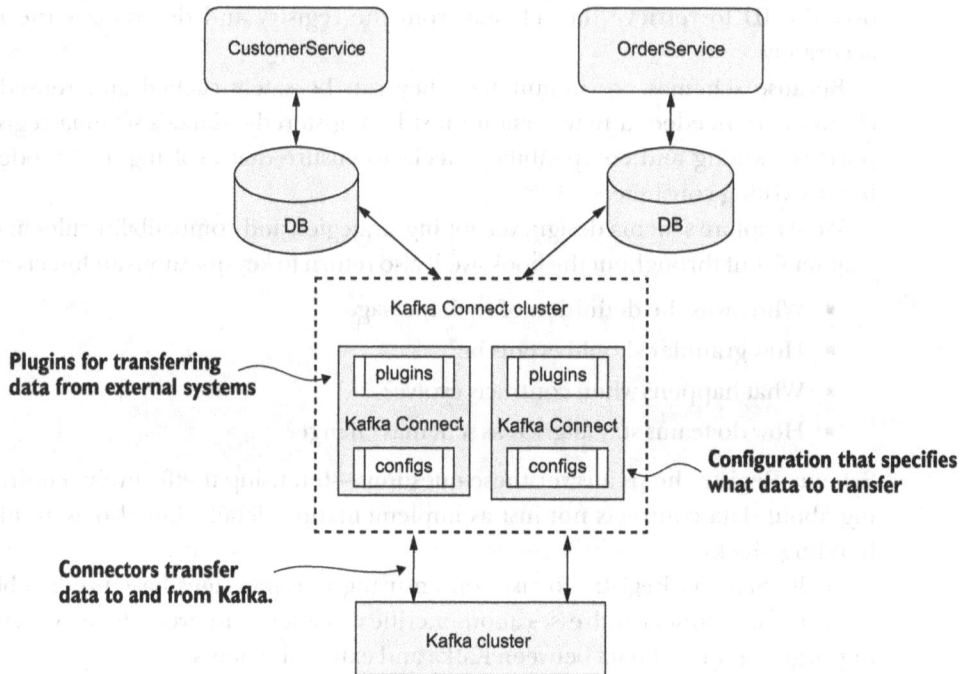

Figure 1.8   The Kafka Connect architecture: connectors integrate Kafka with external systems, moving data in and out.

In our case, we could do the following:

- Use a source connector (based on the JDBC source plugin) to stream address changes from the CustomerService database into Kafka.
- Use a sink connector to push those updates from Kafka into OrderService's database.

This approach avoids writing custom producer and consumer code, relying instead on Kafka Connect's configuration-driven pipelines.

We'll explore this in more depth in chapter 7, including the operational concerns and design patterns.

1.5.3   *Streaming frameworks: Processing data in real time*

In the publish-subscribe pattern, multiple consumers receive the same event, but they may not all need it in the same form. A common question in event-driven architecture is where and how to transform messages so they're useful to different services.

You might start with simple transformations. Kafka Connect, for example, supports basic stateless operations—like renaming fields or filtering values—during data transfer. But Connect has limits: it can't perform complex logic or transformations that depend on previous events or external context.

Suppose `CustomerService` emits address change events. Both `BillingService` and `OrderService` consume them, but with different needs: one wants billing address updates, and the other only cares about shipping changes. Kafka brokers can't help here—they don't inspect message content. So where should the logic live?

You have several options:

- *In the producer*—`CustomerService` could send two different messages to two topics, but that adds complexity to upstream logic.
- *In each consumer*—Every service could filter the messages it receives—but that's inefficient because many services must handle irrelevant data.
- *In a processing layer*—A standalone service could read the raw event, apply routing logic, and publish tailored messages to downstream topics.

This is where stream processing frameworks come in. An example of a streaming application, `RoutingService`, is shown in figure 1.9.

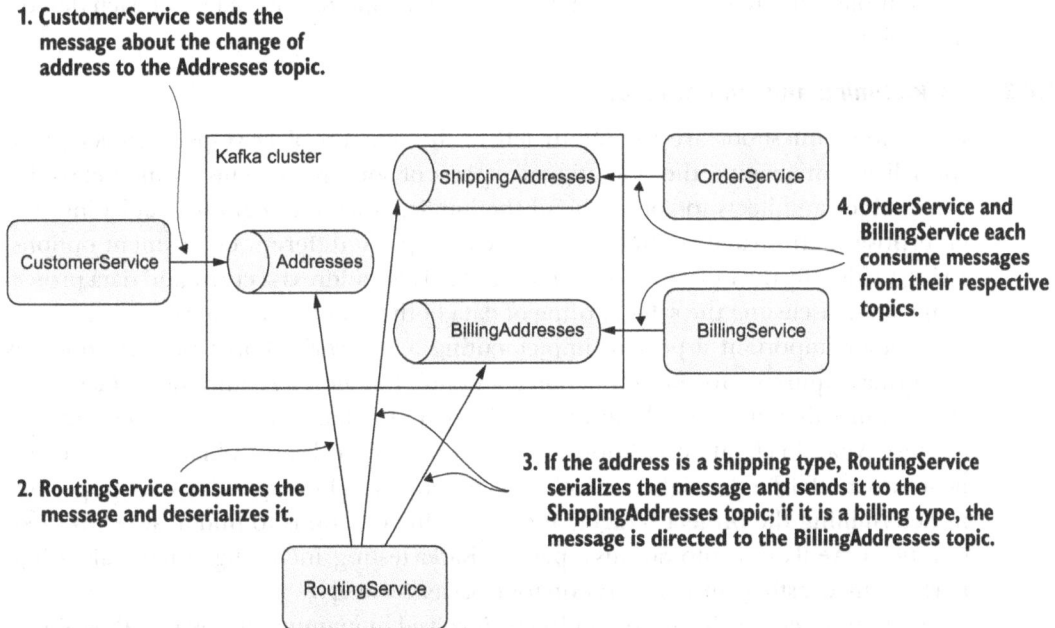

1. CustomerService sends the message about the change of address to the Addresses topic.

Kafka cluster

CustomerService → Addresses

ShippingAddresses ← OrderService

BillingAddresses ← BillingService

4. OrderService and BillingService each consume messages from their respective topics.

2. RoutingService consumes the message and deserializes it.

3. If the address is a shipping type, RoutingService serializes the message and sends it to the ShippingAddresses topic; if it is a billing type, the message is directed to the BillingAddresses topic.

RoutingService

Figure 1.9　An example of a streaming application. `RoutingService` **implements content-based routing, consuming messages from** Addresses **and, based on their contents (e.g., address type), publishing them to** ShippingAddresses **or** BillingAddresses**.**

Frameworks like Kafka Streams and Apache Flink help you build applications that consume, transform, and re-emit data, whether you're filtering, aggregating, joining, or maintaining state across time windows. These tools integrate directly with Kafka and support exactly-once semantics, making them well-suited for everything from simple routing logic to complex event pattern detection.

We'll explore these frameworks and their architectural patterns in chapter 8. For now, what matters is this: Kafka isn't just about moving events—it's about shaping them into something meaningful, at the right place in the pipeline.

1.6 Addressing operations and infrastructure

When architects design a system, they must find a solution that not only meets functional requirements but also ensures operability, supportability, and maintainability throughout its lifecycle. Efficient operational and support practices are vital for ensuring the long-term success and sustainability of systems, while also managing costs effectively. Processes for proactive monitoring and preventive maintenance play a crucial role in preventing costly system failures and repairs.

A critical decision architects face today is whether to deploy a solution in the cloud or on-premises. This decision entails considering factors such as cost, scalability, performance, security, and compliance. It's essential to assess the specific needs and objectives of the project and to carefully weigh the advantages and disadvantages of each deployment option.

1.6.1 Kafka tuning and maintenance

Operational questions are frequently left to the domain of DevOps engineers, who specialize in managing the operational aspects of software systems. Nonetheless, it's essential for architects to comprehend the implications of integrating Kafka into the enterprise's infrastructure. In chapter 9, we'll explore different deployment options, trying to identify the most suitable solution. We'll also address security and data protection issues, discussing the safeguarding of data both in motion and at rest.

Another important aspect of implementing a successful Kafka project concerns gathering requirements. Both functional and non-functional requirements play a crucial role in estimating the solution's cost. What are the hardware requirements for the cluster? What do client applications need in terms of hardware? What key metrics are necessary to define the right service level agreement? These questions are important in determining the project budget, and the architect's job is to find answers to these questions. We'll delve into various aspects of Kafka testing, including functional testing, performance testing, and preparation for disaster recovery.

While architects typically aren't directly involved in maintenance issues, they aim to create sustainable solutions. We strive for systems to be decoupled, but this increases complexity, posing challenges for debugging. If an incident occurs, how can we pinpoint the exact problem? If data doesn't reach the target system, how can we trace where it was lost? What tools do we need for monitoring the system's behavior?

For long-term infrastructure planning, it's crucial to understand opportunities for extending the solution. Requirements may evolve, and if the existing setup cannot adapt, restructuring the cluster may become necessary. Later in the book, we'll explore the process of strategizing for infrastructure changes.

1.6.2   On-premises and cloud options

Nowadays, deploying Kafka on-premises remains the prevailing approach. This gives you control over the cluster, but it also entails responsibility for monitoring, maintenance, and potential troubleshooting. While it might be perceived as somewhat old-fashioned in the current landscape, opting for this method can be a cost-effective solution, especially if the company has a proficient team of system administrators. However, it's important to consider the costs associated with on-premises deployment, such as hardware procurement, infrastructure setup, physical security, and ongoing maintenance by in-house personnel.

The opposite solution is to opt for Kafka as a managed service from a cloud provider. This significantly simplifies provisioning and administration, eliminating the need for hardware maintenance, and it ensures service level agreements are guaranteed by the provider. However, this approach comes with certain limitations:

- You are stuck with the provided Kafka version; upgrading or downgrading is not within your control.
- Some components of the Kafka ecosystem, like Schema Registry, are distributed under commercial licenses and may not be available as a managed service for every provider.
- Often, you'll lack the ability to fine-tune the low-level configuration of the brokers, although the provider is responsible for ensuring baseline performance.
- You have limited freedom to choose tools for managing your cluster.

1.6.3   Solutions from other cloud providers

While Kafka was a pioneer among the systems capable of handling messages at scale, other companies are not standing still and now offer competing solutions. Some provide options for on-premises installation, while others are exclusively available in the cloud. Notable solutions include Apache Pulsar (https://pulsar.apache.org), Amazon Kinesis (https://aws.amazon.com/pm/kinesis/), Google Pub/Sub (https://cloud.google.com/pubsub), and Azure Event Hubs (https://azure.microsoft.com/en-us/products/event-hubs), each with its own set of advantages and disadvantages. Moreover, because Kafka's protocol is open, some of these services support communication using the Kafka protocol, allowing for greater flexibility and interoperability.

The decision on whether a company should opt for a managed service, an on-premises solution, or perhaps a hybrid approach is crucial. It directly ties to the functionality available within your enterprise and raises financial considerations. This book aims to thoroughly explore the pros and cons to assist you in selecting the most suitable solution.

1.7   Applying Kafka in enterprise

Kafka is not a universal solution for every scenario, and one of the primary tasks of an architect is to assess whether this technology is appropriate for the project at hand. This book delves into the architectural intricacies of Kafka, but let's first take a high-level look at two use cases where Kafka can be effectively applied: message delivery and state storage.

1.7.1   Using Kafka for sending messages

In event-driven architectures, an event serves as a signal indicating that something has occurred. Within an enterprise context, the primary application of an event-driven architecture arises when a service notifies subscribers of a change in its internal state. This event is stored persistently and replicated across the brokers in the cluster to ensure availability in the case of a system failure. Once all subscribers have consumed and processed the event, it becomes irrelevant to the consumers.

In Kafka, events are stored persistently for a duration specified by the configuration. The rationale behind this is to maintain accessibility to these events should a subscriber encounter a failure and need to reprocess them.

1.7.2   Using Kafka for storing data

If we retain an event for a specific duration, is it possible to store it indefinitely, transforming Kafka into an immutable storage solution? By configuring Kafka to retain data permanently, we can adopt this approach in event-sourcing scenarios, where every change in application state is recorded as an immutable event rather than overwriting the current state.

When CustomerService sends notifications containing updates regarding a customer's address, these events collectively form a log of state changes. When a consumer needs to reconstruct the actual state, it can read the entire log from the beginning. In this setup, the entity's state isn't explicitly stored; instead, it's modeled as a sequence of changes, and Kafka serves as the definitive source of truth for the entity's state. Microservices aware of customer addresses can replay this log, storing the final entity state in memory or a local database.

Kafka's capability to retain events indefinitely finds extensive application in real-time processing scenarios. For instance, consider a stream of orders that need to be enriched with customer address information. A streaming application can consume the orders and join them with the address details from the change log topic. In chapter 8, we'll delve into the architecture and implementation of such applications.

But given that we already possess a reliable storage solution for the system's state, is there a necessity for databases at all? In practice, Kafka's architecture has notable limitations that hinder its complete replacement of databases. Efficiently processing queries like "Select all customer addresses close to a specified location" is challenging, as clients would need to read, deserialize, and then apply business logic to messages from the broker. We'll explore these distinctions further when evaluating if Kafka is the right fit for a project.

1.7.3   How Kafka is different

We'll explore the unique aspects of Kafka's architecture throughout this book, but we've already discussed some fundamental concepts that shed light on what sets Kafka apart:

- Unlike most other brokers, Kafka was conceived as a distributed commit log, storing messages as an immutable sequence of events. Its implementation of this log-centric approach enables Kafka to handle substantial data volumes and high-throughput workloads efficiently.

- Message replication between brokers and the persistence of the messages enhance its durability and fault tolerance, distinguishing it from some traditional message brokers.

- Kafka's capability to retain historical data makes it a good choice for event-sourcing use cases.

- Kafka brokers are integral components of an actively evolving ecosystem, complemented by connectors for integration with external data sources and frameworks for building real-time stream-processing applications.

These characteristics make Kafka not just a messaging system, but a foundational platform for building reliable, scalable, and data-centric architectures.

Field notes: Getting started with a Kafka project

After Eva's presentation at their next meeting, the team—Max Sellington (sales), Rob Routine (architect), and Eva Catalyst (data engineer)—pauses, glancing at the whiteboard covered in notes.

Max: Appreciate the presentation, Eva—good coverage of the Kafka pieces we need. It looks promising; let's start small and stay within budget. What's the next move?

Rob: First things first, we'll need to define the key use cases for Kafka in our architecture. What are the primary events we want to capture and process for a holistic view of our customers?

Eva: I'd suggest we start by identifying the data sources. What kind of data are we dealing with? Transactions, customer interactions, social media mentions—we need to understand the variety of events we'll be streaming through Kafka.

Rob: Absolutely, Eva. And that brings us to our second question: how are we going to model these events within Kafka? What should our event schema look like to ensure compatibility and scalability?

Max (taking notes): Event schema—got it. Now, I've heard Kafka can handle massive volumes of data. But how do we make sure that its performance and scalability align with our project as its demands grow?

Rob: Great question, Max. We'll have to consider the number of topics, partitions, replication factors, and Kafka cluster sizing. And speaking of clusters, Eva, any thoughts on how we'll manage and deploy our Kafka clusters?

Eva: Certainly, Rob. We need a plan for monitoring, scaling, and maintaining these clusters. Plus, we'll have to decide if we want to go with a self-managed setup or explore the benefits of a managed Kafka service.

(continued)

Max (writing furiously): Alright, so we've got data sources, event schema, performance considerations, and cluster management. Anything else?

Eva: Security, Max. How are we going to secure our Kafka ecosystem? Encryption, authentication, authorization—we can't afford any breaches in our customer data.

Rob: Spot on, Eva. Security is paramount. And lastly, let's not forget about integrating Kafka with our existing systems. How do we ensure smooth data flow between Kafka and our databases, applications, and analytics tools?

Max: Perfect, team. We've got our marching orders—use cases, data sources, event schema, performance, cluster management, security, and integration. Now, before we dive deep, we should also consider the estimations and costs involved. Rob, any insights on estimating the infrastructure costs?

Rob: Absolutely, Max. We need to calculate the hardware, storage, and network requirements based on our projected data volumes. Also, consider potential costs for third-party tools or managed services we might use.

Max: And Eva, from a data engineering perspective, any thoughts on the development and operational costs?

Eva: We'll need to estimate the development time for building Kafka producers and consumers, as well as ongoing operational efforts for monitoring, troubleshooting, and updates.

Max: Great, so infrastructure, development, and operational costs—let's factor those into our plan. Anything else on the financial front we need to consider?

Rob: License costs for Kafka, Max. Depending on the features we require, we might need to explore different licensing options. It's important to align our needs with the licensing model.

Max: Excellent point, Rob. Let's get a comprehensive understanding of the costs involved in adopting Kafka for our Customer 360 project. With that, we'll have a holistic view—just like our approach to customer data!

1.8 Online resources

- Apache Kafka documentation: https://kafka.apache.org
  The official reference for Kafka's configuration, APIs, and operations—essential for anyone building or managing Kafka systems.

- Confluent platform documentation: https://www.confluent.io
  Produced by Confluent, the company founded by Kafka's original creators, this documentation covers Confluent's products that accompany Kafka and serves as a major source of knowledge promoting Kafka and event streaming.

- "The Data Streaming Event": https://current.confluent.io

This Confluent conference features talks from practitioners and Kafka experts—it's great for exploring real-world streaming use cases.

- *Kafka: The Definitive Guide:* https://www.confluent.io/resources/kafka-the -definitive-guide/
  A comprehensive book by Kafka community members covers architecture, APIs, and best practices.

- *Apache Kafka in Action*, by Anatoly Zelenin and Alexander Kropp (Manning, 2025): https://www.manning.com/books/apache-kafka-in-action
  This practical book is full of examples and modern Kafka design patterns.

- "Microservices, Apache Kafka, and Domain-Driven Design": https://www .confluent.io/blog/microservices-apache-kafka-domain-driven-design/
  This post explains how Kafka supports domain-driven, event-based microservice architectures.

- *Building Event-Driven Microservices*, by Adam Bellemare (O'Reilly, 2020): https:// learning.oreilly.com/library/view/building-event-driven-microservices/9781492 057888/
  A practical book on designing microservices around event-driven architecture and modeling data as streams of events.

- "What is Event Driven Architecture?" https://www.confluent.io/blog/journey -to-event-driven-part-1-why-event-first-thinking-changes-everything/
  This article introduces event-driven principles and their impact on modern system design.

Summary

- Two primary communication patterns between services are: request-response and event-driven architecture.

- In the event-driven approach, services communicate by triggering events.

- The key components of the Kafka ecosystem include brokers, producers, consumers, Schema Registry, Kafka Connect, and streaming applications.

- Cluster metadata management is handled by KRaft controllers.

- Kafka is versatile and well-suited for various industries and use cases, including real-time data processing, log aggregation, and microservices communication.

- Kafka components can be deployed both on-premises and in the cloud.

- The platform supports two main use cases: message delivery and state storage.

Kafka cluster data architecture

This chapter covers

- Organizing related messages through topics
- Utilizing partitions for parallel processing data
- The composition of Kafka messages: keys, values, and headers
- Using replication to ensure availability and fault tolerance
- Working with compacted topics for persistent data storage

Let's step away from the business patterns for applying Kafka and explore the implementation of design ideas from an architectural perspective. We first need to understand Kafka's core abstractions—topics and partitions. Then we can move toward how Kafka provides durability through replication and how data is ultimately stored on disk.

We use topics and partitions to process data in parallel, preserve ordering where it matters, and replicate partitions. Think of topics as destinations where events are sent. They contain individual records—keys, values, and optional headers—and require many configuration decisions, such as batching, offsets, on-disk layout, retention policies, and the number of partitions.

Topics retain messages for a predetermined period, based on time or size, and remove them after the retention period expires. These are called *streaming* topics and are used for event streaming. But for storing state, we also have the option of compacted topics, which retain at least the most recent message for each unique key. They are especially useful for storing externalized state, such as configuration data, or changelogs, where only the most recent value matters.

With a solid understanding of these building blocks, you'll have what you need to grasp Kafka's architecture.

2.1 Inside the Kafka cluster

The core components of Kafka are:

- *Topics*—Destinations events are dispatched to
- *Partitions*—Scalability and redundancy units
- *Messages*—Carriers of event information

We use these three components to configure how data is processed and stored. You can see these pieces in context in figure 2.1 It depicts a cluster of brokers, topics that

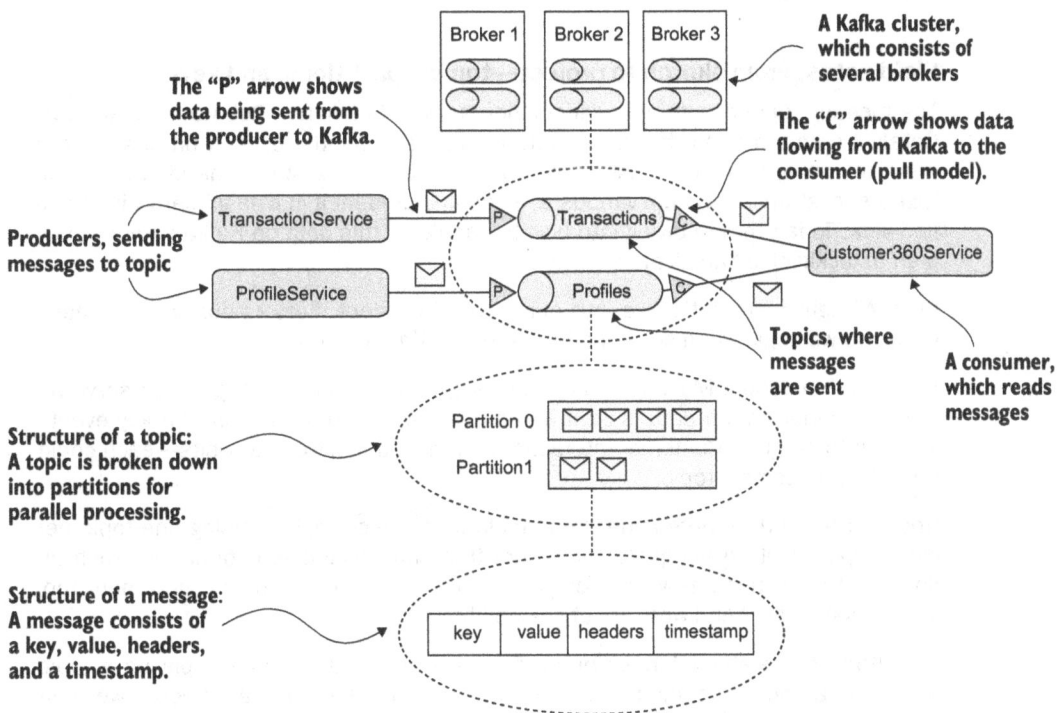

Figure 2.1 An illustration of how data is processed and stored in Kafka. Data is organized into topics, which are further divided into partitions. The basic units of information are messages, which contain keys, values, and headers.

store the data, and messages sent to these topics. Additionally, it highlights the structure of a message, which is composed of keys, values, and headers.

Diagram notation: Clarifying producer and consumer arrows

In Kafka diagrams, arrows can be ambiguous. Do they show who initiates communication or the direction of data flow? In Kafka's case, this can cause confusion, especially since producers *push* data, while consumers *pull* it.

To make this distinction clear, this book uses a custom arrow notation in all architectural diagrams:

- ▶ Arrow with a "P" (for Producer)—Indicates a system that sends data into Kafka
- ▶ Arrow with a "C" (for Consumer)—Indicates a system that pulls data from Kafka

This notation clarifies both the intent and data direction. For example, a consumer initiates a pull, but the data flows from Kafka to the consumer. The "C" arrow always points toward the consumer to emphasize that flow.

With this overview of how data moves, we can begin to design a system for handling all this data on Kafka servers.

Field notes: From sketch to project—topics, partitions, and keys

The meeting room buzzes with anticipation as Max Sellington, Rob Routine, and Eva Catalyst gather around the table, laptops open and minds focused on designing a proof of concept for their Customer 360 operational data store. The idea is to pull together customer info from various sources and present it in a dashboard with a unified view. Today, they're diving into how to handle all this data on Kafka servers; they plan to tackle client applications later.

Max: All right team, let's dive into our proof of concept. Eva, as our data engineer, where do we begin when selecting topics for our Kafka setup?

Eva: Good question, Max. In Kafka, "topics" group related messages and serve as the destination where data is sent and stored. We need to pinpoint the key events we want to capture. Customer interactions, transactions, website visits—each could potentially become a topic.

Rob: But how do we determine the granularity of these topics? Using one topic per event type might be adequate for events that carry business information, such as financial transactions. However, for system events like log messages, how many topics are necessary? And what about scalability?

Eva: Kafka's scalability hinges on partitions—they're just ways to split up a topic so the data can be handled more efficiently. Business data might need fewer partitions, while log data, with lots of volume, may need more partitions for parallel processing. Let's start with a simple setup: a few key events, two topics, and an aggregated view.

Max: Join like in SQL? I don't see any database in your proposal thus far.

Eva: We're exploring various options. One of them involves using a real-time framework to join messages upon arrival. However, I'm currently more concerned with where we'll store the aggregated data, ready for querying. One option is to store them directly in Kafka.

Rob: Eva, let's be clear—Kafka isn't a database; it's merely a commit log with sequential access.

Eva: True, Rob, but it's a commit log with exceptionally fast sequential access, capable of serving as reliable storage. And we will load data into memory for quick access.

Rob: I'm not fully convinced about storage—let's set it aside for now and come back with benchmarks.

Max: Any other challenges we should address?

Rob: In distributed systems like Kafka, ensuring the correct order of events is crucial, especially when dealing with related data. To maintain this order, Kafka divides data within a topic into partitions, which allows for parallel processing. However, if we want to ensure that related events are processed together and in order, they must reside in the same partition. Kafka uses keys for this purpose; for instance, if we use customer IDs as keys, events pertaining to the same customer will be grouped together in a partition, preserving their order.

Max: Excellent insight, Rob. Key selection truly is crucial. Anything else?

Eva: One note on ordering. The partition count is a design-time choice—changing it later can disrupt the ordering. And data replication is another consideration. We'll need to research best practices regarding the number of data copies required, as this will impact the project's cost.

Max: So, to sum up, we need to carefully select topics, consider partition granularity for scalability, explore efficient storage options, address event ordering within partitions, and choose appropriate keys. Let's keep these factors in mind as we proceed with our Kafka-based proof of concept for the Customer 360 project. Don't we have an LLM assistant to handle that?

Eva: For templates and examples, yes. For partitioning, contracts, and ops guarantees—still on us.

The team nodded in agreement, their focus sharpened by the concise summary of their tasks ahead.

First, we need to select topics based on the events we want to capture and decide on how we want to partition them. For the example ODS project, an initial sketch of this arrangement, shown in figure 2.2, has two topics, `ProfileService` and `TransactionService` producing or sending data to the Kafka server. On the receiving end, `Customer360Service` consumer pulls the data.

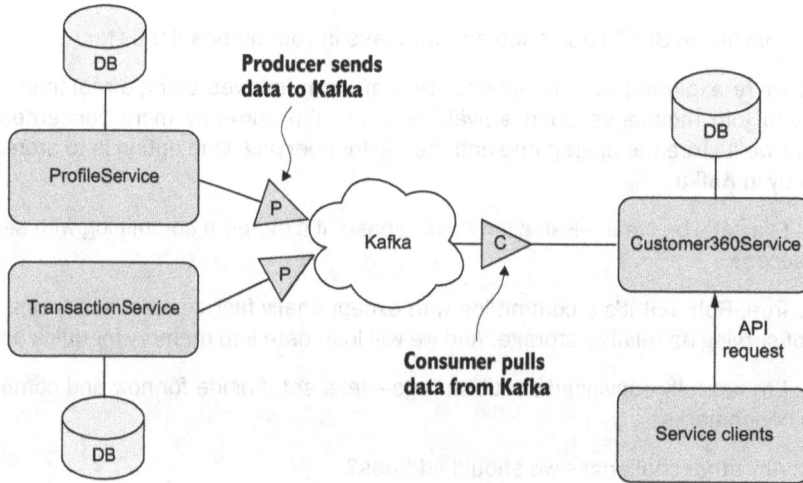

Figure 2.2   The initial draft for a proof-of-concept ODS project. Data from the `ProfileService` and `TransactionService` is transmitted through Kafka. The `Customer360Service` receives and aggregates the data, providing it to clients via an API.

2.2   Core concepts of data processing

While discussing how data is organized on the brokers, we will primarily focus on messages rather than on events. While the terms "event" and "message" can be used interchangeably when discussing logical concepts, it is common practice to refer to *messages* when addressing the physical implementation. *Events* typically describe occurrences or actions within the application domain.

When producers send messages, they route them to a logical destination known as a *topic*. This concept may be familiar to readers with messaging experience. A topic serves to group messages, and the most used pattern is to group messages of the same type under the same topic. Topics are identified by names that are case-sensitive and unique within the cluster. In addition to these names, topics also have unique identifiers (IDs) within the system, though typically producers and consumers use the names when interacting with them. When a producer sends a message, it specifies the name of the topic where the message goes. Similarly, when a consumer subscribes, it specifies from which topics it wants to read messages.

Consider a scenario featuring two producer services: the `TransactionService`, responsible for dispatching events representing customer financial transactions, and the `ProfileService`, tasked with sending updates whenever profile data is modified. Meanwhile, the `Customer360Service` operates as a consumer, aggregating events and presenting them in a dashboard alongside recent transactions and user-related information. This service receives events, stores them locally, and delivers them to the user upon request. The design for this functionality entails employing two distinct topics:

one dedicated to transactions (Transactions) and the other to profiles (Profiles), both depicted in figure 2.3.

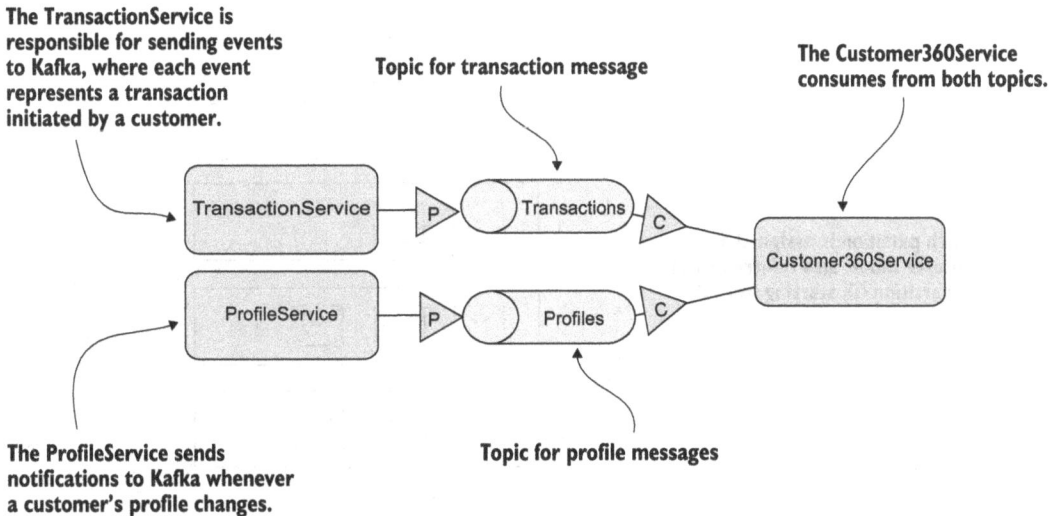

The **TransactionService** is responsible for sending events to Kafka, where each event represents a transaction initiated by a customer.

Topic for transaction message

The **Customer360Service** consumes from both topics.

TransactionService

ProfileService

Transactions

Profiles

Customer360Service

The **ProfileService** sends notifications to Kafka whenever a customer's profile changes.

Topic for profile messages

Figure 2.3   Kafka topics, where each distinct type of message is segregated into its designated topic. Here, we have two services functioning as producers, each sending data to its respective topic. Additionally, a single consumer service subscribes to and consumes data from both topics.

2.2.1   Partitioning the topic

How can we enhance the performance of processing data within a topic? We can break down the data in the topic into multiple segments and process these subsets concurrently. When we create a topic, we choose the number of partitions; this number sets the maximum degree of parallelism for each application reading that topic (one reader instance per partition). Each partition is assigned an index within the topic, represented by an integer starting from 0. Therefore, the combination of the topic name and partition index uniquely identifies a partition.

When a message is dispatched to a topic, the producer directs it to a specific partition within that topic. The message is appended to the end of the partition, forming a commit log—a sequence of immutable records. Each message in a partition gets a unique number called an *offset*, starting from 0 and increasing by 1 each time, which marks its exact position in the partition. This offset allows for precise message retrieval and tracking within the partition. This process is illustrated in figure 2.4.

The selection of partitions is the responsibility of the producer, and we will explore different strategies in chapter 3. For now, it's important to understand that in Kafka, partitions are primarily used to enhance scalability. Consequently, while there is no

The topic is broken down into partitions.

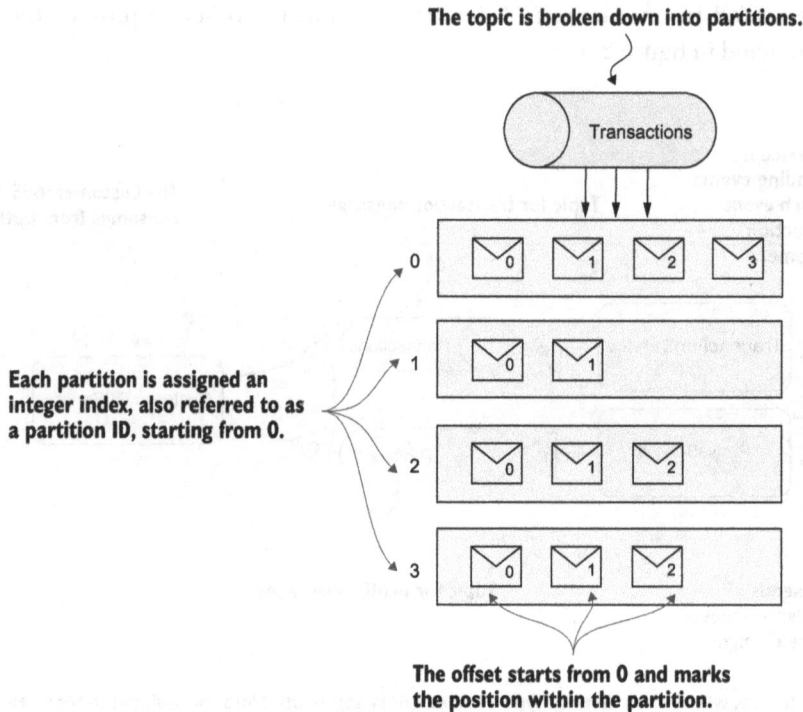

Each partition is assigned an integer index, also referred to as a partition ID, starting from 0.

The offset starts from 0 and marks the position within the partition.

Figure 2.4   A topic is divided into partitions, each with its own index. When a producer sends a message, it specifies the partition to which the message should be directed.

global ordering of messages across the entire topic, ordering is reliably maintained within each individual partition. We will examine this in more detail next.

2.2.2   *Processing data concurrently*

The Kafka client library ensures that the producer has the appropriate number of network connections based on the number of partitions. These connections can be multiplexed, depending on the implementation, meaning that one connection can handle messages for multiple partitions on a broker. In general, splitting a topic into partitions improves the producer's throughput, particularly in scenarios where messages are being produced concurrently.

The number of partitions has an even greater impact on performance on the consumer side. Conceptually, you can think of each partition as being processed by its own "thread" of work. In practice, these threads don't have to be literal OS or Java threads—they simply represent units of concurrent work. To scale out consumption, you can also deploy multiple instances of the consumer application across different machines, forming a consumer group. Each instance within the group manages its specific portion of the data. This functionality can be easily accomplished using Kafka client libraries. The process is depicted in figure 2.5.

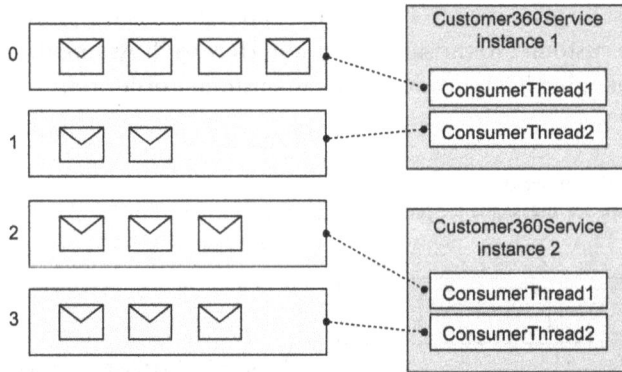

Partitions are consumed in parallel, and processing messages in different partitions does not impact each other.

Figure 2.5 Utilizing partitions for parallel consumption. In this setup, each thread within a service instance is allocated its own partition, with the total number of partitions determining the maximum degree of parallelization achievable.

When high concurrent processing is not required on the consumer side, having just a single consumer is perfectly acceptable. This scenario is depicted in figure 2.6, where all partitions are assigned to a single consumer instance.

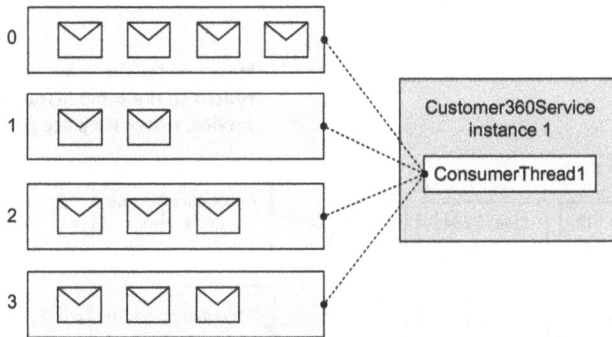

Partitions are assigned to only one consumer instance.

Figure 2.6 All the partitions can be assigned to the same consumer instance.

Now let's discuss message ordering.

2.2.3 Ordering within a topic

When data can be processed independently in parallel, a challenge arises: how can we ensure that data is processed in the correct order? Moreover, how can we guarantee that related messages are processed collectively?

Consider our Customer 360 project as an example, where a service (the producer) sends updates about customer's balance, as illustrated in figure 2.7. Updates about a customer's balance must be processed in strict order, and Kafka ensures this by routing all updates for the same customer to the same partition. Here we'll assume the partition count remains fixed; changing it later can disrupt per-customer ordering.

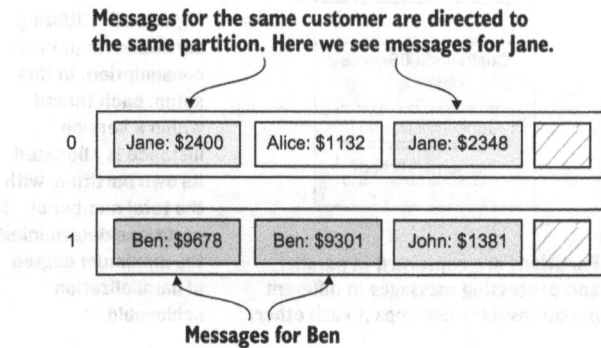

Messages for the same customer are directed to the same partition. Here we see messages for Jane.

| 0 | Jane: $2400 | Alice: $1132 | Jane: $2348 | |

Figure 2.7   Partitioning messages by customer name. This figure shows how messages related to the same customer are directed to a specific partition, ensuring cohesive data management.

| 1 | Ben: $9678 | Ben: $9301 | John: $1381 | |

Messages for Ben

When multiple instances of the consuming service form a consumer group, Kafka similarly assigns each partition to a single consumer instance. This ensures that one instance processes all updates for a given customer, maintaining the order and consistency of the customer's balance (figure 2.8).

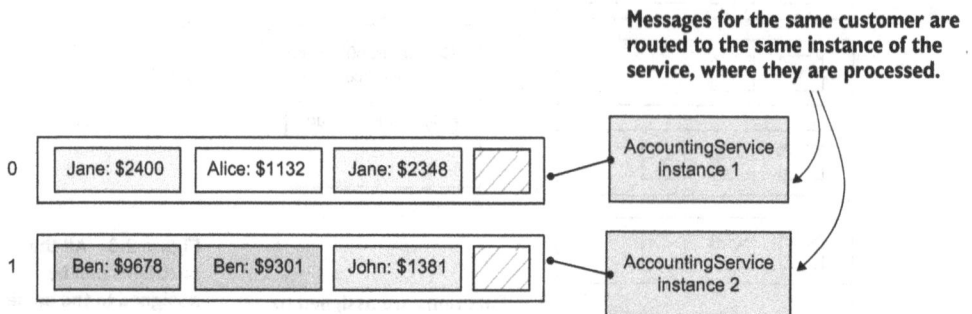

Messages for the same customer are routed to the same instance of the service, where they are processed.

| 0 | Jane: $2400 | Alice: $1132 | Jane: $2348 | | → | AccountingService instance 1 |

| 1 | Ben: $9678 | Ben: $9301 | John: $1381 | | → | AccountingService instance 2 |

Figure 2.8   Routing messages to the same service instance for processing

Without this mechanism, updates for a customer could be processed by different consumer instances, and the balance updates could be applied out of order, leading to incorrect data being displayed to the customer.

2.2.4   *AsyncAPI: Capturing the architecture of topics, partitions, and more*

For our hypothetical ODS, let's say the team opts for the common approach of creating a topic for each type of message. This makes their initial tasks straightforward:

creating topics for profiles and transactions. Next, we'd need to consider replication, the number of partitions, and the partitioning strategy.

The next challenge we'd face is how to document our decisions. We need a way to store and share the topic metadata—such as topic names and their partition counts—so that everyone on the team has a consistent understanding of the system.

Text documents can become outdated quickly, as can pages on the company wiki. Though Kafka had been around for a while, documenting the structure of Kafka clusters is still in its early stages. But there are several emerging open standards for documentation, including AsyncAPI.

AsyncAPI is a specification for defining and documenting event-driven interactions. While it is not designed exclusively for Kafka, it abstracts communication in terms of events, messages, and operations. These abstract definitions can then be refined with bindings specific to concrete protocols like MQTT, Kafka, AMQP, and others, allowing for detailed specification of implementation properties.

AsyncAPI uses YAML or JSON syntax to describe event-driven communication, with all interactions being represented in files that can be stored in version control systems. As a project progresses, you can use AsyncAPI to document architectural decisions, so there's a clear record of the system's event-driven interactions.

To communicate changes to these documents, we can store and share the AsyncAPI files in a repo like Git, using version control to track changes and ensure everyone has the most current information.

A key concept in AsyncAPI is a *channel*, which represents a logical address through which messages are sent and received. In Kafka, a channel corresponds to a topic. A channel has three main attributes:

- *Name*—The identifier used to refer to the channel.
- *Description*—A text explanation of the business purpose of the channel.
- *Address*—In Kafka, this corresponds to the name of the topic.

We can define Kafka-specific properties in the *bindings* section. Configuration properties for the topic, such as the number of partitions, also can be specified there.

From here, we can create a YAML file, shown next. For the proof-of-concept drawing we saw earlier (figure 2.2), the Customer 360 team defines two topics: TRANSACTIONS and CUSTOMER_PROFILES, assigning addresses corresponding to their topic names, and setting the number of partitions for both topics to 9. Since they are unsure of the optimal number of partitions, they choose this number as a starting point, and can experiment later on to find the most suitable configuration.

> **Listing 2.1 An initial configuration for the Customer 360 project**

```yaml
asyncapi: 3.0.0
info:
  title: Customer 360 Project
```

```
version: 1.0.0
description: >
  This project aims to aggregate data from various sources, providing a
  comprehensive view of customer information.

channels:                                              The identification of the topic
  customerProfile:
    description: Storing profile information of customers.    The name of the
    address: CUSTOMER_PROFILES                               topic in Kafka
    bindings:                          Kafka-specific properties
      kafka:
        partitions: 9       Number of partitions for the topic
  transactions:
    description: Information about customer transactions.
    address: TRANSACTIONS
    bindings:
      kafka:
        partitions: 9
```

Next, let's focus on another core concept of Kafka: replication.

2.3 Replicating partitions

Partitions not only facilitate parallelism but also contribute to redundancy by being replicated across multiple machines. To ensure high availability, it's crucial to have multiple copies of data stored on separate machines, ensuring that data remains accessible even if one machine goes down.

When creating a topic, we must specify the desired number of data copies—the *replication factor*. Each partition, which serves as the basic unit of replication, is indivisible. Each copy is stored on a different server in the cluster, so the replication factor can't exceed the number of brokers in the cluster. The replication factor is a property of a topic, so different topics may have different values for this setting. An example of partition distribution is shown in figure 2.9.

Distributing partitions across different brokers helps reduce the load on each server, thereby improving performance. Additionally, the size of each partition is crucial, as it must fit within the available disk space on the broker that hosts it. It's worth mentioning that in the open source Apache Kafka, the default number of partitions is 1, and the default replication factor is also 1. To ensure high availability when using the community version of Kafka, we need to change the default number of partitions and the default replication factor.

2.3.1 Replica leaders and followers

The replicas of the partitions have different roles. Each partition has a primary replica, known as the *leader*, and the remaining replicas are *followers*. Leaders for different partitions may reside on various brokers. During topic creation, Kafka determines the placement of leaders and followers, striving to distribute the load evenly and to ensure that no two replicas of a partition are located on the same machine. An example of this configuration of leaders and followers for a topic is depicted in figure 2.10.

The replication factor for the Profiles topic is set to 3, meaning we maintain three copies of the partitions, each stored on a different broker.

When this broker goes offline, replicas of all its partitions are available on other brokers.

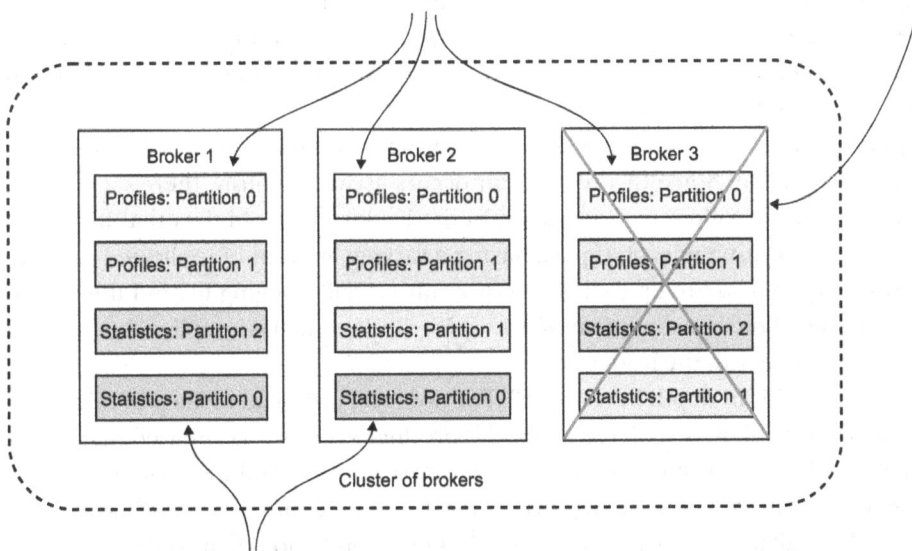

Broker 1
Profiles: Partition 0
Profiles: Partition 1
Statistics: Partition 2
Statistics: Partition 0

Broker 2
Profiles: Partition 0
Profiles: Partition 1
Statistics: Partition 1
Statistics: Partition 0

Broker 3
Profiles: Partition 0
Profiles: Partition 1
Statistics: Partition 2
Statistics: Partition 1

Cluster of brokers

For the Statistics topic, each partition is replicated only 2 times. The replication factor here is 2.

Figure 2.9 Partitions are distributed across various brokers in the cluster. The replication factor, which specifies the number of partition copies, is determined per topic. In the event of a broker failure, the data remains accessible.

One replica of the partitions is the leader and the others are followers.

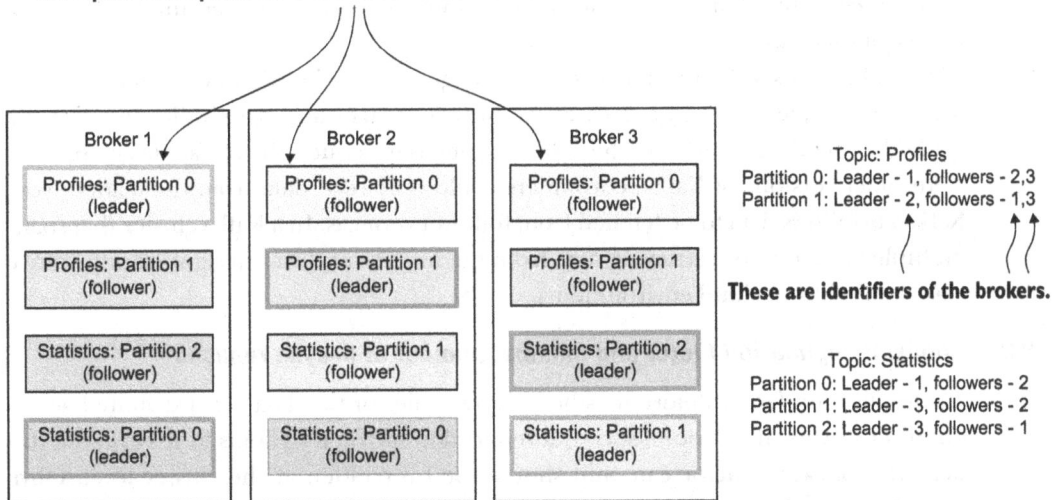

Broker 1
Profiles: Partition 0 (leader)
Profiles: Partition 1 (follower)
Statistics: Partition 2 (follower)
Statistics: Partition 0 (leader)

Broker 2
Profiles: Partition 0 (follower)
Profiles: Partition 1 (leader)
Statistics: Partition 1 (follower)
Statistics: Partition 0 (follower)

Broker 3
Profiles: Partition 0 (follower)
Profiles: Partition 1 (follower)
Statistics: Partition 2 (leader)
Statistics: Partition 1 (leader)

Topic: Profiles
Partition 0: Leader - 1, followers - 2,3
Partition 1: Leader - 2, followers - 1,3

These are identifiers of the brokers.

Topic: Statistics
Partition 0: Leader - 1, followers - 2
Partition 1: Leader - 3, followers - 2
Partition 2: Leader - 3, followers - 1

Figure 2.10 Each partition has one replica designated as the leader, while the others serve as followers.

When a producer sends a message to a Kafka partition, it communicates exclusively with the leader of that partition. Once the message reaches the leader, it is asynchronously replicated to all the followers of that partition. But can data be lost in this scenario? What if the leader fails before the message is distributed to followers? There are different strategies for balancing reliability and performance, and we'll discuss them when we talk about client applications in chapter 3.

Replicas proactively query the leader for new data and pull any unreplicated messages when available. Since this replication occurs asynchronously, there's a delay in data delivery to the followers. Consequently, the leader may hold data that has yet to be replicated, resulting in each replica having a varying amount of replicated data. To identify which replicas are up to date and not substantially lagging behind the leader, Kafka introduced the concept of an *in-sync replica* (ISR), which is a replica that has successfully caught up with the leader.

We'll look at this in depth in chapter 3. For now, you just need to keep in mind that the strongest reliability is achieved when the producer receives acknowledgment that the messages have been successfully replicated to all in-sync replicas (not all replicas, just the in-sync ones). The `min.insync.replicas` setting defines how many in-sync replicas must be available for a successful write. If there aren't enough in-sync replicas, the producer will encounter an exception when trying to send data. In the case of a broker failure, if at least one of the servers where we have a copy of the partition is alive, we won't lose the data.

How does the producer know who the leader of a partition is? Initially, the producer sends a metadata request to get a mapping of partition leaders. As this information doesn't change frequently, it can safely be cached on the producer's side. Each broker maintains leaders for partitions, and if a broker fails, the leaders residing on that broker must be re-elected. This means one of the followers becomes a leader, and the leader of the partition changes.

What happens if the producer sends messages to a broker that no longer holds the leader of the partition? In this case, the broker returns an error, indicating that the leader has likely changed, and the producer needs to request the metadata again.

In older versions of Kafka, consumers could only read data from the leader. Now, Kafka also allows data to be fetched from follower replicas. In a Kafka cluster that spans multiple data centers, retrieving data from the nearest replica can significantly reduce costs, especially in cloud environments.

2.3.2 *Choosing replication factor and minimal number of in-sync replicas*

The replication factor determines how many copies of the data are distributed across different servers. If you don't specify a replication factor, it defaults to 1. However, this default replication factor can, and should, be overridden at the cluster level. Obviously, having only one replica does not ensure high availability. In the event of a failure of the broker holding this partition, data loss will occur.

The `min.insync.replicas` property specifies the minimum number of replicas (including the leader) that must be fully caught up with the leader before a write can be considered successful. Under normal conditions, the number of in-sync replicas equals the replication factor, as all replicas should be in sync. However, replicas might lag if a broker holding a replica fails or is overloaded, causing replication delays. If the count of in-sync replicas drops below this value, producers attempting to send data to this partition will encounter an exception.

The `min.insync.replicas` property is set during topic creation. If this property is not specified at that time, it defaults to the value set on the broker. The default value for `min.insync.replicas` is 1, although this can be overridden.

The choice of this number depends on the cluster's tolerance for failures. For robust fault tolerance and data durability, a recommended configuration is a replication factor of 3 and `min.insync.replicas` set to 2. This setup ensures that even if one broker fails, the cluster remains operational, providing a desired level of resilience.

2.3.3 *Extending topic configuration with replication information*

When setting up replication configurations, you may need to consider how you'll be deploying your Kafka project: on-premises or as a cloud-based solution. One option is to use the cloud and utilize Kafka as a managed service. While this approach could simplify the project's initial setup and conceal Kafka's internal complexities, it does decrease the control you have over the system. If that control is important to your project, consider an on-premises deployment. In designing the Customer 360 dashboard, for instance, the team decides to install a small cluster of brokers locally, settling on three as a starting point.

Once that's settled, you'll need to settle on the replication factor and the number of minimal in-sync replicas. Given that their cluster would contain three brokers, our team opts for a replication factor of 3 to ensure robust high availability, allowing for the failure of up to two brokers without compromising data integrity. As for the `min.insyc.replicas` setting, they select 2, mandating that at least two replicas must acknowledge a write for it to be deemed successful. This redundancy strategy, with data stored in at least two places, mitigates the risk of potential data loss.

Here's how to add that replication factor and minimum number of in-sync replicas to the configuration:

```
asyncapi: 3.0.0
info:
  title: Customer 360 Project
  version: 1.0.0
  description: >
    This project aims to aggregate data from various sources, providing a
    comprehensive view of customer information.

channels:
  customerProfile:
    description: Storing profile information of customers.
```

```
    address: CUSTOMER_PROFILES
    bindings:
      kafka:
        partitions: 9        ◄────┤ The number of partitions
        replicas: 3
        topicConfiguration:              The minimum number
          min.insync.replicas: 2  ◄────┤ of in-sync replicas
  transactions:
    description: Information about customer transactions.
    address: TRANSACTIONS
    bindings:
      kafka:
        partitions: 9
        replicas: 3
        topicConfiguration:
          min.insync.replicas: 2
```

With the replication factor and minimal in-sync replicas now documented, they moved on to the next step: designing the message structure.

> ### Architecture notes: Configuring topics
>
> While working on a proof-of-concept, it quickly becomes apparent that certain key points could be documented and later refined into project guidelines. One way to handle these rules is to publish them on a wiki temporarily, until you find a way to automate the process.
>
> - It's a good practice to keep events of the same type within a single topic. However, the same type of event can be written to multiple topics if needed.
> - The number of partitions is crucial for enabling parallel data processing. This number is specified per topic, with a default value set at the broker level. The team decided to change the default number of partitions to 9.
> - Kafka guarantees message ordering only within a single partition. Therefore, messages that must be delivered in order should be directed to the same partition.
> - To prevent data loss, data should be replicated across multiple brokers. The replication factor is set per topic, with a value of 3 being suitable for most scenarios. The team agreed to set this as the proposed default.
> - The minimum number of in-sync replicas (ISRs) is also important. Since the leader is considered an in-sync replica, setting this value to 2 is sufficient for most use cases. The team decided to adopt this value as the default.

2.4   Inside the topic

We've examined the fundamental components of Kafka, such as topics and partitions, and now we'll explore how Kafka stores and manages data. Beyond the messages themselves, we'll examine how Kafka handles ordering, retention, and the physical representation of data on disk.

2.4.1 Messages: Keys, values and headers

When an event occurs, the system sends a message containing details about the event. However, is this information sufficient? Don't we also need to transmit some technical parameters? If so, how can we do this?

In Kafka, a fundamental unit of information exchange is the *message*. Messages in Kafka consist of *keys*, *headers*, *values*, and *timestamps*. While these terms may correspond to similar concepts in other messaging systems, they can have slightly different meanings in the context of Kafka. Let's delve into their significance within Kafka.

When we discuss messages in an abstract sense, we're referring to their values in Kafka. A value represents the payload of the message—any kind of data that's important to the application or system. Examples of values include

- The current balance of an account for an internet banking application
- The new address of a customer in the case of an address notification service
- Log records of an application for system monitoring

Keys in Kafka are used for selecting a partition. Given that topics are divided into partitions for parallel processing, message order is guaranteed only within a partition. The idea is to assign keys to messages, ensuring that messages with the same key end up in the same partition, as illustrated in figure 2.11. For instance, when updating balances, using the account identifier as a key ensures that related messages go to the same

The account identifier is used as a key. Messages for the same account go to the same partition.

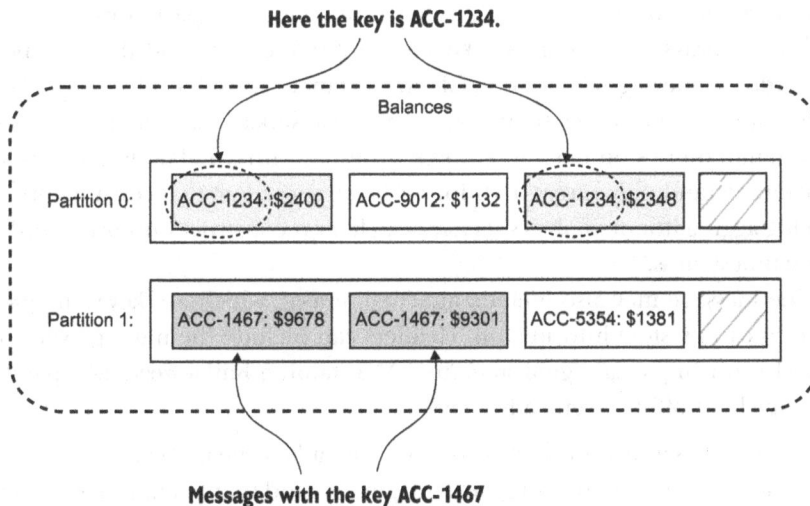

Here the key is ACC-1234.

Balances

Partition 0: ACC-1234: $2400 | ACC-9012: $1132 | ACC-1234: $2348

Partition 1: ACC-1467: $9678 | ACC-1467: $9301 | ACC-5354: $1381

Messages with the key ACC-1467

Figure 2.11 Selecting the key for the Balances topic. The account number is used as the key, ensuring that messages for the same account are routed to the same partition. This setup guarantees that updates for each account are received in the correct order.

partition, preserving their order. This sequential organization allows for the replay of all messages from a partition, which is crucial if data on the consumer side is lost and needs to be restored.

In the example where a service updates customer addresses, using the customer identifier as the key ensures that all updates related to that customer—even if they involve different physical addresses—are sent to the same partition. This guarantees that a customer's address-change history remains in order.

Alternatively, if your use case involves tracking the state of a specific physical address (like a particular warehouse or delivery hub), using a logical destination ID as the key ensures that updates for that physical location are kept together in a single partition.

Keys in Kafka are used to select the partition and are not related to the uniqueness of the messages. Multiple messages can have the same key, but each message is treated as a distinct entity, ensuring individual processing and storage within the partition.

Additionally, keys play a vital role in *log compaction*—a feature that allows Kafka to retain only the latest message for each key in special "compacted" topics. This feature will be explored further in section 2.5.

The choice of key is crucial, because selecting the wrong key can lead to an uneven load of data across partitions. For example, suppose we have a topic with orders that are partitioned based on the order region key (e.g., East, Central, West). If the volume of orders varies significantly by region, with 80% of orders coming from the East region, for example, the partition handling East orders will have significantly more data than the others. In this situation, the East partition might be overwhelmed while the others are underutilized, resulting in an overall imbalance in resource consumption. Heavily loaded partitions can cause increased processing latency for messages, leading to slower response times for consumers dependent on those partitions.

Do we always need keys? No, keys are not mandatory, and they can be omitted if the order of messages is not crucial. For instance, consider a logging scenario where each application instance sends log entries to a Kafka topic. Since each message has a timestamp, there's no need to enforce ordering within Kafka itself—messages can be distributed randomly across partitions. The target system that consumes the logs (such as a log aggregator or analytics service) can later reconstruct the correct order based on these timestamps.

The message may also include attached *headers*, which are key-value pairs typically used to carry system information. Headers can include the message version, an identifier for tracing, or a digital signature. Maintaining Kafka headers separate from the message body offers several advantages:

- It creates a clear distinction between metadata (headers) and the actual data payload (body), simplifying the management and interpretation of metadata by producers and consumers without interfering with the message content.
- It enables applications to append additional information without changing the message body's structure or format, enhancing compatibility. Producers and

consumers can modify headers without affecting the message payload, ensuring existing applications operate smoothly with the introduction of new metadata.

Headers facilitate selective processing, allowing consumers to evaluate the headers and determine whether to process, ignore, or differently route a message, eliminating the need for message deserialization.

An example of Kafka message is shown in figure 2.12.

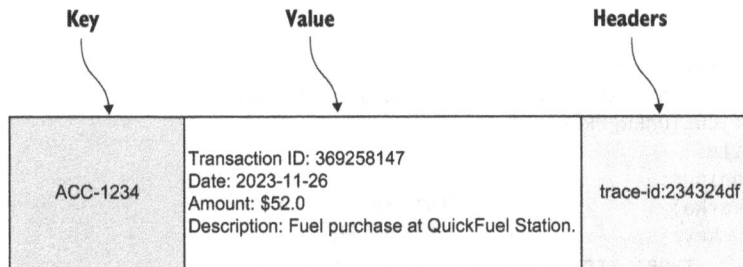

This is a Kafka message representing a financial transaction. The key used is an identifier for the account, while the body contains business information and the header includes system parameters.

Key   Value   Headers

| ACC-1234 | Transaction ID: 369258147
Date: 2023-11-26
Amount: $52.0
Description: Fuel purchase at QuickFuel Station. | trace-id:234324df |

Figure 2.12   An example of Kafka message

2.4.2   First draft for documenting messages in AsyncAPI

Like our ODS project designers, you may have a general idea of what data will populate the topics but postpone deciding on the specifics of the data format until you have a better understanding of how Kafka handles data types. This approach enables them to design a format that optimally serves the needs of their application. But it is still crucial to select appropriate keys for message ordering at the architectural level.

Since Kafka itself does not enforce message structure, you may question the necessity of defining the message structure within the Kafka cluster. It is crucial, however, to clearly communicate the data format between teams. This agreement is vital for establishing a consensus on how to serialize and deserialize values effectively. Since AsyncAPI allows for specifying message structure as part of the channel documentation, you can document it there.

For the ODS project, the team is using the customer ID as the key for the CUSTOMER_ PROFILES topic. This decision makes sense for maintaining order, as updates for each customer need to be processed in sequence. Although the transactions do not require ordering, the team opts to use the transaction ID as the key for the TRANSACTIONS topic. While transaction IDs are unique and don't necessitate order, using them as keys aids in distributing the load across partitions.

The updated configuration, partially shown in the following code, uses AsyncAPI's capability to define messages either as part of the channel or in a separate section for reusability. Our team opts to place them under the channel for simplicity, given the current size of the project. Since keys are specific to Kafka rather than general concepts, they are defined within the bindings of the messages section.

```
asyncapi: 3.0.0
info:
  title: Customer 360 Project
  version: 1.0.0
  description: >
    This project aims to aggregate data from various sources, providing a
    comprehensive view of customer information.

channels:
  customerProfile:
    description: Storing profile information of customers.
    address: CUSTOMER_PROFILES
      profile:
        bindings:
          kafka:                      ┌─── Documented key for
            key:          ◄───────────┘    the Profile topic
              type: string
              description: identifier of the customer
    bindings:
      kafka:
        partitions: 9
        replicas: 3
        topicConfiguration:
          min.insync.replicas: 2
```

2.4.3 *Message batches and offsets*

We discussed sending messages to and reading them from the broker, but, in practice, messages are typically configured to be sent to the brokers as a batch. The Kafka client library groups messages into batches to optimize performance, and the batch becomes the unit of transfer. Hence, whenever messages are transferred to or from the client, it is, in fact, the batch being transferred. Batch parameters are configurable, and we will explore them in chapter 3 when we discuss client applications.

When the message reaches the broker, it is appended to the end of the partition. Its position inside the partition is called the *offset*, which is an integer value. The first message within a partition has an offset of 0. This process is illustrated in figure 2.13.

We can uniquely identify the message with three values:

- Name of the topic
- ID of the partition
- Offset

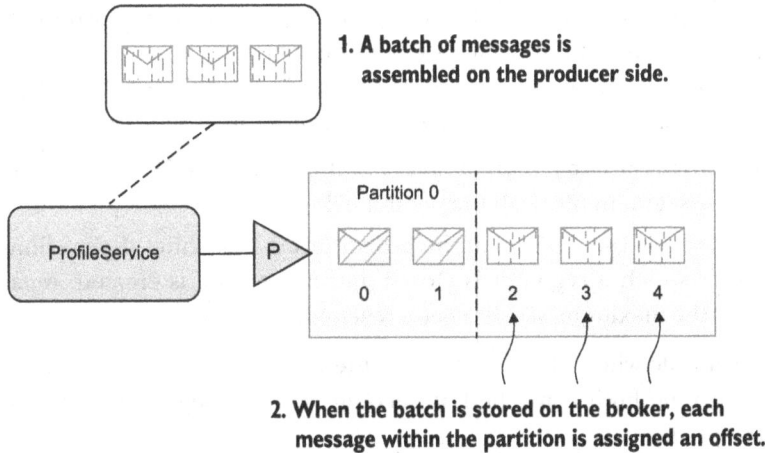

1. A batch of messages is assembled on the producer side.

Partition 0

ProfileService P

0   1   2   3   4

2. When the batch is stored on the broker, each message within the partition is assigned an offset.

Figure 2.13 Each message within the partition is assigned an offset.

The <topic, partition, offset> *tuple* serves as a unique identifier for the message, with no other generated identifiers. The primary purpose of the offset is to keep track of which messages have already been consumed by the consumer application. It's important to note that offsets are not recycled when messages are deleted due to retention policies. Offsets continuously increase, ensuring that this combination uniquely identifies a message, even if it has been removed from Kafka.

2.4.4 *Physical representation of a topic*

In Kafka, messages always persist on the broker's disk, stored in a configurable directory. Figure 2.14 shows the directory where the messages are stored. This directory contains subdirectories for each partition of the topic, where messages are written into files.

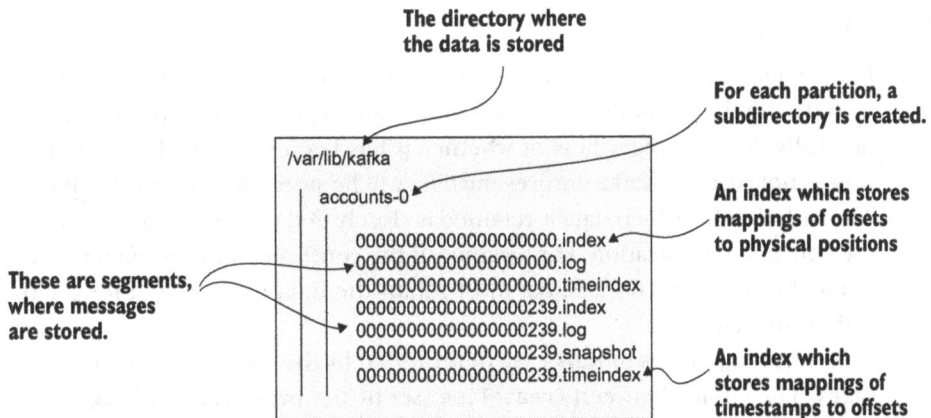

The directory where the data is stored

For each partition, a subdirectory is created.

/var/lib/kafka

accounts-0

00000000000000000000.index
00000000000000000000.log
00000000000000000000.timeindex
00000000000000000239.index
00000000000000000239.log
00000000000000000239.snapshot
00000000000000000239.timeindex

An index which stores mappings of offsets to physical positions

These are segments, where messages are stored.

An index which stores mappings of timestamps to offsets

Figure 2.14 Kafka log files, index files, and other related files (less relevant for the current discussion)

Segments are files on the broker's disk that store partition data. Each partition is divided into multiple segments, but only one segment per partition is active at any time, with new messages being written to it. When a segment reaches a predefined size limit or age, it is closed. This process is controlled by the following properties:

- `segment.bytes` (or `log.segment.bytes` at the broker level)—The maximum size of a single segment file, with the default being 1 GiB.
- `segment.ms` (or `log.roll.ms` at the broker level)—Specifies the maximum duration after which a segment is closed and a new one is created, regardless of whether the maximum size has been reached.

The most recent file where data is actively written is known as the *active segment.* Once its size limit or time limit is reached, it becomes a closed segment, and a new active segment is created.

Kafka creates indices that enable quick access to messages based on specified time-stamps or offsets. These indices let brokers and clients jump directly to a record by off-set or to the first record at or after a given time, without scanning the whole log.

When messages reach the broker, they aren't immediately written to disk; instead, they are placed in the operating system's cache. There is a risk of data loss if the broker crashes before the messages are flushed to disk. However, the likelihood of all brokers crashing simultaneously is low, ensuring that we still retain copies of the messages. The frequency of flushing messages to disk can be configured, allowing a balance between performance and data durability. The messages only become visible to consumers after they are replicated to all in-sync followers.

NOTE There is a useful utility, `kafka-dump-log.sh`, which comes with the Apache Kafka distribution and helps advanced users examine Kafka log files. This script can be used to output the log content in a human-readable format so you can verify the integrity and correctness of the log data.

2.4.5   *Data retention*

For each topic, we define a *retention period*, which determines how long the data will be stored, with the default value set at 7 days. Data older than the specified period is automatically deleted, regardless of whether it has been consumed or not. The deletion time is not strict, as Kafka ensures the data will be stored for at least the defined period. The duration for which data is retained is closely tied to the service level agreements of the consumer application. For instance, if the consumer application might experience a one-day disconnection, Kafka must retain the data for a period longer than a day, with some margin.

Retention periods in Kafka are determined by the timestamps associated with messages. The choice between `CreateTime` (set by the producer) and `LogAppendTime` (set by the broker) is crucial. Using `CreateTime` means the timestamp is fixed when the producer sends the message. On the other hand, `LogAppendTime` assigns a timestamp when the broker receives the message, which can make message deletion more predictable and the system more stable. A good practice is to use `LogAppendTime` for the timestamp and to include the original timestamp from the client in the message's payload.

When `CreateTime` is used as a message timestamp, the broker can impose timestamp restrictions. The `log.message.timestamp.after.max.ms` and `log.message.timestamp.before.max.ms` properties determine the acceptable timestamp range. Messages with timestamps outside this range are rejected, meaning that the records are not appended to the topic log, and the producer receives an error response. These settings can be customized at the topic level.

Alternatively, data retention can be specified based on size. For example, setting a 1 GB retention size means only the latest gigabyte of data is preserved. However, caution is advised when using size-based retention. Consider an application sending notifications for web purchases. After a successful marketing campaign, the application could start generating data at an unexpectedly high rate, potentially overwhelming the consumer application. For critical data, it is safer to opt for time-based retention.

On the other hand, size-based retention is well-suited for use cases where only a limited amount of recent data is relevant, such as page views or user interactions used for real-time personalized recommendations. This approach can also help predict storage costs, which is particularly beneficial in cloud environments where storage expenses can quickly add up.

Both time-based and size-based retention policies can be combined for greater flexibility.

2.4.6 Selecting the number of partitions

If having extra partitions increases parallelism, what is the upper boundary of partitions that makes sense? And how do we select the optimal number of partitions?

While there is no strict upper limit for the number of partitions in Kafka, increasing the number of partitions places higher demands on system resources. Managing more partitions becomes resource-intensive for each broker, as every partition requires its own set of resources. Additionally, there is a practical limit per cluster that defines the system's scalability. Managing metadata can become a bottleneck, especially in setups using a Zookeeper-based controller, which historically could handle up to 200,000 partitions. This limitation was one of the reasons for the introduction of the KRaft (Kafka Raft) controller, which can support clusters with millions of partitions. We will discuss the management of Kafka metadata in more detail in chapter 9.

One of the main reasons for choosing the number of partitions carefully is that changing the number of partitions after creating the topic is highly undesirable. If you use a key-based strategy for message distribution, altering the partition count can disrupt the order of messages. If message order is crucial, a careful process is needed to make this change. For instance, you might stop the producer application, wait until all data is consumed, increase the partition count, and then restart the producer application. Then, new messages will be distributed across all partitions, while previously stored messages will remain in their original locations. Decreasing the partition count is not supported due to the risk of data loss and potential issues with message ordering. The only way to reduce the partition count is to delete and recreate the topic.

Adding more partitions can increase system downtime in the event of a broker shutdown. When a broker goes offline, all leader partitions hosted on that broker must be re-elected among other brokers in the cluster. The greater the number of leader partitions, the longer this re-election process takes. An unclean shutdown, where the broker crashes or stops abruptly, can prolong this process further, as the broker cannot gracefully transfer its leadership roles, requiring additional recovery steps.

In general, using prime number as the partition count for a topic is not recommended, because it can lead to an uneven distribution of data and load among brokers when the number of partitions does not align well with the number of brokers in the cluster.

You can select the partition count based on known throughput, calculating it using the following formula:

$$n=\max(t/p, t/c)$$

where t is the target throughput, p is the throughput per single partition per producer, and c is the throughput per single partition per consumer.

This formula is approximate, as actual throughput depends on producer and consumer configurations. Running tests with different configurations and partition numbers can provide benchmarks for evaluation.

In cases where you don't have specific throughput requirements in advance or can't conduct performance tests, good starting numbers for partition count are often 9, 12, or 15.

2.4.7   Configuring topic metadata

When discussing the specific configuration properties of Kafka, you'll want to consider whether the default values are suitable for your project's needs or if they require adjustment. In the ODS example, the architects customize only the core parameters—partition count, replication factor, and minimum in-sync replicas—while leaving the finer configuration properties unchanged at this early stage of the project.

But defining the retention period requires careful consideration. For the ODS dashboard, the team first needs to set the retention according to the consumers' needs. Second, they realize this property might vary across different environments and stages. While a 7-day retention period seemed reasonable during the development phase, for instance, such long-term storage might not be necessary in production, especially given service-level agreements that require the consumer application to remain highly available. Ultimately, the team decides to set the retention based on time, specifying that data will be stored for at least 5 days, with the understanding that this value might need to be adjusted for production.

Here's that retention policy added to the topic configuration:

```
asyncapi: 3.0.0
info:
  title: Customer 360 Project
  version: 1.0.0
  description: >
    This project aims to aggregate data from various sources, providing a
    comprehensive view of customer information.

channels:
  customerProfile:
    description: Storing  profile information of customers.
    address: CUSTOMER_PROFILES
    messages:
      profile:
        bindings:
          kafka:
            key:
              type: string
              description: identifier of the customer
    bindings:
      kafka:
        partitions: 9
        replicas: 3
        topicConfiguration:
          retention.ms: 432000000    ◄────┘ 5-day retention policy
          min.insync.replicas: 2
```

Architecture notes: Advanced topic configuration

When discussing more advanced aspects of topic creation, there are several key design considerations:

- Messages in Kafka consist of keys, values, and headers. All these components are serialized and deserialized on the client side, and they are not interpreted by brokers. Never assume any logic is performed on the server side.
- Keys are used for partitioning. The main strategy is that messages with the same key are sent to the same partition, ensuring their order is preserved. Therefore, the choice of key is crucial for the design.
- To improve throughput, messages are collected on the client side and sent to the broker in batches, reducing the overhead of individual message transfers.
- Data retention on the broker is governed by policies specified by time or size. The default policy is by time, and the team decided to use mostly default retention values, with adjustments made as necessary based on specific requirements.

2.5 Compacted topics

So far, we have discussed topics as destinations where events are sent. These topics retain messages for a predetermined period, based on time or size, and remove them after the retention period expires. However, Kafka also supports a use case for storing state through what are known as *compacted topics*. These topics retain at least the most recent message for each unique key. This functionality is especially valuable in scenarios where the latest state for each key is critical, such as in stateful applications or for maintaining up-to-date configuration settings.

2.5.1   *The idea of compaction*

By default, Kafka automatically deletes messages based on a time or size policy. However, it's possible to configure Kafka to retain at least the latest value for each key, essentially transforming it into a key-value store. Consider an `AccountService` that sends the new account balance whenever it changes, and a `DashboardService` that consumes these events to display balances to users. The `DashboardService` has the following characteristics:

- It's only interested in the latest balance value.
- It may use Kafka as a storage layer, reading all values from Kafka whenever it starts and storing them in memory.

An example of such a topic is shown in figure 2.15.

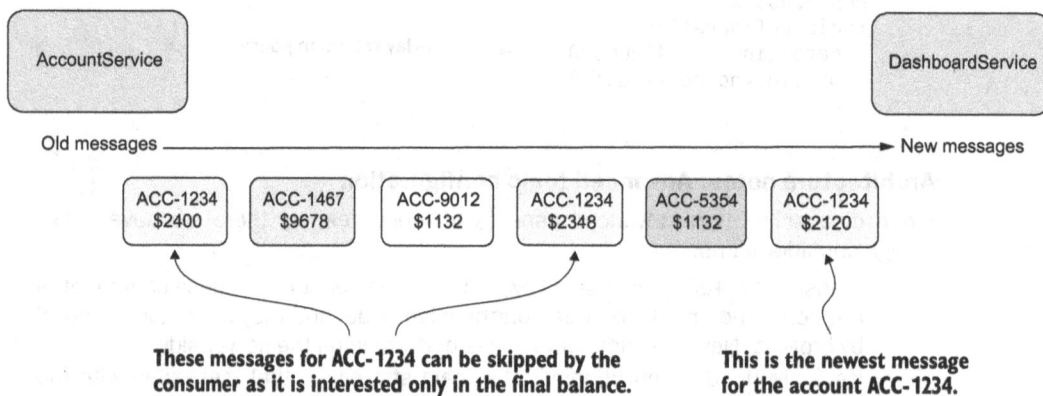

Figure 2.15   A topic where only the final message is important for the consumer. The `DashboardService` is only interested in the latest balances, not their provenance or history.

This can be achieved by storing balances in compacted topics. In this example, the key is the account number, and the value is the balance. To enable compaction, the `delete.policy` property is set to `compact` for the topic. With compaction enabled, Kafka guarantees the availability of the latest value for each account, but not necessarily all historical values. Note that compaction is configured at the topic level, requiring no changes to producers or consumers.

It's important to understand that Kafka does not offer quick access to messages by a specific key. Even with compacted topics, Kafka maintains a commit log with sequential access. To retrieve a particular message, the consumer still needs to read through the log in the usual manner.

Compacted topics retain at least the most recent message for each unique key, but older messages may still exist in the log until they're cleaned up by Kafka's log cleaner. Therefore, getting the latest state for each key requires reading through the log sequentially until the latest entries are reached. For example, at any time, the Dashboard-Service can read the topic from the beginning to get the latest balance values.

Compacted topics have the following features:

- Keys are mandatory (they cannot be null).
- Messages are distributed to partitions based on keys, ensuring that the same key consistently routes to the same partition. A compacted topic in Kafka cannot have a partitioning strategy other than "by key." Partitioning must be done by key to ensure the correct functioning of the log compaction process.
- Messages can be marked for deletion by sending null as a value. If an account no longer exists, the AccountService sends a message with the account number as the key and a null value. These messages are called *tombstone* messages.

2.5.2 *How compaction works*

When discussing the commit log pattern, we've established that messages are immutable, preventing them from being updated, and Kafka does not support deleting messages at arbitrary offsets. So how does Kafka achieve compaction by removing messages? This process is executed by a set of background cleaner threads that rewrite old segments, replacing them with segments containing only the latest value for the key. The compaction process has the following properties:

- Messages in the topic are not reordered; some are removed.
- Offsets remain unchanged after compaction; messages are retained with their original offsets.

Figure 2.16 illustrates how the Balances topic appears after compaction. For all accounts, only the last balance value is retained.

In figure 2.16, the entry for ACC-1447 has been deleted, and if the consumer service is connected and catches up, it will receive the message <ACC-1447, null>. But what if compaction occurred while the consumer service was disconnected? Since there is no message with the key ACC-1447 in the topic, how will DashboardService know that this account no longer exists?

A special property, log.cleaner.delete.retention.ms (which defaults to 1 day), specifies how long tombstone messages must be stored uncompacted. This setting ensures that Kafka retains tombstone messages for the specified period, allowing consumers sufficient time to process these messages. Delaying the removal of tombstones prevents scenarios where consumers might miss them if they have consumed the preceding record but not the tombstone by the time log compaction occurs. This mechanism is crucial for ensuring consumers are aware of deletions within the specified timeframe.

Key	ACC-1234	ACC-9012	ACC-1234	ACC-8345	ACC-1447	ACC-7654	ACC-9012	ACC-1234	ACC-1447
Value	2400	1132	2348	11234	2200	2566	1130	2312	null
Offset	0	1	2	3	4	5	6	7	8

Key	ACC-8345	ACC-7654	ACC-9012	ACC-1234
Value	11234	2556	1130	2312
Offset	3	5	6	7

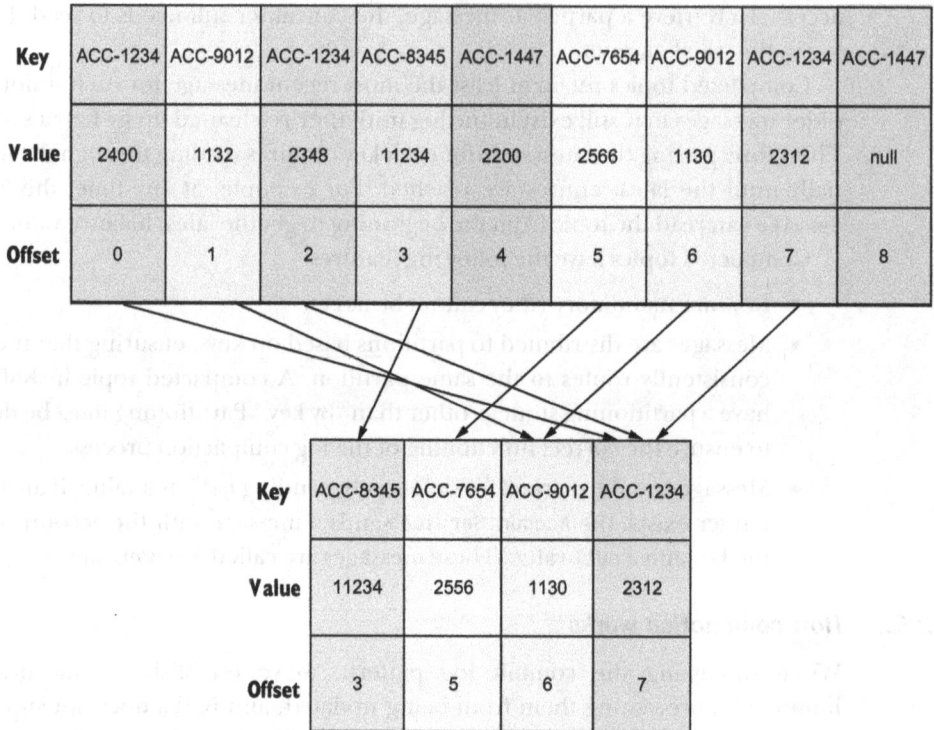

Figure 2.16 During the compaction process, the data within a topic is rewritten. For each key, only the latest value is retained, and messages where the value is null are deleted.

2.5.3 When compaction happens

It is not possible to trigger log compaction explicitly; instead, compaction occurs automatically when certain conditions are met:

- The log.cleaner.enable property is set to true, which is the default value.
- The topic becomes "dirty" based on the ratio specified in the log.cleaner.min .cleanable.ratio configuration property (which defaults to 0.5). In this ratio, the dirty portion of the log is compared to the total log size for a partition. Once this threshold is reached, the topic becomes eligible for compaction.

Additionally, other properties play a role in determining when compaction is triggered:

- log.cleaner.min.compaction.lag.ms—Specifies the minimum time a message must remain uncompacted.
- log.cleaner.max.compaction.lag.ms—Specifies the maximum time a message remains ineligible for compaction.

The log compactor in Kafka considers a log eligible for compaction when either of the following conditions is met:

- The ratio of the size of uncompacted (dirty) data to the total log size exceeds the specified threshold, and the log has contained uncompacted records for at least the duration specified by `log.cleaner.min.compaction.lag.ms`.

- The log has contained uncompacted records for longer than the duration specified by `log.cleaner.max.compaction.lag.ms`.

These configuration options ensure that logs are compacted based on the ratio of changes and the specified time constraints, balancing efficiency with data availability. Additionally, it's important to note that compaction only occurs on closed segments, leaving the active segment untouched to minimize the performance impact.

2.5.4 *Making decisions about the compaction policy*

During the ODS project's initial discussions, the team leaned toward implementing a delete policy for both topics, which would periodically remove data from them. This decision seemed logical for transactions, given their immutable nature, and the team opted to retain only the latest transactions in the aggregated view. However, when considering profile data, the approach isn't as straightforward.

Kafka has traditionally been viewed solely as a transport system between services. Storing all profile data within the topic presented an opportunity to treat it as a key-value storage system, ensuring consistent access to customer data for various stakeholders. While compacted topics are an intriguing feature, the practical implications of working with them on the consumer side remain somewhat uncertain. To explore this possibility further, the designers can configure the topic containing profile data as compacted. The goal here is to retain the latest version of each customer's profile data, making customer data readily available and consistent across applications. The team plans to conduct a series of tests by sending multiple updates to the same keys and tombstone messages for deletion. Then, they can tune the configuration while examining client behavior and monitoring the latency, server performance, and disk usage.

The compaction policy is shown here:

```
asyncapi: 3.0.0
info:
  title: Customer 360 Project
  version: 1.0.0
  description: >
    This project aims to aggregate data from various sources, providing a
    comprehensive view of customer information.

channels:
  customerProfile:
    description: Storing and distributing profile information of customers.
    address: CUSTOMER_PROFILES
    messages:
      profile:
        bindings:
          kafka:
            key:
```

```
                    type: string
                    description: identifier of the customer
        bindings:
          kafka:
            partitions: 9
            replicas: 3
            topicConfiguration:                    The topic uses a
              cleanup.policy: ["compact"]  ◄───── compaction policy
              retention.ms: 432000000
              min.insync.replicas: 2
```

Architecture notes: Compaction

To summarize the key points on compaction:

- When only the latest value for each key is important, a compacted topic is an option. In a compacted topic, only the most recent value for each key is retained, and keys must not be null.
- Access to compacted topics remains sequential, just like with non-compacted topics; Kafka does not provide random access to specific messages.
- Compaction does not occur immediately and cannot be triggered manually; it is initiated periodically based on broker configuration settings and specific conditions, such as the amount of data accumulated or the need to reclaim disk space.
- Typical use cases for compacted topics include maintaining the latest state of a user profile, caching current product prices, or managing configuration data that changes over time.

2.6   Online resources

- "Kafka Replication and Committed Messages": https://docs.confluent.io/kafka/design/replication.html
  This design document explains how Kafka replication works internally, including leader–follower synchronization and message durability guarantees.

- "How to Choose the Number of Topics/Partitions in a Kafka Cluster?" https://www.confluent.io/blog/how-choose-number-topics-partitions-kafka-cluster/
  This Confluent blog post offers guidance and trade-offs for selecting the right number of topics and partitions.

- "Kafka topic partitioning: Strategies and best practices": https://newrelic.com/blog/best-practices/effective-strategies-kafka-topic-partitioning
  This best-practices article from New Relic explores effective partitioning strategies to achieve parallelism and even data distribution.

- "Understanding Kafka Compaction": https://www.naleid.com/2023/07/30/understanding-kafka-compaction.html

Clear and approachable explanation of Kafka's log compaction process illustrates when it happens and how it helps maintain the latest state efficiently.

- "Deep dive into Apache Kafka storage internals: segments, rolling and retention": https://strimzi.io/blog/2021/12/17/kafka-segment-retention/
  This detailed technical post from Strimzi explores Kafka's on-disk storage structure and how segment rolling and retention policies work.

- "Kafka Topic Configuration Reference for Confluent Platform": https://docs.confluent.io/platform/current/installation/configuration/topic-configs.html
  Official Confluent reference which lists topic-level configuration options, essential for tuning performance, reliability, and data retention behavior.

Summary

- Topics act as destinations that group messages together, identified by their unique names.

- Topics are divided into partitions, facilitating parallel data processing. Message order is guaranteed within each partition. However, no ordering is guaranteed across different partitions within the same topic.

- Partitions are replicated across different brokers to ensure redundancy, with the number of replicas determined by the replication factor.

- Messages consist of keys, values, and optional headers, and they also include a timestamp and other metadata. Keys play a crucial role in partitioning, ensuring that messages with the same key are directed to the same partition.

- The offset signifies a message's position within a partition, aiding in tracking which messages have been consumed by the consumer.

- Messages in Kafka are retained based on specific criteria, such as a defined period, the size of the topic, or a combination of both factors.

- Messages are consistently persisted on the disk of the broker in batches. To optimize disk usage, expedite read and write operations, and enforce retention policies, the data is partitioned into segments.

- Specially configured topics, known as compacted topics, store only the latest value for each key in Kafka.

- The organization of Kafka topics can be documented effectively using AsyncAPI.

Kafka clients and message production

This chapter covers

- Connecting to Kafka
- Configuring client applications
- Sending messages using Kafka
- Typical challenges faced by producer applications

Let's shift from the broker internals to how clients talk to Kafka. Client configurations play a significant role in the data-transfer process to and from brokers, so we need to look at the options available to optimize application performance and reliability. First we want to understand the basics of producers: configuring clients, connecting to Kafka, and choosing serializers. Then we can focus on how messages are sent and confirmed, including partitioning, acknowledgments, batching, timeouts, and timestamps. Along the way, we'll note some common pitfalls and how to avoid them. The goal here is to help you send data to Kafka reliably and efficiently, with settings you can justify in production. Then, in the next chapter, we'll examine the intricacies of developing consumer applications.

3.1 Communicating with Kafka

Let's look at how data is transmitted to and from Kafka brokers. In the Customer 360 operational data store project, when a customer profile is created or updated, the new data must be formatted into a message and sent to Kafka. This process is managed by an application that not only receives and validates data from the frontend but also stores it locally and handles the crafting and sending of messages to Kafka. This messaging functionality is embedded within the application's code.

Similarly, another application will consolidate data from various topics—such as profile changes, billing details, and customer interactions—to construct a detailed customer profile. This application will include code that retrieves new messages from Kafka, processes them, and confirms their processing back to the broker. Together, these microservices function as Kafka producers and consumers, incorporating the necessary logic for interacting with Kafka directly into their code.

When developers build these applications, they often opt for using frameworks rather than directly using low-level Kafka client libraries. Popular frameworks like Spring-Kafka or Micronaut-Kafka provide high-level constructs that greatly streamline development, although they may obscure some underlying details. By contrast, low-level Kafka clients expose finer-grained control and enable developers to fine-tune behavior—from custom message conversion and dead-letter routing to precise management of consumer concurrency and offset handling. Since clients are so important to data transmission, we need to fully understand their actions and configuration possibilities.

Field notes: Patterns and pitfalls for Kafka clients

The conference room buzzes with anticipation as Max Sellington, Eva Catalyst, and Rob Routine convene to discuss the intricacies of developing client applications for Kafka integration.

Max: Alright team, let's explore the realm of client applications. What are the requirements for our client teams, and how well-versed should they be in Kafka to effectively integrate with it? Additionally, what are the associated costs we need to consider?

Eva: Integrating with Kafka can be quite direct. Frameworks can simplify many of Kafka's complexities, letting teams concentrate on their specific needs. That said, mastering Kafka does demand time and commitment.

Max: I'm not entirely convinced it's as easy as everyone claims it to be, Eva. Let's consider our proof-of-concept, the Customer 360 project. How do we go about creating the client applications? Will they be structured as microservices? Is programming necessary, or can we rely on configuration? How dependent is this setup on Kafka?

Eva: For our proof-of-concept, we'll have two microservices: one for sending updates about customer data, such as profile changes or new addresses, and another for dispatching the latest transactions. Additionally, we'll have an aggregated service that offers a comprehensive view for customer support. All three services will communicate with Kafka.

(continued)

Max: How feasible is it to implement these services? Do we require a specialized team? Should we consider hiring consultants to kickstart the project?

Eva: Well, with frameworks, programmers can focus on their specific tasks without needing to understand all the complex details of Kafka's internal workings. Let's start with a straightforward approach to our project and assess how it progresses.

Max: I see your point, Eva. Are there any considerations for languages our teams can use for integration?

Rob (interjecting): Currently, Kafka employs its own protocol, but libraries are available for a wide array of programming languages. This flexibility ensures that teams can choose the language best suited to their needs.

Max: And how extensive is this support? By the end of the month, we're down to just a Java programmer and a Python programmer. Will it work?

Rob: Absolutely, Java and Python are among the best-supported languages in the Kafka ecosystem, with a strong community and extensive libraries.

Max: Where might we encounter obstacles?

Eva: Asynchronous communication introduces its own set of challenges. When customer information changes and updates are sent, how do we ensure they're reliably transmitted? What guarantees do we have?

Rob: Perhaps the biggest challenge is understanding all these configuration parameters and finding the optimal combination. They are vital for proper functioning.

Max: I see. So, in summary, our client teams must understand the basics of Kafka, use frameworks for ease of integration, and be prepared to address challenges related to data consistency and governance. With these considerations in mind, let's chart a course for developing robust client applications that seamlessly integrate with Kafka.

As the discussion concludes, the team embarks on a journey to architect client applications that harness the power of Kafka while navigating its complexities.

3.1.1   How producers send messages to brokers

This is a simplified depiction of how messages are sent:

1. Producers encode messages into byte arrays for transmission.
2. A predefined strategy determines the partition to which messages should be sent.
3. For enhanced efficiency, messages are compiled into batches.
4. These batches are then forwarded to the broker when they're ready.
5. Producers have the option to wait for an acknowledgment from the broker, confirming the successful receipt of the batch.

6 In the case of errors or lost acknowledgments, the batch is retransmitted to ensure delivery.

Figure 3.1 provides an overview of the producer routine, and how producers send messages to brokers.

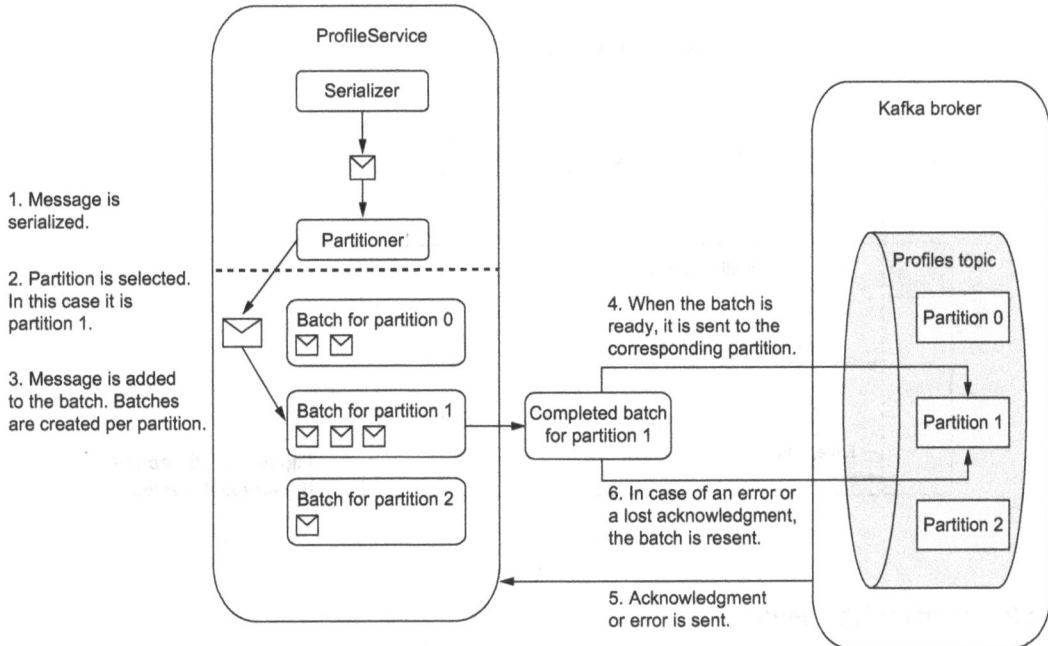

Figure 3.1 Simplified workflow of message transmission by a producer, including serialization, partition selection, batch assembly, and data transmission to the server, with an optional confirmation step

Kafka utilizes its binary protocol over TCP/IP for data transfer, and there are client libraries designed for this protocol. Initially available in Java, Kafka client libraries are now accessible in various popular programming languages, allowing you to code your client application in your preferred language. Regardless of the chosen language, these libraries adhere to the same architectural principles and, crucially, share a consistent set of configuration parameters.

In Kafka, you don't need to be overly concerned about the compatibility of broker and client versions. Kafka features bidirectional compatibility, enabling old clients to communicate with new brokers and vice versa. Before initiating communication, brokers send their supported protocol version (a range of API versions), and the client selects the highest version compatible with both. If there's no such version, an exception is thrown. This approach facilitates independent upgrades of clients and servers while accommodating a diverse range of clients with varying versions. Thankfully, this process is handled automatically by the Kafka library, making it seamless and transparent to developers. This mechanism is illustrated in figure 3.2.

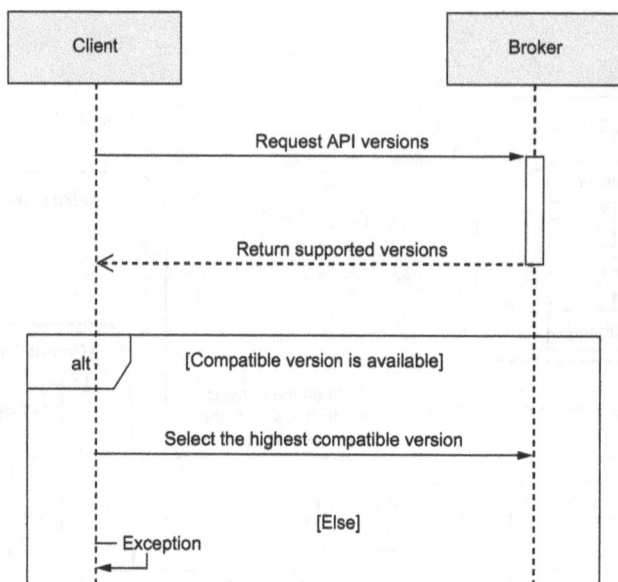

Figure 3.2   Selecting the protocol version

3.1.2   *Configuring clients*

The Kafka client libraries handle numerous tasks behind the scenes, concealed by the functions they expose. For instance, when your application invokes the send method, the library autonomously assembles messages into batches, determines the strategy for distributing messages across partitions, retries sending in the case of errors, and undertakes various other operations. How can you customize and fine-tune the behavior of the client?

Generally, extensive programming is not needed to modify the client. Instead, the client code should remain straightforward, with adjustments made through name-value parameters. Essentially, the client microservice comprises the application code, the client library responsible for low-level communication with Kafka, serialization libraries, other dependencies of Kafka, and configuration files. The number of these parameters is extensive, allowing customization at every step of the client operation without altering the code. Configuration files are separated from the application code, simplifying the supply of different configurations for different environments, and enabling parameter changes without service redeployment. The same set of parameters is supported across various frameworks, with minor variations, and is documented as part of the client configuration. The structure of the client application is shown in figure 3.3.

Application configuration is externalized, so it
can be changed independently of the code.

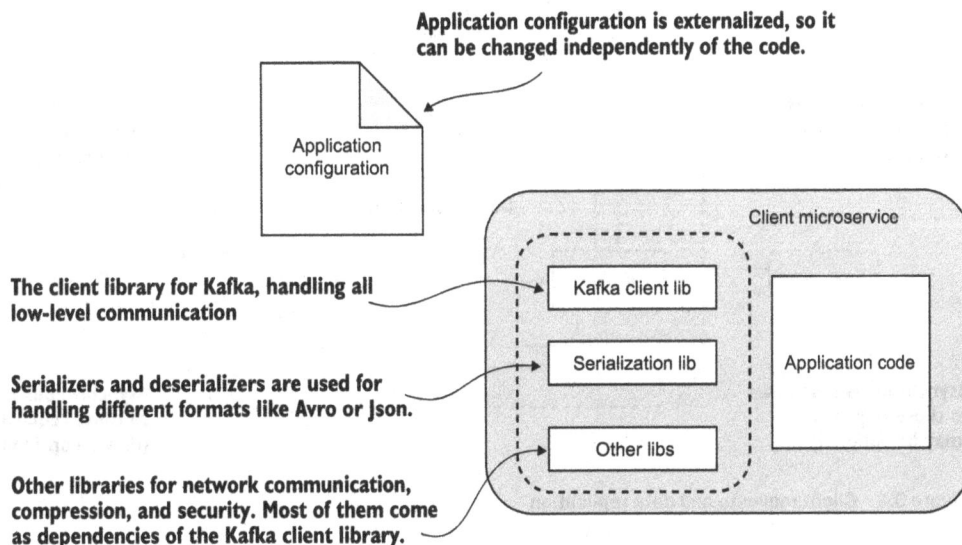

The client library for Kafka, handling all
low-level communication

Serializers and deserializers are used for
handling different formats like Avro or Json.

Other libraries for network communication,
compression, and security. Most of them come
as dependencies of the Kafka client library.

Figure 3.3   A typical structure of a client application for both producers and consumers

The practices of externalizing configurations and using distinct client and serialization libraries are recognized as best practices in application architecture. These approaches enhance the portability and predictability of applications across various environments.

Next, we'll dive into the most important configuration parameters.

NOTE   The configurations and concepts described here apply to all Kafka clients, regardless of the programming language. However, the examples in this chapter—including property examples like class names—are given in Java for illustration.

3.1.3   *Connecting to Kafka*

In Kafka, we have two types of message transfer:

- Brokers replicate data from leader partitions to follower partitions within a topic.
- Producers and consumers send and receive data to and from brokers.

These interactions—shown in figure 3.4—are both handled by the same Kafka service, which processes requests from both producers and consumers, as well as replication requests. This service exposes its functionality to clients via different ports. Typically, we need to expose the service differently because of different security options. The configurations are distinguished by unique listener names, which help to specify and manage the settings for different types of client connections.

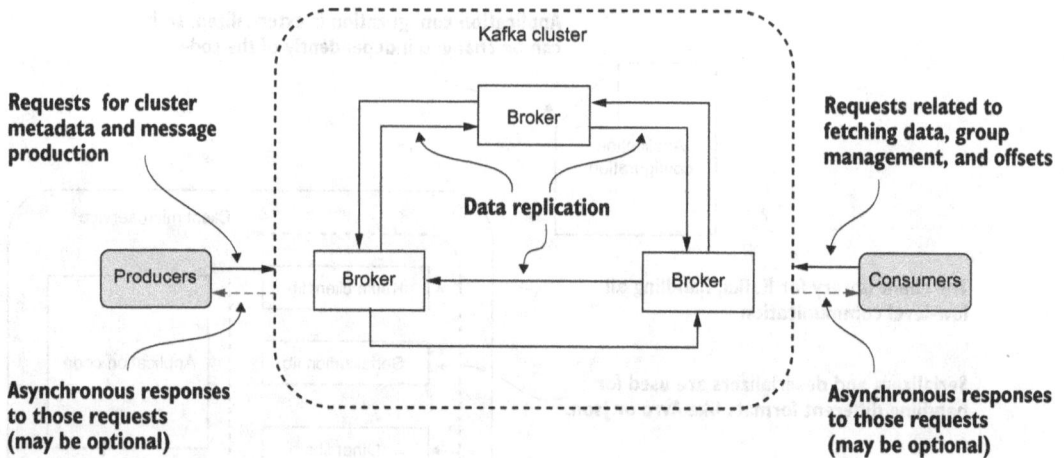

Figure 3.4   Client requests and data replication

Suppose we want to establish connections to Kafka in three different situations:

- *Replicating data between brokers*—Communication will be open without authentication, authorization, and encryption. It will be done through a listener named INTERBROKER.

- *Producers and consumers from the internal network*—These are clients we trust, and there will be no encryption, only authentication and authorization. The listener for this is named INTERNAL.

- *Producers and consumers from the external network*—These are clients we trust less, and there will be encryption, authentication, and authorization. The listener for this is named EXTERNAL.

For this setup, shown in figure 3.5, we would specify three different listeners in the cluster configuration. Each listener is defined in the format ${LISTENER_NAME}://$ {SERVER}:${PORT}, where

- LISTENER_NAME is a nickname for the listener for reference in other properties.
- SERVER is the hostname or IP of the broker.
- PORT is the port where the server listens.

In our example, we'd specify the following:

```
listeners=EXTERNAL://broker1.example.com:9092,
    INTERNAL://broker1:9093,
    INTERBROKER://10.0.0.2:9094
```

Here, the listeners parameter includes three different listeners, each uniquely identified by its name, with associated host and port details.

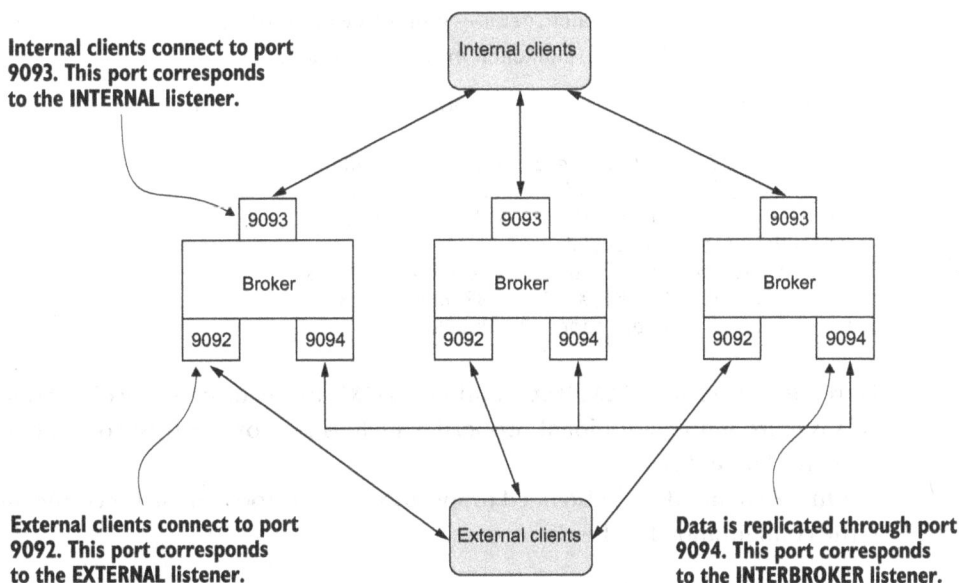

Internal clients connect to port 9093. This port corresponds to the INTERNAL listener.

External clients connect to port 9092. This port corresponds to the EXTERNAL listener.

Data is replicated through port 9094. This port corresponds to the INTERBROKER listener.

Figure 3.5 **Different clients access Kafka through different ports.**

The next important property is `advertised.listeners`. When a client connects to the cluster, it needs to get the addresses of all the brokers. The information returned to the client is contained in `advertised.listeners`, which looks like this:

```
advertised.listeners=EXTERNAL://broker1.example.com:9092,
    INTERNAL://broker1:9093
```

These are the addresses that can be returned to the client. The broker determines which one to return based on the port. If the client connects to port 9092, addresses for the EXTERNAL listener will be returned, and if it connects to port 9093, the INTERNAL listener's addresses will be returned.

On the client side, the `bootstrap.servers` property is specified:

```
bootstrap.servers=broker1.example.com:9092,broker2.example.com:9092,
    broker3.example.com:9092
```

Typically, all brokers are specified here. The client connects to one of the brokers specified in `bootstrap.servers` (if several, the server is chosen randomly), and the bootstrap server returns the addresses of the brokers that correspond to the connected port. In our example, as the client connects to port 9092, metadata with the EXTERNAL listener will be returned. The returned addresses must be resolvable from the client.

Two more properties need configuration on the broker side for a connection:

- `listener.security.protocol.map`—Defines the security protocol per listener.

- `inter.broker.listener.name`—Specifies which listener to use for internal broker communication (`INTERBROKER` in our example).

To summarize, all our connection properties will look like this:

```
listeners=EXTERNAL://broker1.example.com:9092,
    INTERNAL://broker1:9093,INTERBROKER://10.0.0.2:9094
advertised.listeners=EXTERNAL://broker1.example.com:9092,
    INTERNAL://broker1:9093
listener.security.protocol.map=EXTERNAL:SASL_SSL,
    INTERNAL:SASL_PLAINTEXT,INTERBROKER:PLAINTEXT
inter.broker.listener.name=INTERBROKER
```

Here, `SASL_SSL`, `SASL_PLAINTEXT`, and `PLAINTEXT` are security protocols. (Some protocols require setting additional properties such as keystore or truststore; we will cover these in chapter 9.)

On the client side, we also need to specify which protocol to use for connection. This is the configuration for the client:

```
security.protocol=SASL_SSL
bootstrap.servers=broker1.example.com:9092,
    broker2.example.com:9092,broker3.example.com:9092
```

The configuration described here covers client–broker communication—how clients connect to brokers and how brokers exchange data within the cluster. In chapter 9, we'll look at additional internal communication channels used for cluster coordination and management.

3.1.4   *Serializing and deserializing data*

One of Kafka's fundamental features is that brokers merely transfer binary data between clients without any knowledge of the message content. Producers convert the business information they wish to send into arrays of bytes, and consumers, on their end, transform those bytes into meaningful objects. This implies that clients must agree on how serialization and deserialization will be performed—when a consumer receives a message, it needs to know how it was serialized to correctly perform the deserialization. The examples in this chapter use primitive type serializers (e.g., `StrinSerializer`, `IntegerSerializer`, `LongSerializer`, `ByteArraySerializer`) and their matching deserializers. Other formats—schema-based or JSON, will be introduced in chapter 6, when we discuss data contracts.

When configuring a producer, the `key.serializer` and `value.serializer` properties specify which components handle the serialization of the key and value, respectively. For instance, the following configuration indicates that the keys of the message are serialized as integers, and the values are serialized as strings:

```
key.serializer=org.apache.kafka.common.serialization.IntegerSerializer
value.serializer=org.apache.kafka.common.serialization.StringSerializer
```

Serializers always have corresponding deserializers, so on the consumer side, we would specify

```
key.deserializer=
   org.apache.kafka.common.serialization.IntegerDeserializer
value.deserializer=
   org.apache.kafka.common.serialization.StringDeserializer
```

The agreement on the data format is solely determined by the configuration on the client side, and there is no registry to verify if these properties are specified correctly. If the components do not match the data format, an error is thrown at runtime.

Kafka's client library provides numerous ready-to-use serializers and deserializers, some of which may require additional property settings. You also have the option to specify custom serializer and deserializer implementations. In Java, this is achieved by implementing the corresponding interfaces.

3.1.5   Setting quotas

The Kafka cluster is shared among several clients, and it's essential to ensure that our clients do not consume resources excessively. We can set *quotas* to restrict the resource consumption for clients. There are options to specify the rate at which producers and consumers send data and the percentage of used broker threads. If the quotas are exceeded, the broker delays the response, initiating throttling for the client. The clients will receive the responses after the delay is over.

To assign specific quotas to clients, it's essential to identify them accurately. This can be achieved through two primary methods:

- *Utilizing user principals*—Kafka facilitates user authentication via various mechanisms. Upon successful authentication, a user principal, representing the user's name, is linked with client requests. This association enables the allocation of quotas at the user level, managing access and resource usage more finely.
- *Using the* `client.id`—The `client.id` is a user-defined string in the client configuration that accompanies every request to the broker. This ID enables the allocation of quotas to specific client applications. However, relying on `client.id` is not recommended, as it can be any arbitrary string provided in the configuration or even automatically generated by frameworks. For consistency and better management, using principals (such as the client's authentication credentials) is preferred.

The quotas are specified per broker and are calculated over multiple small windows. There can be default quotas, which apply to all clients, or the quotas can be assigned based on `client.id` or user principal (if the clients are authenticated).

3.1.6   Field notes: Setting up the Customer 360 operational data store

Returning to our operational data store example, let's see how we'd set up a project like this. First, like our fictional team, we can delegate the programming tasks to the development team responsible for implementing the services, so we can delve into the architectural considerations.

The team then tackles infrastructure decisions, opting for an on-premises cluster with three brokers. To keep things straightforward, they defer discussions on securing communication and access restrictions, opting to keep communication in plain text for the proof-of-concept phase.

Their next task is to define the configuration for the producer application. This configuration consists of a set of properties, represented as name-value pairs, that are specified on the client side and used by the client library to set up the producer. The resulting client configuration is:

```
boostrap.servers=kafka1.ex.com:9092,kafka2.ex.com:9092,
    kafka3.ex.com:9092
```

This configuration implies that clients must establish network connections to all three brokers on port 9092. For seamless communication between the clients and the brokers, they make sure these connections are permitted and not blocked by firewalls.

Then they must tackle serialization. The team contemplates using JSON for data serialization, which would encode data as strings. To kickstart the process, they settle on these specifications for both services:

```
key.serializer=
    org.apache.kafka.common.serialization.StringSerializer
value.serializer=
    org.apache.kafka.common.serialization.StringSerializer
```

Next, the team discusses client IDs, which are essential for tracking producer microservices and troubleshooting issues. According to Kafka's best practices, a client ID should represent the logical application name (like `ProfileService` or `Transaction-Service`), and optionally a stable instance identifier if needed for operational clarity.

To ensure uniqueness and clarity in logs and metrics, the team decides to assign a prefix to each microservice's client ID. For example, the `TransactionService` will use a prefix like `trans.srv-`, and the `ProfileService` will use `profile.srv-`.

They consider appending a unique identifier (like a container or instance name) to the client ID. Since Kafka already logs the host or IP address of the producer, detailed tracing can be done without adding ephemeral IDs to the client ID.

The next step is to determine which parts of the configuration should be publicly documented. Our team agrees that specific implementation details should remain within the client application, while serializers and client identifiers should be documented using AsyncAPI and accompanied by diagram. This is because key and value types are pertinent to the consumer team, whereas client IDs are relevant for the monitoring department.

Keys and values were already outlined in the messages section of the configuration. Here, AsyncAPI introduces the concept of *operations* to describe client actions, whether they involve publishing or receiving messages. Operations are abstractly described, with implementation-specific properties detailed in the bindings section. The current version of the client documentation follows.

Listing 3.1   Specifying producer operations

```
operations:
  updateCustomerProfile:                              ◀── Name of the operation
    title: Customer profile data is updated.
    description:  Notifies about updating the profile data.
    action: send                           ◀
    channel:                                            Type of the action—for the
      $ref: '#/channels/customerProfile'   ◀           producer, the type is send
bindings:
  kafka:                                              Reference to the channel
    clientId:                                         in the channel section
      type: string
      enum: ['profile.srv']     ◀── Client identifier
  newTransaction:
    title: .
    description:  Notifies about new transactions.
    action: send
    channel:
      $ref: '#/channels/transactions'
bindings:
  kafka:
    clientId:
      type: string
      enum: ['trans.srv']
```

> **Architecture notes: Initial producer configuration**
>
> To document the important information that must be communicated between clients:
>
> - Kafka offers strong compatibility across different versions, so it is generally not required for clients to run the same version as the brokers.
> - Clients must be provided with the appropriate connection string and configuration details needed to connect to the Kafka cluster, including any required authentication or security settings.
> - Keys and values are serialized separately, with the serialization algorithms specified in the client configuration. It is important to share this information with consumers to ensure they can correctly deserialize the data.

3.2   Sending a message

Let's explore the realm of producers, the entities responsible for publishing events by dispatching messages to Kafka. We'll explore the entire journey from the creation of a message to the moment the service receives acknowledgment of successful delivery or encounters an error. What aspects should the producer handle autonomously? Which features are guaranteed by the framework, and what requires explicit programming? What are the possibilities for customization?

While Kafka operates on an open binary protocol, enabling interaction at a low level, it is more pragmatic to use client libraries with higher-level APIs. These libraries, available in various languages, share common concepts and interaction patterns. In this chapter, we'll outline the behavior of the client without binding it to any specific programming language.

The producer consistently communicates with the partition leaders, requiring knowledge of the brokers where the partition leaders are located. To acquire this information, the producer sends a metadata request to the cluster and, in response, receives a mapping of brokers and partition leaders. This information remains static and is cached on the producer's side. The duration for which this information is cached is determined by the `metadata.max.age.ms` configuration parameter, which is set to 5 minutes by default. After this period, a metadata refresh is enforced. This process is shown in figure 3.6.

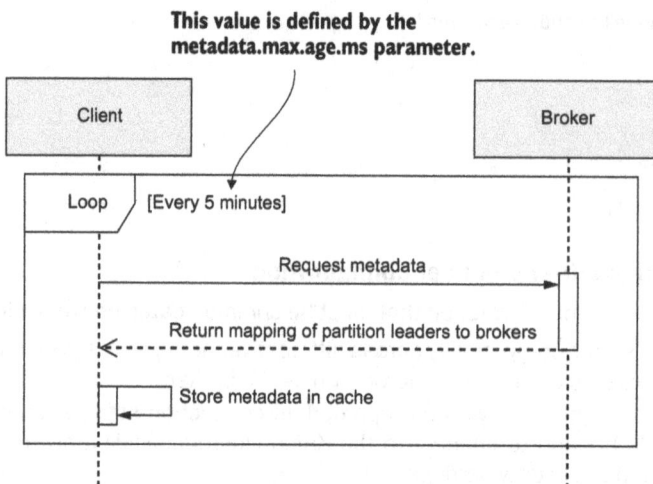

Figure 3.6   The process of receiving and caching metadata

If a leadership change happens and the client sends data to a broker that has lost its leadership status, a temporary error arises. This error is swiftly addressed by the client library, which fetches the latest metadata from the broker and resends the batch to the newly selected leader. Details about this error are written as an informational message in the client application's log.

To send a message from your program, you need to invoke the send method and provide a set of parameters. Note that the actual name of this method may vary depending on the programming language or framework you are using. Typically, at the code level, you specify the following:

- The topic to which the message should be sent (this parameter is required)
- The key for the message
- The value for the message

At least one of the key or value parameters must be present.

Additional parameters, such as message headers, the partition for sending the data, the timestamp for the message, or callbacks for processing message delivery can also be passed. However, these parameters are often omitted or determined by a default strategy.

A lot of background work takes place after the send method is invoked:

1. The message is created with key, headers, and value. All parts are optional, but either key or value must be present.
2. The data is serialized into bytes. Keys and values are serialized independently, potentially using different serializers for each.
3. A partition is selected.
4. The message is added to a batch, which is stored in the memory of the producer application. This optimization helps transfer messages in bulk rather than one by one.
5. When the batch reaches its maximum size, as defined in the client configuration, or when the predetermined timeout for accumulating new messages expires, it is considered ready and is dispatched to the broker leading the chosen partition.
6. The batch is written on the leader and replicated to followers.
7. Upon receiving acknowledgment, the message (actually the entire batch) is considered delivered, and the metadata about the message, such as its offset and partition, becomes available to the client.
8. In the case of an exception, if it's a retriable exception, the batch is sent again until success or until a configurable limit is reached.
9. If an exception is not retriable, it will be thrown on the client side.

The message-sending algorithm is illustrated in figure 3.7.

The good news is that all this behavior is implemented by the library, and the programmer only needs to ensure the right configuration parameters are specified. Now let's explore how we can customize specific steps.

3.2.1 Partitioning strategy

Let's revisit the concept that, within each topic, there are multiple partitions designed for parallel data processing. It's crucial to understand that partitions are treated independently, potentially handled by different consumer instances situated on distinct servers. In general, we should not rely on the assumption that data from different

1. Application creates the message, which contains key, headers, and value.

2. All parts of the message are serialized into byte arrays.

3. The partition is determined based on the chosen strategy.

```
1010
```

Producer → Serializer → Partitioner

9. If retry is not possible an exception is thrown.

Topic Accounts
Partition 0

```
1010   1001   1101
```

4. The message is allocated to the appropriate batch, which is organized by both partition and topic.

Topic Accounts
Partition 1

```
1110   0001
```

8. If the exception is retriable, the number of retries has not been exceeded, and timeouts have not expired, then the batch will be re-sent.

Metadata
(offset,
timestamp ...)

[no]

Retry?   [yes]   Batch ready?   [no]

5. When the batch is ready, it is sent to the cluster.

[yes]   [no]

[yes]

Ok?   ←   Ack   ←   Kafka cluster

7. Once the batch is successfully written, the broker sends an acknowledgment along with metadata.

6. The batch is written on the leader and replicated to followers.

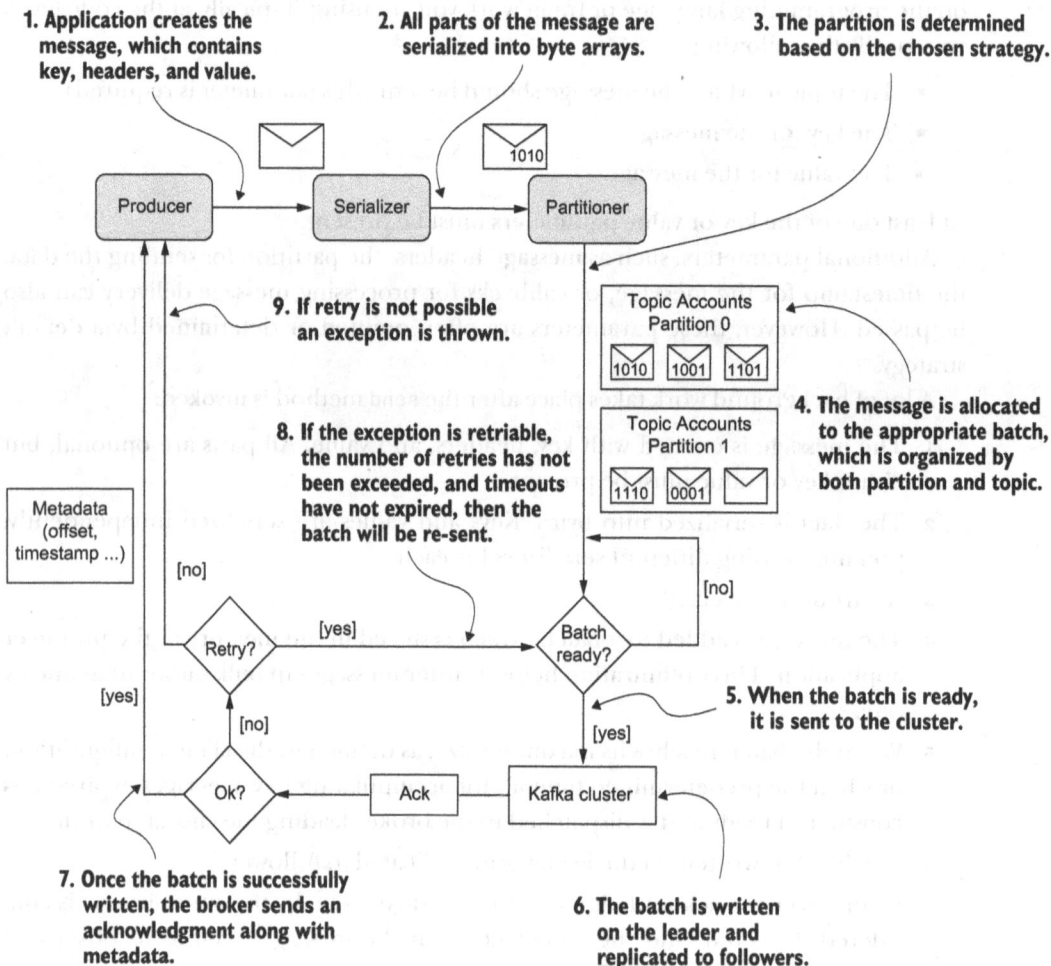

Figure 3.7   Producer message-sending workflow in Kafka

partitions will be processed together. Additionally, it's important to reiterate that message ordering is maintained only within each partition.

The default partitioning strategy in Kafka is based on the message key. This ensures that messages with the same key are directed to the same partition, preserving their ordering. The partition is determined by taking the hash of the key and dividing it by the total number of partitions. If the key is absent (null), the default UniformStick-Partitioner partitioner uses sticky partitioning: it sends each batch of records to a single partition, then switches (rotates) to another partition for the next batch. This means that no per-key ordering or co-location is guaranteed. If you need ordering, co-location, or compaction semantics, you'll need to provide a stable key.

This default strategy is applied when no other partitioning strategy is specified. However, you can override this behavior by setting the `partitioner.class` property in the producer configuration:

```
partition.class=org.apache.kafka.clients.producer.RoundRobinPartitioner
```

With the *round-robin strategy*, the presence of keys is ignored, and messages are evenly distributed across partitions in a cyclical manner. The round-robin strategy processes messages one by one, cycling through available partitions and looping back to the first partition after reaching the last one. This strategy is highly efficient, ensuring an even distribution of messages so that all partitions contain approximately the same amount of data.

The following options are rarely used, but they are available:

- Specify the partition index explicitly in the `send` method.
- Implement your own distribution strategy by creating a custom component.

You can use these strategies if the key-based or round-robin strategies do not satisfy your requirements. This may happen if you have a key for the data, but the data is highly imbalanced, meaning that certain keys are present much more frequently than others. In this case, you might want to assign partitions not based on a hash distribution. Alternatively, you might have information about the current system load and want to balance the load manually for optimal resource utilization.

However, it's important to note that dynamically assigning partitions comes with the cost of not being able to guarantee message ordering for any given key. If ordering is required for messages sharing the same key, they must all be sent to the same partition.

3.2.2 *Field notes: Partitioning strategy for the Customer 360 ODS*

Let's see how our team comes up with a partitioning strategy for their ODS. They determine that partitioning by key is essential for the `CUSTOMER_PROFILES` topic, as maintaining the order of updates is critical. Therefore, they select the customer identifier as the key for this topic. As for transactions, the natural ordering is governed by the business timestamp, an attribute of the transaction object. There may be some debate on the necessity of a key for this topic, but incorporating a key would enhance data organization and streamline processing. So, they opt to use the transaction identifier as the key for the `TRANSACTIONS` topic.

Now it's time to document the partitioning strategy. In this case, AsyncAPI may not be the best option because it doesn't provide a standard way to describe how messages should be partitioned. One possibility is to include it in the description attribute, but you may want a visual approach as well. In figure 3.8, you can see an initial diagram illustrating all pertinent information to convey the decisions made.

3.2.3 *Acknowledgment strategies*

How does the client determine that the message has been successfully delivered to the cluster, and what does "successfully" actually mean? Kafka provides several ways to

specify acknowledgment strategies with
different guarantees. Essentially, you
need to choose between latency (how
quickly the acknowledgment is delivered) and durability (the confidence
that you will not lose the data).

The acknowledgment strategy is
specified on the producer side by setting the `acks` parameter. Therefore, if
you have several producers writing data
to the same topic, they may have different acknowledgment strategies. The following options are available:

topic:
CUSTOMER_PROFILES
key: Customer ID
key type format: JSON
value type format: JSON
partitioning: by key
client.id = profile.srv-

ProfileService

P

Kafka

TransactionService

P

topic: TRANSACTIONS
key: Transaction ID
key type format: JSON
value type format: JSON
partitioning: by key
client.id = trans.srv-

Figure 3.8   Draft diagram for producer services

- `acks=0`—This is the fastest and, at
  the same time, the least reliable
  strategy. In this case, the producer does not wait for acknowledgment from the broker and
  considers the message acknowledged once it has been sent
  through the network. The offset
of the message is not known. If an error happens and the message is not saved on
the cluster, the producer considers it sent anyway and does not attempt to retry.

- `acks=1`—The acknowledgment is sent by the broker when the message is
  received by the leader but before it is replicated to the followers. While the leader's response is requested, replication is not guaranteed as it occurs in the background. If the leader fails before the replication is completed, the message is
  physically lost, but from the point of view of the producer, it has been delivered.
  Before Kafka version 3.0, this value was the default strategy, making a compro-
  mise between good latency and durability.

- `acks=all` *or* `acks=-1`—This option provides the strongest guarantee in terms of
  durability. The acknowledgment is sent when the data is replicated to all in-sync
  followers. The parameter value is called `all`, and it can be a bit misleading
  because you might assume that replication to all followers is necessary for client acknowledgment. However, if some followers are lagging, the leader does
  not wait for them and sends the acknowledgment after the message is delivered
  to the in-sync followers. Here the `min.insync.replicas` property, which was discussed in chapter 2, comes into play. It's worth remembering that the leader is
  also an in-sync replica, and the default value of `min.insync.replicas` is 1. Therefore, if only one in-sync replica is required, this option may function similarly
  to the `acks=1` strategy. For critical data, the `min.insync.replicas` parameter
  must be adjusted. This setting can be configured both at the broker level and

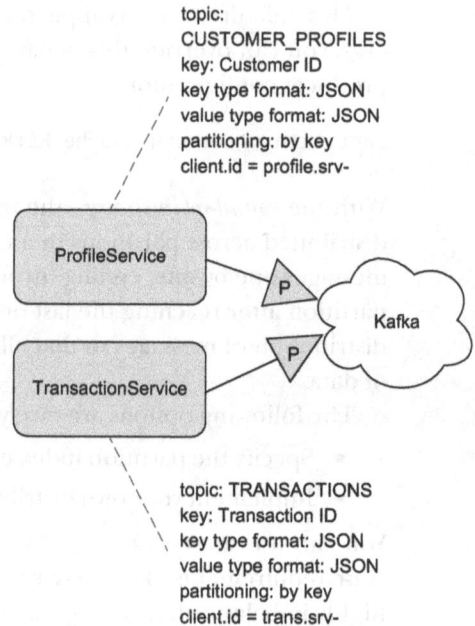

for individual topics. Commonly, the value is set to one less than the `replication`
`.factor` to ensure high durability while maintaining availability.

The replication factor and the acknowledge strategy are settings that significantly
impact the performance of the application. In chapter 11, we'll explore how Kafka's
performance and availability are influenced by configuration settings, which will help
us understand the trade-offs between throughput, latency, and data integrity in different
scenarios.

3.2.4 *Field notes: Implementing an acknowledgment strategy*

Coming up with an acknowledgment strategy means weighing the options between all
acknowledgment and just leader acknowledgment. Considering the critical nature of
the business data and the acceptable latency levels, for our Customer 360 ODS, we'd
chose to implement all acknowledgment. This ensures comprehensive processing
before advancing, aligning with the project's requirements.

The acknowledge property gets added to the documentation. Here is what the part
for the `updateCustomerProfile` operation looks like:

```
operations:
  updateCustomerProfile:
    title: Customer profile data is updated.
    description:  Notifies about updating the profile data.
    action: send
    channel:
      $ref: '#/channels/customerProfile'
bindings:
  kafka:
    clientId:
      type: string
      enum: ['profile.srv']
    acks: all                    ◀──────┘ Specifying acknowledgment
```

3.2.5 *Batches and timeouts*

When you pass a message to the client library, the message is not sent immediately. In
the background, messages are packed into batches to optimize network transfers, as
was illustrated in figure 3.7. Batches are prepared per partition of the topic, ensuring
that each partition will have its own batch, and they are sent in the background thread.
When the broker sends an acknowledgment, it always acknowledges the entire batch.
If an acknowledgment is not received, the entire batch is re-sent. Error handling varies
depending on the client framework, but the client application typically needs to implement
a callback to handle exceptions effectively.

Batches are created in the memory of the client. The amount of memory is configured
by the `buffer.memory` property, and it should be adjusted to meet the project
requirements. If the client application crashes, the unsent batches will be lost, and it is
the responsibility of the client to handle this situation. The producer should consider
messages as delivered only after the acknowledgment is received.

The maximum batch size is determined by the batch.size property in the producer configuration, with the default value being 16 KB. When data is continuously arriving, the batch is sent out when it is full. But what happens if there aren't enough records to send? How long should we wait for additional records to accumulate? This delay is regulated by the linger.ms property, representing the additional number of milliseconds to wait for messages to accumulate. By default, linger.ms is set to 0, meaning the batch is sent immediately when the sender thread is free and available to send requests.

If acknowledgment is not received, the batch is re-sent, and the number of retry attempts before a successful send is determined by the retries property. In the latest versions of Kafka, the default value for this property is 2,147,483,647, which is the maximum value of the integer type in Java. However, this doesn't imply that the client will retry indefinitely; rather, it indicates that timeout properties should be employed. Various properties for timeouts exist, and their values are interconnected:

- delivery.timeout.ms sets an upper limit for reporting success or failure. This timeframe encompasses the entire cycle, including retries and waiting for acknowledgment.
- request.timeout.ms specifies the time the producer awaits a response from the server for each individual request, highlighting its focus on the timing of a single response rather than on the overall process. This property affects various types of producer requests, such as sending messages, receiving acknowledgments, or performing metadata lookups.
- max.block.ms determines the upper limit for blocking in the case where there isn't enough memory for buffering records. If the timeout specified by this property expires, an exception is thrown.

Asynchronous processing can lead to challenging scenarios. For instance, what if a batch is successfully written to the broker, but the acknowledgment is lost? Could this result in duplicate data? What if a batch is delivered after multiple retries? Could this cause reordering, even within a single partition?

We'll explore delivery guarantees in detail in chapter 7. For now, it is important to note that Kafka provides producer idempotence and ordering guarantees with certain configurations. By default, settings like enable.idempotence=true, acks=all, and an appropriate configuration of retries and max.inflight.requests.per.connection ensure that batches are delivered exactly once, in the order they were sent, and without duplicates. If these key settings remain properly configured, you can rely on Kafka's strong delivery guarantees.

Architecture notes: Configuring producers for the Customer 360 ODS

To summarize the key considerations for configuring producers in the client applications of the ODS:

- *Serializers*—key.serializer and value.serializer are set to use string serialization, aligning with the JSON data format.

- *Partitioning*—Data will be partitioned using keys, with entity identifiers chosen as the keys.
- *Client identifiers*—Each service is assigned a unique prefix for the `client.id` property for monitoring purposes. These identifiers must be unique to each producer instance.
- *Acknowledgment strategy*—The acknowledgment strategy is configured as `all`, providing assurance against data loss.

3.2.6 Common producer challenges

In the following sections, we'll outline several common challenges encountered when working with Kafka producers. Understanding these pitfalls will help prevent data loss, performance degradation, and unexpected message behavior. We'll also discuss how to address and mitigate them effectively.

WRONG PARTITIONING STRATEGY

Selecting an appropriate partitioning strategy is a critical responsibility for producer applications. When message ordering is necessary, partitioning by key is an effective approach. It's essential to choose the key wisely, as it ensures that related messages are directed to the same partition and thus preserved in sequence.

A well-designed partitioning strategy also evenly distributes messages across partitions, promoting a balanced workload. If message order isn't a priority, achieving even distribution can be accomplished using a round-robin approach. Therefore, partitioning demands careful consideration of your application's particular requirements in terms of message sequencing, load distribution, and processing parallelism.

NOT ENOUGH MEMORY

In Kafka, messages are grouped into batches and stored in the client's memory, so having enough memory is critical. The `send` method waits for acknowledgments from the Kafka broker before freeing up memory, which means that until a batch is acknowledged, memory cannot be released for new messages. It's important to understand the client's memory needs and to adjust the `buffer.memory` and `batch.size` settings to match. Also, the application must adhere to the maximum permitted batch size to avoid errors.

Monitoring is crucial for maintaining Kafka's performance on both the client and broker sides. In chapter 11, we will explore how to set up effective monitoring to ensure optimal performance.

INCORRECT TIMESTAMPS

If the producer system's clock is unsynchronized or inaccurate, it could assign incorrect timestamps to messages, and correct timestamps are vital for determining when data should be removed according to retention policies. Inaccurate timestamps might lead to premature deletions or overly prolonged retention of messages, potentially causing compliance problems or inefficient storage use. Accurate timestamps also affect log compaction, particularly under time-based cleaning policies.

Moreover, even when timestamps are accurate, batching and compressing messages will result in a single timestamp being applied to the entire batch if the `message` `.timestamp.type` is set to `LogAppendTime` (as discussed in chapter 2). This can cause the loss or inaccurate representation of individual timestamps within the batch.

It's crucial for all system components to agree on the source of the timestamp, whether it's from the producer or the broker. Mismatched configurations across systems can disrupt the expected sequencing and timing, leading to inconsistencies in data processing.

SEVERAL PRODUCERS WRITING CONCURRENTLY

Managing a Kafka topic that receives input from multiple applications requires careful planning and coordination. Kafka guarantees that messages appended to a partition are stored in order. However, when several producers write to the same partition simultaneously, their messages may arrive interleaved at the broker, resulting in an overall sequence that doesn't match the order in which each producer sent them. Achieving a consistent global ordering among all producers can be challenging.

Additionally, Kafka lacks a native feature for indicating the origin of each message; messages don't automatically include metadata to identify their producer. Consequently, if a problem arises—such as data being submitted in an incorrect format—pinpointing the responsible party for the error can prove difficult.

To mitigate these challenges, a best practice is to embed an identifier of the producing application within the message headers. This identification should be implemented within the producer service's code, enabling easier tracing and accountability of messages.

TRANSACTIONS WITH OTHER SYSTEMS

Consider the following scenario: an entity's state changes within a system, and we aim to both update the new state in the database and emit a notification about this change to Kafka. For data consistency, these actions must be atomic—either both succeed or neither occurs. However, deciding which action to prioritize can be challenging, especially since Kafka does not support distributed transactions. If we first send the message to Kafka and then attempt to update the database, there's a risk that the database update might fail, resulting in an erroneous event. Conversely, if we update the database first but fail to send the notification, consumers won't be aware of the update. This dilemma highlights the need for a strategy to manage such situations, a topic we'll explore in chapter 7.

Architecture notes: Advanced producer configuration

While Kafka's default settings are well-suited for most use cases, advanced configurations allow you to optimize the producer's behavior for your specific requirements.

- To ensure message ordering, messages must be distributed to partitions using keys. If ordering is not required, keys are not necessary, and other partitioning strategies can be employed.
- The default settings for acknowledgments and retries are generally optimal and should not be modified without careful consideration.
- The default settings for batch size (batch.size) and timeouts (such as linger.ms) are typically acceptable. However, benchmark testing should be conducted to determine if adjustments are needed for your specific use case.
- It is important for the producer to have a designated client.id to enable tracking and monitoring requests back to the source.
- By default, the timestamp of each message is set on the producer side.

3.3 Online resources

- "Kafka Protocol Guide": https://kafka.apache.org/protocol.html
  This official Kafka documentation details the wire protocol, message formats, and request-response flows—essential for anyone implementing low-level Kafka integrations or debugging communication problems.

- "Kafka Listeners—Explained": https://www.confluent.io/blog/kafka-listeners -explained/
  This Confluent blog post clarifies how to set up internal, external, and inter-broker communication in various deployment environments.

- "Kafka Producer Configuration Reference for Confluent Platform": https:// docs.confluent.io/platform/current/installation/configuration/producer -configs.html
  This official Confluent reference describes all producer configuration parameters, invaluable for fine-tuning reliability, batching, and throughput.

- "Kafka Acks Explained": https://betterprogramming.pub/kafka-acks-explained -c0515b3b707e
  This article breaks down Kafka's acknowledgment modes, helping readers understand how they affect message delivery guarantees and latency.

- "Understanding Kafka partition assignment strategies and how to write your own custom assignor": https://medium.com/streamthoughts/understanding -kafka-partition-assignment-strategies-and-how-to-write-your-own-custom -assignor-ebeda1fc06f3
  This deep-dive post explains Kafka's consumer group rebalancing and partition assignment logic, including practical guidance for implementing custom assignors.

- "Spring for Apache Kafka": https://spring.io/projects/spring-kafka

The official Spring project page and documentation, providing resources for integrating Kafka into Spring applications using high-level abstractions and annotation-driven configuration.

- "Spring Cloud Stream": https://spring.io/projects/spring-cloud-stream
  This official Spring project page introduces Spring Cloud Stream, a framework that simplifies building event-driven microservices by abstracting messaging middleware.

Summary

- The Kafka service can be exposed to clients on various ports and protocols, primarily to accommodate diverse security requirements.

- Client applications utilize a library to manage communication with Kafka, with its behavior customized through configuration parameters.

- Producers and consumers must align on the data format, employing specific components for serialization and deserialization, which are specified through configuration parameters.

- Producers prepare messages by serializing them, selecting appropriate partitions, batching them together, and sending them to Kafka brokers, awaiting acknowledgment.

- In the event of retriable errors, producers resend data seamlessly without manual intervention.

Creating consumer
applications

This chapter covers

- Receiving messages from Kafka
- Principles of parallel message reception
- Common challenges in Kafka consumer handling
- Accessing Kafka via HTTP
- Utilizing data compression in Kafka

Here we'll shift from producers to the other half of the pipeline: consumers. We need to understand how they read at scale, coordinate, and stay correct. How are messages received and processed in parallel, how do applications subscribe to topics or explicitly position themselves in a stream, and how do batching and timeouts shape throughput and latency? To answer these key questions, we need to make consumer groups concrete, explore rebalances, and highlight the most common problems, which are lag, duplicates, and ordering. We also want to consider Confluent REST Proxy as a lightweight integration option. By the end of this chapter, you'll know how to design consumer logic that is reliable, efficient, and easy to operate.

In our ODS example, we'll focus on the next stage of the project: developing the consumer application. With topics set for customer profile data and transactions, the

Customer 360 team will now delve into the intricacies of data aggregation, determining how best to handle and merge the incoming streams. After discussing the various trade-offs, the next step is to start designing the consumer application, focusing on data aggregation and processing it in the client code.

Field notes: Consumer patterns and trade-offs

Max: Alright, let's dive into the consumer application for our project. We've got those two input topics—one for customer profile data and the other for transactions. And we settled on using customer ID as the key for profile data and transaction ID for transactions. Now, we're looking at aggregating data by customer ID. So what's the plan for the consumer service? How's it going to handle and mash up all that data?

Eva: Easy, it's just going to stash the data away in the relational database.

Rob: The consumer side isn't straightforward at all. How many instances of our aggregated service should we have? It will pull data, but how much data should it receive in one request to avoid memory issues? And if it fails, how quickly will the cluster detect it?

Eva: Just like with the producers, a lot of configuration is required to make the application work properly. We need to examine all these properties.

Max: I have a feeling that you're going to ask for more time for research, as usual. But this seems much more complex than it looked at the beginning. Do we have any backup scenarios at all?

Rob: In the worst-case scenario, teams can use a REST proxy, which provides a simple HTTP interface for producing and consuming messages. It acts as a gateway between applications and Kafka, facilitating integration in diverse environments.

Max: So opting for REST is viable? That sounds like a universally approachable method. After all, REST is familiar territory for most.

Eva: Exactly. But it's crucial to weigh the trade-offs. Using Kafka's native libraries provides full feature access, and considering HTTP's overhead, the native protocol offers better throughput and lower latency.

Rob: Hey, one more thing. Can we handle the data aggregation in the Java app that sits in the middle?

Eva: Oh, absolutely. We can totally pull that off, but it's going to involve a bit of stream programming magic. That's something we'll tackle in the next phase of our project.

Rob: Got it. I'm always thinking about ways to streamline our process.

4.1   *Organizing consumer applications*

Let's discuss *consumers*, the components responsible for reading messages from the Kafka cluster. First and foremost, recall that Kafka operates on a pull basis, meaning that the server doesn't autonomously send messages to the client. Instead, the client actively queries the server in a loop to check for the availability of new messages. To facilitate this, the client must establish a connection with the cluster and specify from which topics it wants to retrieve data.

The simplified consumer behavior process is as follows:

1 The consumer subscribes to one or several topics and regularly requests new messages.

2 When the consumer polls, it receives a batch of messages either when enough data is available or when the configured timeout expires.

3 The consumer deserializes the messages.

4 The consumer processes the messages based on its specific logic.

5 The consumer updates its offset in Kafka, marking the position of the last-read message. This doesn't necessarily mean the messages have been fully processed—it just marks them as read.

Figure 4.1 illustrates the behavior of the consumer application.

Messages are pulled by the consumer and deserialized before processing. Arrows indicate the direction of data flow, not request initiation.

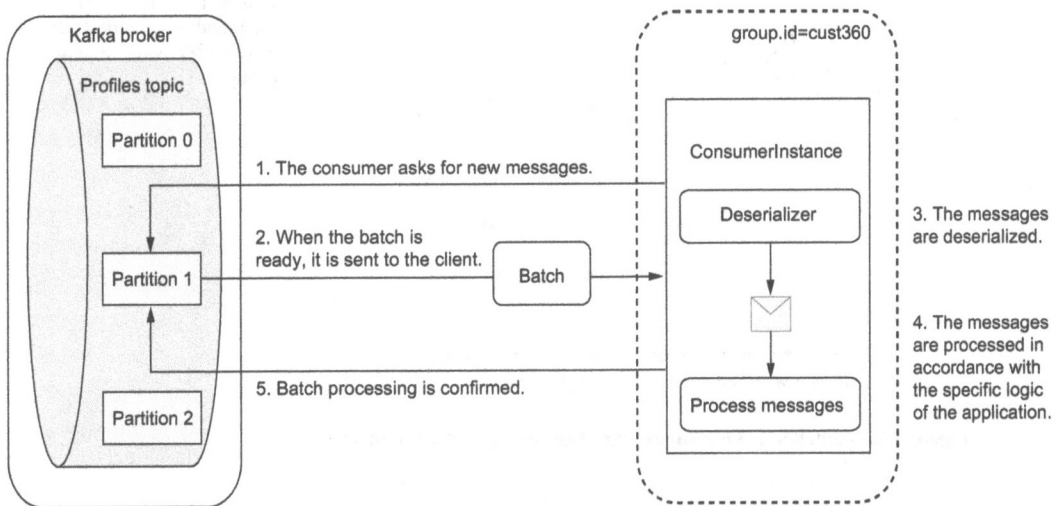

Figure 4.1 Consumer message reception involves periodically requesting new data, receiving messages when available, deserializing and processing the messages, and acknowledging their processing.

The important part of consumer application development is reading topics in parallel. This is where Kafka introduces a key differentiator: *consumer groups*—an essential component of distributed message consumption.

In Kafka, consumers form consumer groups to enable parallel processing of data. While this isn't necessarily tied to services—because a service can operate multiple consumer groups, and a group can span multiple services—thinking in terms of services as separate consumer groups can be a helpful mental model for understanding how the system works.

Figure 4.2 illustrates the concept of different consumers in different consumer groups reading from the same topic. Within a consumer group, multiple consumers share partitions of the topic, with each partition assigned to only one consumer at a time. We'll explore various configurations later in this chapter, but it is crucial to understand that each partition is exclusively handled by a single consumer instance within a consumer group.

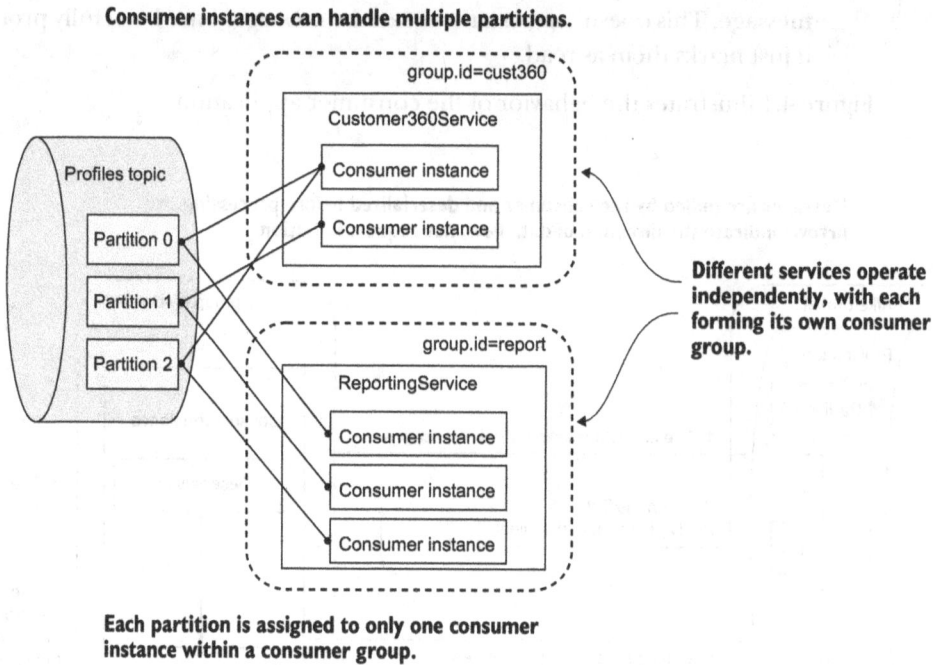

Figure 4.2   Each service consumes data from the topic independently.

In the previous chapter, we explored fundamental concepts applicable to all Kafka client applications. We delved into the structure of client applications, the process of connecting to Kafka clusters, and the serialization of data for transmission. Now we are going to look into the details of programming and configuring the consumer applications.

4.2   Receiving a message

The reading cycle mirrors the sending process. The client requests data, and if there are new unprocessed messages on the broker, the server sends them to the client in a batch. Subsequently, the client deserializes and processes them and then commits the offsets to mark the messages as processed, though this does not necessarily imply that the processing was successful.

Here's an explanation of the typical workflow of a Kafka consumer:

1 The consumer requests partition assignments from the Kafka cluster, effectively asking which partitions it should read.

2 The consumer then enters a loop, repeatedly polling the broker for new messages. If messages are available, the broker batches and sends them to the consumer. If not, the broker may wait for more messages to arrive or until a specified timeout is reached before returning a batch.

3 Upon receiving the messages, the consumer typically deserializes them, translating the data from an array of bytes into objects or other structures used in the application.

4 The consumer processes each message according to the application's unique requirements. This processing could involve a range of actions, such as updating a database with incoming data or performing specific calculations.

5 After processing, the consumer commits its position—the offset of the next record to read. By default, these offsets are stored in a special topic on the broker, allowing Kafka to track which messages have been read by the client. A commit just records your place in the stream (where to start next time); it does not acknowledge each message individually. This ensures that the consumer can resume from the correct position in the event of a restart or failure.

The consumer workflow is shown in figure 4.3. Note that this workflow can vary based on different consumer configuration settings, allowing for customization according to the specific needs of your application.

Now let's explore each part of the workflow.

4.2.1 Reading data in parallel

We partition data to enable the parallel processing of messages. On the client side, multiple consumer components are typically employed to read and process data from the same topic. The central concept here is a *consumer group*, which brings collaborating consumers together.

The term "consumer" can be somewhat perplexing, as we initially referred to consumers as entire applications retrieving data from Kafka. In this chapter, our focus is predominantly on consumer components, which are integral elements of consumer applications. For consistency with other literature, we will refer to these components as consumers. You can envision these consumers as threads, but it's essential to note that this isn't the sole possible implementation. The crucial point is that the consumer group collectively receives all messages from the topic, and each message is processed by a designated member of the group.

Start polling for new messages, continuously asking for new messages.

Consumer

Ask for new messages.

Init

Polling loop

Kafka cluster

After messages have been processed, offsets need to be committed. Subsequent fetch operations will then retrieve messages starting from the last committed offset.

Committing offsets

[no]

[yes]

Messages ready?

[no]

Success?

[yes]

Message processing

Deserializer

Application processing logic, such as saving data into the database

Messages are deserialized into objects.

If there are new messages, they are sent to the client in batches.

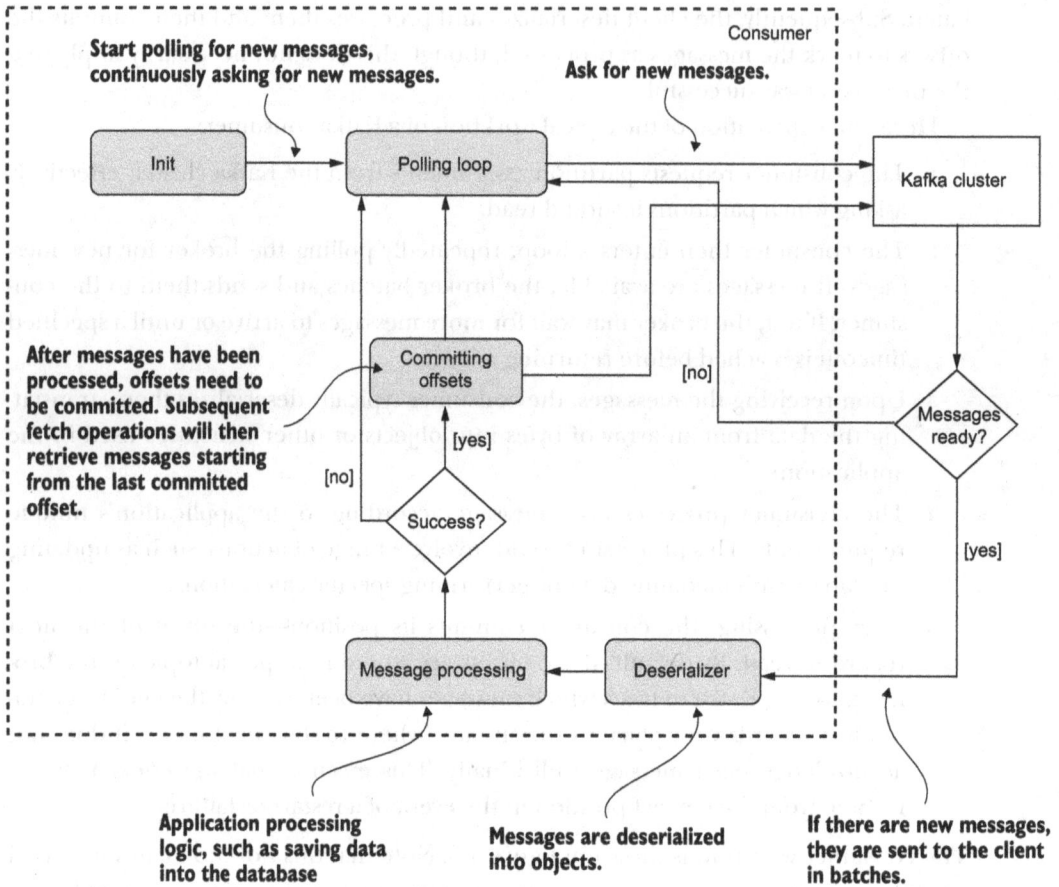

Figure 4.3   Workflow of the consumer application

Let's consider a scenario where `Customer360Service` is responsible for processing notifications about address changes. This microservice defines the consumer group, ensuring that the group collectively receives all messages from the topic. Within this microservice, several consumer components (hereafter referred to as *instances*) may exist, with each handling its designated portion of the data. In Kafka, the distribution of work is organized so that each partition within the topic is assigned to only one consumer instance within the consumer group. An example of partition assignment is shown in figure 4.4.

The consumer group is a fundamental concept in implementing the publish-subscribe pattern. Subscribers are not aware of each other, and each subscriber is expected to receive all messages for processing. In Kafka, this is achieved using consumer groups. If you have multiple microservices that need to independently process messages from the same topic, each microservice will have its own consumer group. A consumer

Here we have one instance of Customer360Service with two consumer instances inside. Four partitions are assigned to two consumer instances.

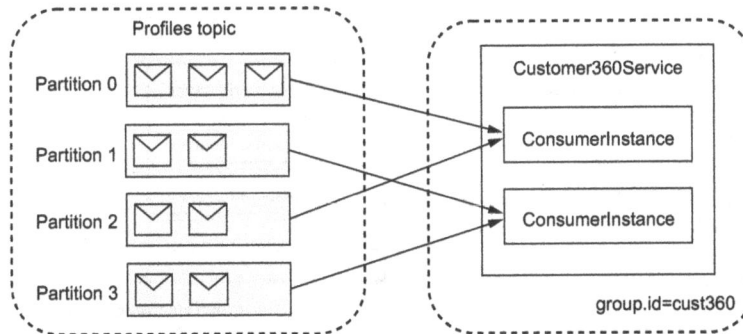

Figure 4.4 Assignment of the topic partitions to the consumer instances within a consumer group

group is defined by the group.id property, which is simply a string value set as part of the client configuration.

We may have multiple instances of a microservice sharing the same consumer group and collaborating. The number of partitions within the topic determines the degree of parallelism, as each partition can be assigned to only one consumer from the group. Various deployment configurations are possible, some of which are illustrated in figure 4.5.

What happens if you have more consumers than partitions? It is indeed possible, but some of them will not receive any partitions, rendering them idle. Conversely, if a group has fewer consumers than partitions, more than one partition may be assigned to some consumers, as illustrated in figure 4.4.

In previous examples, all consumers within a consumer group read data from one topic. It is also possible for a consumer to read data from multiple topics. Client libraries allow consumers to subscribe to a list of topics or to topics matched by a regular expression. In this case, consumers will be assigned partitions from different topics. An example of a subscription is shown in figure 4.6.

Subscribing to multiple topics is common for streaming applications, where the logic of data processing depends on data coming from multiple topics. The strategy for partition assignment is configurable, and we'll cover the provided strategies later in this chapter.

4.2.2 Setting initial consumer configuration for the Customer 360 project

The discussion about client configuration has begun, focusing on ensuring alignment with the producer configuration. Similar to the producer setup, the consumer configuration needs to include information on how to connect to the Kafka cluster. Consequently, the connection endpoint was added to the consumer properties:

```
bootstrap.servers=kafka1.ex.com:9092,
kafka2.ex.com:9092,kafka3.ex.com:9092
```

All consumer instances are inside one service instance. They share the same group.id property.

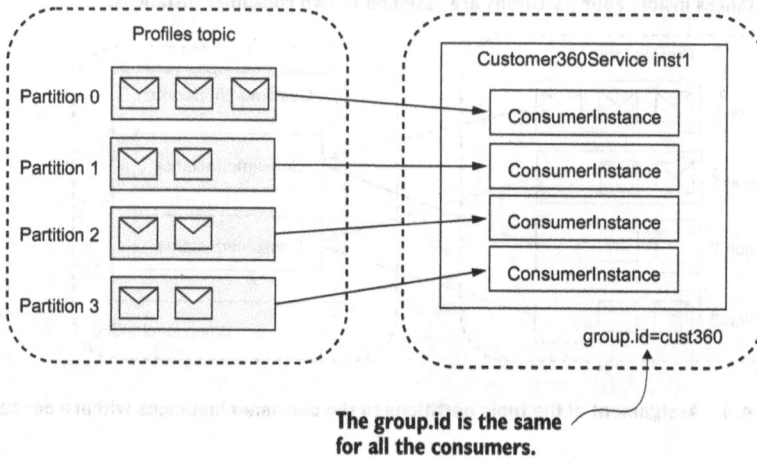

Profiles topic

Partition 0

Partition 1

Partition 2

Partition 3

Customer360Service inst1

ConsumerInstance

ConsumerInstance

ConsumerInstance

ConsumerInstance

group.id=cust360

The group.id is the same for all the consumers.

Here we have two instances of the Customer360Service, each with two consumer instances inside. Each consumer has the same group.id, so all the partitions are distributed between them.

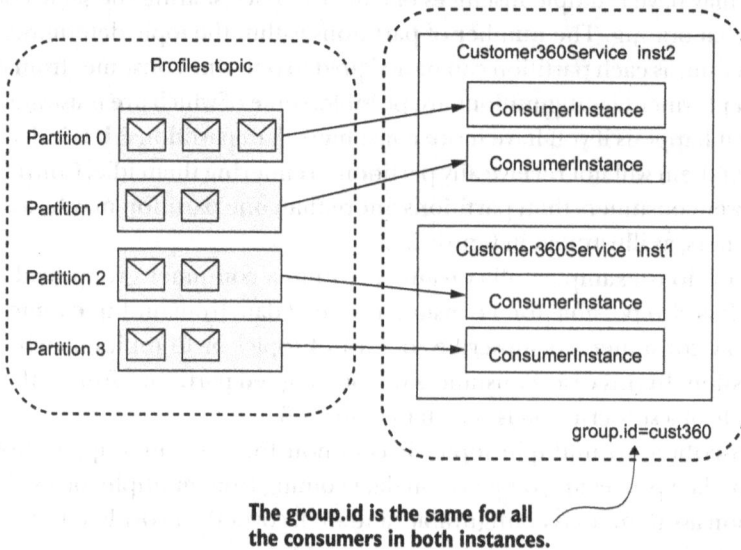

Profiles topic

Partition 0

Partition 1

Partition 2

Partition 3

Customer360Service inst2

ConsumerInstance

ConsumerInstance

Customer360Service inst1

ConsumerInstance

ConsumerInstance

group.id=cust360

The group.id is the same for all the consumers in both instances.

Figure 4.5   Various consumer topologies

With the producer services already defined, it's imperative to ensure that the consumer services adhere to the established contract. Given the agreement that producers will send keys and messages in JSON format, the consumer application must be configured to handle JSON. Thus, deserializers were added:

```
key.deserializer=
   org.apache.kafka.common.serialization.StringDeserializer
value.deserializer=
   org.apache.kafka.common.serialization.StringDeserializer
```

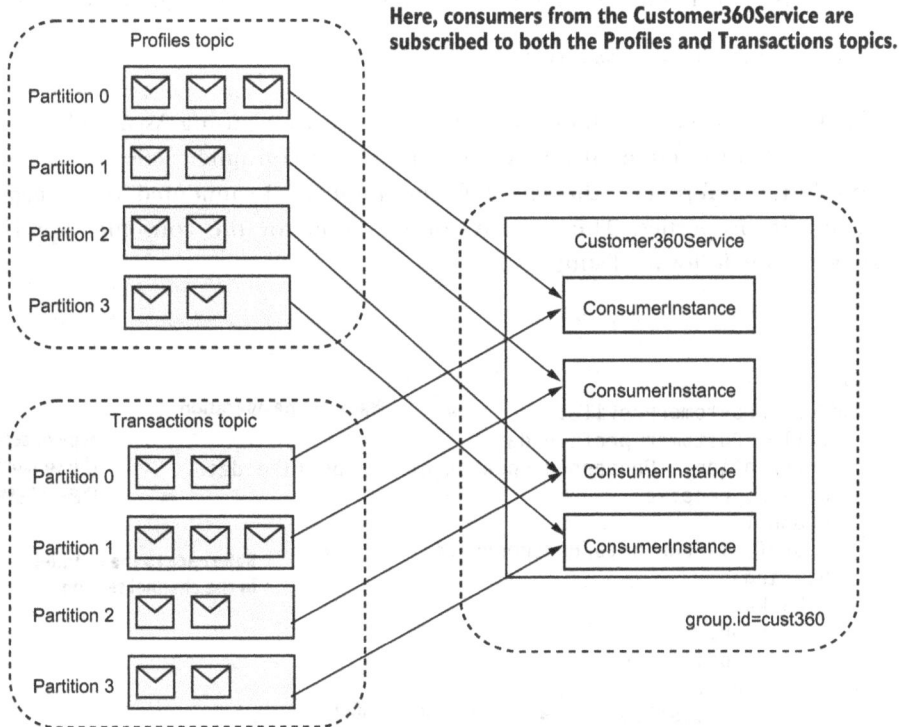

Figure 4.6 Subscribing to multiple topics

Next, the team turned their attention to specifying the consumer group property. This identifier is crucial, as it will be used for all consumers within the Customer360Service. The team agreed on the following setting:

```
group.id=cust360
```

Within the application, there will be two sets of consumers: one reading from the CUSTOMER_PROFILES topic and another from the TRANSACTIONS topic. Kafka supports having multiple consumers subscribing to different topics within the same consumer group. This ensures that each message in each partition of each topic is consumed by only one consumer within the group, allowing for parallel processing of messages across different topics while still maintaining consumer group semantics.

In addition to the group.id property, consumers also utilize the client.id property for monitoring and debugging consumer behavior.

For example, consumers reading from the CUSTOMER_PROFILES topic are configured with

```
client.id.prefix=cust360-profile
```

And consumers reading from the TRANSACTIONS topic are configured as follows:

```
client.id.prefix=cust360-trans
```

The team proceeded with documenting their decisions using AsyncAPI. Once again, they needed to define an operation to represent consumer actions. The consumer application referenced the channel and publicly documented the group.id and client.id properties. The current configuration for the consumer application is shown in the following listing.

Listing 4.1   Documenting the consumer configuration

```
operations:
  onUpdateCustomerProfile:          ◀──┤ Name of the operation
    title: Customer profile data.
    description:  Processed updates of the profile data.      Type of action—for
    action: receive               ◀──┤ the consumer, the
                                       type is receive
    channel:
      $ref: '#/channels/customerProfile'   ◀──┐ Reference to the channel
    bindings:                              │ in the channel section
      kafka:
        groupId:
          type: string
          enum:
            - cust360           ◀──┤ Group identifier
        clientId:
          type: string
          enum:
            - cust360-profile       ◀──┤ Client identifier

  onNewTransaction:
    title: Transaction data.
    description:  Processed updates of the profile data.
    action: send
    channel:
      $ref: '#/channels/transactions'
    bindings:
      kafka:
        groupId:
          type: string
          enum:
            - cust360
        clientId:
          type: string
          enum:
            - cust360-trans
```

4.2.3 *Group leader and group coordinator*

In Kafka, two roles are essential for data consumption: the group coordinator and the group leader.

The *group coordinator*, which is one of the brokers within the Kafka cluster, manages consumer groups and handles the coordination of consumers within these groups. This role is dynamic, and different consumer groups may have different coordinators. When the coordinator goes down or becomes unreachable, a new coordinator is elected. The group coordinator is the one who orchestrates the actual partition assignments for the consumers.

The *group leader* comes into play in partition assignment. Like many other configurations, the partition assignment strategy is set on the client side, and the group leader, which is one of the consumers within the group, is tasked with managing consumers on the client side.

Here's what occurs when a consumer group initiates:

1 As consumers start, they send a request to determine which broker will serve as their coordinator. This is shown in figure 4.7.

Each consumer in the group sends a request to a broker, asking which broker is the group coordinator for its group. This request may be directed to any broker in the cluster.

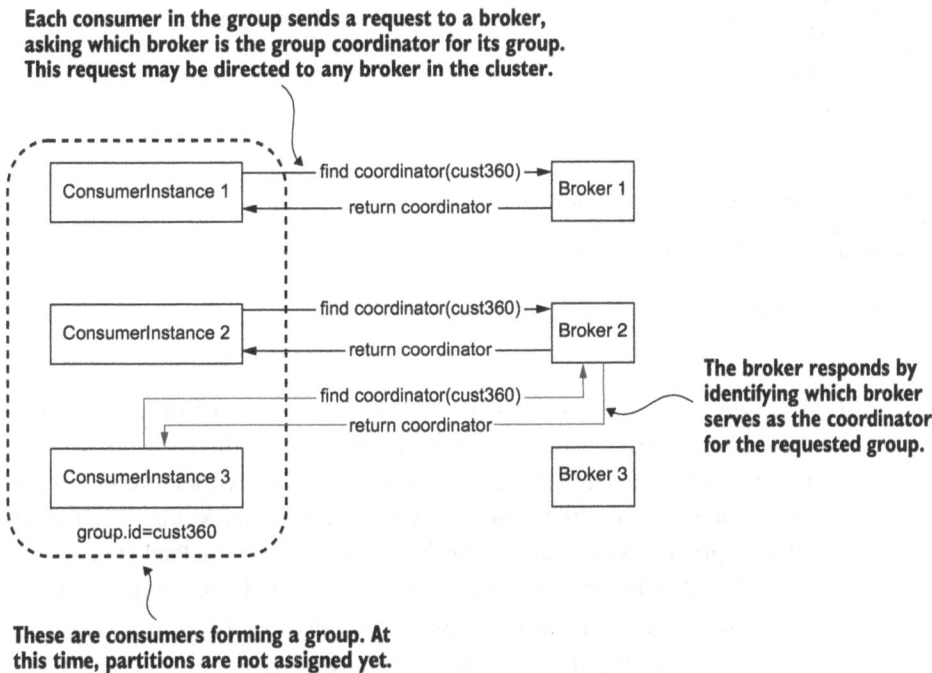

The broker responds by identifying which broker serves as the coordinator for the requested group.

These are consumers forming a group. At this time, partitions are not assigned yet.

Figure 4.7 Finding the group coordinator

2 Upon receiving the response, each consumer sends a request to the coordinator asking to join the group (sending a JoinGroup request), and one of the consumers

sending the request becomes the group leader. The group leader then receives information about the group members and their subscriptions (see figure 4.8).

All consumers send requests to the coordinator to join the group. In response, each consumer receives a member ID, while the group leader also gets the complete list of members and the subscription details.

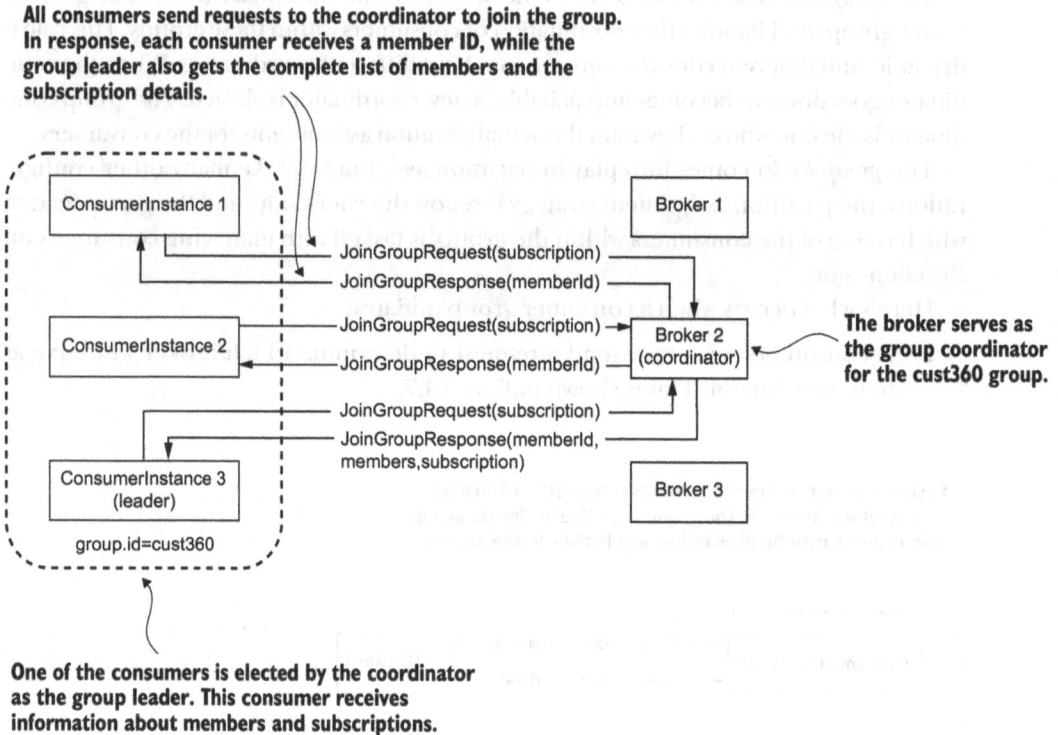

One of the consumers is elected by the coordinator as the group leader. This consumer receives information about members and subscriptions.

Figure 4.8   Joining the group

3 The group leader then calculates the assignment of partitions to consumers using a configured strategy, returning the assignment to the coordinator. The strategy is defined by the `partition.assignment.strategy` property, which is set as a part of the consumer configuration. Several strategies are available, and it is also possible to provide a custom strategy by implementing the `PartitionAssignor` interface. We will explore these strategies in more detail later in this chapter.

4 The coordinator informs the consumers which partitions they are assigned. The distribution of assignments is shown in figure 4.9.

It's important to note that within a consumer group, individual consumers don't need direct interaction with each other. They communicate solely with the group coordinator, and once they've received their partition assignments, they fetch data directly from the partition leaders. This streamlined communication simplifies consumer coordination and enables efficient data consumption.

Consumers ask the coordinator for their assignments.

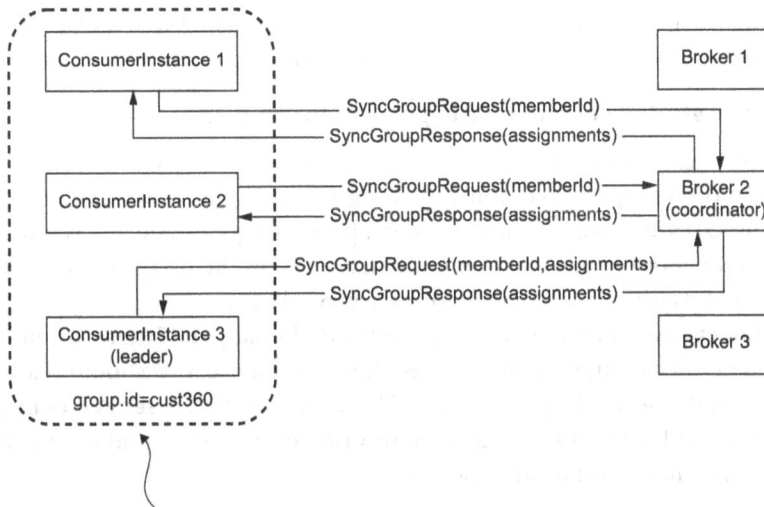

The group leader calculates the partition assignments using
the configured strategy and sends them back to the group
coordinator for distribution to all group members.

Figure 4.9 Distributing the assignments

Another vital function of the group leader is to conduct health checks on the consumer group and keep track of the consumed data. We will delve into these functions later in this chapter.

4.2.4 Committing the offsets

The consumer application subscribes to various topics by specifying their names, either explicitly or through a regular expression, and continuously requests new messages from the server. However, a crucial question arises: How do the brokers determine which data has not been processed yet? This is accomplished by tracking the offsets of the processed messages.

As discussed in chapter 2, in Kafka, each message in a partition is assigned a unique offset that reflects its position. When a consumer processes data, it informs the broker about the processed messages by committing their offsets. Offsets can be committed explicitly through a dedicated method or automatically in the background thread. By default, messages are automatically committed periodically, regardless of whether they were processed. This behavior is controlled by the enable.auto.commit configuration property, which is likely to be adjusted for most use cases. If an error happens and messages are not committed, those messages will be read again in the next call.

The committed offsets are tracked per consumer group and stored within the internal topic named __consumer_offsets. What if a consumer group doesn't have any committed offsets? This can occur when consumers in the group are reading from the topic for the first time. In such cases, the behavior is determined by the `auto.offset.reset` property. By default, it will reset to the latest committed offset. Additionally, there are options to read the topic from the beginning or to throw an exception if no committed offset is found.

4.2.5 Specifying the strategy for committing offsets for an ODS

While the ODS team opts to leave the partition assignment strategy at default settings, they face a more complex decision regarding offset committing. Given the critical nature of the ODS dashboard's business data, preventing message loss is crucial. Consequently, they choose to manually commit offsets within the programming code. This means setting the `enable.auto.commit` property to `false`.

The architects also need to determine what should happen if there are no committed offsets. They decide that, in these cases, the consumer service should read all existing events from the beginning of the topic. Thus, `auto.offset.reset` gets configured to `earliest`. This can lead to rereading previously processed events if offsets are absent or cleared, so consumers must be idempotent.

4.2.6 Creating batches

When transferring data from Kafka brokers to consumers, messages are grouped into batches to improve the efficiency of the data transfer process. Selecting the right batch size is important—it should be large enough to enhance throughput but small enough to avoid overloading the consumer's memory. Let's examine the configuration properties that play a crucial role in this balancing act.

In Kafka, control over the size of these batches primarily resides on the consumer side, which has settings that ensure the data volume is manageable and prevents system overload. Here are the properties that influence the size of the batch:

- `fetch.min.bytes` specifies the minimum amount of data the broker should transfer to the client. It allows the consumer to wait until more data accumulates at the broker, enabling larger batches and fewer fetch requests. The default setting prioritizes quick response times, with a default value of 1, meaning data is sent immediately as it becomes available, without waiting for additional messages. Increasing this value improves throughput over latency.

- `fetch.max.wait.ms` addresses how long the broker should wait before sending a batch if the `fetch.min.bytes` threshold hasn't been met, balancing the trade-off between batch size and response time. This allows us to calibrate the batch size, as more records are likely to accumulate during the wait period.

- `fetch.max.bytes` limits the amount of data returned in a single fetch operation. However, Kafka ensures that at least one message is sent per fetch request to maintain progress, even if it exceeds the `fetch.max.bytes` limit.

- `max.poll.records` controls the number of messages fetched per request. This is particularly useful for scenarios where messages are of a consistent size, providing an alternative way to manage data flow based on message count rather than size. In practice, the broker will wait according to `fetch.max.wait.ms` to accumulate at least `fetch.min.bytes` of data but not exceed `fetch.max.bytes` in size or `max.poll.records` in message count, whichever limit is reached first.

- `max.partition.fetch.bytes` specifies the maximum amount of data the broker will return per partition in each fetch request, ensuring manageable amounts of data per partition. However, if the first record batch in a partition exceeds this limit, it will still be returned to ensure the consumer can make progress.

Together, these properties play a critical role in fine-tuning consumer performance, balancing throughput and latency, and managing resource utilization efficiently. Since each property influences batch size from slightly different angles, it's important that their values be aligned and not contradictory. This coherence ensures that one setting does not counteract another, allowing for efficient data processing. It may be useful to experiment with these settings in your environment and adjust them based on the observed performance characteristics. We will discuss performance tests in chapter 10.

4.2.7 Timeouts and partition rebalance

Under normal circumstances, consumers in a Kafka group are each allocated a set of partitions from which they process messages and confirm their processing. Each partition of a topic is assigned to only one consumer in the group. But what happens if a consumer fails? Who will take care of the partitions assigned to that failed consumer?

Another scenario arises when there are fewer consumers than partitions, requiring some consumers to handle more than one partition. What happens if an additional consumer joins the group? In such cases, should the partitions be redistributed among all consumers to ensure a more even distribution of the load?

Kafka addresses these issues by automatically triggering a rebalance of partitions among consumers when changes occur in a consumer group. This can happen under several circumstances:

- When a new consumer joins the group, such as when an instance of the application starts and requests to join.
- When a consumer leaves the group, gracefully notifying the coordinator—typically when the application shuts down.
- When a consumer fails or is too slow to process messages, which can be self-detected, prompting the consumer to notify the coordinator that it is leaving the group. Alternatively, the coordinator might detect an unhealthy consumer and remove it from the group.

In any of these scenarios, Kafka ensures that partitions are reassigned among the remaining healthy consumers through a process known as a *rebalance*. This mechanism helps Kafka maintain high availability and fault tolerance while ensuring efficient data processing across the consumer group. In figure 4.10, each partition is assigned to a single consumer. Figure 4.11 demonstrates the process of partition redistribution following a consumer instance failure.

Here we see two instances of the service, both belonging to the same consumer group. Each instance operates with two consumers, allowing each consumer to manage one partition exclusively. This configuration represents a typical setup under normal operating conditions.

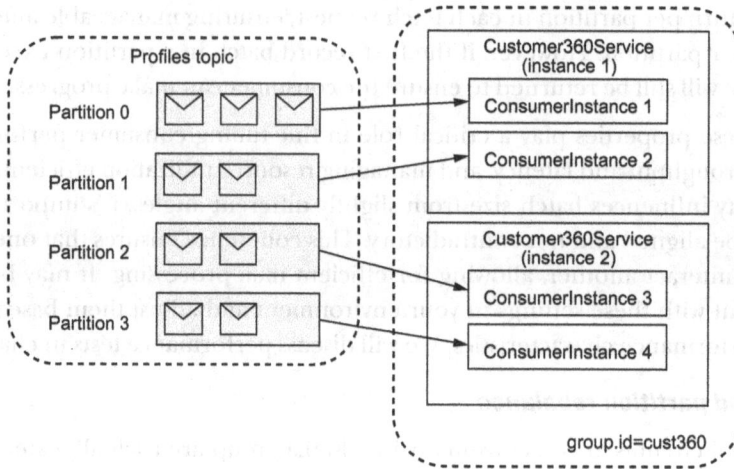

Figure 4.10   Assignment of the partitions under normal circumstances

After a rebalance, partitions are redistributed among the remaining healthy consumers.

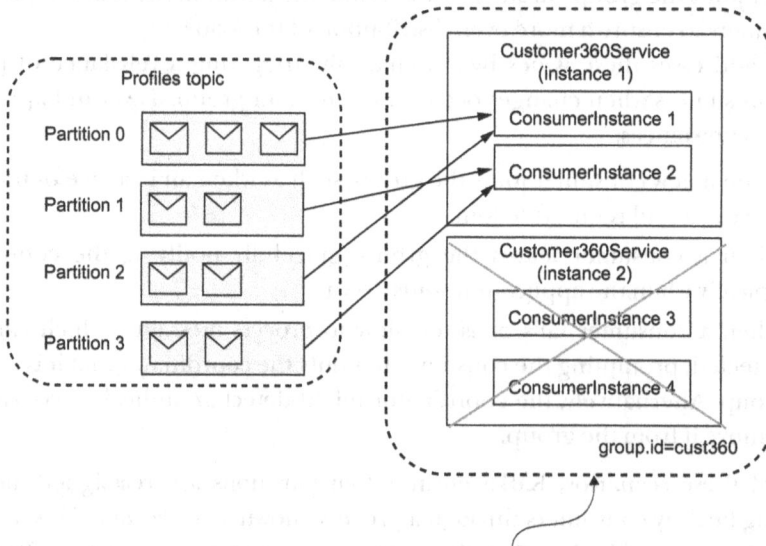

This is a failed service instance. The detection of this failure triggers a rebalance of the partitions among the remaining healthy consumers.

Figure 4.11   Redistribution of the partitions after a failure

Rebalance strategies vary based on the method of partition assignment, and they can be categorized into two types:

- *Eager rebalances* (often referred to as "stop-the-world")—Triggered upon detecting a need for rebalance, this approach temporarily halts message processing for all consumers. Partitions are then revoked and reassigned from scratch based on the chosen strategy, ensuring only healthy consumers receive partitions. Message processing resumes post-rebalance, resulting in a temporary pause in activity.

- *Cooperative rebalances*—Characterized by their incremental approach, these strategies focus on adjusting ownership for a subset of partitions that require new owners, allowing partitions with unchanged assignments to continue processing messages without interruption. This method minimizes processing downtime by ensuring only the necessary partitions are involved in the rebalance.

Each rebalance strategy has implications for system throughput and consumer downtime, with the choice between eager and cooperative rebalances influencing how a Kafka consumer group adapts to changes and handles failures. The default rebalance strategy, `RangeAssignor`, is an eager strategy, meaning it pauses all consumers during a rebalance to reassign partitions, which can result in temporary consumer downtime.

When a consumer joins a group at startup or exits a group before shutting down, it notifies the coordinator, which triggers a rebalance. However, detecting unexpected failures of consumer instances requires a different approach. Kafka employs health-check mechanisms based on timeouts, configured via properties. These properties help determine the response to consumer timeouts and failures:

- Consumers periodically send heartbeats to the coordinator to signal their health. The frequency of these heartbeats is set by `heartbeat.interval.ms`. Regular heartbeats indicate a healthy consumer.

- The `session.timeout.ms` property determines the maximum time the system will wait for a heartbeat before considering a consumer unhealthy. This value must be set higher than `heartbeat.interval.ms`, typically three times higher, ensuring the broker receives at least one heartbeat out of three attempts. If the broker doesn't receive any heartbeats within this timeframe, the coordinator considers the consumer to have failed and initiates a rebalance. In this scenario, the rebalance is initiated by the broker.

- The `max.poll.interval.ms` property sets the maximum allowed time between data polls by the consumer. This defines the time a consumer has to process the data it receives from the broker. By default, this value is set to 5 minutes. Therefore, after the consumer receives a batch of messages, it has 5 minutes to process them before it must send another fetch request to the broker. If this limit is exceeded, the consumer marks itself as inactive and sends a request to leave the consumer group, signaling a need for rebalance. In this scenario, the rebalance is initiated by the consumer itself.

These timeout configurations are pivotal for maintaining the robustness and reliability of consumer groups in Kafka.

4.2.8   Static group membership

Whenever a consumer joins or leaves a group, a rebalance is triggered, which can be a time-consuming process. However, it is possible to avoid rebalances during temporary consumer outages, such as restarts, by using static group membership.

To enable static group membership, consumers must be configured with a `group.instance.id`, a unique identifier that serves as the consumer's member ID. When a consumer with static membership leaves the group and rejoins within the `session.timeout.ms` period, the group coordinator recognizes its `group.instance.id` and retains its previous partition assignments. This allows the consumer to resume processing from the last committed or processed offset before it left the group.

By using static group membership, unnecessary rebalances caused by temporary restarts can be effectively avoided, leading to more stable and efficient consumer group behavior.

4.2.9   Partition assignment strategies

Now, let's explore how the group leader assigns partitions to consumers. Customizing this process by implementing the `ConsumerPartitionAssignor` interface is an option, but it's not a necessity for every deployment. Kafka comes equipped with several default strategies that are ready to use, catering to a variety of needs and scenarios.

Let's look at the strategies included with the Kafka client library:

- The `RangeAssignor` strategy, shown in figure 4.12, is the default in Kafka. It orders consumers by their `memberId` and assigns partitions sequentially starting from the first consumer. This method ensures that if several topics each have the same number of partitions, the partitions with the same index across these topics will be assigned to the same consumer instance. This can be crucial for applications that need to correlate data across multiple topics.

  In figure 4.12, we have the `Invoices` and `Profiles` topics, and for each customer, we want to process them with the same consumer instance. To achieve this, both the corresponding invoice and profile messages must be sent to partitions with the same index. The simplest way to ensure this is by using the same key—such as the customer identifier—for both topics. Kafka's partitioning logic will ensure that records with the same key are routed to the same partition (by index) in each topic, which in turn ensures those messages are consumed by the same instance.

- The `RoundRobinAssignor` strategy distributes partitions evenly among all the consumers in the group, as illustrated in figure 4.13. This method ensures optimal utilization of all available consumers, potentially enhancing performance. However, one drawback is that if a rebalance occurs, it can lead to significant movement of partition assignments among consumers. Keys are ignored in this strategy.

The RangeAssignor strategy ensures that partitions with the same index are assigned to the same consumer. ConsumerInstance 1 has partitions with index 0 and ConsumerInstance 2 has partitions with index 1 for both topics.

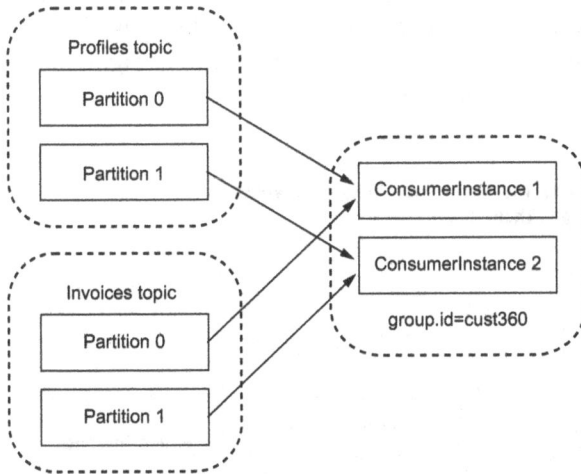

Figure 4.12 The `RangeAssignor` **strategy**

The RoundRobinAssignor strategy distributes partitions across consumers as evenly as possible. Here, partitions are distributed in this order: Profiles-0, Profiles-1, Invoices-0, Invoices-1. With three consumer instances, Invoices-1 is assigned to ConsumerInstance 1.

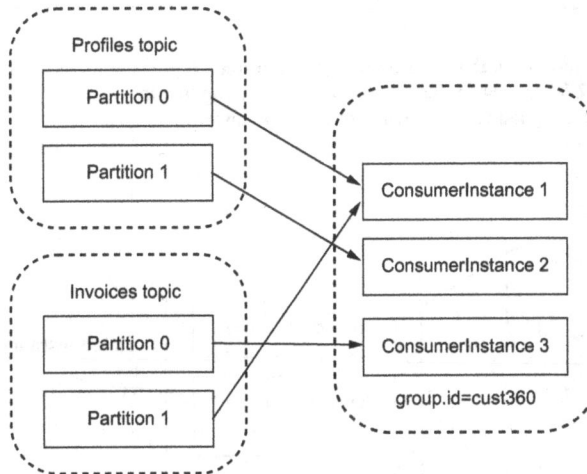

Figure 4.13 The `RoundRobinAssignor` **strategy**

- The `StickyAssignor` strategy assigns partitions in a manner similar to Round-RobinAssignor but prioritizes maintaining existing partition assignments to consumers wherever possible. When all consumers are active, the assignment is the same as with RoundRobinAssignor, as shown in figure 4.13. However, during a rebalance, the RoundRobinAssignor reassigns partitions to active consumers from scratch. In contrast, StickyAssignor attempts to distribute partitions evenly while preserving existing assignments wherever possible. This strategy minimizes disruptions and improves overall system performance. Figure 4.14 illustrates the difference in rebalance behavior.

When a rebalance happens, the RoundRobinAssignor revokes all assignments and assigns them again.

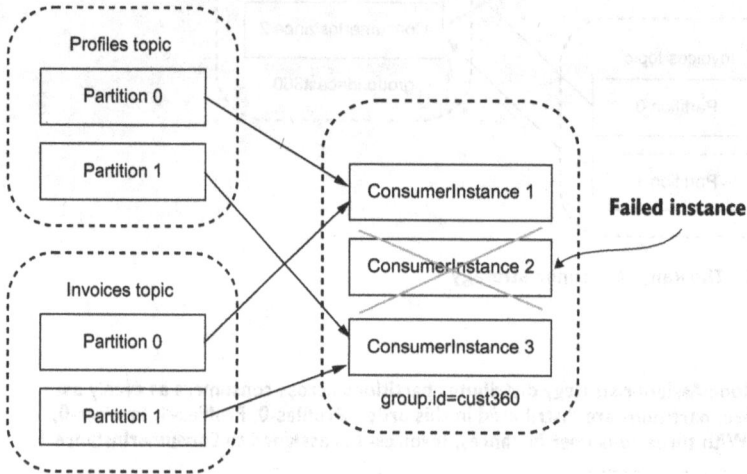

The StickyAssignor minimizes the reassignment of partitions. If ConsumerInstance 2 fails, only Profiles-1 receives a new assignment, as it was previously assigned to the failed consumer instance.

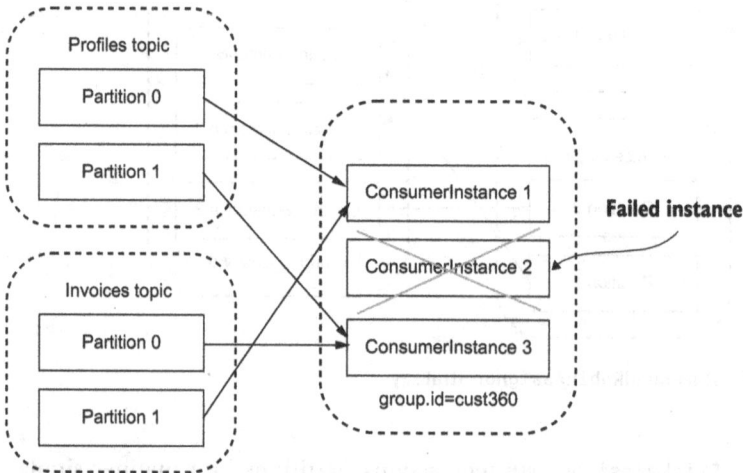

Figure 4.14   Different assignments after rebalancing with the RoundRobinAssignor and StickyAssignor strategies

- The `CooperativeStickyAssignor` strategy builds on the `StickyAssignor` approach by providing an even less disruptive rebalance process. While the `StickyAssignor` aims to minimize changes to partition assignments, it still triggers a full revocation and reassignment of partitions during a rebalance. In contrast, the `CooperativeStickyAssignor` performs rebalances incrementally. Instead of revoking all partitions at once, it only revokes and reassigns the partitions that need to move. This allows consumers to continue processing their existing partitions during the rebalance, minimizing downtime and improving availability.

Choosing the right strategy depends on the structure of your topics and the requirements of your application. The default `RangeAssignor` distributes partitions in contiguous blocks and is useful when you need correlation in data from multiple topics. For more balanced distribution across consumers, the `RoundRobinAssignor` is better suited for unrelated topics or when even load distribution is more important than data locality. If stability during rebalancing is a priority, the `StickyAssignor` and `Cooperative-StickyAssignor` minimize partition movement across rebalances. In more advanced scenarios, you can also implement a custom assignor to control how partitions are allocated based on specific business logic.

4.2.10 *The next-gen consumer rebalance protocol*

Kafka is designed to keep the broker simple and efficient by implementing much of the logic on the client side, including partition assignment. In this model, consumers are responsible for calculating assignments and maintaining state. However, this approach has several drawbacks:

- *Troubleshooting and bug fixes*—When a misbehavior occurs, client-side logs must be examined to diagnose the issue. While this may be manageable when all systems are in the same data center, it becomes more challenging as more applications move to the cloud. If a bug is identified, all affected clients must be updated, which can be complex and time-consuming.

- *Inconsistent views of metadata*—Clients are responsible for monitoring metadata changes and triggering rebalances. However, this can lead to inconsistencies, as different clients might have different views of the metadata, causing coordination problems.

- *Limited operations during rebalances*—Even with cooperative rebalancing, certain operations—such as committing offsets—are not available, which can disrupt normal consumer operations.

The challenges associated with client-side partition management have led to the development of a new approach: centralizing assignment management on the brokers to achieve greater efficiency and consistency. This shift is the foundation of the next-generation consumer rebalance protocol, which, at the time of writing, is in the preview stage.

While the new protocol still allows for client-side assignments (including custom logic through the `PartitionAssignor` interface), its real strength lies in the use of server-side assignors. These assignors are designed with several strategies in mind:

- *Even distribution*—Distributes partitions across consumers as evenly as possible
- *Stickiness*—Minimizes reassignments by retaining existing partition assignments wherever feasible
- *Rack awareness*—Attempts to assign partitions so that consumers and their corresponding partitions are located within the same rack, improving performance and fault tolerance

The new protocol consolidates partition assignment and heartbeats into a single API, the `ConsumerHeartBeat` API. A consumer sends a request containing the following metadata:

- *Member information*—Includes group ID, member ID, and rack ID
- *Subscription information*—Specifies the topics to which the consumer is subscribed
- *Currently owned partitions*—Lists the partitions the consumer currently owns
- *Rebalance timeout*—The maximum time allowed for rebalancing
- *Preferred server-side assignor*—Indicates the server-side assignor the consumer wishes to use

The group coordinator then calculates the partition assignments and returns a response to the consumer. This response includes

- *Target assignment*—The desired partition state for the consumer
- *Heartbeat interval*—The interval at which the consumer should send heartbeats

Most fields in the response are optional and are only sent when there are changes. When the group is stable, the consumer request serves primarily as a simple heartbeat.

Figure 4.15 illustrates the process when a new consumer joins the group. It is also worth mentioning that the new protocol introduces a timeout for partition revocation. If a consumer does not revoke its partitions within the time specified by `max.poll.interval.ms`, it is removed from the group.

With server-side assignors moving the logic of computing assignments to the server, several properties must now be defined on the broker side:

- `group.consumer.assignors`—Specifies the server-side assignors available for use. The client can also indicate its preferred assignor; if not specified, the most common assignor is used by default.
- `group.consumer.max.session.timeout.ms`—Sets the maximum allowed session timeout for consumers.
- `group.consumer.heartbeat.interval.ms`—Defines the heartbeat interval for consumers.
- `group.consumer.max.heartbeat.interval.ms`—Specifies the maximum allowable heartbeat interval.

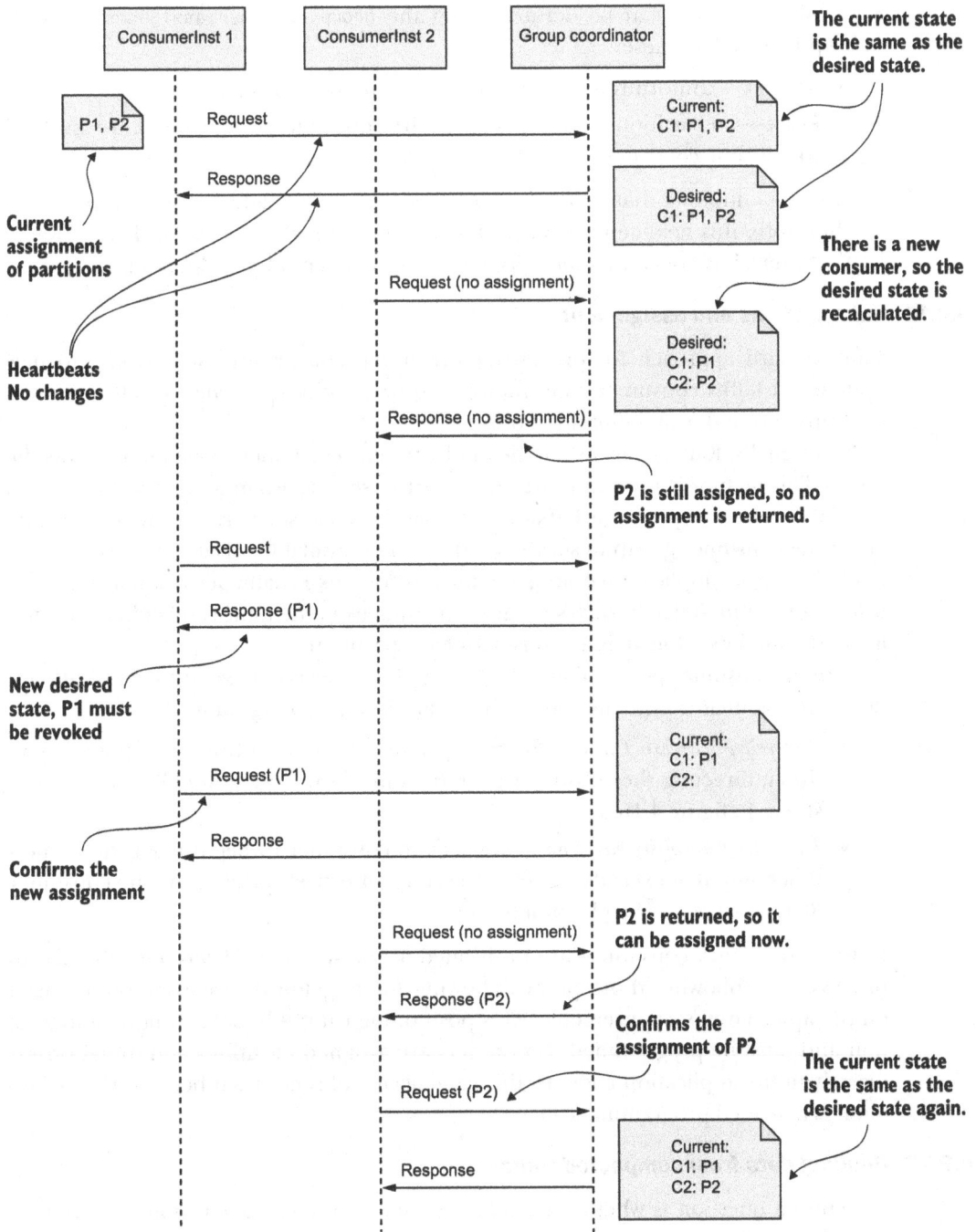

Figure 4.15 An example of the next-generation rebalance protocol. ConsumerInst 2 joins the group, and this triggers the rebalance.

Server-side assignors can be defined using the `group.consumer.assignors` property with options such as these:

- `Uniform`—Uniformly distributes partitions among consumers
- `Range`—Co-partitions topics, ensuring partitions with the same index are assigned to the same consumer

It's worth mentioning that there is no concept of a group leader in the new protocol. Furthermore, this next-generation protocol is only available for use in KRaft (Kafka Raft) clusters; it is not compatible with Kafka clusters that still use ZooKeeper.

4.2.11 Subscriptions and assignment

The standard approach for processing streaming data involves subscribing to new updates—a Kafka consumer continuously requests and receives new batches of data, beginning from the last committed offset.

Additionally, Kafka provides the flexibility to set a consumer's position to a specific offset. This feature is useful in various scenarios, such as when a microservice needs to read an entire topic from Kafka to populate its local store, requiring all consumers in the consumer group to start from the earliest available offset. Another use case might involve an application opting to manage offsets externally, perhaps in a database, instead of within Kafka. In such situations, reading from the topic can begin at any designated point by setting an initial offset for each partition.

Explicit consumer positioning in Kafka can be achieved in two ways, and both are done programmatically in the code rather than through configuration:

- *By specifying an exact offset*—Assign a specific value as the offset for each topic partition, directing the consumer to start from this precise point. This situation is shown in figure 4.16.
- *By finding an offset based on time*—Set the consumer to begin from the earliest timestamp that exceeds a given timestamp, effectively positioning the consumer at the start of a particular timeframe.

In these scenarios, consumers are positioned at the specified offsets and proceed to process data following those points, allowing for targeted data consumption based on the application's requirements. This positioning cannot be set through configuration and must be programmed. Consumers are assigned partitions and initial offsets directly in the application code. In this case, `group.id` is not used because the assignment is managed programmatically.

4.2.12 Reading data from compacted topics

A common question is whether consuming data from compacted topics is different than that from regular topics. In practice, the client-side API usage remains identical, with no changes in the programming code.

However, clients need to be mindful that compacted topics only guarantee that at least the most recent message for each key will be retained. You may also receive older

Message offsets
Assigned consumer position: partition 0
is set to begin reading at offset 24.

21 22 23   24 25 26 27

Partition 0

21 22   23 24 25 26

Partition 1

Partition 1 is set to begin reading at offset 23.

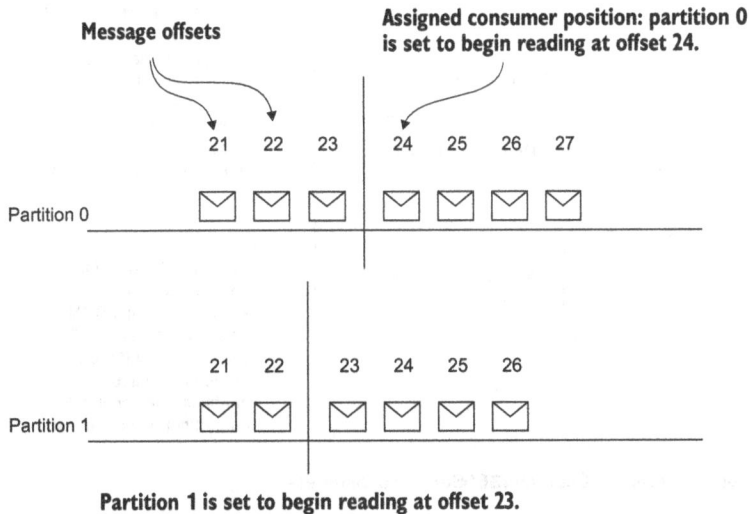

**Consumer assignment determines the offset from which
the consumer will start reading in the partition.**

Figure 4.16 Specifying consumer assignment by offsets

messages for the same key if the log cleaner hasn't fully compacted the log yet. So while you won't see the entire history of every key, you may also see more than one message per key during consumption.

Since keys are critical to how compaction works and are determined by the producer, they should be designed carefully to ensure that compaction functions as expected.

4.2.13 Consumer considerations for the ODS project

For the Customer 360 dashboard, we'll finalize the configuration of the consumer application along these guidelines:

- Both `key.deserializer` and `value.deserializer` will use string deserializers, ensuring consistency with the producer specifications.
- A consumer group identifier is designated to coordinate the collaborative efforts of the consumers.
- The service will deploy two sets of consumers: one for reading from the CUSTOMER_ PROFILES topic and the other from the TRANSACTIONS topic. Each set will be assigned a distinct prefix for the `client.id` property.
- Manual offset committing will prevent message loss. In cases where no offset is specified, data will be retrieved from the beginning.

Figure 4.17 depicts this current setup.

topic: CUSTOMER_PROFILES
key: Customer ID
key type format: JSON
value type format: JSON
client.id = cust360-profile
group.id = cust360
enable.autocommit=false
auto.offset.reset=earliest

Customer360Service

ProfileConsumers

Kafka

TransactionConsumers

topic: TRANSACTIONS
key: Transaction ID
key type format: JSON
value type format: JSON
client.id = cust360-trans
group.id = cust360
enable.autocommit=false
auto.offset.reset=earliest

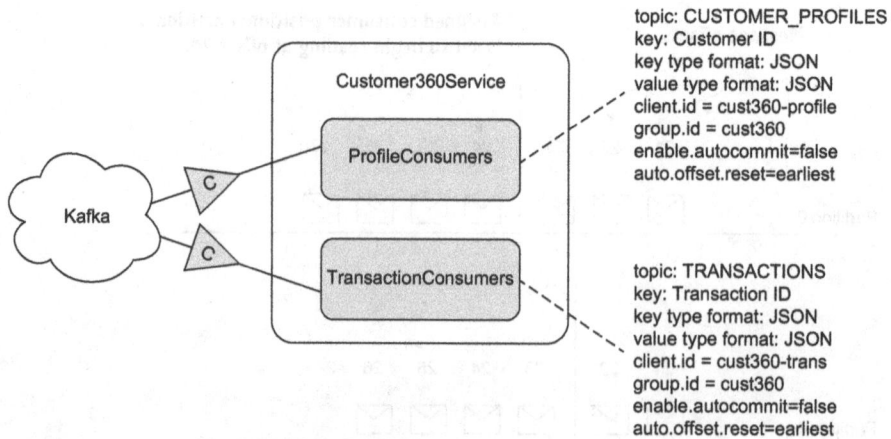

Figure 4.17   Current setup for Customer360Service consumers

The data engineer on the ODS project suggests providing guidance for the team on implementing the consumer microservice, as some aspects might be tricky. There will be independent consumers reading from the TRANSACTIONS and CUSTOMER_PROFILES topics, potentially updating the same aggregated object. With a straightforward implementation, consumers might inadvertently overwrite data, as illustrated in figure 4.18.

Let's summarize the overwriting process:

1   Consumer X reads data from the CUSTOMER_PROFILES topic for the customer with ID = 123.
2   Consumer Y reads data from the TRANSACTIONS topic for the customer with ID = 123.
3   Consumer X retrieves the current aggregate from the database for the customer with ID = 123.
4   Consumer Y retrieves the current aggregate from the database for the customer with ID = 123.
5   Consumer X updates the aggregate and writes it back to the database.
6   Consumer Y updates the aggregate and writes it back to the database, overwriting the update made by Consumer X.

To prevent both sets of consumers from overwriting the aggregated object when updating simultaneously, the team decided to employ a technique called *optimistic locking*. The process is shown in figure 4.19.

Optimistic locking is a concurrency control mechanism used to ensure data consistency. It involves maintaining a version number or timestamp for each data record. When a consumer updates the record, it checks that the version number hasn't changed since it was read. If the version is unchanged, the update proceeds, and the version

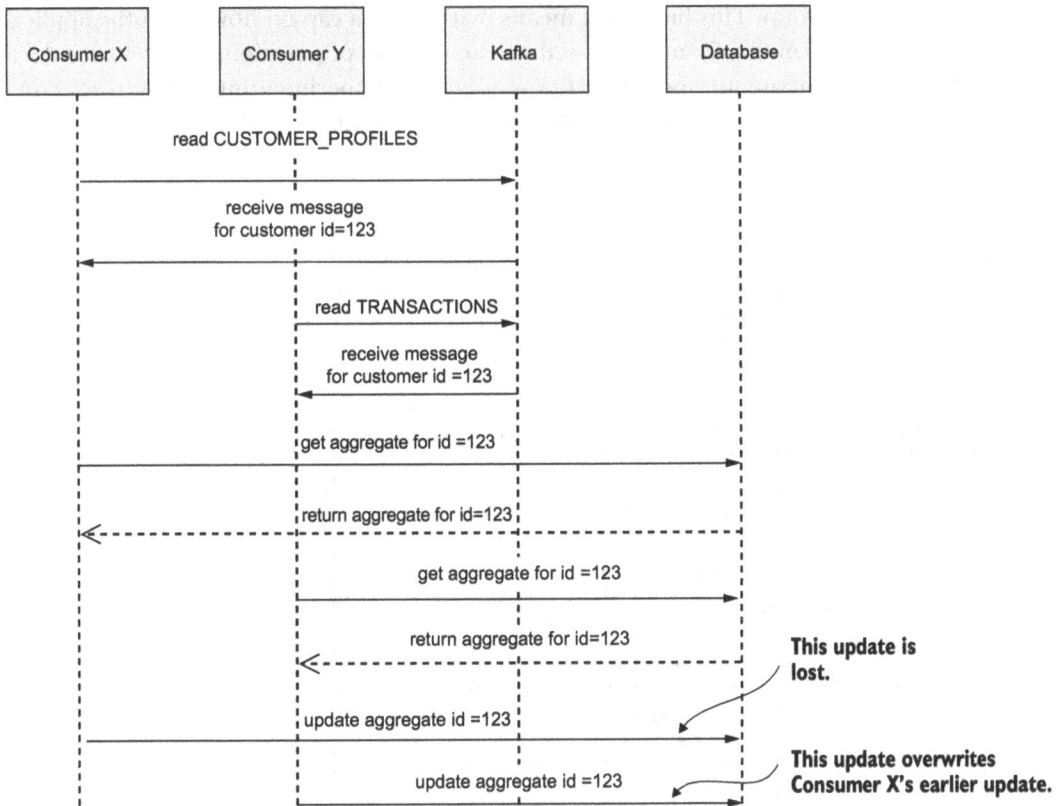

Figure 4.18 Overwriting data by different consumers

number is incremented. If the version has changed, the update is aborted, and the consumer retries the operation. This approach helps prevent data overwrites caused by simultaneous updates.

Another common approach is to use a single microservice by utilizing a streaming framework to centrally handle all updates. This can help reduce the risk of data overwrites and ensure greater consistency. However, this approach also has trade-offs, such as potentially introducing a central processing bottleneck or making the system more complex to scale and maintain. We'll explore these trade-offs and the role of streaming frameworks in more detail in chapter 8.

4.3 Common consumer problems

Let's look at some of the complcations that you may face when dealing with consumers.

4.3.1 Consumer scalability challenges

The scalability of consumer applications is fundamentally linked to the number of partitions, since each partition can only be assigned to a single consumer instance within a consumer group. This limitation means that there's a cap on how much the application can scale on the client side based on the number of partitions. Therefore, selecting the appropriate number of partitions is crucial. Experimenting with and selecting an optimal number of partitions will be covered in chapter 10.

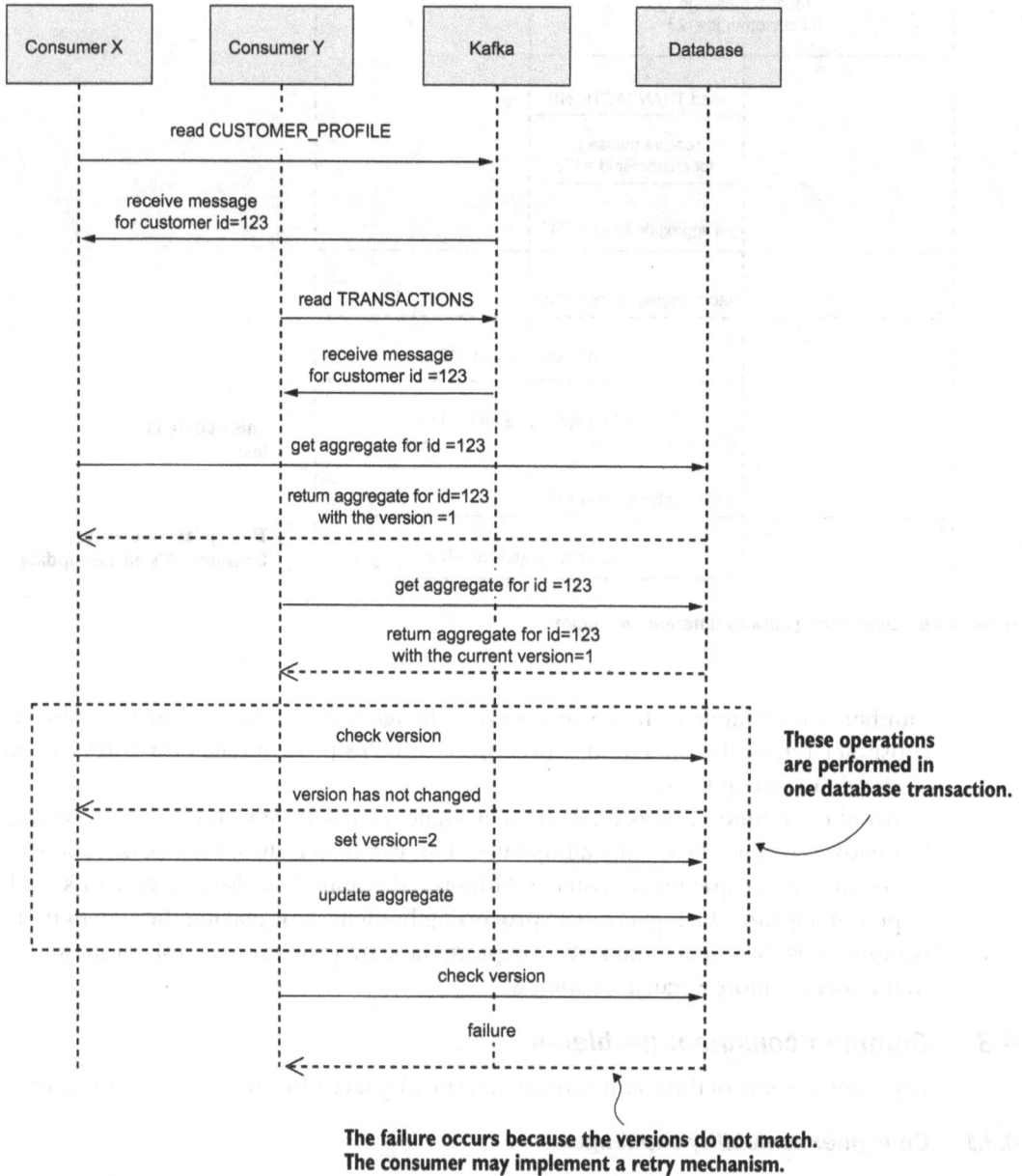

Figure 4.19   Using optimistic locking

To optimize workload distribution and ensure continuous processing, it's common practice to deploy multiple instances of consumer applications that share the same consumer group. This approach allows for efficient scaling and workload management across the consumer instances.

Given that workload patterns can change, monitoring whether consumer instances keep pace with the load is crucial. A key metric in this context is *consumer lag*, which indicates how far behind a consumer group is in processing messages. Consumer lag can be determined in two ways: either by using the JMX metric provided by Kafka or by calculating the difference between the latest offset committed by the consumer group for a specific partition and the latest offset produced to that partition in the Kafka broker. However, the latter method is approximate because offsets may be missing—compaction is the primary reason for missing offsets, but other factors can also contribute to this. Figure 4.20 shows how the consumer lag is calculated.

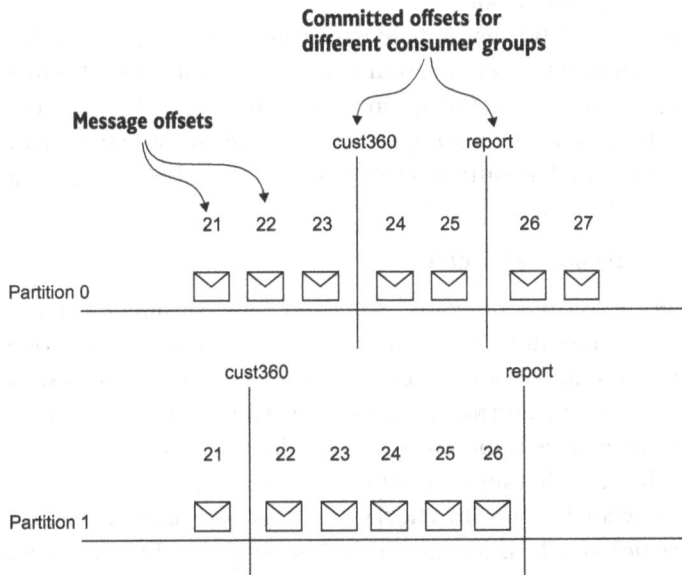

Lag is determined by calculating the difference between the last committed offset and the last produced offset for each partition within a consumer group. For the consumer group cust360, the lag for partition 0 is calculated as 4 (27−23), and for partition 1, it is 5 (26−21).

Lag for the report group is 2 for partition 0 and 0 for partition 1.

Figure 4.20 Calculating consumer lag

This metric reflects the number of messages that have been published to the partition but not yet been processed by the consumer group, providing insight into the group's processing backlog. Consumer lag is vital for making informed decisions about scaling up consumer instances to ensure efficient processing.

Another way to scale is to dispatch read records to a bounded worker pool sharded by key (all messages with the same key go to the same worker). This preserves per-key ordering while allowing parallelism across different keys. In this model, offset commits require care: because the workers finish out of order, you can only advance the commit to the highest contiguous offset that has fully completed—the effective "watermark."

4.3.2   *Optimizing batch size configuration*

Determining the ideal batch size necessitates a careful balance of various factors, tailored to the unique needs of each application. To control the amount of data delivered to the client, system configurations need to be aligned, with `max.poll.records` commonly used to set the maximum number of messages fetched in a single request. However, since message sizes can vary, accurately predicting a batch's actual size based on the number of messages is hard. This makes careful memory management essential to avoid running out of resources.

Both latency and throughput demands must be weighed, as larger batches can increase latency due to accumulation delays but simultaneously enhance throughput by reducing overhead. Also, the optimal batch size might change over time as workload patterns evolve, requiring ongoing monitoring and adjustment to maintain the desired performance levels. The intricacies of monitoring and adapting to these changes will be explored in detail in chapter 11.

4.3.3   *Timeout management strategies*

Configuring the various timeouts associated with consumer behavior is critical and requires careful attention. When the record processing involves long-running operations, such as interacting with external systems or generating files, properties such as `max.poll.interval.ms` and `max.poll.records` need to be fine-tuned to avoid triggering unnecessary rebalances. Optimizing these values often involves system benchmarking to achieve a balance that supports efficient processing.

Timeouts related to health checks (such as `heartbeat.interval.ms` and `session .timeout.ms` described earlier) are critical because they help strike a balance between promptly detecting failures and avoiding unnecessary rebalances. These settings directly impact how quickly the system can respond to problems without causing instability in the consumer group.

Proper configuration of these timeouts is vital for enhancing consumer performance, managing failures effectively, and preserving the Kafka ecosystem's stability. Inadequately configured timeouts can result in preventable rebalances, processing bottlenecks, and extra strain on the Kafka cluster, highlighting the importance of a thoughtful setup.

4.3.4   *Error-proof deserialization processes*

Since brokers do not deserialize messages, they cannot validate their content. Consequently, consumers must trust that producers send messages in the expected format. If consumers encounter messages they cannot deserialize, they must implement proper error handling. Without such mechanisms, a single malformed message could disrupt the entire process, causing the consumer to fail and halt further processing.

Thankfully, client-side frameworks offer deserialization error handlers that can be customized to manage these errors effectively. The schema registry, discussed in chapter 6, helps maintain data contracts by storing schemas centrally, allowing producers and consumers to agree on the schema format and compatibility over time.

4.3.5 *Offset initialization strategies for new consumers*

It's important to remember that when a consumer first starts reading from a topic, there may already be existing data in the topic. Therefore, a key decision is whether the consumer should process all data from the start or only messages that arrive after it connects. Many use cases necessitate reading from the beginning, but the default setting for auto.offset.reset is latest, which means the consumer only receives the newest messages by default. Different behavior is shown in figure 4.21.

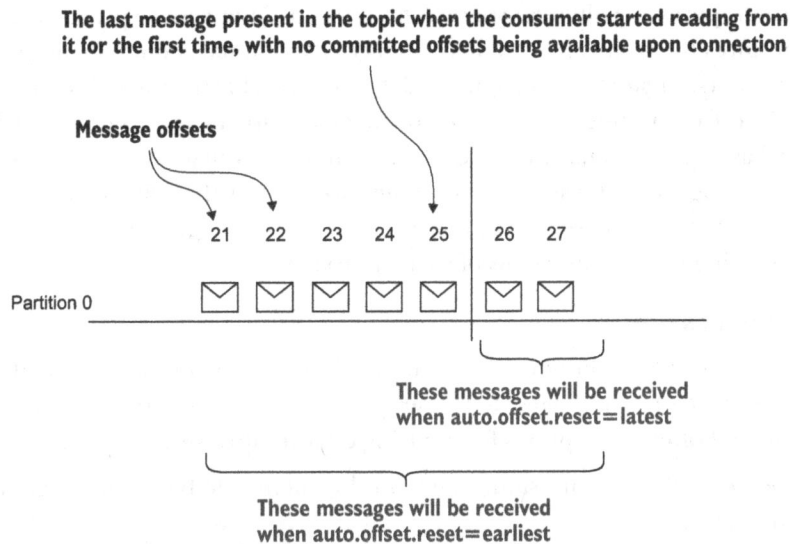

Figure 4.21 Different configurations of the auto.offset.reset **property**

Moreover, offsets for a consumer group are subject to their own retention period, governed by the offset.retention.minutes setting, which defaults to a 7-day timeframe. Offsets may expire if the consumer group is inactive for a certain time. If a consumer reconnects after this period, and the offsets have expired, the auto.offset.reset setting becomes relevant once more, determining where the consumer starts reading from. To accommodate the potential unavailability of consumer applications, it is advisable to adjust the `offset.retention.minutes` property to align with the maximum expected downtime. This adjustment ensures that consumers can resume operations without data loss or redundancy when they reconnect after a period of inactivity.

4.3.6   *Accurate offset commitment practices*

The default setting for `enable.auto.commit` is `true`, allowing offsets to be committed automatically at set intervals. While this configuration simplifies the consumer code, it introduces a potential risk of losing messages if offsets are committed before their associated messages are fully processed. Should a failure happen after an offset is committed but before message processing is finalized, the consumer will start consuming from the subsequent offset upon restart or rebalance, thus bypassing the unprocessed messages. To avoid data loss, especially in critical applications, developers may opt to manually manage offset commits, ensuring messages are fully processed before their offsets are considered committed.

4.3.7   *Coordinating transactions across external systems*

Since Kafka does not support distributed transactions, synchronizing operations with other systems poses a challenge. Specifically, if a consumer service processes messages and then stores the results in a database, it faces a dilemma: should it commit the offsets to Kafka first or store the data in the database first? Each approach carries its own risk of failure. Committing offsets before the database update means potential data loss if the database operation fails, as Kafka would consider those messages processed. Conversely, updating the database first but failing to commit the offsets afterward could result in message duplication. Chapter 6 will delve into strategies to address these challenges, weighing the pros and cons of each approach.

4.4   *Data compression*

Let's look at how Kafka supports data compression to boost network throughput and save storage space for messages. Kafka supports message compression using various algorithms and offers two options for applying data compression:

- *Producer level*—Compression occurs on the client side before messages are sent to Kafka.
- *Broker level*—Compression takes place on the Kafka broker side.

Let's start with the scenario where compression is applied at the producer level but not at the broker level, which is generally the recommended approach. This can be configured by setting the `compression.type` property in the producer's configuration to one of the following codecs: `gzip`, `snappy`, `lz4`, or `zstd`. If `compression.type` is set to `none`, data is sent without compression; otherwise, the specified codec compresses the data.

On the producer side, messages are gathered into batches. The entire batch is then compressed by the producer before being sent to the broker. Batch compression is particularly effective because batches are more likely to contain similar data, enhancing the compression ratio. The broker stores this data in its compressed form. When a consumer requests the data, it is transmitted in its compressed state and then decompressed by the consumer application automatically, without any specific configuration needed by the consumer. This setup is shown in figure 4.22.

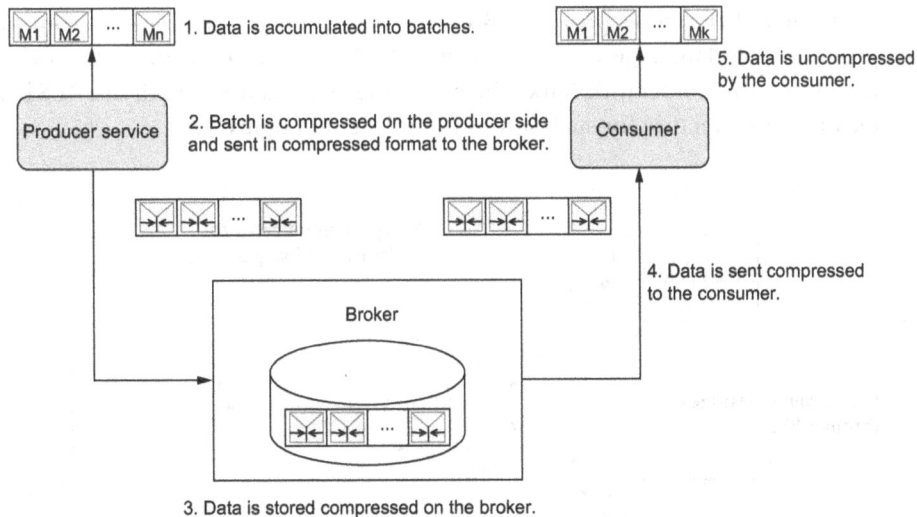

Figure 4.22 Compressing the data on producer side

What occurs when compression is configured at the broker level? This setting is adjustable via the compression.type property in the server's configuration and can be further customized for each topic. On the broker, this property accepts the following values:

- uncompressed—Data is stored without any compression.
- producer—Utilizes the compression codec specified by the producer.
- zstd, lz4, snappy, gzip—Specifies a codec for the broker to compress the data.

The default setting is producer, indicating that the broker retains the data in the compressed format applied by the producer, which is generally the recommended approach. However, if the broker is set to use a different codec than the producer, it first decompresses the batch and then recompresses it using the chosen codec before storage. This extra step introduces additional overhead.

Compression techniques generally perform better on text-based formats like JSON due to the repetitive nature of text, which compression algorithms can efficiently reduce. In contrast, binary formats like Avro, which are already optimized for size, typically see less benefit from compression. Compressing already-encrypted data is ineffective because encryption makes data appear random to others, removing the predictable patterns that compression algorithms rely on, plus it introduces a minor increase in CPU usage. For aggregated data, such as logs, employing compression is highly beneficial, particularly when the goal is to optimize throughput rather than minimize latency.

4.5 Accessing Kafka through the Confluent REST Proxy

Until now, we've discussed building Kafka client applications with libraries that operate using Kafka's native protocol. But what if libraries compatible with your preferred programming language aren't available? While it's a rare occurrence, you still have the option to interact with Kafka through a more familiar method: the REST API. The example architecture for such setups is illustrated in figure 4.23.

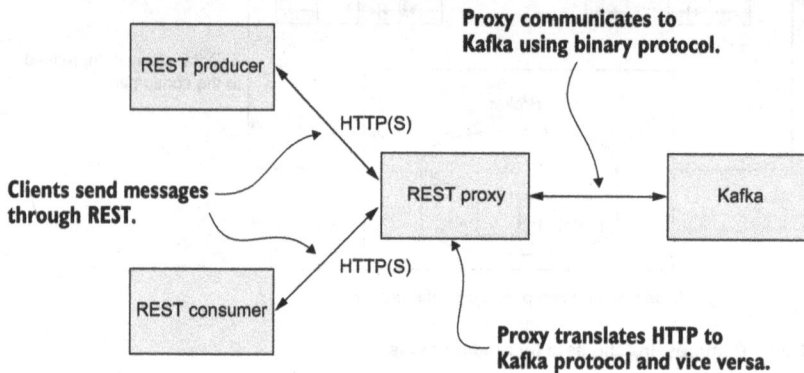

Figure 4.23   Communicating to Kafka through REST

In this setup, the Confluent REST Proxy acts as an intermediary between the clients and Kafka. When clients need to send messages to or receive them from Kafka, they communicate with the REST Proxy using the REST API via the HTTP/HTTPS protocols. The REST Proxy then relays these requests to Kafka using the Kafka protocol and returns the operation's results to the client as an HTTP response. Conceptually, the client application performs the same operations as a typical application would, but it does so using HTTP REST.

Various products implement the pattern of interfacing with message brokers through protocols like HTTP, and some of the products also support alternative (not HTTP) protocols, such as AMQP. A prominent example of such a product is the *Confluent REST Proxy*, designed specifically to offer an HTTP interface to Apache Kafka. This tool enables the production and consumption of messages, in addition to providing an administrative interface for managing topics, brokers, configurations, and other Kafka cluster entities. Another notable solution is Kafka Bridge, part of the Strimzi project. *Kafka Bridge* offers functionality similar to that of Confluent REST Proxy but is geared toward cloud-native environments, particularly Kubernetes.

In a cloud environment, the Confluent REST Proxy can be effectively combined with gateway solutions provided by cloud vendors. For instance, using Amazon API Gateway in conjunction with the REST Proxy enhances integration capabilities with AWS services. This setup allows for seamless integration with AWS Identity, which simplifies the authentication and authorization processes for API access. Furthermore, it facilitates publishing of APIs, making them more accessible to developers and applications within the AWS ecosystem.

Accessing Kafka through REST is particularly beneficial in situations where the client is implemented in a programming language that lacks native support for Kafka client libraries. It's also advantageous for quickly creating prototypes or in use cases where low latency isn't a critical requirement, such as performing administrative tasks to manage the Kafka cluster. These scenarios highlight the flexibility of using REST with Kafka, making it easier to work with Kafka across different programming languages and for a variety of tasks.

4.6 Online resources

- "Kafka Consumer Configuration Reference for Confluent Platform": https://docs.confluent.io/platform/current/installation/configuration/consumer-configs.html
  A comprehensive reference guide detailing all configuration options available for Kafka consumers in Confluent Platform.

- "Understanding Kafka partition assignment strategies and how to write your own custom assignor": https://medium.com/streamthoughts/understanding-kafka-partition-assignment-strategies-and-how-to-write-your-own-custom-assignor-ebeda1fc06f3
  An in-depth article explaining Kafka's partition assignment strategies, their tradeoffs, and how to implement a custom assignor tailored to specific consumer group requirements.

- "Consumer Group Protocol": https://developer.confluent.io/courses/architecture/consumer-group-protocol/
  An online course that explains how Kafka's consumer group protocol works under the hood.

- "Apache Kafka Message Compression": www.confluent.io/blog/apache-kafka-message-compression/
  An insightful blog post exploring how message compression works in Apache Kafka.

- "Confluent REST Proxy for Apache Kafka": https://docs.confluent.io/platform/current/kafka-rest/index.html
  Official documentation for the Confluent REST Proxy, detailing how to produce, consume, and manage Kafka topics over HTTP using a RESTful interface.

- "Strimzi Kafka Bridge Documentation": https://strimzi.io/docs/bridge/latest/
  Official documentation for the Strimzi Kafka Bridge, which enables HTTP and
  WebSocket clients to interact with Kafka clusters by exposing a REST API.

- "What Are Apache Kafka Consumer Group IDs?" www.confluent.io/blog/
  dynamic-vs-static-kafka-consumer-rebalancing/
  A detailed blog post comparing dynamic and static Kafka consumer rebalancing,
  explaining how static membership can reduce downtime and improve consumer
  group stability.

- "KIP-848: The Next Generation of the Consumer Rebalance Protocol": https://
  cwiki.apache.org/confluence/display/KAFKA/KIP-848%3A+The+Next+
  Generation+of+the+Consumer+Rebalance+Protocol
  The official KIP-848 proposal outlining the next generation of Kafka's consumer
  rebalance protocol.

Summary

- Consumers continuously request data, deserialize incoming messages, process
  them according to application-specific logic, and then commit the message offsets back to Kafka.

- To facilitate parallel processing, consumers operate within a consumer group,
  where partitions are equitably distributed among group members.

- Consumers can either subscribe to topics to dynamically receive partition assignments or explicitly assign specific partitions for targeted data processing.

- Each consumer group has a group coordinator, which is a broker, responsible for
  managing the members of the group and facilitating rebalances.

- Within each consumer group, a group leader is designated to manage partition
  assignments and coordinate with the group coordinator.

- Timeouts are set to efficiently detect and manage consumer inactivity or failures.

- Messages can be compressed by either the producer or the broker to enhance
  network throughput and reduce storage space. By default, compression is handled by the producer, which specifies the compression type in its configuration.

- When utilizing the Confluent Rest Proxy, clients can interact with Kafka via HTTP
  REST. The Rest Proxy serves as a mediator, converting requests and responses
  between the HTTP REST format and Kafka's native protocol.

Part 2

Solving problems with Kafka

Now that you understand how Kafka works, we'll turn to how it can be applied to real-world challenges. This part of the book is about bridging architecture with practice—seeing where Kafka fits, where it doesn't, and how to design responsibly around it.

In chapter 5 we'll explore concrete use cases and also highlight when Kafka is not the right tool, comparing it with alternative systems. Chapter 6 moves into the design of data contracts, examining event definitions, governance, and the role of schema registries. Chapter 7 focuses on architectural interaction patterns, from microservices and data mesh to request-response and transactional outbox designs. Finally, chapter 8 introduces frameworks for real-time processing, showing how they can help build streaming applications.

Kafka in real-world use cases

This chapter covers

- Key scenarios where Kafka excels
- Identifying situations where Kafka may not be the ideal choice
- Comparing Kafka with other technologies that serve similar purposes

When considering the introduction of new technology, it's crucial to understand both its potential applications and its limitations. Messaging solutions, for instance, vary widely, and different scenarios may be better addressed by specific technologies. However, it's often advisable to use existing products for new challenges instead of adopting a new solution for every distinct use case.

Now that you understand the basics of how Kafka works, it's time to put that knowledge to work so you can turn uncertain "should we use Kafka?" conversations into confident, defensible decisions grounded in clear patterns and trade-offs. In this chapter, we'll walk through high-impact use cases—notifications, external data integration, real-time analytics, and log aggregation—showing when Kafka's guarantees help and what they cost. To pick the right tool for each job, it's also crucial to understand antipatterns and edge cases. We'll also look at alternatives to using Kafka—RabbitMQ, Pulsar, and managed cloud services. You'll leave this chapter with a practical checklist for evaluating Kafka's capabilities and appropriateness, a solid mental model of its limits, and implementation pointers for both Kafka-first and Kafka-free designs.

Field notes: When to choose Kafka—and when not to

Max: Alright team, let's talk about the use cases for Kafka. Are there any alternatives we should consider? Maybe we want to test something else alongside Kafka?

Eva: Good point, Max. The closest competitor to Kafka is Apache Pulsar. It has some technical advantages, like multitenancy and geo-replication. However, its community is smaller than Kafka's.

Rob: Another popular option is RabbitMQ, especially for microservices communication. It's known for its simplicity and reliability.

Max: So, besides microservices, what are the other use cases for Kafka?

Rob: Well, Kafka excels in log and metrics collection because it's designed to handle high message rates efficiently.

Eva: Exactly. Kafka is also great for data integration, serving as a central hub to stream data between different systems. In fact, one of the most important uses is change data capture (CDC)—capturing changes from databases and making them available in real time to other systems.

Rob: And let's not forget real-time processing. Kafka's great for streaming data in real time, even though the processing and analytics happen outside of Kafka. It works perfectly as a broker for real-time applications.

Max: That makes sense. The chief problem we're trying to address is the time that the current batch process takes to run. Are there other alternatives that could help with more parallel processing while we think about real-time streaming?

Eva: Absolutely. While technologies like RabbitMQ, ActiveMQ, or Redis Streams are more about alternative approaches than intermediate steps, they can be useful in scenarios where a concurrent worker queue is needed to handle large-scale data processing in parallel. They can provide more flexibility than traditional batch jobs.

Max: So we have quite a few options and use cases. It's clear Kafka is versatile, but we should keep an eye on other technologies as well.

5.1   *Navigating real-world implementation*

In my experience teaching Kafka courses to business consultants, a common sentiment emerges: "We don't care about the implementation details; we'd rather understand where Kafka can and cannot be effectively utilized." However, achieving a nuanced understanding of Kafka's applicability—and whether it's the best fit for the business problem—requires familiarity with its architecture.

5.1.1 Event-driven microservices

Let's go back to our example ODS project, Customer 360, where we are creating a unified view of each customer by integrating data from various sources. We'll consider two microservices in particular:

- `ProfileService`—Manages customer information, such as creating, updating, or deleting customer profiles
- `Customer360Service`—Aggregates information from various sources to maintain an updated and comprehensive customer profile

How does `Customer360Service` receive updates about customer changes? This mechanism is depicted in figure 5.1.

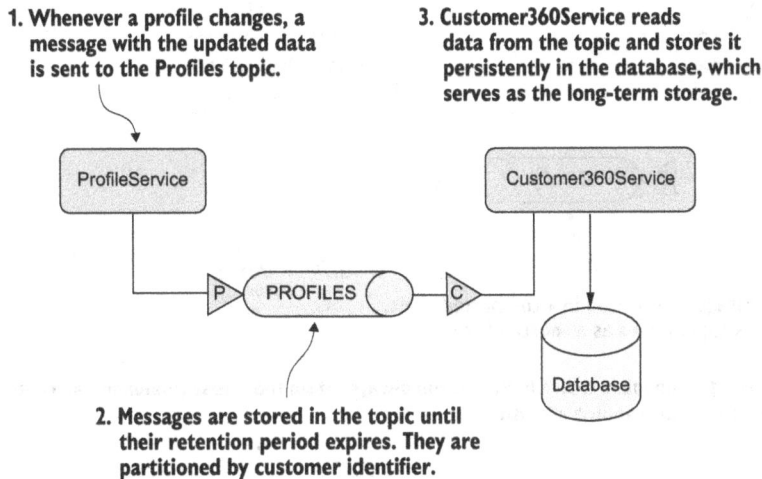

1. Whenever a profile changes, a message with the updated data is sent to the Profiles topic.

3. Customer360Service reads data from the topic and stores it persistently in the database, which serves as the long-term storage.

ProfileService

Customer360Service

P | PROFILES | C

Database

2. Messages are stored in the topic until their retention period expires. They are partitioned by customer identifier.

Figure 5.1 Flow diagram illustrating how `ProfileService` sends notifications about profile changes to `Customer360Service` through Kafka

Whenever customer information changes, `ProfileService` publishes a message with the updated customer state to a Kafka topic designated for customer events. In this approach, the customer identifier is used as the key, ensuring the chronological ordering of events for each specific customer.

Kafka then ensures the seamless transmission of updated customer states between services. Concurrently, `Customer360Service` subscribes to and consumes these events from the Kafka topic, integrating them into its local storage. This local storage acts as the repository for compiling an aggregated view of each customer's information. As new events are processed, `Customer360Service` updates the customer profile with the latest changes conveyed by the messages, bypassing the need for detailed context or a record of the sequence of those changes.

In this scenario, events consumed by `Customer360Service` are stored in its persistent storage, acting as the primary data source. Events are removed from Kafka topics following the expiration of their retention period. Consequently, once the events are deleted, there is no longer a record of historical changes, making it impossible to audit changes or revert to previous states.

An alternative communication strategy between these two services is depicted in figure 5.2, which is slightly different from figure 5.1. Here we utilize a topic configured with a compact retention policy.

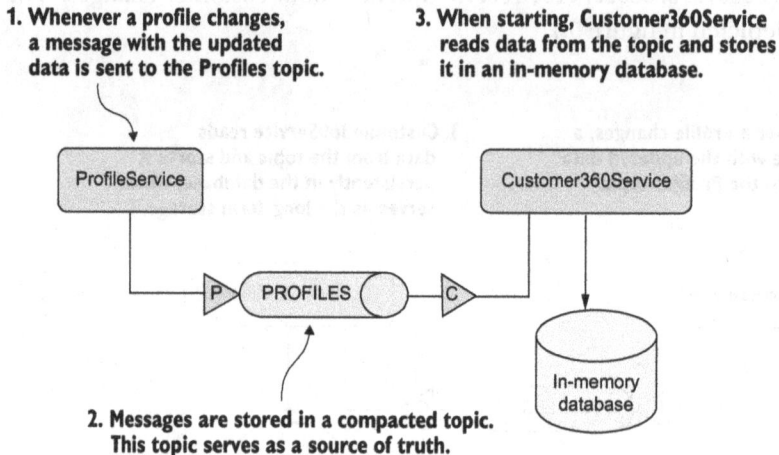

1. Whenever a profile changes, a message with the updated data is sent to the Profiles topic.

3. When starting, Customer360Service reads data from the topic and stores it in an in-memory database.

ProfileService

Customer360Service

P ▷ PROFILES ◁ C

In-memory database

2. Messages are stored in a compacted topic. This topic serves as a source of truth.

Figure 5.2   Using compacted topics in Kafka: you always retain the latest version of each event, allowing Kafka to act as a source of truth.

This setup guarantees that only the most recent state for each key is maintained, with older states of the same key being removed. Consequently, `Customer360Service` doesn't depend on its own durable persistent storage but can use an in-memory database for immediate access, with Kafka acting as the durable persistence layer. This setup allows for state reconstruction while ensuring data durability through Kafka.

Another approach involves employing Kafka's delete retention policy but configuring it to essentially never delete messages, thereby preserving the data indefinitely. This method is effective for keeping a full record of changes without enabling log compaction. By setting retention times or sizes to exceptionally high values, messages can be kept for an exceedingly long time, achieving a "forever" retention within the bounds of available storage. This setup ensures the availability of a comprehensive event history within the topic, providing a simple yet effective means of safeguarding historical data in Kafka.

Additionally, Kafka's tiered storage feature can be used to offload older messages to cheaper, long-term storage (such as cloud-based object storage) while keeping more recent data on high-performance disks. This allows Kafka to retain massive volumes of data cost-effectively without overwhelming primary storage.

Such a strategy is especially beneficial in contexts where retaining historical data is critical for analytical purposes, auditing, or meeting regulatory compliance demands, where losing historical messages could be harmful. With this configuration, Kafka acts once more as the definitive source of truth, allowing `Customer360Service` to reconstruct state by replaying all events.

While Kafka can be used for event storage, it isn't a replacement for a database. It provides an append-only log with sequential access and lacks referential integrity, strong consistency, secondary indexes, and full SQL querying. Designs that treat Kafka as storage must plan for retention/compaction trade-offs and the latency of rebuilding state from events. They should keep the system of record in a database or read store, and use Kafka as the change feed.

ALTERNATIVE APPROACHES

The most prevalent alternative to event-driven services is the synchronous request-response communication pattern. Unlike the event-driven example, `Customer360-Service` does not passively receive notifications but instead proactively requests data by sending a synchronous request and awaiting a response. The data received can be locally cached, with `Customer360Service` determining the appropriate timing for updates.

For services requiring access to shared data, indirect communication through a shared database is another option. For example, in a catalog and inventory system, sharing the database between the catalog service and the inventory service ensures that information regarding product availability is always synchronized. Another example is a configuration management service, where configuration settings are stored in a shared database and can be accessed by various services during initialization or runtime. While this approach is less common in microservices architectures—primarily due to concerns about tight coupling and scalability—it remains a feasible option when services can manage schema coupling effectively.

For situations demanding complex and nested data retrieval, GraphQL (https://graphql.org) presents an alternative to traditional REST APIs. GraphQL's flexible query language allows clients to specify precisely what data they need, mitigating the common problems of over-fetching and under-fetching associated with REST. Additionally, GraphQL supports subscriptions for real-time data updates, further enhancing its utility for dynamic, data-driven applications. This approach is particularly effective for highly interconnected data structures, such as social media platforms. For example, in an application like LinkedIn or X (formerly Twitter), users are connected in a network, and each user has posts, comments, and reactions from others, forming a complex graph of relationships.

Lastly, it's important to note that event-driven microservices aren't inherently tied to Kafka. Microservices architectures existed well before Kafka's widespread adoption, and they can use a variety of messaging systems depending on their specific needs and trade-offs. Kafka is just one of the more popular options today.

The market offers other products with similar capabilities, with RabbitMQ (www
.rabbitmq.com) being one of the most prominent alternatives. While Kafka and
RabbitMQ differ in their feature sets, both can serve as robust backbones for modern
event-driven architectures. We'll compare the two in more detail later in this chapter.

IMPLEMENTATION CHALLENGES

In the request-response pattern, each request is made with the expectation of receiving a response signifying success or failure. If no response arrives, the absence itself is
treated as an error. Trace identifiers help correlate requests and responses for auditing, and erroneous outcomes are logged with appropriate alerts. This predictable feedback loop gives teams confidence: every request ends with a clear, observable result.

Event-driven messaging presents a different set of challenges. The primary concern
is guaranteeing that all messages reach their intended consumers without disappear-
ing within the complex distributed system. Messages are eventually deleted after their
retention period expires, leaving no direct means to verify whether a specific message
was successfully delivered to the broker or the client. Nonetheless, Kafka offers well-
defined and predictable delivery guarantees, which are dependent on specific configurations. Understanding how these settings affect message preservation across the
system's various components is crucial to preventing message loss. We will talk about
delivery guarantees in chapter 7.

Another challenge arises from the fact that once a message is written to Kafka, it
cannot be modified or deleted until it reaches its expiration. Kafka does not perform
message validation at the broker level, meaning corrupted messages will be recorded
in the topic and subsequently delivered to consumers. If a consumer is unprepared to
handle such errors, it may fail and be unable to continue processing. In chapter 6, we
will discuss strategies for managing data contracts between producers and consumers,
which are essential for preventing such situations.

As projects evolve, new requirements emerge that call for changes in the structure
of events. Unlike the evolution of REST APIs, where new versions typically introduce a
fresh set of endpoints, the event-driven architecture operates without endpoints. This
raises important considerations: Is it feasible to send events of different versions to a single topic, or is it necessary to create a new topic for each version? These questions and
their implications will be explored in chapter 6.

As event-driven systems are decoupled and distributed, it is hard to trace events
through the system, especially when trying to identify a failure point. In particular, bugs
related to network latency, timing issues, or the ordering of events are very hard to
reproduce. These characteristics make quality monitoring more challenging, a topic we
will discuss in detail in chapter 11.

ADVANTAGES

Despite the challenges, event-driven services communicating through Kafka offer significant advantages:

- *Continuous updates*—Unlike services that request data on demand and receive
  only a snapshot of the current state, event-driven consumer services receive a

continuous stream of changes—either incremental deltas or event-carried state transfer (see chapter 6). This continuous stream of updates allows consumers to maintain a more dynamic and up-to-date view of the data, reflecting changes as they happen.

- *Decoupling of services*—Services are decoupled, allowing for the addition or update of services without necessitating changes in others, if event contracts are preserved.

- *Optimized latency*—Kafka is engineered to minimize end-to-end latency, enabling real-time responsiveness in consumers that can keep pace with the workload.

- *Resilience*—The architecture enhances system resilience, as the failure of one component does not directly affect others. Replicating data across multiple brokers ensures the system can withstand server failures, while persistent messaging safeguards against any consumer failures by allowing messages to be reconsumed.

- *Scalability and flexibility*—Independent operation of services means the system can more effectively manage workload variations, facilitating scalability and operational flexibility.

DISADVANTAGES

Employing event-driven services with Kafka also presents several drawbacks:

- *Complexity for simple use cases*—Asynchronous communication and the distribution of components add complexity that may not be beneficial for use cases necessitating direct interactions. Scenarios where immediate knowledge of responses (including errors) is crucial to progress are less suited to the event-driven model. A common example is when a user fills out a form in an application and needs an immediate response to proceed, or a real-time stock trading platform where users need immediate feedback on their buy or sell orders.

- *Transactional communication needs*—For transactional communication between services that demands strong consistency, the asynchronous nature of event-driven architectures might pose challenges. An example is e-commerce order processing, where the system needs to simultaneously process a payment, update inventory, and generate an order confirmation. While an asynchronous implementation of this scenario is possible, it introduces the risk that the payment might be processed but the inventory not be updated due to a failure, resulting in orders for out-of-stock items. The issue of ensuring consistency within such systems will be explored in chapter 7.

5.1.2 Data Integration

When discussing event-driven microservices, we explored a scenario where the `ProfileService` creates an event and sends it as a message to a Kafka topic. This event is crafted in the application code, with its attributes populated with the updated profile values, and it's dispatched using a Kafka producer method. This approach is favored by developers who require precise control over data production as well as detailed handling of message acknowledgments and retries.

However, in addition to profiles, we also need to replicate reference tables, which might include data like marital status, occupation, education levels, and geographical information such as country codes. This type of data is either static or changes infrequently and is typically updated directly in the data source rather than through application logic. In such cases, creating services specifically for managing data updates and notifications can be unnecessary, and a simpler data transfer solution with minimal coding would be advantageous.

When we need to replicate data from one system to another, we can do this in two broad ways:

- By reading the current state of the data source (snapshot-based replication)
- By employing the change data capture (CDC) pattern, which captures every change—insertions, updates, and deletions—as an event from the source system's change logs

Instead of designing specialized events for each type of change, CDC uses a uniform event representation to show what has been modified.

Kafka Connect, part of the Confluent platform, is a general-purpose data integration tool that can be used for both approaches. It uses connectors and configurations (no custom code needed) to transfer data in either of two ways:

- By reading the current state (like using JDBC Source Connector for snapshot-based replication)
- By integrating with a CDC tool like Debezium (https://debezium.io) to stream changes from the source system's change logs

For our needs—transferring reference tables such as those for occupations and education levels—Kafka Connect can streamline the process efficiently. The setup for implementing this solution is illustrated in figure 5.3.

To enable the data replication process, a Kafka Connect cluster is required, and this cluster must be configured with the appropriate plugins for each participating system. Databases are often used as examples when discussing Kafka Connect because they're the best-known technology, but the source and destination systems can be of any kind.

Source and sink connectors are completely decoupled and operate independently. The flows for each are shown in figures 5.4 and 5.5, respectively.

Each connector will be configured with parameters detailing how to connect to the database, which tables to transfer, and the frequency for polling the external system for new data, among other settings. We will explore Kafka Connect and its configuration in more detail in chapter 7.

ALTERNATIVE APPROACHES

An obvious alternative to using Kafka Connect is to write applications that directly publish to and consume from Kafka topics. This approach is feasible when you have

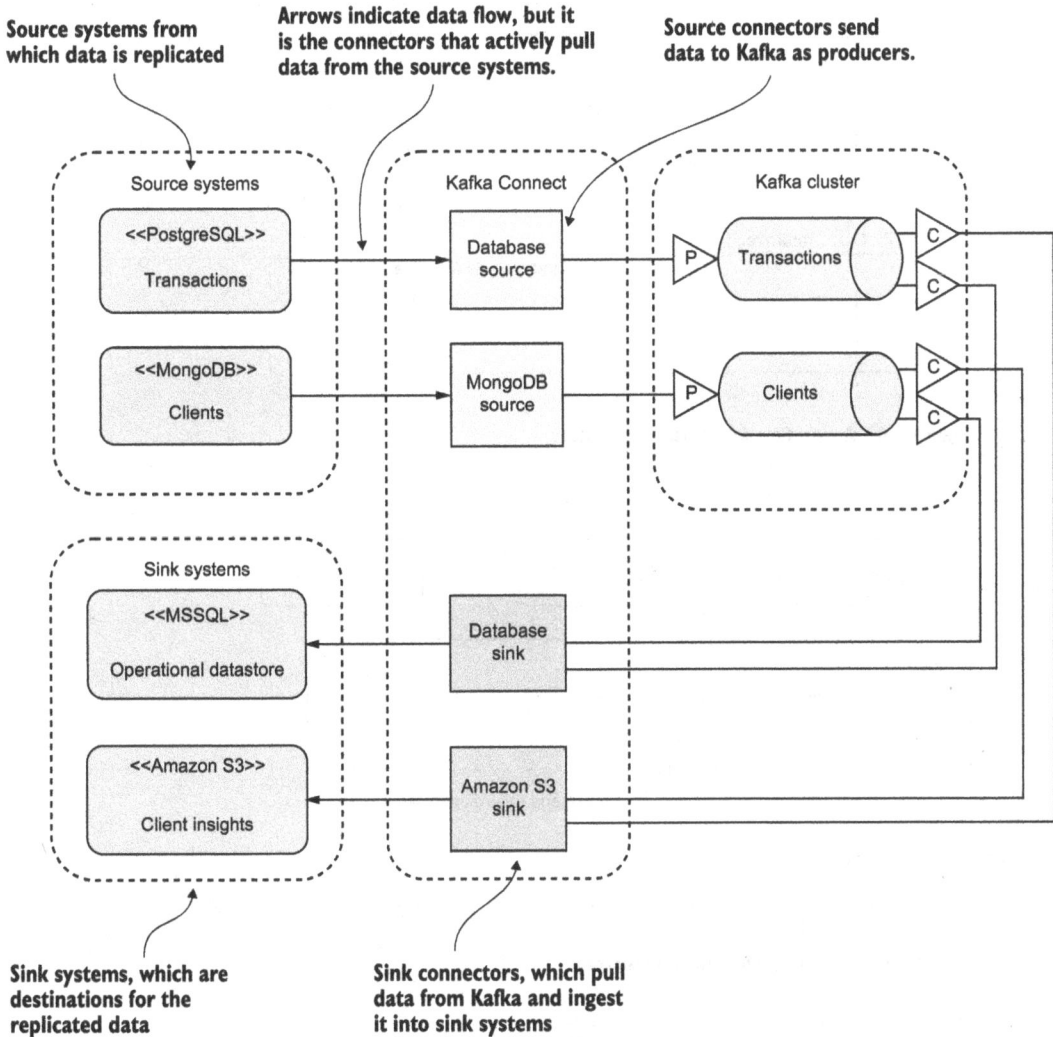

Figure 5.3 Setting up Kafka Connect for data replication involves using PostgreSQL and MongoDB as source systems. Source connectors are responsible for pulling data from these systems and inserting it into Kafka topics. In turn, sink connectors pull the data from Kafka and insert it into the target systems. In this setup, both sink connectors consume data from the same topics, with one inserting the data into an MS SQL database and the other into Amazon S3.

applications written in programming languages for which Kafka clients are available. However, integrating systems like mainframes, which may not have straightforward Kafka integration capabilities, can be more complex.

Database tools often offer functionality that can synchronize data transparently between databases or even with other systems, thus potentially bypassing the need for Kafka entirely. Examples of such tools include Debezium for CDC or Oracle GoldenGate

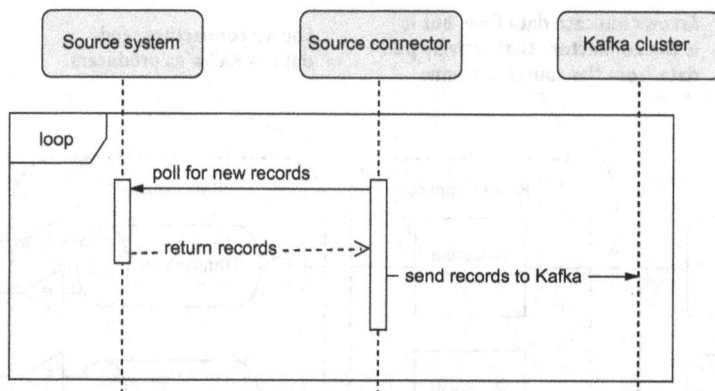

Figure 5.4   A workflow for source connectors

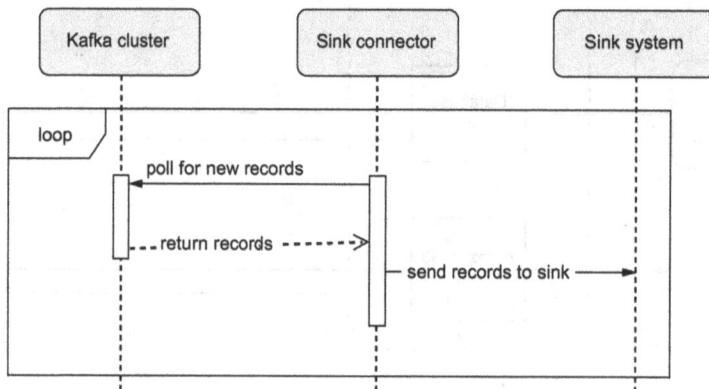

Figure 5.5   A workflow for sink connectors

for database replication. These tools offer stronger consistency guarantees than Kafka Connect. However, they typically emit raw change events (row-level inserts, updates, and deletes) rather than domain events with business context and enrichment. Kafka Connect's advantage is a uniform integration path that publishes into Kafka, where stream processing can enrich, transform, and fan out data to many consumers.

Various extract, transform, load (ETL) tools provide capabilities to create data transfer pipelines, often through visual interfaces that facilitate connection to a wide range of data sources and robust data transformation features. These tools support data transfer either in batches on a scheduled basis or in real time. Such ETL platforms are designed to meet diverse integration requirements, providing extensive transformation capabilities and high customizability, making them suitable for a wide range of large-scale use cases. Compared to Kafka Connect, traditional ETL tools typically have limited real-time capabilities. Additionally, Kafka's open source nature often makes it a more cost-effective solution for data integration.

IMPLEMENTATION CHALLENGES

Integrating data through Kafka Connect necessitates setting up an additional Kafka Connect cluster. This added complexity can pose a significant barrier, particularly for teams lacking extensive operational expertise in managing Kafka environments.

Often, data transfer involves not just a simple pass-through but may require modifications. While Kafka Connect supports basic message transformations—such as masking a credit card number—its capabilities may fall short for more complex data manipulation. For instance, when transformations involve combining multiple messages or more advanced logic, Kafka Connect alone is insufficient.

To handle more sophisticated transformations and aggregations, teams typically turn to streaming frameworks (discussed in chapter 8). These frameworks enable real-time processing of data streams and are designed to support advanced transformation and enrichment use cases that go beyond the built-in features of Kafka Connect.

Managing error handling robustly is challenging within Kafka Connect. Issues like transient network failures or errors in the source or target systems need to be gracefully handled to ensure data integrity and continuity. Ensuring that the system can recover from failures and continue processing without data loss is a critical challenge.

ADVANTAGES

Kafka Connect boasts a robust marketplace filled with ready-to-use connectors that can greatly simplify integration processes. Kafka Connect efficiently manages common tasks such as data type conversion and executes them reliably at scale, making it ideal for scenarios where custom coding for data ingestion or export is impractical, such as syncing data between databases or streaming logs to an analytics platform. This gives it a substantial advantage over traditional ETL tools, which are generally designed for batch processing at predefined intervals. This streamlined approach allows Kafka Connect to facilitate continuous, real-time data flow, enhancing integration efficiency and reducing the need for intensive manual coding.

DISADVANTAGES

Using Kafka Connect comes with certain disadvantages that should be considered:

- Many connectors are distributed under a commercial license, which can increase the overall cost of integration. Even when using open source connectors, the operational costs associated with running Kafka Connect can be significant. Efficient resource utilization and cost optimization become essential, especially when dealing with large volumes of data. The operational and planning pitfalls of Kafka Connect are covered in chapter 7.

- Another issue inherent to low-level data replication is the direct exposure of raw data rather than abstracted services. This raises security concerns, as sensitive data might be transferred without proper masking or encryption, and not all users or systems should have access to all data.

- Kafka Connect pipelines are fragile in the face of schema changes. Many organizations lack a systematic way to notify all dependent systems when table structures or formats change. As a result, a connector configured for an older schema may suddenly fail when a reference table evolves. These failures are often hard to predict and even harder to prevent, causing unexpected disruptions in data processing.

5.1.3   *Collecting logs*

From the moment computer systems were first developed, it was necessary to log application events to analyze errors and understand the causes of failures. For many years, systems logged messages to plain text files stored on local filesystems. As technology evolved and architectures became more complex, particularly with the proliferation of microservices in distributed environments, the limitations of this approach became apparent—it became increasingly difficult to track events and pinpoint the sources of troubles. This complexity necessitated the development of centralized logging systems, enabling real-time oversight and a unified view of what is happening across all the services.

In our Customer 360 ODS, we have multiple services generating data and a single service tasked with aggregating this data. These services may utilize various programming languages and frameworks, but it's crucial for us to standardize the way we collect log events to simplify tracking activities over time. How should our applications format and emit events, and where should these logs be stored?

As shown in figure 5.6, the proposed setup includes multiple applications emitting events, which are processed through Kafka and then transferred to Elasticsearch (or an open source fork like OpenSearch) for indexing and analysis. Kibana (or OpenSearch Dashboards) is used as a visual interface to interact with the log data. This high-level overview does not dive into implementation details but offers an understanding of the data flow.

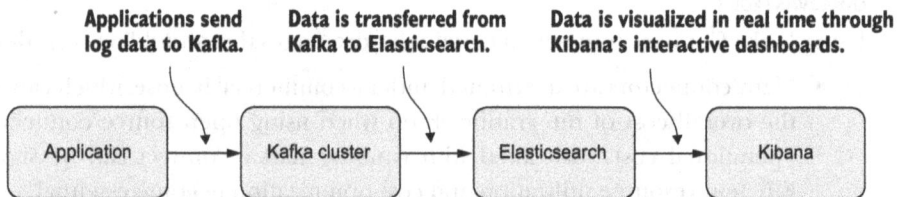

Figure 5.6   Conceptual flow for log data collection: log data is sent from the application to Kafka for processing, then indexed in Elasticsearch, and finally visualized in Kibana.

Elasticsearch (www.elastic.co) is one popular solution for managing and analyzing log data, known for its ability to efficiently handle large volumes of information and index new data within seconds. It offers robust search capabilities that enable users to perform complex queries on log data and quickly extract meaningful insights. Additionally, Elasticsearch is relatively easy to install and maintain, making it a favored choice among organizations of various sizes.

Once log events are collected in Elasticsearch, they can be accessed through its REST API or via Kibana, a visual interface designed for interacting with the data. Kibana offers an SQL-like query interface and features for building dashboards that update in real time as the data changes. This setup suggests that Elasticsearch, or a similar system, meets our requirements for handling log data effectively, but how do we transfer the data there?

This is where Kafka comes into play. Kafka serves as an intermediary for log data before it is processed by systems like Elasticsearch. When an application encounters a significant event, it generates a log event, which can be sent to Kafka in one of two ways:

- *Direct invocation of producer's methods*—The application utilizes a client library to format the log event as a Kafka message, incorporating all the necessary producer-specific configurations. This method involves directly embedding Kafka producer calls within the application code that sends the log messages. For example, a microservice handling user authentication may directly send login events to Kafka by calling the producer's send() method.
- *Integration with logging frameworks*—More commonly, Kafka producers are integrated with existing logging frameworks such as log4j, logback, or SLF4J. The application simply logs events using the common log method, while the configuration—external to the application—specifies where to send the logging data. Transmission is handled by appenders, and for Kafka, a specialized Kafka appender is required. This approach is preferred because it decouples Kafka interaction from the application's logging system, allowing easy modifications by adjusting appender configurations without changing the application code.

These methods ensure that log data is efficiently managed and transferred to Kafka, providing a robust, scalable solution for logging in complex systems. One of the possible implementations is illustrated in figure 5.7.

This is a common setup for log transfer using the open source data collector Fluentd (www.fluentd.org). The process for sending log data works as follows:

1 The application generates log events through a generic logging framework, keeping the code independent of the underlying logging system.
2 Fluentd agents collect the log data from files and forward it to Kafka as log events.
3 The data is then moved from Kafka to Elasticsearch using a Kafka Connect server.

ALTERNATIVE APPROACHES

Although Kafka is commonly used as an intermediary buffer for sending data to centralized log systems, various alternative methods are also available. For instance, using a syslog server is another popular approach. A syslog server implements the Syslog

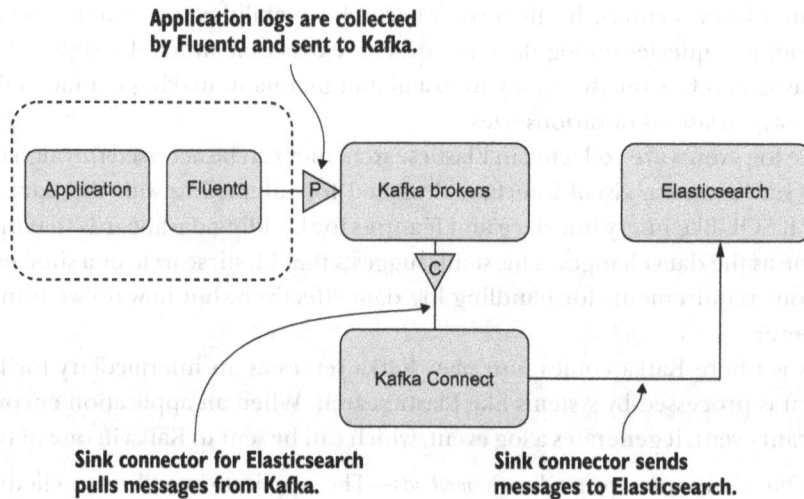

Figure 5.7   Sending log data via Kafka to Elasticsearch

protocol, a standard for message logging across different devices and applications within a network. Applications can employ a syslog agent to send out notification messages that include a timestamp, a severity rating, an identifier of the application, and event-specific information.

In the scenario we discussed earlier in this section, data is transferred to a centralized log system via Kafka. However, depending on the system requirements and architecture, data could be routed to systems like Elasticsearch using several other methods, including these:

- *Logstash*—This open source data ingestion tool collects data from various sources, transforms it according to predefined rules, and sends it to destinations like Elasticsearch.

- *Fluentd and Fluent Bit*—These tools collect data from various sources, enrich it, and forward it to log management systems. In the previous example, Fluentd sends data to Kafka, but it can also send data directly to Elasticsearch, depending on the desired setup.

- *Direct integration*—Applications can also send logs directly to Elasticsearch using the REST API, bypassing intermediate brokers like Kafka.

Another increasingly popular alternative is to use cloud-based observability platforms like Datadog (www.datadoghq.com) or New Relic (https://newrelic.com). These platforms are widely utilized for log management, monitoring, and troubleshooting, providing real-time insights and comprehensive visibility into system performance.

These alternatives provide flexibility in designing log management systems that can adapt to different operational environments, such as containers, virtual machines, or cloud services, while also meeting various technical requirements, like message transformation or enriching logs with metadata.

IMPLEMENTATION CHALLENGES

Using Kafka for logging introduces several challenges that require strategic management and careful planning:

- *Resource intensity*—Kafka demands substantial memory and CPU resources to effectively handle high data volumes and throughput. Operating and maintaining a Kafka cluster, particularly in environments with high data volumes, can be costly. It necessitates not only physical resources but also skilled personnel for effective management.

- *Distinct nonfunctional requirements*—Log data management has different priorities than business data management. For logs, the focus is on optimizing throughput rather than latency. The importance of reliability also differs; losing log messages, while not ideal, is generally less critical than losing financial transaction data. As a result, a separate Kafka cluster for logging is often warranted. This dedicated cluster can be tailored to meet high-throughput requirements without impacting the latency-sensitive tasks of other business applications. This cluster is typically focused on higher disk I/O throughput rather than on low-latency storage, and on utilizing servers with more memory and network bandwidth to handle the increased volume of log data.

- *Resource isolation*—Establishing a separate Kafka cluster for logs helps isolate log traffic, preventing it from interfering with the performance of critical business data streams. This segregation ensures that resource consumption for logging does not affect other applications and allows each cluster to be optimized according to its specific operational demands.

These considerations highlight the need for a thoughtful approach to using Kafka in logging scenarios, ensuring that the system's architecture aligns with the requirements of log data management.

ADVANTAGES

Using Kafka as an intermediary for log data before it reaches a centralized logging system provides several key advantages that significantly enhance the reliability, scalability, and manageability of log processing systems:

- *Decoupling of applications from logging solutions*—Applications simply send data to Kafka without needing to be aware of the downstream centralized logging system. This separation adds flexibility to the architectural setup, allowing for changes in the logging infrastructure without impacting application code.

- *Reliability and durability*—Kafka offers robust durability and fault tolerance through data replication and retention policies. This ensures that log-producing applications continue to operate smoothly without being affected by the performance issues or downtime of log-processing systems. Even if the logging system experiences downtime, data is not lost and can be replayed or reprocessed once the system is restored.

- *High throughput*—Kafka can manage high volumes of log messages, ensuring that log data is processed and transferred to systems like Elasticsearch without delay. This capability is crucial for maintaining real-time data flow and timely log analysis.
- *Buffering*—Kafka acts as a buffer to even out load spikes, preventing data loss during periods of high traffic. This buffering ensures that downstream systems are not overwhelmed, maintaining stability and performance across the logging infrastructure.

These benefits underscore why Kafka is increasingly favored as an intermediate layer in log management architectures, facilitating a more resilient, flexible, and efficient logging operation.

DISADVANTAGES

Using Kafka as an intermediary for sending logs to a centralized logging system has certain disadvantages that organizations should consider when designing their logging architecture:

- *Overkill for small systems*—For smaller systems with less frequent log data, implementing a Kafka-based logging pipeline may be excessive. It demands more infrastructure and management effort than simpler alternatives like directly logging to files or using data transfer agents like Fluentd.
- *External dependencies*—Although Kafka is effective at transporting log data, it lacks built-in capabilities for log analysis and processing. This necessitates the integration of additional systems such as Elasticsearch for log analysis, which can increase the complexity and introduce more potential points of failure into the logging infrastructure.

5.1.4   Real-time data processing

Traditionally, data analysis was performed in a batch manner. Data was collected in storage, and a periodic process would run at set intervals, querying a slice of data to obtain analytical information. However, there are numerous use cases where it is critical to react to events with minimal delay. For instance, detecting potential fraudulent transactions, predicting equipment failures, identifying anomalies, and issuing timely alerts are all scenarios where swift responses are essential. Delayed processing in these cases can result in significant financial losses and operational inefficiencies.

The Customer 360 ODS dashboard is a prime example of how reacting to events in real time can significantly enhance the client experience. Customers browse web pages, write comments on social media, and visit brick-and-mortar stores. By collecting and analyzing these activities, businesses can gain a deeper understanding of their customers and make personalized recommendations. For instance, if a customer is browsing a page with new mobile phone models, all the gathered information—including purchase history, social activities, and recent actions—can be used to suggest the product that best suits their needs.

The travel industry demands real-time data analysis. Flights are canceled or delayed, customers request upgrades, and travel plans are connected to hotel reservations and insurance policies. If something unexpected happens, it triggers a chain of changes that must be resolved in real time.

Although Kafka, as a message broker, does not interpret data or directly support real-time analytics, it can be integrated with frameworks that do. These frameworks receive data from Kafka, process it, and then send the output back to Kafka for consumption by interested parties. Real-time processing involves creating an application—figure 5.8 shows a fraud-detection example.

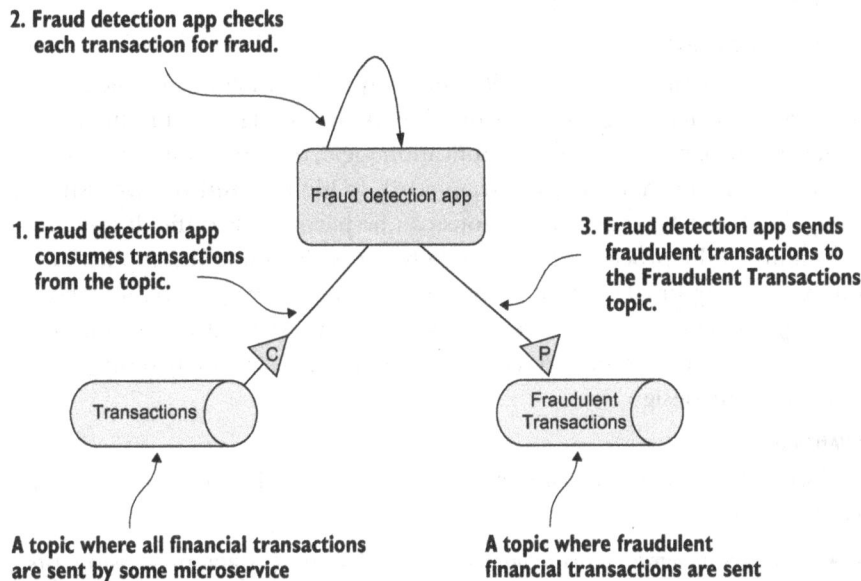

Figure 5.8 The fraud detection application acts as a producer and a consumer for Kafka topics. It reads messages from the Transactions topic, processes them, and sends the output results to the Fraudulent Transactions topic.

The common approach to implementing real-time processing applications is to use a framework that provides high-level constructs for processing while abstracting away the low-level communication with message brokers. Several frameworks are available, with Kafka Streams being one of the best known.

Kafka Streams (https://kafka.apache.org/documentation/streams/) is a library that helps implement processing logic in Java. It offers many convenient functions for stateless processing, like filtering and transformation, as well as stateful processing, such as calculating functions over aggregated data in real time. While the logic can be implemented in plain Java, Kafka Streams simplifies development by providing useful functions and ensuring exactly-once semantics for data processing. We will examine this in more detail in chapter 8.

ALTERNATIVE APPROACHES

In contrast to real-time data processing, data can also be processed in batches. The extract, transform, load (ETL) process extracts the data, processes it, and finally loads it into another storage system. For many use cases, processing data once a day is sufficient. Batch processing can be more efficient for large volumes of data that do not require immediate analysis.

Additionally, some use cases require data to be collected over time, such as organizing datasets for machine learning model training. While real-time processing provides immediate insights, batch processing is often simpler and more cost-effective for long-term data aggregation and analysis.

IMPLEMENTATION CHALLENGES

Developing real-time applications is a relatively new paradigm, and the most significant challenge is the learning curve for developers. While high-level framework constructs simplify the programming of the application logic, developers still need to understand the underlying mechanics of the framework to identify and resolve issues effectively. Debugging Kafka Streams applications can be particularly difficult due to the distributed nature of the processing. Additionally, properly tuning the application configuration to achieve optimal performance is challenging and requires careful consideration.

Managing state in Kafka Streams, especially for stateful processing, can be complex. Ensuring that the state remains consistent and is correctly restored after failures requires careful design.

ADVANTAGES

Processing data in real time can provide significant market and operational advantages to organizations:

- *Seamless integration with microservices*—Real-time data processing fits perfectly into a microservices architecture. These applications typically implement well-defined pieces of logic that can be deployed and scaled independently.
- *Immediate insights and decision making*—Low-latency processing of data in real time enables businesses to react quickly to events and make timely, informed decisions.
- *Enhanced responsiveness*—Real-time systems are more responsive and adaptive to changes, ensuring better performance, reliability, and customer satisfaction.

DISADVANTAGES

There are several disadvantages of using real-time processing frameworks that need to be carefully considered when deciding whether real-time processing is the right choice.

- *Shortage of skilled professionals*—Compared to traditional batch processing, it is harder to find professionals with expertise in real-time processing.
- *Limited programming language support*—Many real-time processing frameworks are Java-centric, which can be a limitation for teams using other programming languages.
- *Operational overhead*—Launching a microservice for every data processing task can lead to organizational challenges and increased complexity.
- *Lack of robust tool support*—The tooling ecosystem for real-time processing frameworks—such as IDE plugins, testing frameworks, and code generators—is not as mature, making development and maintenance more difficult.

5.2 Differences from other messaging platforms

Kafka is widely recognized as a robust messaging platform, but it's not the optimal choice for every messaging scenario. Other message brokers vary in their offerings, with some features overlapping those of Kafka. Let's explore a few instances where other options could be more suitable.

To facilitate our comparison with other solutions, we'll start by highlighting key characteristics of Kafka. We'll look at the alternatives in section 5.3.

5.2.1 Publish-subscribe model

Kafka is designed around the publish-subscribe pattern and does not natively support the point-to-point messaging pattern. In the publish-subscribe model, when a message is published to a Kafka topic, it becomes available to all consumers subscribed to that topic. Each consumer that subscribes to the topic can receive and process the message independently.

In contrast, the point-to-point communication model involves messages being sent to a specific queue, where each message is exclusively designated for a single consumer. In this model, once the designated consumer processes and acknowledges the message, the message is removed from the queue, ensuring it is not processed by any other consumer.

Point-to-point communication is essential for use cases that require exactly-once processing semantics. In such scenarios, if multiple consumers attempt to receive the same message, the broker must ensure that only one of them succeeds. Implementing this behavior in Kafka is challenging and typically requires explicit assignment of partitions to consumers. Examples of use cases that benefit from point-to-point communication include push notifications and task assignments to specific workers.

5.2.2 Partitioned data

In Kafka, data is partitioned, and when messages are sent to different partitions, we cannot rely on them being processed together by the same consumer instance. This makes Kafka less suitable for use cases where data from the entire topic needs to be processed together. For example, calculating statistical functions over all messages requires collecting and processing all the data in one place. Suppose we want to find the ten most expensive orders for each day in a topic containing customer orders. To perform this calculation, all orders need to be aggregated in a single location.

This problem can be mitigated by configuring the topic to have only one partition. However, this approach limits the benefits of parallel processing and scalability that Kafka typically provides.

5.2.3 Lack of broker-side logic

Kafka brokers do not perform operations based on message content, as messages are not deserialized at the broker level. This means that any kind of message processing is performed on the consumer side. Consumers need to receive messages and deserialize them to make them ready for processing. It is important to understand that brokers in Kafka cannot perform functions like the following that are available in other messaging systems:

- *Content-based routing*—If this functionality is required, an intermediate service must be created to read, deserialize, and then route the message to the appropriate output topic based on its content. Frameworks for stream processing, like Kafka Streams or Apache Flink, are well-suited for implementing such services.

- *Message validation*—Since brokers do not know the content of messages, they cannot verify if the content adheres to a specific data format. Validation can only occur on the client side. This obstacle and possible solutions will be discussed in chapter 6. This is a significant limitation of the Kafka technology, as receiving messages with an unexpected structure can be problematic for consumers.

5.2.4 Sequential data access

Consumers in Kafka retrieve data sequentially, following the order of messages within a partition. As mentioned in chapter 4, it is possible to position a consumer explicitly if the offset or timestamp of the message is known. However, it is not possible to position a consumer based on the content of the message, as the message content is not indexed.

If an application requires access to data based on content, Kafka cannot be used as the primary storage solution. Instead, messages should be offloaded into a datastore that supports random access to data, such as a relational database, a NoSQL database (including options like Elasticsearch), or similar solutions.

5.2.5 Message persistence

Kafka does not support in-memory topics; all messages are persistent and stored on disk. Kafka allows messages to be retained for a predetermined duration or indefinitely, based on configuration. Clients must account for the fact that data will be removed after the retention period expires, regardless of whether it has been processed. This differs from systems where messages are removed based on consumer acknowledgment.

Storage capacity should be planned carefully, and disk usage should be monitored to avoid running into disk space shortages. The retention period for storing data should be aligned with the nonfunctional requirements of the client application, ensuring that clients are not disconnected for longer than the data is retained in the topics.

5.2.6 Limitations in handling large messages

Kafka is not designed to support large messages, with the default maximum message size (the `message.max.bytes` property) set to 1,048,588 bytes (slightly larger than 1 MiB). If a message exceeds this size, it will be rejected by the broker. There are two reasons for this limitation:

- *Resource utilization*—Producers need to allocate memory for handling larger batches per topic and partition because batches are formed on the producer side. Consumers also must be prepared to process large messages in memory. Additionally, when data is replicated, followers act as clients, pulling data from the leaders, which means large messages impact the replication process as well.
- *Network efficiency*—Transmitting large messages can consume significant bandwidth, reducing the efficiency of data transfer.

To handle large messages, producers can split messages into parts and attach sequence numbers to them. These message parts must be sent to the same partition to ensure they are processed by the same consumer. The system must also be prepared for consumer failures, ensuring that received parts of messages are not lost if a consumer fails.

Another (preferred) solution is to use referenced messages, where the content of the message is stored in external store and a reference to that stored content is sent through Kafka, as illustrated in figure 5.9.

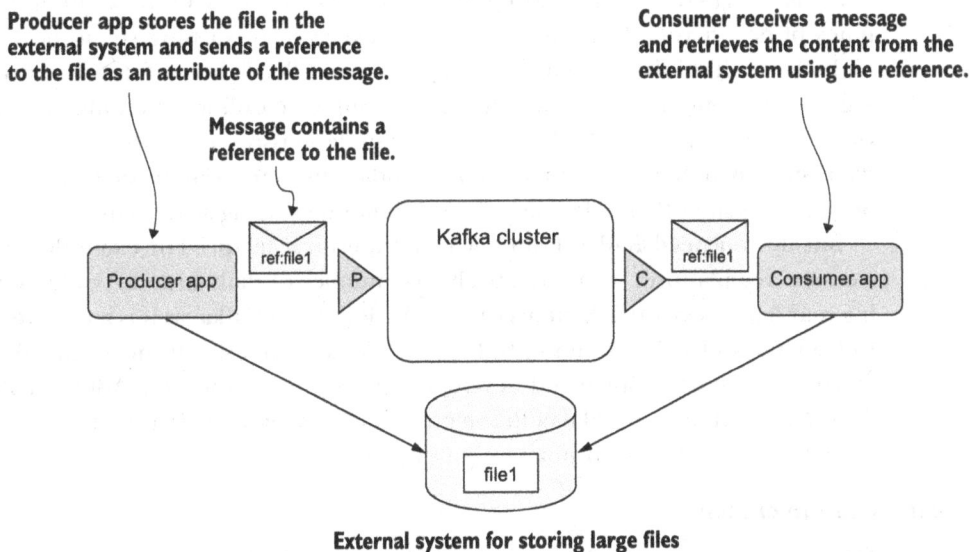

Figure 5.9 Passing messages with references to content stored externally

However, this approach comes with a caveat: if the message in Kafka expires before it's consumed (due to the topic's retention policy), the reference might outlive the actual Kafka message. In that case, the external store may retain data that no longer has a valid pointer, leading to potential orphaned data that must be cleaned up separately.

If the solution is to increase the maximum message size, the following properties must be adjusted on the broker:

- `message.max.bytes`—The largest record batch size allowed by Kafka after compression (if enabled). This can also be set per topic with the `max.message.bytes` property.
- `replica.fetch.max.bytes`—The number of bytes of messages to attempt to fetch for each partition when replicating.

The following properties must be adjusted on the consumer side:

- `max.partition.fetch.bytes`—The maximum amount of data per partition the broker can send to the client. If a single message batch exceeds this size, the entire batch will be returned to the client to prevent blocking progress.
- `fetch.max.bytes`—The maximum amount of data the broker can send to the client. Similarly, if a single message batch exceeds this limit, the full batch is returned to ensure the client can proceed.

The following property must be adjusted on the producer side:

- `buffer.memory`—The amount of memory the producer uses for buffering records.

5.2.7 *Scalability and high throughput*

Kafka is designed for high throughput and scalability, efficiently handling large volumes of data across distributed systems. It excels at processing small messages at a high rate with minimal latency, making it an excellent choice for systems requiring high-throughput message processing. For example, in online streaming platforms like video or music services, Kafka is used to handle massive amounts of real-time event data, such as user interactions, recommendations, and content delivery. Numerous benchmarks show that Kafka outperforms other messaging systems in these areas.

But do you need Kafka if latency is not a critical factor? For example, in a small e-commerce platform with a relatively low number of daily orders, real-time processing may not be essential. Systems can still benefit from Kafka, as it is a mature solution with a large and active community. However, Kafka's complexity means that the cost of expertise for maintenance and development must be considered. Additionally, Kafka provides robust features like fault tolerance and scalability, which can be valuable even when low latency is not a primary requirement.

5.2.8 *Fault tolerance*

Many use cases involving the streaming of business data do not tolerate data loss. Financial, healthcare, and e-commerce systems require fault tolerance to ensure that the failure of one component does not result in losing any data. This is typically achieved by duplicating components.

Kafka ensures fault tolerance by replicating partitions across different brokers, which guarantees that, with the correct configuration, at least one copy of the data always remains available. Replication is built into Kafka and does not require the installation of additional products.

5.2.9 Batch processing

The idea of real-time processing is to handle events immediately as they occur, with minimal delay. However, many business workflows today are still designed to process data in batches. This means that data is collected over a period and then processed in large chunks. For instance, a DWHUploadService might collect client transaction events and upload them to a data warehouse in bulk on a daily basis, as shown in figure 5.10.

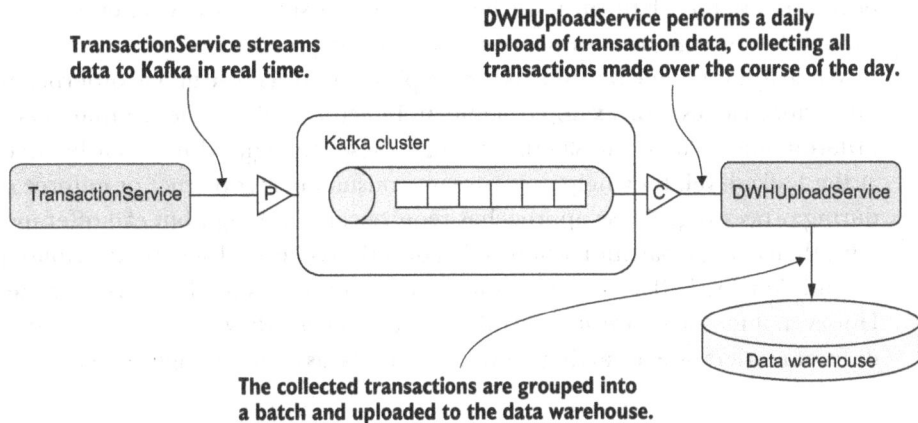

Figure 5.10 Time-based batch load to the data warehouse: the consumer buffers records and, at fixed intervals, bulk-loads a batch to the data warehouse (rather than per-message processing).

Although it's possible to implement batch processing in Kafka, this approach presents several challenges:

- *Data partitioning*—Kafka partitions data to distribute it across multiple consumers. To collect all the data for a batch job, the consumer responsible for forming the bulk upload must aggregate data from all partitions. This can be complex and resource-intensive.

- *Streaming nature of data*—Kafka's data is inherently streaming, making it difficult to define clear batch boundaries. Using system timestamps, a consumer can start from the first record older than the provided timestamp. However, determining the last record for the batch is challenging because events may arrive with delays. Thus, a mechanism is needed to handle late-arriving events.

- *Handling failed records*—If some records in a batch fail during upload, there may be a need to resubmit only the failed records. However, Kafka does not natively support retrieving specific failed records; it retrieves data sequentially. This necessitates implementing custom logic on the application side to handle partial failures and retries.

These challenges highlight the complexities involved in adapting Kafka for batch processing, which inherently contradicts its design for real-time, continuous data streams.

5.2.10 *Lack of global ordering*

Partitioning data also leads to a lack of global ordering, since ordering is only guaranteed within a single partition. If a use case requires global ordering, this can be achieved by using only one partition, but this sacrifices the benefits of parallelism. For example, in an e-commerce flash sale event, ensuring fairness means all customer orders across the platform must be processed in strict sequence, even if they come from different regions or devices—global ordering is critical.

While using a single partition is the simplest way to achieve global ordering, there are other approaches. For example, some architectures add sequence numbers or other ordering metadata to messages. Although these strategies don't coordinate ordering at the Kafka level, they help downstream consumers reconstruct or enforce ordering during processing. These approaches require careful design but can offer more flexibility than a single partition when global ordering is needed across a distributed system.

Additionally, Kafka maintains the order of messages as they arrive at the broker. However, if messages are sent by different producers, they may arrive at the broker in different orders due to varying network latencies, as shown in figure 5.11.

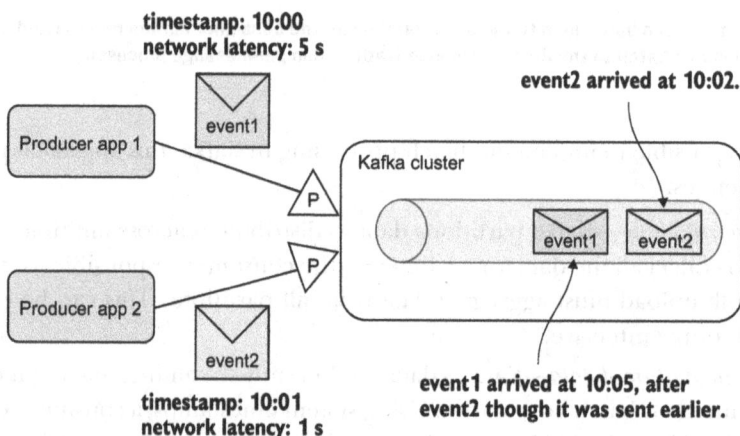

Figure 5.11 Unexpected ordering. Earlier timestamped messages can arrive later because of network delays.

Systems that require strict ordering in such situations must implement a streaming component that reorders messages based on their timestamps.

5.3 Kafka alternatives

Numerous messaging solutions are available today, both open source and commercial. Additionally, cloud providers offer their own managed messaging services. Let's briefly look at the main competitors to Kafka.

5.3.1 RabbitMQ

One of the most frequent questions I receive is how Kafka compares to RabbitMQ (www.rabbitmq.com). While both are open source distributed message brokers, they have different architectural approaches and offer distinct capabilities.

RabbitMQ supports three primary messaging patterns:

- *Point-to-point (queues)*—A producer sends a message intended for a single consumer. Once consumed, the message is removed from the queue, ensuring that no other consumer can process it.
- *Publish-subscribe (topics)*—A message is sent to multiple subscribers, ensuring all subscribers receive the message. This is typically achieved using exchanges and bindings.
- *Request-reply*—This approach is used when a client sends a request and expects a response. It involves creating a queue for replies, which can be specific to a request or client, or it can be non-exclusive. The client includes a correlation ID with the request message; then the server processes the request and sends a reply to the reply queue with the same correlation ID. The client retrieves the reply using the correlation ID, which matches the response to the original request.

RabbitMQ supports various messaging protocols, including Advanced Message Queuing Protocol (AMQP), Streaming Text Oriented Messaging Protocol (STOMP), and Message Queue Telemetry Transport (MQTT).

The architecture of RabbitMQ is illustrated in figure 5.12. Producers and consumers are decoupled and communicate through message brokers. Unlike Kafka, producers in RabbitMQ do not send messages directly to brokers but to an Exchange. The Exchange routes messages to the appropriate queues based on routing rules and message content. This additional layer allows for more granular control over message flow compared to Kafka's direct producer-to-topic model.

When deciding whether to use RabbitMQ or Kafka as a messaging platform, various aspects need to be carefully evaluated, including non-functional requirements and team expertise.

The primary architectural difference lies in the pattern used for handling message logic:

- *Smart endpoints/dumb pipes (implemented in Kafka)*—Kafka brokers do not perform any logic on the messages. They do not interpret message structure; they simply

Producer application sends messages to the Exchange component of RabbitMQ.

Queues are destinations where messages are sent.

Consumers retrieve messages either by pushing or pulling them.

Exchange routes messages to the queues.

Bindings specify how messages are routed.

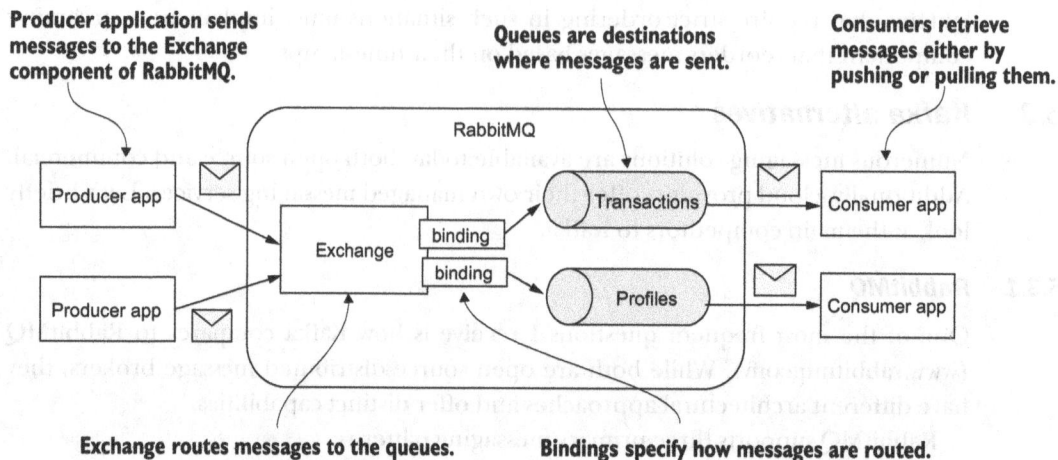

Figure 5.12   RabbitMQ architecture

store messages on disk and dispatch them between clients. All logic happens on the consumer side, allowing Kafka to handle a high throughput of messages efficiently.

- *Dumb endpoints/smart pipes (implemented in RabbitMQ)*—Exchanges in RabbitMQ apply a set of rules for message routing, enabling complex routing scenarios. This pattern allows RabbitMQ to perform sophisticated routing and processing within the messaging infrastructure.

The following requirements are critical for the choice of the platform:

- *Throughput and latency*—Evaluate the throughput and latency requirements of your system. Kafka is typically preferred for high-throughput, low-latency use cases.

- *Message routing complexity*—Consider the complexity of your message routing needs. RabbitMQ excels in scenarios requiring complex routing rules and message transformations.

A powerful new extension for the RabbitMQ system is RabbitMQ Streams (www .rabbitmq.com/docs/streams), which offers functionality similar to Kafka. RabbitMQ Streams enables working with an append-only persistent log of data, which is replicated for fault tolerance. By supporting durable storage, efficient data access, and consumer offset management, RabbitMQ Streams provides a robust solution for real-time data processing applications.

Both RabbitMQ and Kafka are mature systems with strong development communities, providing robust support, extensive documentation, and a variety of tools and extensions.

5.3.2 Apache Pulsar

Probably the closest product to Apache Kafka in terms of functionality is Apache Pulsar (https://pulsar.apache.org). Like Kafka, Apache Pulsar is an open source messaging system capable of supporting high-rate message processing. Released after Kafka, Pulsar aims to address some of the user-friendliness and optimization limitations found in its predecessor.

The architecture of Apache Pulsar, as shown in figure 5.13, implements a publish-subscribe pattern similar to Kafka. It supports the concepts of producers, consumers, and topics. Publishers and subscribers exchange messages, which are the basic units of information. To enable parallel processing of data, topics are partitioned.

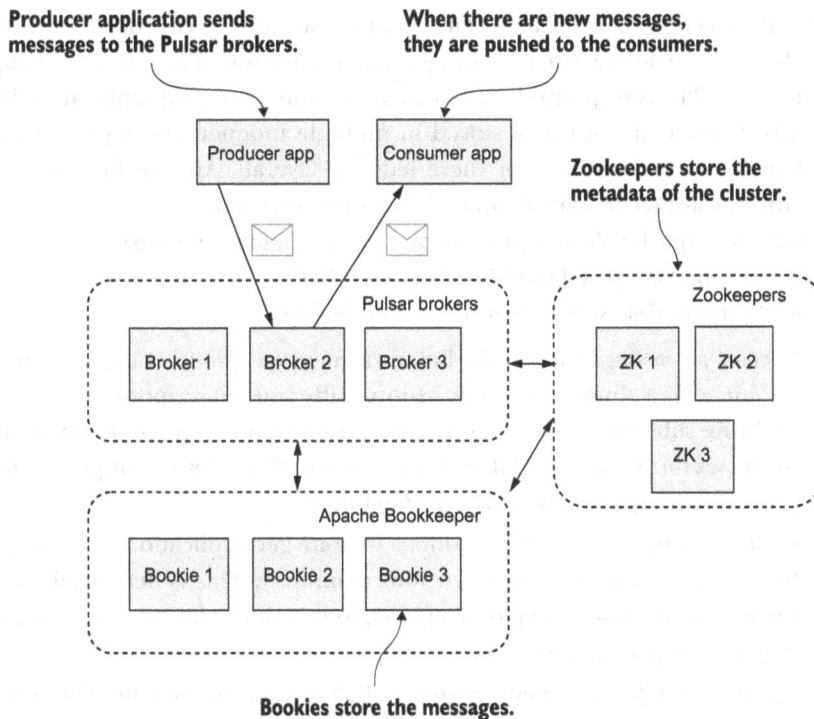

Figure 5.13   Apache Pulsar architecture

The main architectural difference between Apache Kafka and Apache Pulsar is the separation of storage and processing of messages. In Pulsar, message processing is handled by stateless brokers, while storage is managed by the Apache Bookkeeper (https://bookkeeper.apache.org) project. This separation brings an additional level of scalability, as stateless brokers can easily be scaled independently of the storage layer, leading to more efficient resource management. Stateless brokers also simplify failover and load balancing, as they do not hold state, allowing for faster recovery and rebalancing compared to Kafka, where brokers manage both message processing and storage.

In Kafka, brokers are responsible for communicating with producers and consumers, as well as for message persistence. Brokers in Kafka are stateful and store messages on local disks. Each partition is stored in its entirety on a single node, whether that node is a leader or a follower. Partitions cannot be split across multiple nodes.

In contrast, Apache Pulsar brokers are stateless and have the following functions:

- Receiving messages from producers
- Communicating with Apache Bookkeeper for message persistence
- Dispatching messages to consumers
- Performing various administrative tasks for cluster maintenance

Apache Bookkeeper is a scalable, fault-tolerant storage service optimized for write-ahead logging, real-time stream storage, and replication. The primary component, known as a bookie, is responsible for storing data and managing replication. In Pulsar, the log is distributed, with data stored in multiple independent logs called ledgers. Each bookie stores fragments of these ledgers. Overall, Apache Bookkeeper offers more efficient storage management and faster recovery times.

Pulsar uses Apache Zookeeper (https://zookeeper.apache.org) for storing metadata, like the approach used by older versions of Kafka.

Apache Pulsar offers several features out of the box:

- *Support for message queues*—In Pulsar, a message queue is implemented using a topic with a single consumer group. Different subscription modes exist. An exclusive subscription ensures that only one consumer in the subscription group processes the messages, while a shared subscription allows multiple consumers to process messages in a load-balanced manner.

- *Built-in geo-replication*—Pulsar offers built-in geo-replication, allowing data to be replicated across multiple regions seamlessly. This is beneficial for disaster recovery and for serving global applications with low latency. In contrast, Kafka requires a separate product for geo-replication.

- *Ephemeral non-persistent message storage*—Pulsar supports ephemeral non-persistent message storage, enabling temporary storage of messages that do not require persistence.

- *Multitenancy*—Pulsar supports multitenancy, allowing different components to operate securely in a shared environment. This ensures resource isolation and security for various tenants.

- *Dead letter topics*—Pulsar supports dead letter topics, where unprocessable messages can be routed for further inspection and handling.

It is possible to enable a Kafka protocol handler on Pulsar brokers. This allows Kafka clients to communicate with Pulsar without any modifications. Additionally, there are client-side libraries that act as wrappers to adapt existing Kafka client code seamlessly.

When comparing Kafka and Pulsar, it's important to note that Kafka has a more developed ecosystem. This includes a large user community, active forums, numerous conferences, and various providers offering Kafka as a managed service. Additionally, Kafka benefits from a wide array of extensions, libraries, and tools.

5.3.3 Solutions from cloud providers

Given the widespread use of message communication, it's no surprise that each major cloud provider offers its own messaging solution. The following services are available as managed cloud services, where the service provider handles the underlying infrastructure, maintenance, and management tasks. These services cannot be installed in on-premises environments:

- Amazon Kinesis (https://aws.amazon.com/kinesis/) is a service designed to process big data in real time. It implements the publish-subscribe pattern, where a Kinesis stream maps to a Kafka topic and a shard maps to a partition, with ordering guaranteed within a shard. Like in Kafka, messages are distributed to shards using partition keys. Messages are persistent and removed based on retention settings, with a maximum retention period of 7 days. Kinesis stores data in three replicas and includes preconfigured fault-tolerant settings that cannot be changed. When using On-Demand mode, capacity automatically scales in response to varying traffic.

- Google Pub/Sub (https://aws.amazon.com/kinesis/) is a serverless, message-oriented service available on Google Cloud that provides large-scale event delivery and messaging analytics. Scalability in Pub/Sub is automatic, adjusting to the current system load. Messages are persistent, and exactly-once delivery semantics are guaranteed. Messages can be delivered using either push or pull modes. Once all subscribers have acknowledged receipt of a message, it becomes unavailable. However, acknowledgments can be modified, allowing the replay of previously acknowledged messages in bulk.

- Azure Event Hubs (https://azure.microsoft.com/en-us/products/event-hubs) is a service from Microsoft designed for processing high volumes of events. Clients can interact with Event Hubs via the Kafka protocol, allowing existing Kafka clients to communicate with it without any changes. It also supports the Advanced Message Queuing Protocol (AMQP) and HTTP protocols. The concept of an Event Hub is similar to a Kafka topic, with data distributed across multiple partitions within it. Event Hubs dynamically adjusts resources based on the incoming workload, ensuring scalability and performance. It also provides features like capture, which allows automatic storage of streaming data in Azure Blob Storage or Azure Data Lake for long-term retention and batch processing. Additionally, Event Hubs offers built-in support for event retention, allowing you to configure the retention period for your events.

5.4   Online resources

- "Top 5 Kafka use cases": https://blog.bytebytego.com/p/ep92-top-5-kafka-use-cases

  A short guide to the five most popular ways companies use Kafka.

- "Event Sourcing using Apache Kafka": www.confluent.io/blog/event-sourcing-using-apache-kafka/

  An overview of how Kafka enables event-sourced application design.

- "When NOT to use Apache Kafka?" www.kai-waehner.de/blog/2022/01/04/when-not-to-use-apache-kafka/

  An overview of use cases that are a poor fit for Kafka.

- "Beyond Limits: Produce large records without undermining Apache Kafka?" https://conduktor.io/blog/beyond-limits-produce-large-records-without-undermining-apache-kafka

  An explanation of how to send large records without hurting Kafka's performance.

- "Does Apache Kafka really preserve message ordering?" https://aiven.io/blog/kafka-real-ordering

  A clear explanation of what Kafka can—and cannot—guarantee about message ordering.

- "Ensuring Message Ordering in Kafka: Strategies and Configurations": www.baeldung.com/kafka-message-ordering

  An overview explaining how client settings influence message ordering guarantees in Kafka.

- "Kafka vs. Pulsar: Streaming data platforms compared": https://quix.io/blog/kafka-vs-pulsar-comparison

  A concise comparison of Kafka and Pulsar across architectures, performance, and ecosystems.

Summary

- Microservices that communicate through events can use Kafka as an underlying integration platform, providing decoupled communication between services, improving scalability and fault tolerance. Kafka offers an efficient and scalable solution for integrating microservices in distributed architectures.

- Kafka's ability to process events with high throughput makes it ideal for collecting logs and metrics, as Kafka can handle vast amounts of data at a high rate.

- Data replication can be implemented using Kafka Connect, a key component of the Kafka ecosystem. Kafka Connect provides a flexible and scalable way to implement data replication without extensive custom development.

- Various frameworks tightly integrated with Kafka allow building applications that process data in real time, empowering businesses to react to data as it is generated, enabling advanced real-time use cases.

- RabbitMQ and Apache Pulsar are messaging platforms that compete with Kafka, each serving its own niche. RabbitMQ excels in low-latency, transactional messaging, while Pulsar's architecture with stateless brokers and separate storage makes it more scalable for certain use cases. The choice between Kafka, RabbitMQ, and Pulsar depends on non-functional requirements such as scalability, real-time processing, and transactional guarantees.

- Kafka excels at processing small messages at a high rate with minimal latency, making it a top choice for real-time event-driven systems. Examples include clickstream analytics, fraud scoring on card transactions, IoT telemetry ingestion, and real-time operational alerting.

- Kafka may not be the best choice for use cases requiring strict ordering, batch transfers, or random data access (e.g., a single-sequence financial ledger or nightly bulk file/table transfers for ETL).

Defining data contracts

This chapter covers

- Event design principles
- Supporting data contracts in Kafka
- Type evolution and schema changes
- Common challenges in managing data contracts

We've looked at the fundamentals of Kafka and its real-world fit, so let's turn to a practical question: how can we define events and express them as durable, evolvable data contracts. To address this, we need to set event boundaries and granularity, compare state versus delta events (and when each fits), and map domain events to Kafka messages without losing business meaning. We'll explore the tools and techniques for managing contracts over time: type evolution and compatibility, format choices, ownership, and how teams communicate changes. Then we can turn to implementation with Schema Registry and survey practical alternatives. This should set you up with a clear path from whiteboard models to production-ready schemas that teams can rely on.

Field notes: Turning business facts into schemas

The team gathers to discuss an important question about how to define data contracts.

Max: Alright team, we haven't really talked about events yet. What exactly is an event, and how do we define it when systems communicate through Kafka? It's not like a service with a clear endpoint and parameters, so how does a consumer know what data to expect?

Eva: Good question, Max. Let's break it down. An event is a record of something that has happened in the system. It's immutable, meaning it can't be changed once it's created, and it includes a timestamp to show when it occurred. The context of the event gives it meaning and relevance. In Kafka, you define the schema for the events. The schema acts as the contract between the producer and the consumer. It specifies the structure of the data being exchanged. This is the most important topic for us as architects because it ensures consistency and reliability across our systems.

Max: Got it. So are these schemas defined in XML?

Rob (laughing): XML? Nobody uses XML anymore, Max. That went out with dial-up internet. We use more modern formats like Avro, JSON Schema, and Protobuf. But if you're feeling nostalgic, you could always define custom serializers.

Max (chuckling): Alright, I get it. So is there a way to manage these schemas? Like a service catalog, but for data?

Eva: Yes, there is. It's called the schema registry. The schema registry stores and provides access to schemas for your Kafka topics, ensuring that producers and consumers use the same data contract.

Max: That sounds useful. But what exactly is a schema registry, and how does it relate to Kafka?

Rob: The schema registry is a separate cluster of servers in the Kafka ecosystem. It serves as storage for schemas and provides an API for managing them. This way, producers and consumers can fetch the schema and ensure they are using the correct format.

Max: That makes sense. But how do we manage sharing these contracts, agreeing on what data is exposed, and communicating changes?

Eva: There's a lot to organize. You need a process for sharing contracts, getting agreements on the data structure, and communicating any changes. This ensures that everyone stays on the same page.

Max: Can business analysts create these schemas, or is it too technical?

Eva: One of the important questions is how to map the business representation of the event to the technical one. The tools don't help much with that, so it's a collaborative effort between business analysts and developers.

Rob: It's mostly a technical contract, so it's probably best handled by developers or data engineers. Business analysts can provide input on the data requirements, but the actual schema definition is usually a technical task.

6.1 How Kafka handles event structure

Although Kafka brokers do not interpret data, there must be an agreement between producers and consumers on the structure of the data being exchanged. This raises important questions: What are the best practices for designing events? Who is responsible for defining the event structure? And if the structure of an event changes, how do you notify all relevant parties about the changes?

Before diving into these questions, let's first review the commonly accepted practices in the Kafka ecosystem, as illustrated in figure 6.1. In Kafka, schemas are stored separately from the brokers in a specialized server known as the Schema Registry (https://docs.confluent.io/platform/current/schema-registry/index.html). Schemas are managed through a REST API, and each time a schema is updated, a new version is created. Arrows A and B in figure 6.1 depict the process of creating schemas through the REST API.

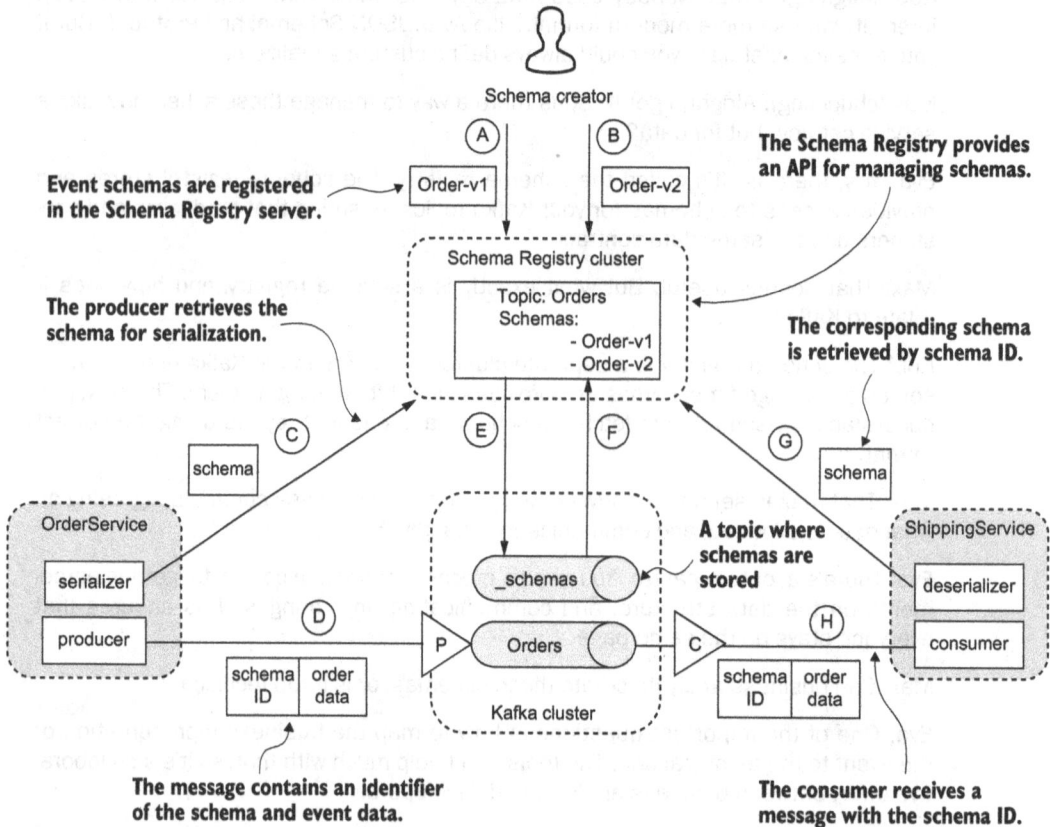

Figure 6.1 Managing schemas in Kafka. Schemas are deployed via a REST API and stored in a Kafka topic. The Schema Registry provides access to these schemas through its API, allowing clients to retrieve and cache the necessary schemas locally.

The Schema Registry operates as a cluster, to handle failovers. One server acts as the primary, handling writes, while the others serve as secondaries, handling reads. If the primary server fails, another server in the cluster is automatically elected to take over as the new primary. The Schema Registry does not have its own database; instead, it stores schemas in a compacted topic in Kafka, named _schemas by default. The rules governing how schemas are assigned to topics are configured within the Schema Registry (discussed later). Arrows E and F in figure 6.1 illustrate how schemas are stored in and retrieved from the _schemas topic. Records in _schemas use structured keys encoding the record type, name, and version.

When producers send messages, they retrieve the appropriate schema from the Schema Registry and serialize the message structure, embedding the schema identifier within the message along with the actual data. Schema Registry currently supports three serialization formats—JSON Schema, Avro, and Protocol Buffers (Protobuf)—each with its corresponding serializer. In figure 6.1, arrow C represents how the schema is retrieved from the Schema Registry, and arrow D illustrates how the serialized message is sent to Kafka.

On the consumer side, when a message is received (arrow H in figure 6.1), the consumer knows how to extract the schema ID from the message. This ID is then used to retrieve the corresponding schema from the Schema Registry (arrow G in figure 6.1), which is subsequently used to deserialize the message.

It's important to understand that the Schema Registry does not eliminate the consumer's responsibility for understanding the data format. A consumer must still be written with prior knowledge of the message structure—it cannot "discover" business semantics from the registry. The registry simply provides the means to look up the schema safely and consistently, ensuring that producer and consumer remain compatible over time, even as schemas evolve. Without the Schema Registry, each service would need to manage this compatibility manually.

While using the Schema Registry is not mandatory—serialization and deserialization can be entirely managed by the clients—adopting the Schema Registry is considered a best practice. It offers standardized schema management and helps ensure compatibility and consistency across different services.

Now let's dive deeper into the design and implementation considerations for schemas.

6.2 Designing events

The architect's most important task is to define the contract for the interaction between systems. While this is the standard practice for services, the path is less traveled for events.

6.2.1 Challenges in event design

An *event* is a single, immutable fact that something happened, accompanied by a timestamp. In an event-driven system, an interface defines the structure and attributes of these events, clearly describing what occurred. When an architectural team designs such an interface, they should specify the attributes, including their names, data types, and metadata, such as versioning information or tracking IDs. Additionally, the interface should define the channels through which events can be published, subscribed to, or accessed.

Defining the structure of an event can be challenging, especially when dealing with complex entities like a user. Consider an event that carries information about changes to a user profile. In the producer service, the user profile might be represented as a composite entity, which could include a collection of Address entities or SocialAccount entities, as shown in figure 6.2.

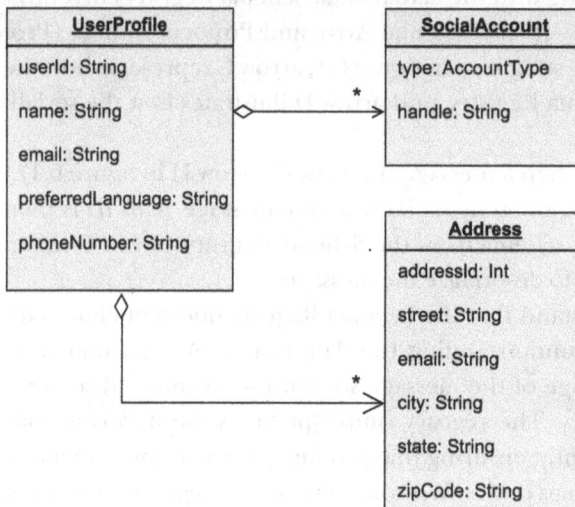

Figure 6.2   An example of a composite entity. The UserProfile aggregates a collection of SocialAccount and Address entities. Together, they represent the complete state of a UserProfile.

Suppose the user's address has changed. What information should the event contain in this scenario? One approach is to include all components of the user profile in the event, regardless of which specific attribute was modified. In this case, each event will contain an entire structure, as shown in figure 6.2.

The approach where each entity update is treated as a distinct event is illustrated in figure 6.3.

Similarly, when only a single attribute, such as the preferred language, changes, the key question arises: should we capture the entire user object or just the specific attribute that was updated? The fine-grained approach is shown in figure 6.4.

Defining the structure of an event is one of the key challenges in event design, and we will explore this topic further later in the chapter.

Another important consideration is whether technical attributes such as the timestamp, version, and source of the event should be embedded within the event's structure or handled separately as event metadata.

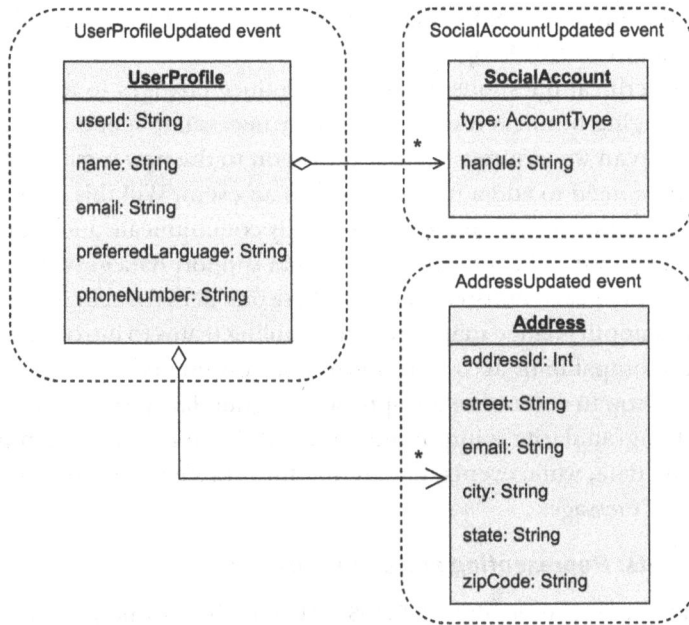

Figure 6.3 Each entity is mapped to a distinct event. For example, if an address changes, only an `AddressUpdated` event will be sent, without any information about the `UserProfile` or `SocialAccount`.

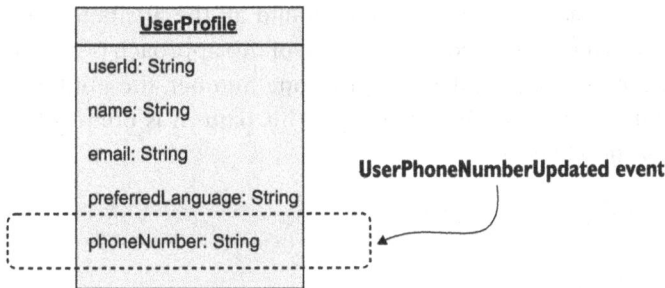

Figure 6.4 The `UserPhoneNumberUpdated` event contains only the one changed attribute.

During the analysis phase of a project, events are often defined abstractly, without direct mapping to a specific serialization format. Analysts typically use diagramming tools like Enterprise Architect (www.sparxsystems.eu) or DrawIO (https://app .diagrams.net) to visualize event structures or specify them in YAML using specifications like AsyncAPI. In some cases, even Microsoft Excel has been used for this purpose.

However, when the project moves into the implementation phase, the team must transition these abstract definitions into concrete serialization formats such as JSON or Avro. At this stage, there are several important considerations: What data types are supported by the chosen format? Can attributes be marked as nullable? Does the format support nested structures like lists or maps? These questions are crucial for ensuring that the serialized events faithfully represent the originally defined structures. Unfortunately, there is currently no tool on the market that seamlessly maps event definitions from their logical models to implementation-ready structures, leaving a gap that teams must bridge manually during development.

One of the most critical questions is how to introduce changes to an event. As a project evolves, changing business requirements may necessitate modifications to the event structure. How can we ensure a smooth transition to the new version for all participants? Suppose we need to add a new attribute to an event. Will this change break the consumer's code? How should the team effectively communicate and manage this update? In this chapter, we will explore how tools that support data governance, such as Confluent Schema Registry, enforce rules and best practices for schema evolution. These rules ensure smooth change management, enabling teams to introduce changes safely and maintain compatibility across producers and consumers.

Now let's explore how to determine the appropriate granularity for an event. Choosing the right level of granularity is important: events that are too coarse-grained may include unnecessary data, while events that are too fine-grained can result in an overwhelming number of messages.

6.2.2　*Fact and delta events: Representing state changes*

When a user updates their profile, the `ProfileService` publishes a notification indicating that the data has been changed. How should this event be structured? There are two common patterns for event structures: fact events and delta events.

Fact events, also known as *state events*, always contain all the attributes of an entity, regardless of which ones have changed. An example of this approach is shown in listing 6.1. For instance, if the user only updates their phone number, the notification event will still carry the entire set of profile attributes. This pattern is often referred to as *Event-Carried State Transfer* (ECST).

> **Listing 6.1　`UserProfileUpdated` event carrying all the attributes from the user profile**

```
{
  "eventType": "UserProfileUpdated",
  "eventId": "123e4567-e89b-12d3-a456-426614174003",
  "timestamp": "2024-09-26T12:00:00Z",
  "userProfile": {
    "userId": "12345",
    "name": "Alice Johnson",
    "email": "alice.johnson@example.com",
    "preferredLanguage": "en",
    "addresses": [
      {
        "addressId": "98765",
        "street": "456 Elm St",
        "city": "Metropolis",
        "state": "NY",
        "zipCode": "10001"
      }
    ],
    "socialAccounts": [
```

```
    {
      "type": "twitter",
      "handle": "@alicejohnson"
    }
  ],
  "phoneNumber": "+1-555-123-4567"
}
}
```

This pattern aligns with the publish-subscribe model, where the publisher notifies consumers of changes without knowing which specific information each consumer is interested in. While the producer does not expose its internal domain object directly, the event interface must include attributes that are potentially relevant to other systems.

Fact events are designed by the producer team, which possesses the necessary domain knowledge to create a consistent and comprehensive interface. Given the longevity and level of integration of an application, it may be impossible for message or event producers to anticipate all potential consumers of their events. This unpredictability is, in fact, a fundamental aspect of the decoupling inherent in the event-driven paradigm.

Advantages of fact events:

- *Ease of design and maintenance*—Fact events fully represent the state of an entity at a specific point in time, providing a complete picture with each event. This consistency simplifies onboarding new consumers, who can rely on a clear and stable contract.

- *Resilience*—Consumers can obtain the current state by simply reading the latest event, which is particularly useful if they have missed previous events due to failures.

- *Decoupled consumer logic*—The producer service does not need to be concerned with the specific logic required by different consumers. If a consumer needs additional attributes, they must be added consistently, making them available to all consumers. All event-specific logic is implemented on the consumer side.

However, there are also some drawbacks:

- *Access control*—All consumers have access to all attributes of the event, which could pose a security risk in certain use cases.

- *Redundancy*—The event may include information that no consumers need, leading to unnecessary data exposure.

- *Increased disk space and network traffic*—Sending the entire state of an entity increases network traffic and requires more disk space, which can become a problem, especially in high-throughput systems.

In contrast, *delta events* carry only the identifier of the changed entity and the specific attributes that have been modified. An example of a delta event, where the user changes only their phone number, is shown in listing 6.2. While delta events are smaller in size, the concern about managing multiple schemas for different combinations of attributes isn't necessarily valid. In fact, a single schema can be used where all attributes are defined as optional. In this schema, only the modified attributes need to be included in the event, making it both flexible and scalable without the need for multiple schemas.

Listing 6.2   Phone number change as a separate event

```
{
    "eventType": "UserPhoneNumberUpdated",
    "eventId": "123e4567-e89b-12d3-a456-426614174007",
    "timestamp": "2024-09-26T12:30:00Z",
    "userId": "12345",
    "newPhoneNumber": "+1-555-987-6543"
}
```

In many systems it's common to design multiple event types. This allows producers to emit different kinds of events for different update scenarios, rather than tailoring one message to the exact needs of each consumer.

However, in some scenarios multiple attributes must be updated together to maintain consistency. For example, if a user's address is updated, changes to the street, city, and ZIP code must be applied atomically. Emitting them as separate delta events might result in invalid intermediate states on the consumer side, particularly if those events are processed out of order or with delay. In such cases, either a fact event containing the full address or a grouped delta event with all address fields is preferable.

Delta events have some advantages:

- *Smaller message size*—Since delta events carry only the changed information, they result in more efficient use of network bandwidth and storage.
- *Selective exposure*—Only the relevant domain attributes are exposed, allowing other attributes to change without impacting data contracts, thereby enhancing security and flexibility.

However, delta events also come with certain drawbacks:

- *Limited reusability*—Delta events are often tailored to specific consumer needs, making them less reusable across different contexts.
- *Complex state reconstruction*—Because delta events do not include the full state, consumers cannot rely on reading just the latest event to obtain the current state. Instead, they must apply each delta event in sequence to accurately reconstruct and maintain the state, which increases the complexity of the consumer logic. This is common in event-sourced systems, but it's typically mitigated with periodic snapshots (and "snapshot + tail" recovery) to keep replay time bounded.

Publicly available cloud services or off-the-shelf products typically utilize fact events, making them well-suited for a wide range of consumers. In contrast, when microservices are integrated within a specific project, delta events are more commonly used, as they are often tailored to meet the specific requirements of that project.

In our Customer 360 ODS, implementing fact events appears to be the better option, as events like financial transactions and profile updates have broad applicability and will be consumed by multiple services.

6.2.3 Composite, atomic, and aggregate events: Representing event structure

A microservice's domain model represents entities that are related to one another. When sending notifications about changes, it's important to determine how to slice the model and define the boundaries of each event. For example, if our microservice has a `UserProfile` entity that aggregates social account entities, we must decide whether changes should be conveyed as one event covering the entire composite or as separate events for each part of it.

In event-driven systems, three primary types of events can be used depending on the complexity and needs of the system: composite events, atomic events, and aggregate events. Each type serves a specific purpose and is suited to different scenarios:

- *Composite events*—A composite event represents the combination of multiple related changes into a single event. These typically correspond to entities that are interrelated within a domain model. When multiple entities change within one microservice as part of a single use case, composite events are generally the better choice. For instance, if a social account changes, the entire profile is sent as one event.

- *Atomic events*—Atomic events are small, specific, and reflect a single interaction or change. However, they can be more challenging to manage due to the need to process them in the correct order. For example, if a new user is created, you might send two events: `UserProfileCreated` and `SocialAccountCreated`. If these events are sent through different channels, consumers must be prepared for the possibility that `SocialAccountCreated` might arrive before `UserProfileCreated`, even though the social account references the user profile. When correlation between events is required, composite events might be a better choice, as atomic events can complicate processing logic on the consumer side.

- *Aggregate events*—Aggregate events are generated by combining multiple smaller events into a final, higher-level event, signaling that a higher-level outcome has been achieved. For example, as shown in figure 6.5, an `OrderCompleted` event is emitted after the `OrderCreated`, `InventoryChecked`, and `ShipmentScheduled` events have occurred. While the logic for aggregating events could be implemented on the consumer side, a more effective approach is to use an intermediate service that assembles the final event and emits it.

  This approach makes the `OrderCompleted` event available to multiple consumers. These services are typically implemented using stream-processing technologies, which we will cover in chapter 8.

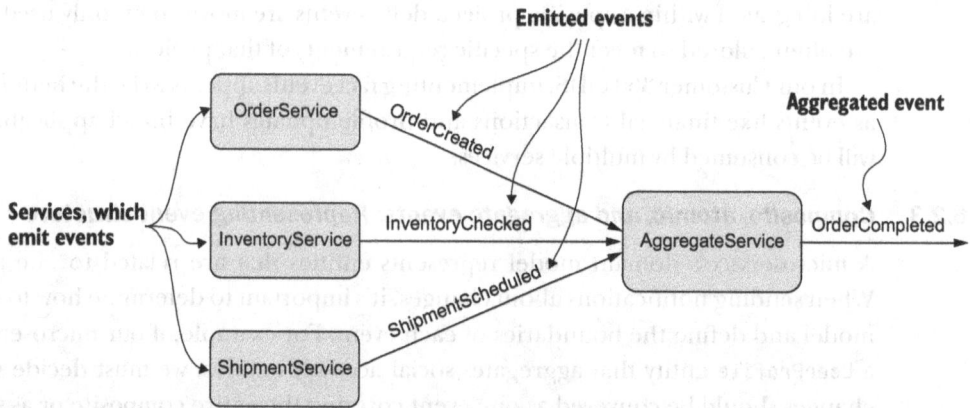

Figure 6.5   An intermediate service aggregates three events into one.

6.2.4   *Pulling state on notification*

Another pattern involves one service notifying another that a state change has occurred, without sending the actual changes. Instead, the consumer service, upon receiving the notification, pulls the updated state from the producer.

An example of this approach is illustrated in figure 6.6. This method typically combines event-driven communication with the invocation of synchronous services. It's often used because the events are small, and the producer doesn't need to be aware of the specific data requirements of the consumer.

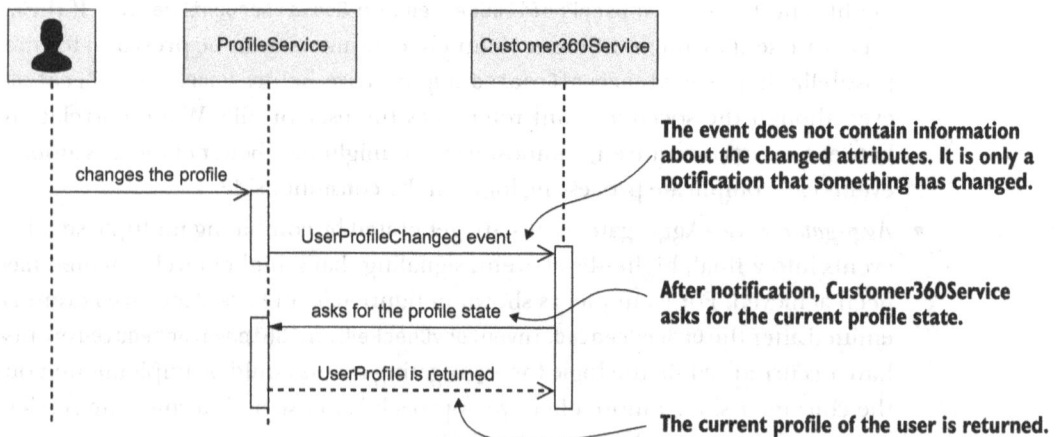

Figure 6.6   The UserProfileChanged event does not contain details about which attributes were modified. Instead, it serves as a simple notification indicating that a change has occurred. Upon receiving this notification, the client calls a synchronous service to retrieve the current state.

This pattern is sometimes chosen for its simplicity, especially when the notification payload is lightweight and the producer doesn't need to be aware of specific consumer requirements. However, it combines asynchronous event delivery with synchronous state retrieval, which can lead to data consistency challenges.

These challenges are not unique to this pattern—they reflect the general difficulties of working in eventually consistent systems. Even systems with transactional guarantees must accept some ambiguity in the meaning of "latest state," particularly in high-concurrency environments.

What makes this pattern more fragile is the tight coupling between event receipt and state retrieval. For instance, as shown in figure 6.7, a consumer might receive a `User-ProfileChanged` event but find the profile already deleted when attempting to fetch it. Avoiding such issues requires versioning, coordination, or fallback handling—each of which adds operational complexity.

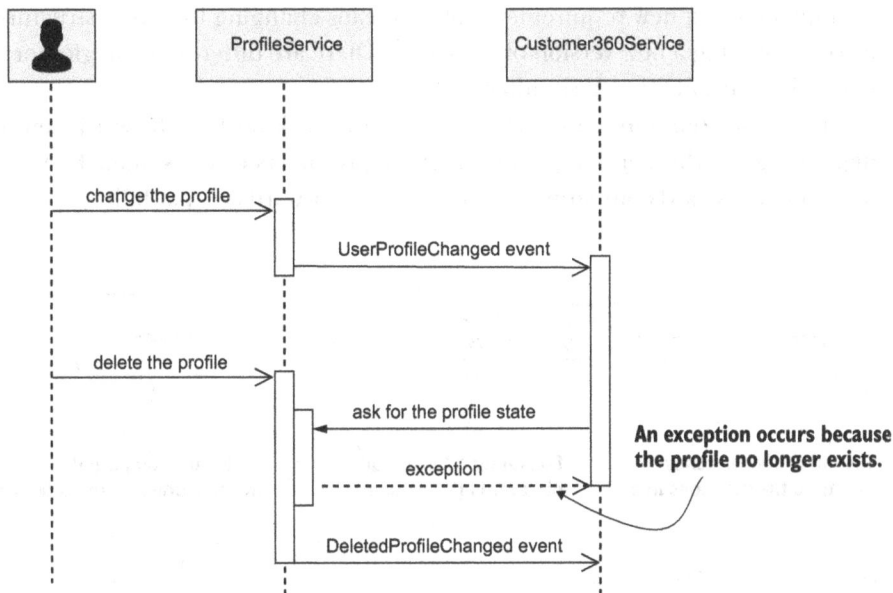

Figure 6.7 Due to the asynchronous nature of events, a service might request a profile that no longer exists.

This pattern often requires additional coordination between services to ensure that consumers pull the correct state and handle any potential versioning issues—an implementation that can be complex and difficult to manage effectively.

6.2.5 *Evolution of types*

Over time, new project requirements emerge, and applications must adapt accordingly. As new versions of applications are developed, new events may be introduced, some events might be deprecated, and the structure of existing events may change. How can we ensure a smooth transition to new application versions?

In the past, a new release rollout often meant downtime for the applications involved. Systems were shut down, new versions were deployed, and data was migrated using scripts, causing temporary unavailability. However, today's systems are expected to evolve without interrupting the user experience. So what are the best practices for managing changes in data contracts between systems to ensure seamless upgrades?

A key best practice is to avoid replacing applications all at once. Instead, new versions should be introduced gradually, with functionality incrementally added, while older functionality is retired over time. In software engineering, this gradual migration is often referred to as the *strangler fig* pattern. In the world of events, this means producers and consumers of different versions of events can coexist and work simultaneously.

Implementing new requirements often means changing the event structure, which involves creating a new version of the event. There are different strategies for supporting multiple event formats simultaneously.

The most common approach is to ensure backward or forward compatibility, depending on whether you plan to upgrade producers or consumers first. Figure 6.8 illustrates backward compatibility, and 6.9 shows forward compatibility.

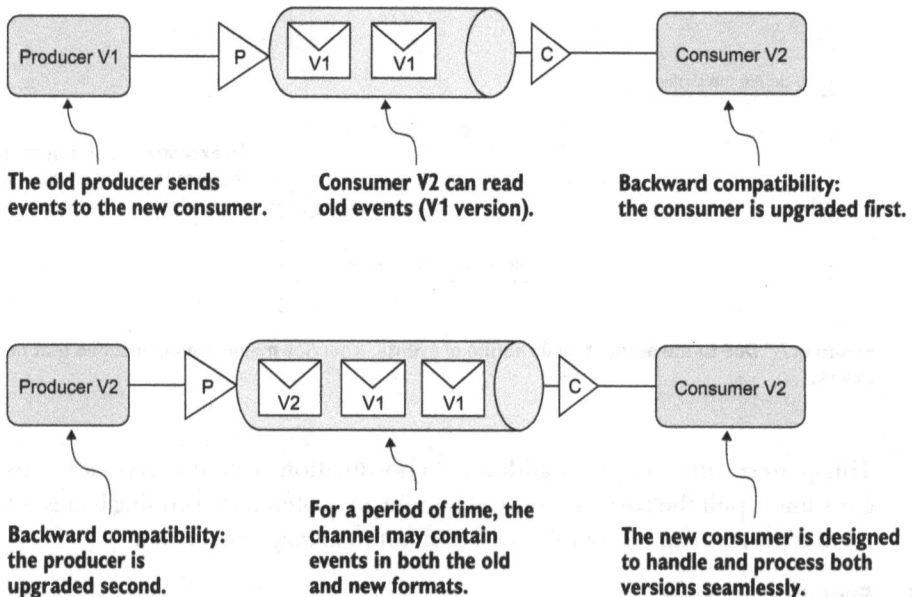

The old producer sends events to the new consumer.

Consumer V2 can read old events (V1 version).

Backward compatibility: the consumer is upgraded first.

Backward compatibility: the producer is upgraded second.

For a period of time, the channel may contain events in both the old and new formats.

The new consumer is designed to handle and process both versions seamlessly.

Figure 6.8   When using backward compatibility, consumers are upgraded first. The new version of the consumer can handle the old messages.

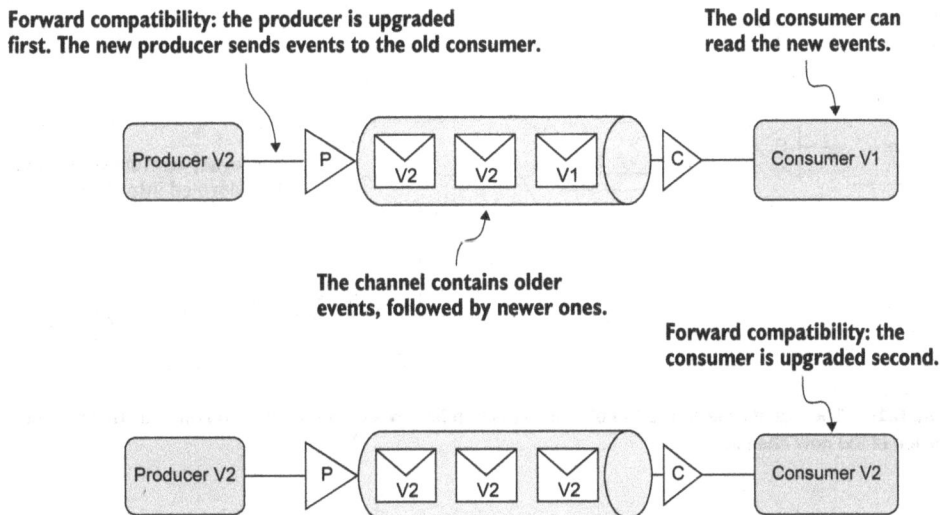

Figure 6.9 With forward compatibility, producers are upgraded first and the old consumer must handle the new events.

- In backward compatibility, consumers are upgraded first, meaning the new version of the consumer must still be able to read older versions of events.
- In forward compatibility, producers are upgraded first, so older versions of consumers must be able to process the new events.

Ensuring schema compatibility guarantees that no exceptions occur due to incorrect schema versions. This is essential, as errors that prevent consumers from deserializing messages are particularly disruptive. Schema repositories must validate that schemas adhere to the selected compatibility strategy to prevent such issues.

This compatibility is achieved through defined rules, rather than through custom code for each new version. However, it also places restrictions on the types of schema changes that can be made. For example, if a new field is added to an event, an older consumer can safely ignore it. However, changes like renaming fields or altering their data types are not allowed, as they could break compatibility. We will discuss backward and forward compatibility in more detail later in the chapter, especially as this strategy is strongly supported within the Kafka ecosystem.

Another strategy involves introducing a transformation component between systems to handle the conversion between different versions of events. This approach, illustrated in figure 6.10, allows client components to remain agnostic to compatibility rules, as the transformation logic is centralized in a dedicated intermediary. The transformation component can either transform new events into the old version for legacy consumers (as in figure 6.10) or, less frequently, convert old events from legacy producers into the new format.

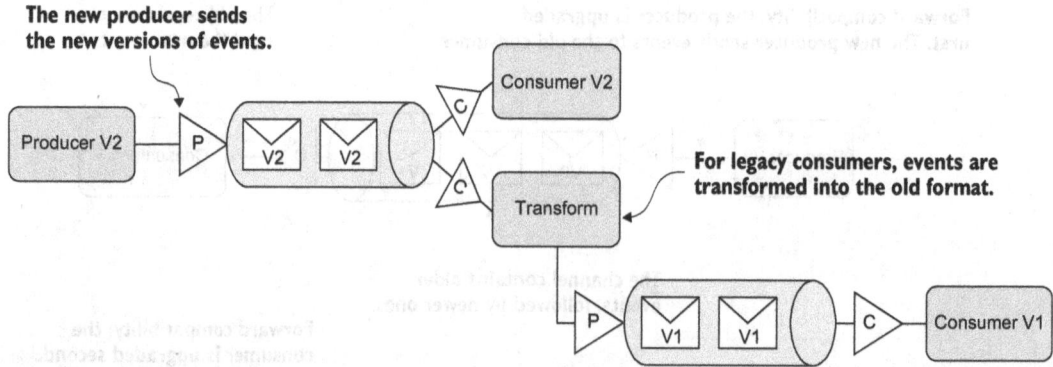

Figure 6.10 The transformation to the old format is handled by a component in the middle. This assumes the creation of the new channel.

The Transform service can act as a temporary solution, serving as a bridge to enable smooth migration during a transitional phase. In this case, it ensures that existing consumers (e.g., Consumer V1) can continue functioning while the system evolves to a new schema or version. This approach requires creating separate channels (e.g., Kafka topics) for each version of the event. Custom transformations ensure that both old and new producers and consumers can operate simultaneously without being burdened by version compatibility concerns. This approach can be particularly useful in complex systems where multiple consumers rely on different schema versions, allowing a smooth transition to new data formats without disrupting the overall system architecture.

Another variation of this transformation strategy involves the transformer applying consistent processing rules across all versions, treating messages agnostically to ensure uniformity. In this case, all other consumers (including those working with newer versions) consume from topics where the transformer acts as the producer. This approach simplifies maintenance by centralizing transformation logic in a single component, reducing the complexity of managing version compatibility across multiple consumers.

However, if a newer version of an event omits certain fields that were present in earlier versions, transforming from new to old becomes problematic or even impossible without additional context. In such cases, data fidelity may be compromised, and the transformation component must either supply default values, raise errors, or fall back to partial compatibility. This highlights the importance of careful schema evolution practices, especially when relying on transformation-based strategies to maintain backward compatibility.

Another potential strategy is to deploy a separate pipeline with a new version of the producer, consumer, and channel, as shown in figure 6.11. This creates two parallel systems: one that handles the old format and another that processes the new format.

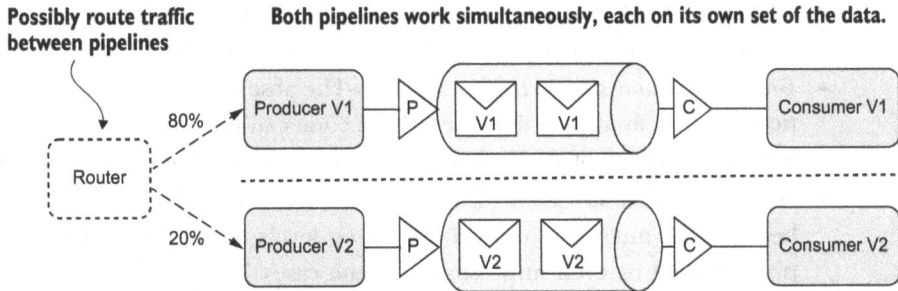

Figure 6.11 The new version of producer, consumer, and channel are deployed in the same environment as the old ones. After validation of the new version, the old one can be retired.

This approach is particularly effective if there is a mechanism to route new traffic or a portion of existing traffic to the new pipeline. Gradually migrating traffic to the new system allows for a phased transition, minimizing risk. Once the new pipeline has been fully validated and all traffic has been successfully migrated to the new producer, consumer, and channel, the old versions can be safely decommissioned.

6.2.6 Mapping events to Kafka messages

The data contract consists of three main components:

- *The structure of the event*—In Kafka, this is represented by a schema format.
- *The channel for event transfer*—In Kafka, this corresponds to a topic.
- *The logic behind when and why an event is sent*—Unfortunately, the triggering mechanism is typically described in text during analysis and is not directly mapped to Kafka concepts.

In Kafka, events are mapped to messages, making it essential to define a clear and consistent message structure. The best practice for achieving this is to define a *schema*, which serves as a strict contract between the producer and consumer. A schema is a formal description that outlines how data is organized, specifying the structure of the data, the fields it contains, their types, and any constraints. Schemas are independent of programming languages and are typically defined using formats such as JSON Schema, Avro, or Protobuf. When it comes to implementation, code generators are often used to produce auxiliary artifacts, like Java classes, based on these schemas.

Using a schema as a contract between the producer and consumer in Kafka, ensures that both sides have a consistent understanding of the data structure. This is crucial for avoiding errors and misinterpretations in data exchange.

When business analysts define events, they often detail the structure in specifications or company Wiki pages. Although tools like those in the AsyncAPI ecosystem can generate different schema formats from specifications, it's common for these analytical documents to remain disconnected from the actual code. This disconnection leads to several serious problems:

- *Lack of an event catalog*—Without a centralized event catalog, users struggle to easily discover the available events within the integration.
- *Gap between analysis and implementation*—The absence of automatic synchronization between analytical documents and code can lead to inconsistencies, creating a gap between business requirements and technical implementations.
- *Inconsistent data structures*—Data types, structures, and constraints may differ between the analytical and programming levels, making straightforward mapping difficult or even impossible in some cases. This can lead to serious challenges in ensuring data integrity and correctness.

To address this gap, a formal process is needed (manually crafted for now) for managing schema evolution, ensuring that all changes undergo compatibility checks, are communicated across teams, and are clearly documented.

6.2.7   *Data strategies for the Customer 360 ODS*

In the early discussions of the Customer 360 ODS, the team wasn't entirely sure how to define the structure of the events. They initially agreed to use JSON as the data format, given its wide support, but the lead architect, who has a background in database development and prefers precise data structures insisted that formal data contracts were necessary. At this stage, they have two services: `ProfileService` and `Transaction-Service`, each emitting its own type of event. For `ProfileService`, the team decides to send fact events that include the entire profile information, as profile updates are infrequent. Similarly, since transactions are immutable, `TransactionService` also uses fact events for its data.

Next, the team tackles the question of data governance—who will be responsible for defining the events, topics, and overall structure. Again, the architect emphasizes the importance of governance, insisting that clear rules are necessary for the definition of events, and that without these guidelines, the system could quickly become disorganized. On this point, the data engineer agrees, stressing that defining the right process early can help maintain consistency as the system grows.

At the same time, the team realizes that some flexibility at the early stage of development could be beneficial. Requirements are still evolving, and too much rigidity could hinder rapid experimentation. Allowing loosely defined schemas with optional fields gives the developers room to iterate quickly. But this flexibility must be temporary and intentional. As more services and teams begin to rely on the events, they'll need stronger schema validation and version control.

6.3   *Event governance*

So far, we have focused on the conceptual design of events. But what concrete artifacts do we need to create so that software developers can implement these designs? Specifically, where should we define the event's structure, its name, and its attributes?

The standard approach is to use a schema definition language that enforces structure and provides clear guidelines for development. Common formats for this purpose include Avro (https://avro.apache.org), JSON Schema (https://json-schema.org), and Protocol Buffers (https://protobuf.dev). Each of these formats enables consistent event serialization, validation, and communication across systems and is enforceable in the application code.

6.3.1 Data formats

We need to define the event schema in a language-independent format, which will act as a contract for communication between systems. This schema will specify the structure of the event and the associated rules for its data, such as field types and optionality. However, the underlying serialization framework will define how this data is serialized, how the schema is processed, and how code is generated for various programming languages. The schema can either be transmitted alongside the data or shared between producers and consumers.

One of the most widely used data formats for event serialization is *Avro*, a framework developed as part of the Apache Hadoop project. Avro serializes events into a compact and efficient binary format. Instead of storing field names with the data, Avro relies on the schema to define the structure, which makes the serialized data smaller in size. The following listing shows an example of an Avro schema for a Client.

Listing 6.3   An example of the Avro format

```
{
  "type": "record",                           A record defines a composite type.
  "name": "Client",
  "namespace": "com.example",                 A namespace groups related objects.
                                              In Java it corresponds to a package.
  "fields": [
    { "name": "clientId", "type": "string" },   An attribute has a
    { "name": "clientName", "type": "string" }, name and a type.
    { "name": "age", "type": "int" },
    { "name": "email", "type": ["null", "string"], "default": null },
    { "name": "isPremium", "type": "boolean", "default": false },
    { "name": "address",
      "type": {                             The structure of Address    It is possible to
        "type": "record",                   entity is inlined, but it is also   specify optionality
        "name": "Address",                  possible to use a reference.  and a default value.
        "fields": [
          { "name": "street", "type": "string" },
          { "name": "city", "type": "string" },
          { "name": "postalCode", "type": "string" }
        ]
      }
    },
    { "name": "createdAt", "type": "long", "logicalType": "timestamp-millis" }
  ]
}
```

The schema itself is written in JSON and consists of the following key elements:

- `type`—Defines the type of an object. A composite object is represented by the `record` keyword.
- `namespace`—Groups related types to prevent name collisions and organize schemas.
- `fields`—Describes the attributes of the object, which can be primitive, composite, or structured types such as arrays or maps. Fields can also be marked as optional, allowing for more flexibility.

How can we work with a `Client` object in our code? Two primary approaches exist:

- *Generate language-specific structures*—For example, in Java, a `Client` class could be generated from the Avro schema as part of the build process, allowing you to interact with the object using native classes.
- *Work directly with name-value pairs*—This approach allows you to manipulate the event data dynamically, without needing predefined classes, by handling the attributes as a map of key-value pairs with direct get/put access.

Another popular serialization format is Protocol Buffers (Protobuf), developed by Google. It defines schemas in a way similar to other formats like Avro. Listing 6.4 shows an example of a Protobuf schema.

Listing 6.4   An example of the Protobuf format

```
syntax = "proto3";          ◄──────  The version of the Protobuf format

package com.example;        ◄──────  A package groups objects, similar
                                     to a namespace in Avro.

message Client {            ◄──────
  string clientId = 1;      ◄──────  A message defines a structured
  string clientName = 2;             object, similar to a record in Avro.
  int32 age = 3;
  string email = 4;                  An attribute has a name,
  bool isPremium = 5;                a type, and a tag.

  message Address {
    string street = 1;
    string city = 2;
    string postalCode = 3;
  }

  Address address = 6;
  int64 createdAt = 7;
}
```

In Protobuf, fields are optional by default, and in the latest version (proto3), the concept of required fields has been removed. This decision was made to enhance backward compatibility, ensuring that older clients can safely ignore any newly added fields without breaking deserialization. Each field is assigned a unique *tag number*, which is used in the binary encoding to represent the field. The number should never change once it is set, to maintain backward compatibility.

Unlike Avro, which includes the schema alongside the data by default, Protobuf keeps the schema separate. This means that the schema, or the code generated from it, must be available on both the client and server sides to enable serialization and deserialization.

Like Avro, clients working with Protobuf can either use the generated language-specific classes or manipulate the event as a set of name-value pairs. This flexibility allows developers to integrate Protobuf seamlessly into various environments while maintaining efficiency and compatibility.

Sending data in JSON format without a schema offers flexibility, but it lacks any formal structure or validation. However, JSON Schema can be used to define a strict data contract, ensuring that the structure and content of the data conform to specific rules. Listing 6.5 shows an example of a JSON Schema.

Listing 6.5 An example of JSON Schema

```
{
  "$schema": "http://json-schema.org/draft-07/schema#",   ◄── Specifies the version
                                                              of JSON Schema
  "title": "Client",
  "type": "object",                                       ◄── Defines a composite object
  "properties": {.          ◄── An attribute has a name,
    "clientId": {               a type, a default value,
      "type": "string"          and possible constraints.
    },
    "clientName": {
      "type": "string"
    },
    "age": {
      "type": "integer",
      "minimum": 0
    },
    "email": {
      "type": ["string", "null"],
      "format": "email"
    },
    "isPremium": {
      "type": "boolean",
      "default": false
    },
    "address": {
      "type": "object",
      "properties": {
        "street": {
          "type": "string"
        },
        "city": {
          "type": "string"
        },
```

```
      "postalCode": {
        "type": "string"
      }
    },
    "required": ["street", "city", "postalCode"]
  },
  "createdAt": {
    "type": "string",
    "format": "date-time"
  }
},                                                    Specifies mandatory fields
"required": ["clientId", "clientName", "age", "address", "createdAt"],  ◀
"additionalProperties": false                         ◀
}                                                         Ensures no extra
                                                          properties are allowed
```

Like Avro and Protobuf, JSON Schema defines the structure of an object and supports various validation constraints, such as data types, required fields, and value ranges. These constraints are enforced to guarantee that the exchanged JSON data adheres to the expected format.

JSON Schema supports an open content model, allowing events to include additional attributes not explicitly defined in the schema. This is configured using the `additionalProperties` attribute, which can specify whether extra fields are permitted. You can also restrict these additional properties to specific types or names.

Unlike Avro or Protobuf, JSON data is serialized as plain text, which makes it less efficient in terms of size and speed. However, the human-readable nature of JSON makes it more suitable for scenarios where readability and ease of debugging are prioritized over performance. Table 6.1 shows a comparison of the different data formats.

Table 6.1   Comparison of different data formats

Feature	Avro	JSON Schema	Protobuf
Data serialization format	Binary	Text (JSON-based)	Binary
Schema definition language	JSON-based schema definition or Avro IDL (Interface Definition Language)	JSON-based schema definition	Protobuf-specific syntax
Compatibility	Strong compatibility rules	Less robust due to open content model	Strong compatibility rules
Data size	Compact	Larger size	Compact
Human readability	Schema is human-readable; data is not	Both schema and data are human-readable	Schema is human-readable; data is not
Performance	High	Lower	High
Support for complex types	Supported	Limited	Supported
Programming language support	Broad (Java, Python, C++, Go, etc.)	Broad (any JSON-supporting language)	Broad (Java, Python, C++, Go, etc.)

6.3.2 Selecting a data format for the Customer 360 ODS

At this point, we need to choose which format to use for defining schemas. While JSON may seem more familiar and straightforward, Avro offers a more mature ecosystem, strong community support, and numerous libraries and tools across popular languages. These advantages can be beneficial for rapid prototyping and troubleshooting in a proof-of-concept. Avro balances performance with schema flexibility and can be integrated into a project like this with minimal setup. So we'll go with Avro.

6.3.3 Data ownership

When a ready-to-use product or service is integrated into an enterprise environment, it typically offers various customizable interfaces to facilitate integration. For instance, a customer relationship management (CRM) system, whether deployed on-premises or in the cloud, stores critical information about a company's current and potential customers. This *CRM system* provides interfaces for create, read, update, and delete (CRUD) operations on customer data, and it may also emit events when customer data changes. In this scenario, the CRM system acts as the data owner, managing and controlling access to the customer information it holds.

In-house service development is primarily driven by business requirements. Service contracts and integration methods are typically discussed and agreed upon by all stakeholders. However, the team responsible for exposing the service often has greater influence, as they possess deep domain knowledge. In the context of event-driven systems, this means the event producer takes ownership of the data contracts. While new interfaces are created to meet specific business needs, their reusability should also be considered, as the same events may be consumed by multiple services across the organization.

During the proof-of-concept implementation of the Customer 360 ODS, our team is responsible for integrating services through Kafka. When it comes time to create data contracts, they need to collaborate closely with the domain teams, who hold the expertise needed to design reusable data contracts. This deep understanding of domain data ensures that the data contracts will meet both immediate project needs and broader organizational requirements.

6.3.4 Organizing data and communicating changes

Data owners must provide accessible data contracts, ensuring that schemas are defined in a central repository managed by the producer team. This repository should also be available to other teams, allowing them to review the emitted events and assess their relevance to their services.

Event consumers need access to the event schemas to generate code that integrates with their applications. They must be notified when a new schema version is released, so they can either migrate their code to align with the changes or rely on backward compatibility. Additionally, consumers should have a mechanism to propose changes to the data contracts, which can be managed through pull requests or a similar collaborative process.

6.3.5 *Designing events for the Customer 360 ODS*

Let's say the architect and data engineer finally arrive at the design for their events. For their proof-of-concept project, they will use fact events. This approach is straightforward for profile update events if you store them in a compacted topic, which is also better suited for storing the entire state. Fact events are also a natural fit for transaction events, which are immutable. As for the target format, it's safe to go with Avro, which is the most common format for Kafka. On these points, the decisions are relatively easy to make.

The more challenging question is where to define the structure of the events. A data engineer who favors clear and precise abstract models might want to define the event structure directly in the AsyncAPI files. This arrangement means that the business analysts could be responsible for these definitions, making them self-contained and serving as the "source of truth." AsyncAPI does allow event structures to be defined abstractly, without being tied to a specific data format. In this case, the structure for the User-ProfileUpdated event would look like the example shown in listing 6.6. As you can see, the event structure is defined abstractly and can be reused across multiple operations by referencing it.

Listing 6.6   Referencing abstract event structure across multiple operations

```
asyncapi: 3.0.0
info:
  title: User Profile API
  version: 1.0.0
components:
  messages:
    UserProfileUpdated:
      payload:
        schemaFormat: 'application/vnd.apache.avro;version=1.9.0'
        schema:
          type: record
          name: UserProfile
          namespace: com.company
          doc: User Profile information
          fields:
            - name: userId
              type: int
            - name: userEmail
              type: string
```

This is not the only approach. An architect may be concerned that AsyncAPI models are less readable, particularly for developers, and that while tools can generate Avro schemas from these models, there could still be gaps in translating them into concrete technical formats. They also lack certain features, such as the ability to define precise data constraints, even for optional values. An alternative is to define the schemas directly in Avro, store them in Git, and reference them from the AsyncAPI specifications. This approach is feasible because AsyncAPI supports referencing external resources, either locally or remotely. Listing 6.7 shows an example of this approach.

Listing 6.7 Referencing an Avro schema from another file

```
asyncapi: 3.0.0
info:
  title: Customer 360 Project
  version: 1.0.0
  description: >
    This project aims to aggregate data from various sources, providing a
    comprehensive view of customer information.

channels:
  customerProfile:
    description: Storing and distributing profile information of customers.
    address: CUSTOMER_PROFILES
    messages:
      userProfile:
        payload:
          schemaFormat: 'application/vnd.apache.avro;version=1.9.0'
          schema:
            $ref: './path/to/submodule/path/to/UserProfile.avsc'
```

Finally, the team agreed to move forward with this second approach to streamline the process and reduce potential obstacles for developers.

6.4 Schema Registry

So far, we have discussed how data contracts should be created and who is responsible for them. Now we'll move on to the implementation phase and explore how schemas are managed, where they are stored, and how they are incorporated into an event-driven architecture. In this context, we will focus on the Schema Registry, a key component within the Kafka ecosystem. The Schema Registry is provided by Confluent, one of the leading providers of Kafka-related services and tools.

The Schema Registry can be installed on-premises at no cost, and it's also available as a managed service in cloud environments where Kafka is used. Today, it is widely regarded as the primary method for managing and enforcing data contracts in Kafka-based architectures, ensuring that producers and consumers adhere to consistent data formats as they evolve over time.

6.4.1 Schema Registry in Kafka ecosystem

Figure 6.12 illustrates how the Schema Registry fits into an enterprise landscape that incorporates Kafka. To ensure high availability, the Schema Registry operates in a cluster and provides interfaces for storing and retrieving schemas. It does not manage its own storage but instead persists schema data in a Kafka topic. Clients interact with the Schema Registry via the HTTP protocol.

Schemas are versioned, and whenever a change occurs, a new version is created. These versions are immutable, meaning they cannot be altered after creation, allowing them to be safely cached on the client side. The Schema Registry supports schemas in

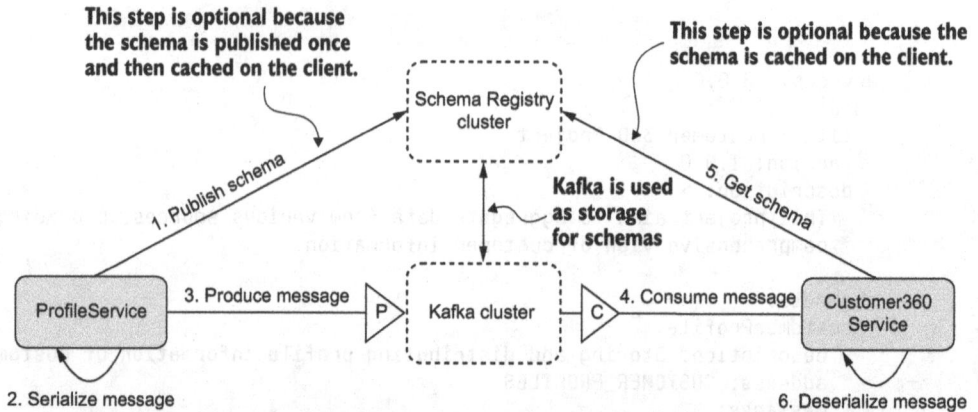

Figure 6.12   Interactions with the Schema Registry. The schema is registered with the Schema Registry server, which stores it in Kafka. Producers use this schema to serialize messages, and consumers retrieve the schema from the Schema Registry to deserialize messages.

three formats: Avro, Protobuf, and JSON Schema. For simplicity in this chapter, we will assume that schemas are defined in Avro, as it is the most used format.

In the Schema Registry, schemas are managed via a REST API, with endpoints for tasks such as registering and retrieving schemas, checking compatibility, and more. Any HTTP client, such as curl, can be used to perform these operations.

For example, this is how the schema version is retrieved by ID:

```
curl http://schema-registry:8081/schemas/ids/1
```

And this is how the schema is registered:

```
curl -X POST http://schemaregistry:8081/subjects/Client-value/versions
```

To apply built-in schema management, clients must include the appropriate libraries and specify the data format in their configuration. Here's a snippet of a producer configuration.

Listing 6.8   A producer configuration with keys and values serialized in Avro

```
key.serializer = io.confluent.kafka.serializers.KafkaAvroSerializer
value.serializer = io.confluent.kafka.serializers.KafkaAvroSerializer
schema.registry.url = http://registry.example.com:8081
```

In this configuration, we specify that data will be serialized in Avro format and provide the URL for the Schema Registry server. Here Avro is used for both keys and values; however, it is not very common to use complex structures for keys.

Similarly, the following listing shows a consumer configuration.

```
key.deserializer = io.confluent.kafka.serializers.KafkaAvroDeserializer
value.deserializer = io.confluent.kafka.serializers.KafkaAvroDeserializer
schema.registry.url = http://registry.example.com:8081
```

In Kafka, the schema is not sent with the message. Instead, schemas are registered with the Schema Registry, and each version is assigned a unique identifier (a schema ID) during registration. When a producer sends a message, it contains the schema ID along with the serialized data. This format is depicted in figure 6.13.

When this contains 0, it
indicates that the message
is associated with the schema.

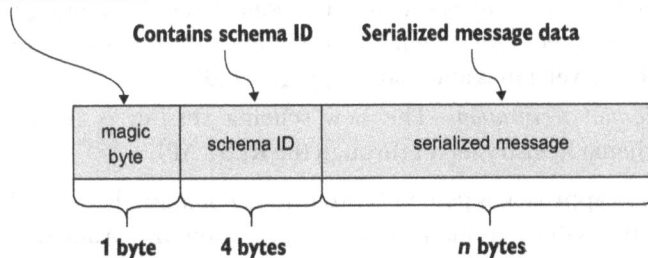

Contains schema ID   Serialized message data

magic byte	schema ID	serialized message

1 byte   4 bytes   *n* bytes

Figure 6.13   How a message, containing a schema, is serialized. Consumers decode a schema ID and use it to retrieve the schema from the Schema Registry, which they then use to deserialize the data.

When a consumer receives a message, it knows from its configuration that the data is serialized in the format supported by the Schema Registry. The schema ID is stored in a specific part of the message, allowing the consumer to retrieve the correct schema version from the Schema Registry (unless it is already cached on the consumer side). Once the schema is obtained, the consumer can deserialize the message according to the schema.

Before a message is sent to Kafka, it is validated against the schema. If the message does not conform to the schema, an exception is thrown on the producer side, and the message is not sent. Similarly, if a consumer receives a message that does not match the schema (commonly referred to as a "poison pill" in the context of Kafka), it will fail to deserialize the message and will throw an exception.

It's important to note that all validation happens on the client side. Kafka brokers do not inspect the contents of messages; they treat them as raw byte arrays. This means that if a producer is incorrectly configured, it can bypass validation and send invalid or nonsensical messages to a topic, which will be accepted by the broker.

In such cases, the consumer will typically fail during deserialization when it encounters invalid data. Whether this failure results in message loss or service disruption depends on how the consumer is implemented. Many consumer applications catch deserialization exceptions and either log the error, send the message to a dead-letter queue, or apply retry logic. However, if the application follows a "let it crash" approach—failing fast to signal an unprocessable message—the consumer instance may terminate abruptly.

The fact that Kafka brokers accept data without performing any validation can be a significant concern for architects. This lack of server-side validation introduces risks, as it allows improperly structured or invalid data to enter the system undetected, creating potential problems for downstream consumers. For many, this behavior is a major obstacle in adopting Kafka for critical use cases.

6.4.2   Registering schemas

Two ways to register a new schema version are:

- *Automatic registration*—When a producer sends a message, the producer client library checks the schema compatibility. If no violations are detected, the new schema version is automatically registered.
- *Manual registration*—The new schema version is registered directly on the Schema Registry server through the REST API.

The second approach is generally preferred, as it aligns better with a controlled release process. To disable automatic schema registration, the producer should set the following properties:

- `auto.register.schemas=false`—Disables automatic schema registration
- `use.latest.version=true`—Instructs the serializer to always look up and use the latest schema version in the subject for serialization

These properties are specific to the Confluent Platform, not Apache Kafka itself. Additionally, the `use.latest.version=true` property can be set at the consumer level, ensuring that consumers always use the latest schema version for deserialization.

6.4.3   A concept of subject

So far, we have focused on modeling events and defining their structure using a selected data format. However, it is equally important to understand how these events are mapped to Kafka topics. Should we create a separate topic for each type of event? Can multiple event types be placed in the same topic? What general rules govern this mapping?

This is where the concept of a *subject* comes into play. A subject represents the domain model of an event—essentially, the type of the event that is initially registered in the Schema Registry. When the event's structure changes, a new version of the subject is created. Compatibility rules—which specify what kinds of changes are allowed or forbidden—are defined at the subject level.

But why use the term "subject"? Why isn't the concept of an event sufficient? The answer lies in the relationship between events and Kafka topics, which can vary depending on the chosen strategy. Different organizations or systems may employ different strategies to map events to topics. For example, some may prefer a one-to-one relation-ship, where each event type gets its own topic, while others may opt to group related event types within the same topic.

This flexibility in event-to-topic mapping is why the term "subject" is used. It decou-ples the domain model of the event from the specifics of how it is organized in Kafka, allowing for more nuanced strategies in how events are managed and evolved over time.

Let's consider three different strategies that are offered by the Schema Registry server.

TopicNameStrategy

The default strategy in Schema Registry is `TopicNameStrategy`, which means that a sub-ject evolves within the context of a specific Kafka topic. Listing 6.10 shows an Avro schema for an event about client modifications. When events based on this schema are published to the `CLIENTS` topic using `TopicNameStrategy`, the Schema Registry will group all schema versions for these events under the subject associated with that topic. This ensures the topic contains only messages which follow compatible versions of the same schema, giving consumers confidence that the structure of the data remains con-sistent as it evolves.

Listing 6.10 An example of the client event in Avro format

```
{
  "type": "record",
  "name": "ClientEvent",
  "namespace": "com.example",
  "fields": [
    {
      "name": "eventId",
      "type": "string",
      "doc": "Unique identifier for the event"
    },
    {
      "name": "eventType",
      "type": "string",
      "doc": "Type of event (e.g., 'ClientCreated', 'ClientUpdated')"
    },
    {
      "name": "timestamp",
      "type": "long",
      "logicalType": "timestamp-millis",
      "doc": "Event timestamp in milliseconds"
    },
    {
      "name": "clientId",
      "type": "string",
      "doc": "Unique identifier for the client"
    },
    {
      "name": "clientName",
      "type": "string",
```

```
        "doc": "Name of the client"
      }
    ]
}
```

When the schema com.example.Client is first registered for the CLIENTS topic, the Schema Registry creates the subject, which becomes closely tied to that topic by naming convention. The subject will have the name CLIENTS-value, indicating that the schema applies to the value portion of the message. While it's possible to define a schema for the key as well, it's less common. In such cases, the subject name would be CLIENTS-key.

Each version of the schema will be addressable via the Schema Registry's REST API at {schema_registry_url}/subjects/CLIENTS-value/versions/{version-number}, allowing for easy retrieval of specific versions as needed.

If the same com.example.Client schema is registered for another topic (e.g., PERSONS), a completely new subject named PERSONS-value will be created by the Schema Registry. This subject will be independent of CLIENTS-value and will evolve separately. For example, if we want to add an address attribute to the CLIENTS-value schema, we can modify and register the new schema version under CLIENTS-value. A new version will be created for CLIENTS-value, but this change will not affect PERSONS-value, which will retain its original structure.

This approach is like how types are managed in a database—one can have two tables with the same structure but different names. Each table can evolve independently, and changes to one do not automatically propagate to the other.

RECORDNAMESTRATEGY

It's also possible to model a subject as an event type that is entirely independent of Kafka topics. For architects who practice domain-driven design, this approach is likely the most intuitive. This can be achieved using the RecordNameStrategy. In this case, when we register the schema, the subject will be named according to the fully qualified class name, such as com.example.ClientEvent, and its lifecycle will not be tied to any specific Kafka topic.

This strategy enables the creation of polyglot topics, which are so named because they can contain multiple types of events. This is particularly useful when maintaining the order between events of different types is essential. For instance, let's consider different schemas for client-related events: ClientCreated, ClientUpdated, and Client-Deleted. With TopicNameStrategy, these events could not be placed in the same topic because they have different schemas. However, if the order of these events is critical—such as when tracking changes to a client's data—RecordNameStrategy can be used. By selecting the client identifier as the key for partitioning, all client modification events will be delivered to consumers in the correct order.

In this case, a specific version of the schema can be accessed via the Schema Registry's REST API at the following URL: {schema_registry_url}/subjects/com.example .ClientEvent-value/versions/{version-number}.

In this scenario, consumers need to be equipped to handle multiple event types from the same topic and to deserialize them into different objects based on the event type.

TopicRecordNameStrategy

There is also a hybrid approach called `TopicRecordNameStrategy`, which combines elements of both `TopicNameStrategy` and `RecordNameStrategy`. Like in the `TopicNameStrategy`, the subject is registered for a specific topic and evolves alongside that topic. However, similar to `RecordNameStrategy`, it allows multiple types of events (or subjects) to be placed within the same topic.

For example, if we register the `com.example.ClientEvent` schema for the `CLIENTS` topic using `TopicRecordNameStrategy`, the subject will be named `CLIENTS-com.example.ClientEvent`, addressable at `{schema_registry_url}/subjects/{client-com.example.ClientEvent}/version/{version-number}`. This means that while the subject is associated with a specific topic, it also retains its fully qualified name, allowing multiple event types to coexist within the same topic under distinct subjects.

This strategy is particularly useful for polyglot topics that need to evolve their schemas independently within each topic, rather than applying schema changes globally.

6.4.4 Compatibility rules

Earlier in this chapter, I introduced the concept of type evolution. Now let's explore how type evolution is managed within the Schema Registry. Type evolution is closely tied to the concept of a subject, so it's important to understand what kinds of changes can be made without breaking existing consumers.

Compatibility mode is configured on a per-subject basis. If a new schema version is incompatible with the selected compatibility mode, it cannot be registered in the Schema Registry—the registration will be rejected.

BACKWARD COMPATIBILITY

The default compatibility mode for subjects in Schema Registry is backward compatibility, where consumers are upgraded first. This means that consumers can still read messages produced with a previous version of the schema. In this mode, consumers are typically upgraded first, ensuring they can handle both the old and new message formats. An example of backward compatibility is illustrated in figure 6.14.

In this example, we have two versions of the `ClientProfile` entity: V1 and V2. In version V2, one formerly mandatory attribute (`age`) is removed, and one optional attribute (`score`) is added. Since the consumer is upgraded first, it can read the old version by ignoring the `age` attribute and assigning a default value to `score`.

In backward compatibility mode, the following changes are allowed:

- *Deleting fields*—If a field is removed in the new version, consumers receiving older messages with the deprecated field will simply ignore it.
- *Adding optional fields*—When a new field is added, it must have a default value. If a consumer receives a message that doesn't contain this new field, it automatically fills in the default value.

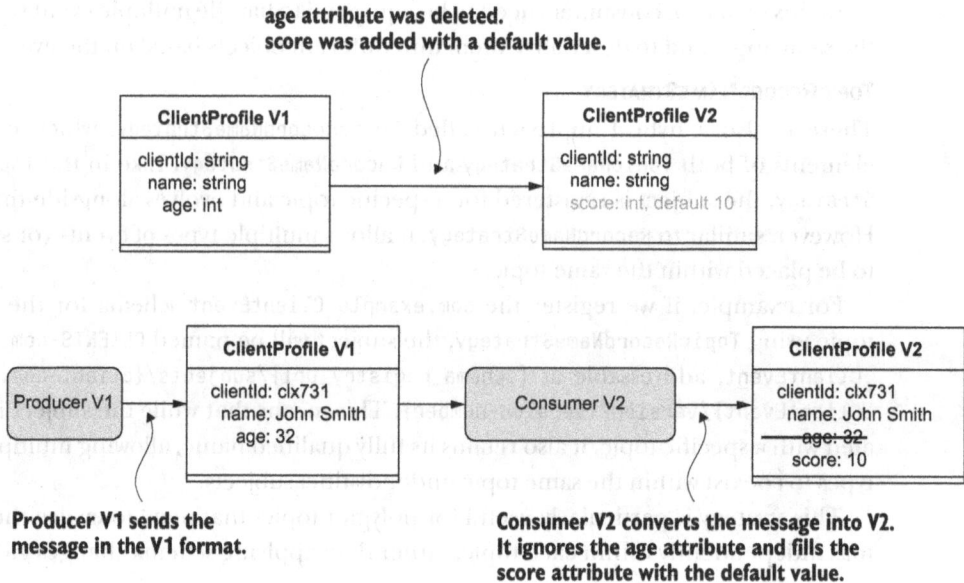

Figure 6.14 An example of backward compatibility. The new consumer must understand the previous version of the schema.

However, this approach can be challenging, especially in environments with many independent consumers, some of which may be owned by different teams or even outside the organization.

FORWARD COMPATIBILITY

Forward compatibility mode means that producers are upgraded first and older consumers must be able to read messages produced with the new schema version.

In the example shown in figure 6.15, schema version V2 is created from version V1 by removing one optional attribute (score) and adding one mandatory attribute (address). The producer is upgraded first, and the old version of the consumer interprets the message as V1 by ignoring the address attribute and assigning a default value to score.

The following changes are allowed in forward compatibility:

- *Adding fields*—Older consumers will receive messages with new fields that they do not recognize, but they will simply ignore the unknown fields.
- *Deleting optional fields*—If an optional field is removed, older consumers will automatically fill in the missing field with its default value.

OTHER COMPATIBILITIES

The Schema Registry also supports several other compatibility modes, which are less common than BACKWARD and FORWARD compatibility:

score attribute was deleted.
address attribute was added.

ClientProfile V1
clientId: string name: string score: int, default 10

ClientProfile V2
clientId: string name: string address: string

Producer V2

ClientProfile V2
clientId: clx731 name: John Smith address: 'Oak Lane, 1'

Consumer V1

ClientProfile V1
clientId: clx731 name: John Smith address: 'Oak Lane, 1' score: 10

Producer V2 sends the
message in the new V2 format.

Consumer V1 converts the message into V1.
It ignores the address attribute and fills the
score attribute with the default value.

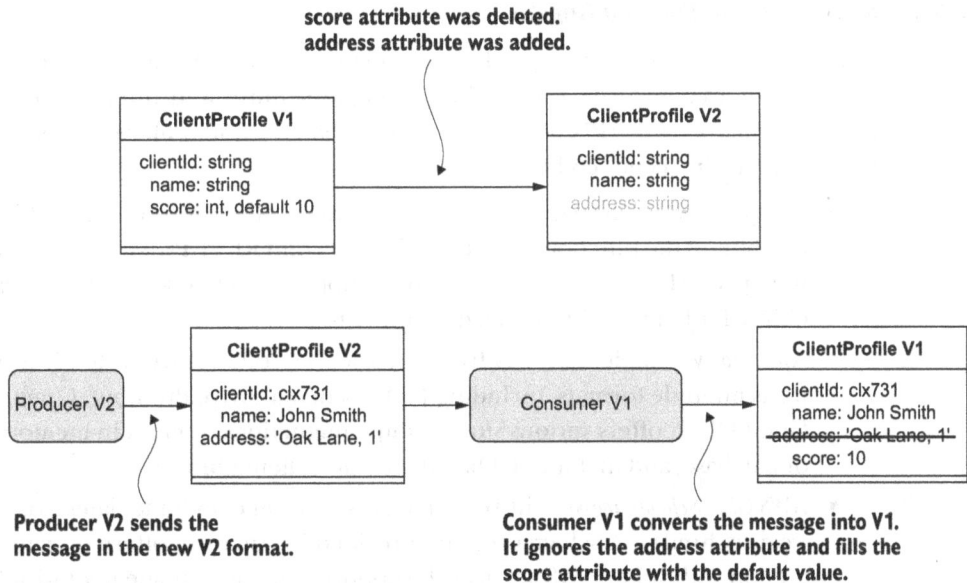

Figure 6.15   An example of forward compatibility. The old consumer must understand the new version of the schema.

- FULL *compatibility*—This mode ensures both backward and forward compatibility simultaneously. Adding and deleting optional fields is allowed, and both producers and consumers can be upgraded in any order without breaking functionality.

- *Transitive compatibility*—By default, backward and forward compatibility modes only check compatibility between the new version and the immediate previous version. However, with BACKWARD_TRANSITIVE, FORWARD_TRANSITIVE, and FULL_TRANSITIVE modes, compatibility is checked across all previous versions. For example, version V10 must be compatible not only with V9 but also with V8, V7, and so on, down to V1. This is especially useful in data lakes and analytics platforms, where data is stored long-term and may be consumed by various services or tools over time. It's also beneficial in large organizations with distributed teams, where some consumers might not be updated as frequently but still need access to new data.

- NONE *compatibility*—In this mode, no compatibility checks are enforced, allowing all changes to be made freely. Although this mode is rarely used in regular workflows, it can be helpful when incompatible changes are required. For instance, if a breaking change is necessary, you can temporarily switch the compatibility mode to NONE, apply the change, and then revert to the previous mode, such as BACKWARD.

6.4.5   *Alternatives to Schema Registry*

There are several alternative products for managing schemas and data contracts in event-driven architectures, each offering unique features and integrations. Many of these alternatives are API-compatible with Schema Registry, allowing you to switch without modifying client code.

- *Karapace* (www.karapace.io)—An open source alternative developed by Aiven, combining the functions of Schema Registry and REST Proxy. Distributed under the Apache License, it is fully API-compatible with Schema Registry and is a good choice for lightweight, simple deployments.

- *Apicurio* (www.apicur.io)—A free, open source solution from Red Hat that supports multiple formats, including JSON Schema, Avro, Protobuf, OpenAPI, and GraphQL. It offers various storage implementations, such as in-memory, Kafka, or database, and includes UI-based tools and client libraries.

- *AWS Glue Schema registry* (https://docs.aws.amazon.com/glue/latest/dg/schema-registry.html)—A schema registry provided by Amazon, offering seamless integration with other AWS services. It supports schema management with features like versioning and compatibility, making it ideal for organizations within the AWS ecosystem.

6.4.6   *Handling data contracts without the centralized server*

Schema Registry provides a valuable way to define and control data contracts, but it also introduces some challenges:

- *Lack of server-side validation*—Since Kafka brokers do not inspect message contents, it is the client's responsibility to ensure correct interaction with schemas. This can lead to issues if producers bypass schema validation, sending invalid data.

- *Overly restrictive compatibility modes*—While compatibility modes allow adding or removing fields, many necessary schema changes do not fit within these constraints. Common examples include renaming an attribute (perhaps because the previous name no longer reflects its meaning or due to a change in naming conventions), changing an attribute's type (such as from a string to an enumeration), or restructuring entities. Upgrading to a new schema version may require a carefully planned migration process to avoid breaking consumers.

- *Environment-specific schema identifiers*—When schemas are registered, they are assigned unique identifiers, which differ across environments (e.g., development vs. production). This discrepancy can cause complications when transferring messages between Kafka clusters, as the same schema may have different IDs in different environments. Such situations are often addressed with migration components that read messages, replace the schema identifier at the byte level, and write the message to the target cluster.

Given these issues, the question arises: do we really need Schema Registry, or could we rely on smarter clients capable of managing custom type handling more effectively?

An example of such a solution is illustrated in figure 6.16, where all schema management is handled on the client side. Schemas are packaged and distributed to interested clients as part of libraries, with fixed identifiers, custom serializers, and tailored migration rules. Whenever a schema changes, a new version is distributed to the clients.

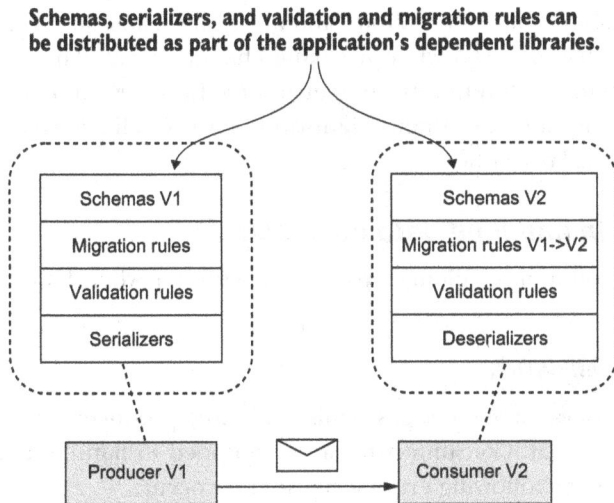

Figure 6.16 Distributing schemas, serializers, and migration and validation rules as a part of the client package

However, this approach also comes with some drawbacks:

- *Limited integration with message browsers*—Standard UI tools for browsing and searching Kafka messages often rely on centralized schema management and may not support custom serializers or deserializers. As a result, you lose the ability to effectively use these tools for inspecting and querying Kafka messages.
- *High development overhead*—Implementing this custom solution requires significant effort, including maintaining schema distribution, serializers, and migration logic.

6.4.7 *Commercial extensions for data contracts*

The Confluent Platform enterprise distribution includes several advanced features that enhance the capabilities of data contracts:

- *Integrity constraints*—Fine-grained integrity constraints can be applied to schema elements to enforce data quality. These rules are defined using the Google Common Expression Language (CEL), allowing for flexible validation logic applied directly on the data structure.

- *Enhanced metadata*—Data contracts can be enriched with additional metadata properties, providing more context about the data. This can include information such as data lineage, ownership, or processing history, enhancing transparency and governance.
- *Rules and policies*—Data contracts can specify detailed rules, such as the encryption of sensitive fields, and policies for handling invalid messages. For example, you can define how to mask or reject records that violate specific data protection requirements.
- *Migration rules*—Migration rules allow smooth transformation of messages between schema versions, even when breaking changes occur. This eliminates the need to switch to a different topic for versioning. In the event of a problem, rollbacks are supported by Confluent Platform to ensure reliable version management and minimal disruption.

6.5   Common problems in handling data contracts

Let's explore the most common challenges you may encounter when handling data contracts.

6.5.1   Absence of server-side validation

Since Kafka brokers do not validate messages, a misconfigured producer can send data to a topic in the wrong format. Consumers must be equipped to handle improperly serialized data; otherwise, the following error scenarios may occur:

1 The consumer reads a message in the wrong format, causing an exception to be thrown.
2 If the exception is not properly handled, the consumer fails, and the offset is not committed.
3 Upon restarting, the consumer reads the same invalid message again, causing the failure to repeat in a loop.

This behavior is one of the most frustrating in production, especially since it cannot be easily fixed on the server side—Kafka does not allow deleting individual messages from a topic. The usual fix is to manually adjust the consumer offset using command-line tools.

In this scenario, the offset of the poison message should first be identified, either by examining logs or using browsing tools. Once the offset is determined, the `kafka -consumer-groups.sh` script, included in the Kafka distribution, can be used to reset the offset to the specified value.

It is crucial to test consumers for their ability to handle messages in the wrong format. A "wrong format" doesn't necessarily mean the message is nonsense; it could be as simple as missing required fields that prevent the consumer from deserializing the data. A policy should be in place to deal with these cases. A common solution is to redirect problematic messages to a dead-letter topic for manual review and processing. It is essential to actively monitor these dead-letter topics so that any incorrect messages can be addressed promptly.

6.5.2 Handling incompatible changes for non-compacted topics

When a new schema version is incompatible with the previous one, a custom migration process must be implemented. A high-level approach could be as follows:

1 Stop producing data with the old schema version.
2 Consume all remaining messages from the topic.
3 Temporarily switch the schema compatibility to None.
4 Register the new schema version in the Schema Registry via the REST API.
5 Restore compatibility to Backward or Forward mode.
6 Upgrade producers and consumers to handle the new schema.
7 Resume producing and consuming data using the new schema version.

Another approach is to create separate topics for each schema version, such as CLIENTS .V1 and CLIENTS.V2. The migration process would be as follows:

1 Stop producing messages to the old topic (CLIENTS.V1).
2 Consume all remaining messages from the CLIENTS.V1 topic.
3 Upgrade producers and consumers to support the new schema.
4 Redirect producers and consumers to the new topic (CLIENTS.V2).

In both cases, managing incompatible schema changes requires careful planning, as Kafka does not automatically handle schema evolution of such cases. The migration process must be well thought out to ensure smooth transitions between schema versions.

Both approaches can imply downtime or require careful orchestration. In practice, maintaining availability during schema-breaking changes is non-trivial. The system may need to operate in a dual-write or dual-read mode temporarily, where producers send data to both old and new topics, or consumers read from both until the migration is complete.

6.5.3 Migrating state

In the previous section, we discussed handling incompatible schema changes for topics where messages expire after the retention period. However, if you're using compacted topics for storing state and need to upgrade to an incompatible schema version, all messages must be migrated. This requires developing a custom migration application, as illustrated in figure 6.17.

The migration process follows these steps:

1 A new topic is created, and messages are migrated to it by a dedicated migration component. During migration, keys and timestamps must be preserved to maintain data consistency.

Phase 0: Both producers and consumers work with version V1.

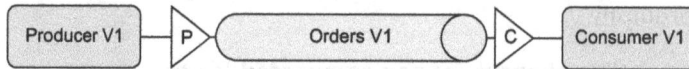

**Phase 1: MigrationService transforms the data from Orders V1 to Orders V2,
acting both as a consumer for Orders V1 and as a producer for Orders V2.**

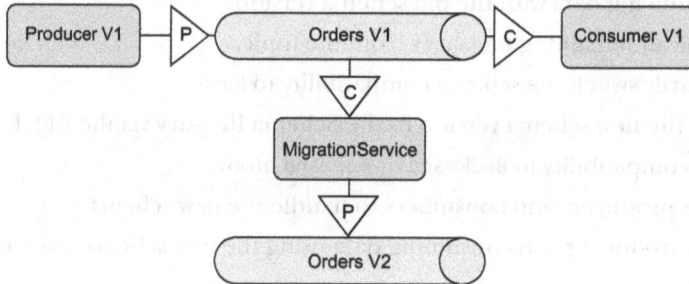

Phase 2: Both producers and consumers have been switched to version V2.

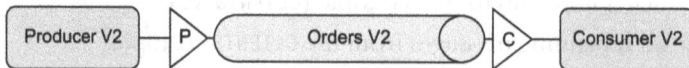

Figure 6.17
Migrating
messages
using a special
transformation
service

2 Once all messages are migrated, the producer is upgraded and starts sending
   data to the new topic.

3 Finally, consumers are upgraded and begin consuming data from the new topic.

This approach ensures a smooth migration while preserving data integrity when dealing with incompatible schema changes in compacted topics.

6.5.4 *Automatic registration of schemas*

As previously mentioned, schemas can be registered either explicitly through the
Schema Registry's REST API or automatically with the producer's first message.
However, if an issue is identified after the first schema is registered, resolving it
often involves re-registering a new schema version or manually cleaning up data
already written to Kafka—tasks that can be operationally complex. Additionally,
if the first producer registers a schema without prior validation, it may introduce
incompatibilities with the expected schema evolution strategy. The solution is to
establish a process where schemas are registered in advance in a controlled and
validated manner.

It's also critical to restrict write access to the _schemas topic, where schemas are
stored, to prevent unauthorized changes. Additionally, creating a backup of this topic is
essential, as corrupted schemas can render the entire cluster nonfunctional.

6.6 *Online resources*

- "Schema Registry Concepts for Confluent Platform": https://docs.confluent.io/platform/current/schema-registry/fundamentals/index.html

  An introduction to the core concepts of Confluent Schema Registry, explaining how schemas are stored, versioned, and used to ensure compatibility in Kafka-based systems.

- "Building an Event-Driven Data Mesh": https://learning.oreilly.com/library/view/building-an-event-driven/9781098127596/

  A guide to designing and implementing event-driven architectures, covering patterns, workflows, and best practices for building scalable, loosely coupled systems.

- "What do you mean by Event-Driven?" https://martinfowler.com/articles/201701-event-driven.html

  An overview of event-driven architecture, explaining its key concepts, styles, and challenges, and when it is an appropriate architectural choice.

- "Should You Put Several Event Types in the Same Kafka Topic?" https://www.confluent.io/blog/put-several-event-types-kafka-topic/

  A discussion of when and how to place multiple event types in a single Kafka topic, including the trade-offs, compatibility concerns, and design considerations involved.

- "Schemas for Kafka topics: Multiple Schemas vs. Composite Schemas—Comprehensive Comparison": https://medium.com/@bryan_56456/schemas-for-kafka-topics-multiple-schemas-vs-composite-schemas-comprehensive-comparison-b34880e81987

  A comparison of approaches for structuring schemas in Kafka topics, contrasting multiple independent schemas with composite schemas and examining their trade-offs in real-world use.

Summary

- Designing events is challenging; it requires careful consideration of the right attributes and optimal granularity to balance flexibility, performance, and data relevance for consumers.

- Establishing clear rules for defining, updating, and communicating event changes is crucial to avoid chaos as systems scale. A best practice is maintaining a centralized, version-controlled schema repository to facilitate collaboration between developers and business analysts, and ensure consistent event structures.

- State events capture the full state of an entity, while delta events convey only the changes. Each approach offers trade-offs: state events provide simplicity and completeness, while delta events reduce message size and bandwidth usage but increase consumer complexity.

- Data contracts in Kafka are represented by schemas, which act as agreements between producers and consumers to define the structure of shared data, ensuring consistency and preventing misinterpretation across systems.

- The Schema Registry manages event schemas and ensures compatibility between schema versions, supporting both forward and backward compatibility to allow producers and consumers to evolve independently without causing system failures. It stores schemas in Kafka topics for versioning.

- Kafka brokers do not enforce schema validation—all message validation happens on the client side, making it critical for producers and consumers to correctly implement schema checks.

- As requirements change, schemas must evolve gracefully. Following best practices such as backward or forward compatibility ensures that new schema versions can coexist with old ones without disrupting the system.

- When breaking changes are unavoidable, migration strategies should be implemented, including phased deployments and transformation components to convert older event formats into newer ones, ensuring a smooth transition without service downtime.

Kafka interaction patterns

Now that you have seen some real-world use cases, let's look at how Kafka fits into architectural patterns, so you can choose it deliberately, not by default. To make these choices, it's important to know where Kafka excels in microservices, including smart endpoints, data mesh, CQRS, and event stores, and where it's a poor match (request-response).

Then there's the issue of how to move data in and out—for this we can turn to Kafka Connect, which we met briefly in chapter 5. We'll explore in detail how this product can be effectively used for data integration within an enterprise environment, examining both its potential and common challenges.

Finally, we need to protect our system from the risk of undetected data loss—always a concern in asynchronous message transfer—using Kafka's guarantees. How do we ensure durability (no data loss), exactly-once processing, and ordering, and what do these semantics actually guarantee?

This chapter helps turn patterns into practical choices you can defend in production, backed by clear checklists and trade-offs.

Field notes: When Kafka helps—and when it hurts

The team gathers once again in the meeting room, with the whiteboard cluttered with diagrams of their Kafka setup.

Max: You know, one thing's been bothering me. Not too long ago, service buses were all the rage. And they worked pretty well. Those tools let you visually define the data flow between services and even create transformations right there. But where are we now? It feels like we've taken a step back to low-level programming. Why? Is this all just for performance?

Eva: It's not just about performance, Max. Those service buses never worked perfectly. The visual tools were useful, but they were never as expressive as code. Every time we needed to make a more complex change, it felt like we were fighting the tool's limitations. And don't forget, small changes often required redeploying the whole service bus pipeline, which wasn't flexible at all. Flexibility is one of the main things we gain with Kafka and microservices.

Rob: Flexibility, sure, but have we gone too far in the other direction? Now Kafka is just a set of pipes, and all the logic is handled by the consumers. Is putting all that logic at the endpoints really the best approach? Sure, we can add intermediate services, but at some point, won't this many microservices become an unmanageable mess?

Max: Hmm, so are you saying Kafka isn't enough by itself? I thought Kafka was so good that we could use it everywhere.

Eva: I wouldn't go that far, Max. Kafka excels at certain patterns, but it's not a one-size-fits-all solution. For example, Kafka doesn't naturally fit with request-response patterns. It's great for asynchronous, publish-subscribe workflows, but trying to use it for request-response would feel forced.

Rob: Exactly. Trying to implement request-response using Kafka is not a pattern—it's an antipattern. And while we're talking about events—storing all of them? Sure, disks are cheap, but they're not free. Do we really need to keep last year's events? Who's going to need that?

Eva: Storing all the events isn't as much of a problem anymore, especially with tiered storage options. We can offload older events to cheaper storage like S3. But what does concern me is the performance of the event sourcing pattern. If we just treat Kafka as a storage system and load data into microservices on demand, we'll run into serious performance bottlenecks.

Max: That's a good point. There's a lot to think about. We need to make it clear to ourselves and the other teams which patterns Kafka is good for, and which ones we should avoid.

7.1   Using Kafka in microservices

Let's start by exploring architectural patterns commonly used in microservices and evaluating how effectively Kafka can address them. While Kafka excels in many scenarios, it may not be the ideal solution for certain patterns, and we will highlight these limitations.

7.1.1   Smart endpoints and dumb pipes

In a Kafka-based architecture, the *smart endpoints, dumb pipes* pattern emerges naturally as the only viable approach. Since Kafka brokers merely transport messages and do not interpret them, all processing logic must reside at the endpoints. This makes the pipes truly "dumb," serving purely as communication channels, fully decoupled from any processing logic. An example of such a decentralized architecture is illustrated in figure 7.1.

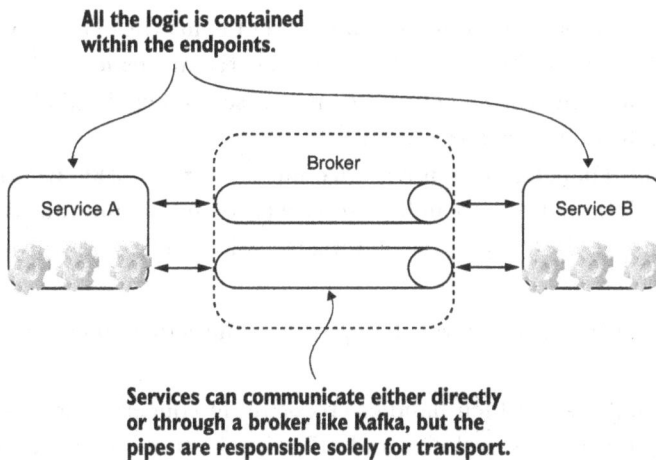

Figure 7.1   All the logic resides on the smart endpoints; the pipes serve only for transport.

This contrasts sharply with the *enterprise service bus* (ESB) pattern, where microservices communicate through middleware that not only transports messages but also performs additional tasks. These tasks may include data validation, enforcing authorization rules, encryption, dynamic routing, and auditing, as shown in figure 7.2.

Modern architectural approaches often consider ESB an antipattern for two primary reasons:

- Centralizing logic in the ESB creates a bottleneck, slowing down development.
- Deploying the ESB as a monolithic product introduces a single point of failure— even if it's clustered, it remains a logically unified component in the architecture.

If an ESB centralizes too much logic and becomes an antipattern, this raises an important question: What about integration logic that isn't directly related to business

Endpoints are responsible solely for business logic.

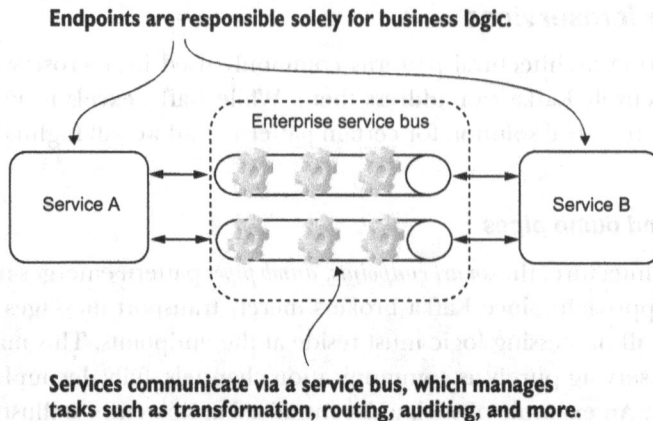

**Services communicate via a service bus, which manages
tasks such as transformation, routing, auditing, and more.**

Figure 7.2   Integration
logic is handled by
smart middleware (the
enterprise service bus).

functionality? For instance, data transformation might be considered business logic unique to each endpoint, but should we also implement concerns like encryption or auditing within each service? These cross-cutting concerns are typically integration-related, and need to be standardized across the enterprise, so they should be configurable rather than hardcoded at each endpoint.

The solution to this challenge lies in a service mesh. A *service mesh* introduces an infrastructure layer designed to streamline service-to-service communication in a microservice architecture. In this approach, a microservice is effectively divided into two components:

- The business logic component, which implements the actual functionality of the service.
- The system component, which handles cross-cutting concerns such as encryption, auditing, retries, observability, and other integration-related responsibilities not directly tied to the service's core business logic.

The system component is designed to be reusable across multiple microservices and is configurable to suit specific needs.

A service mesh uses the *sidecar* pattern, where each microservice consists of two containers: one for the business logic, and another, the sidecar, for managing integration logic. All network traffic to the business logic container is routed through the sidecar proxy. The sidecar handles system-level concerns, such as encryption, retries, load balancing, and others, before forwarding requests to the business logic container. This separation offloads integration and infrastructure responsibilities from the business logic, enabling cleaner, more focused code.

An example of a service mesh architecture is illustrated in figure 7.3. These sidecar proxies are typically off-the-shelf components that perform predefined tasks based on configuration. One of the most widely adopted implementations of this pattern is

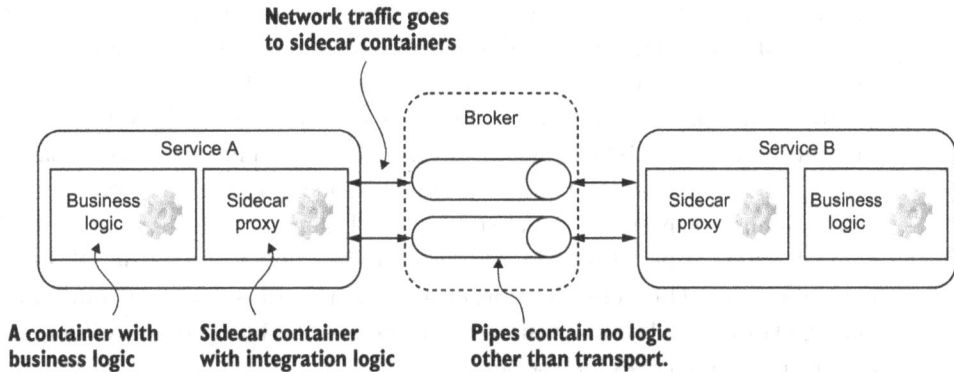

**Network traffic goes
to sidecar containers**

Broker

Service A

Business
logic

Sidecar
proxy

Service B

Sidecar
proxy

Business
logic

**A container with
business logic**

**Sidecar container
with integration logic**

**Pipes contain no logic
other than transport.**

**Figure 7.3   An example of a service mesh architecture. Business logic and integration logic are
separated into different containers. All network traffic flows through the sidecar component, which acts
as a proxy to the component's pure business logic.**

Envoy (www.envoyproxy.io), a high-performance, open source proxy that powers many
service mesh frameworks.

How are these sidecars configured? When integration logic is managed by a product like a service bus, these products typically provide tools such as a service catalog. A
service catalog offers visibility into all available services and allows users to configure
complex integration logic in a centralized manner. In a service mesh, this functionality
is handled by a dedicated component known as the *service mesh control plane*, which is
shown in figure 7.4.

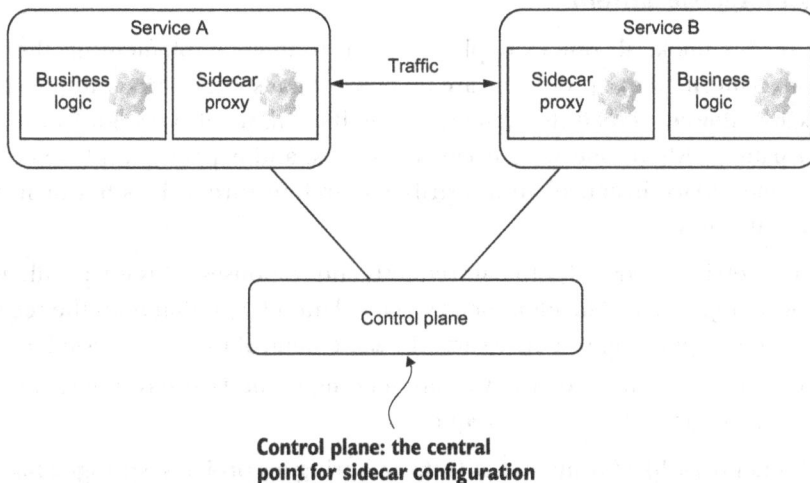

Service A

Business
logic

Sidecar
proxy

Traffic

Service B

Sidecar
proxy

Business
logic

Control plane

**Control plane: the central
point for sidecar configuration**

Figure 7.4   Configuring sidecar containers through the control plane

The control plane is a critical concept in a service mesh architecture, responsible for the centralized management of all sidecar proxies. It provides the functionality to configure, deploy, and manage the behavior of the network across the entire mesh. The control plane enables you to define traffic policies, security configurations, load balancing rules, and observability features, ensuring consistent behavior across participants.

In practice, the control plane is often implemented as a product or a set of components—examples include Istio's control plane (https://istio.io) and Linkerd's control plane (https://linkerd.io)—that provide a user interface or API for configuring these rules. This centralization ensures that service-to-service communication is managed in a scalable and dynamic way, without embedding complex integration logic directly into the services themselves.

But how do services which communicate through Kafka relate to a service mesh? In earlier chapters, you saw that much of the Kafka-related integration logic is handled by client libraries. For example, functionality like batching messages on the producer side or retrying message delivery if an acknowledgment is not received are implemented within the Kafka client library, not directly in the services themselves. This raises the question: Should this functionality be moved to the sidecar container instead of being handled by the client library?

This is where the overlap between Kafka client libraries and sidecar proxies becomes evident, making Kafka-enabled services less compatible with traditional service mesh designs. The community is actively discussing and exploring ways to make these concepts compatible. Experimental efforts, such as the Kafka mesh filter, aim to bring Kafka communication into the service mesh paradigm. However, this remains a hot topic at the cutting edge of microservices architecture, with no definitive solution yet widely adopted.

7.1.2 *Request-response pattern*

So far in this book, all our examples have been about implementing the publish-subscribe pattern, where producers are unaware of consumers and multiple consumer groups are allowed to read the same message. But can we also use Kafka for a *request-response* pattern, where one service sends a request and expects a reply to come back to the same service instance? In a distributed architecture, this behavior introduces several challenges:

- The service needs a way to pair requests and responses. This is typically achieved by setting a special header, such as a correlation ID, so that both the request and the corresponding response carry the same value of the correlation ID.
- If multiple instances of a service are sending requests, the response must return to the instance that sent the request.

Some frameworks, like Spring Kafka (https://spring.io/projects/spring-kafka), implement this pattern, allowing users to avoid dealing with the complexity of the implementation details. An example of this flow is shown in figure 7.5.

1. **RequestResponseService sends a request message to a Kafka topic using a Kafka producer and waits for a reply. It sets a correlation ID in the message header.**

2. **ResponderService receives a message with a Kafka consumer and generates a response.**

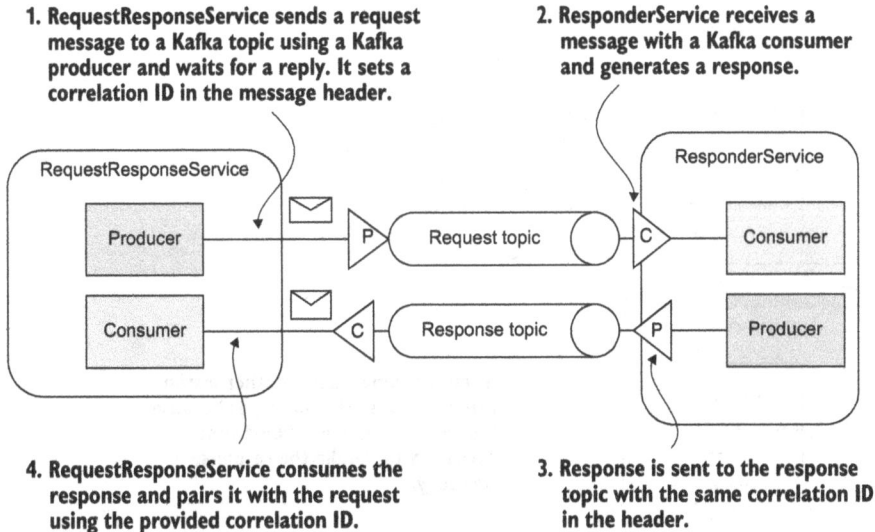

4. **RequestResponseService consumes the response and pairs it with the request using the provided correlation ID.**

3. **Response is sent to the response topic with the same correlation ID in the header.**

Figure 7.5 Both services participating in the request-response pattern have a producer and consumer container. The request and response are matched using the correlation ID, specified in the message header.

When a request is sent, a special CORRELATION_ID header is added, and the service expects it to be echoed back in the response. The trickiest part of this pattern is ensuring that the response is delivered to the correct instance of the service.

In a typical consumer group scenario, when a consumer instance fails, its partitions are reassigned to healthy consumers. However, in the request-response pattern, the consumer instance that takes over the partition after a failure cannot process the response correctly because it lacks the request context. This situation is illustrated in figure 7.6.

There are several approaches to resolving this challenge, and different client frameworks implement various strategies:

- *Manual partition assignment*—In this approach, partitions for the consumers in RequestResponseService are assigned manually. When a request is sent, the headers include information about the response topic and partition where the response should be delivered. The assignment of the consumer instance to the partition is done manually, and if the consumer instance fails, no automatic recovery happens. Custom logic needs to handle any failures in consumers reading replies. An example of this approach is shown in figure 7.7.

- *Broadcasting responses to all consumers*—Another approach (shown in figure 7.8) is to simulate broadcasting by having each instance of RequestResponseService use a different consumer group. This ensures each instance receives all responses, allowing it to select only those that match its own requests and ignore the rest. If an instance fails and is restarted with the same consumer group, it can still read the messages (although it may lose the request context). This approach improves availability, but it may require additional filtering logic.

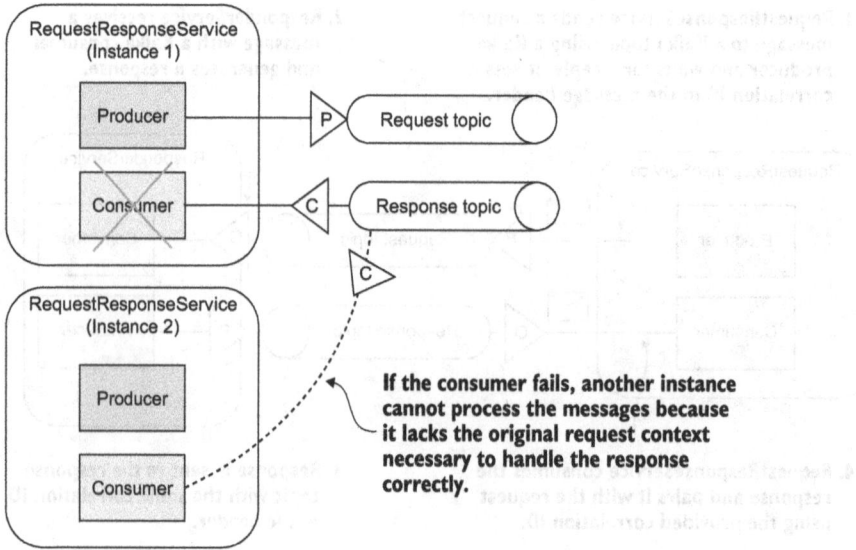

Figure 7.6 The availability of `RequestResponseService` is problematic, as another instance does not have the original request context.

If the consumer fails, another instance cannot process the messages because it lacks the original request context necessary to handle the response correctly.

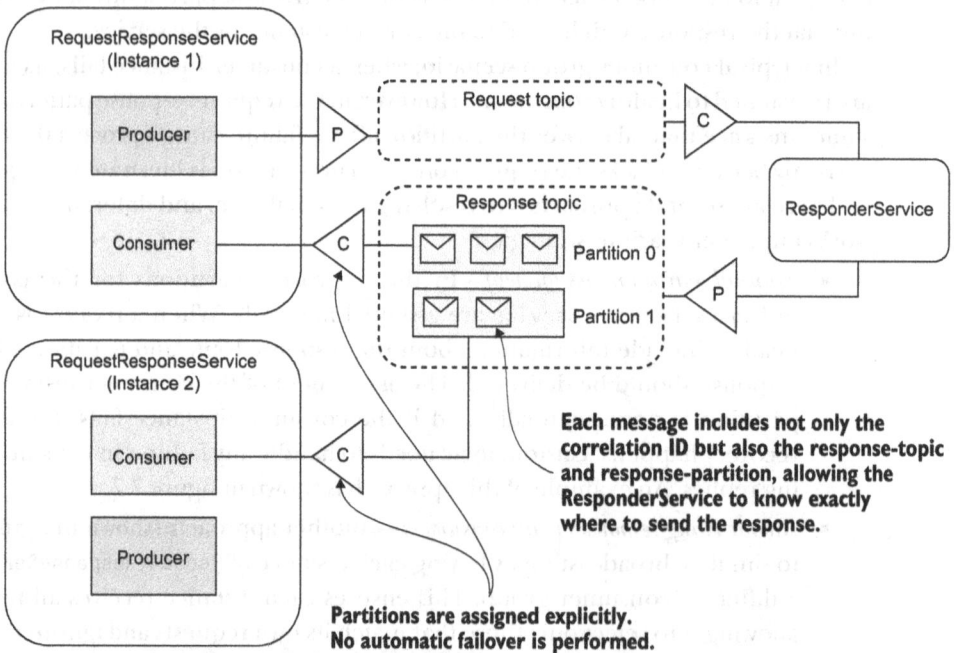

Each message includes not only the correlation ID but also the response-topic and response-partition, allowing the ResponderService to know exactly where to send the response.

Partitions are assigned explicitly. No automatic failover is performed.

Figure 7.7 Each message carries a correlation ID, a topic, and a partition so that `ResponderService` knows where to send the response.

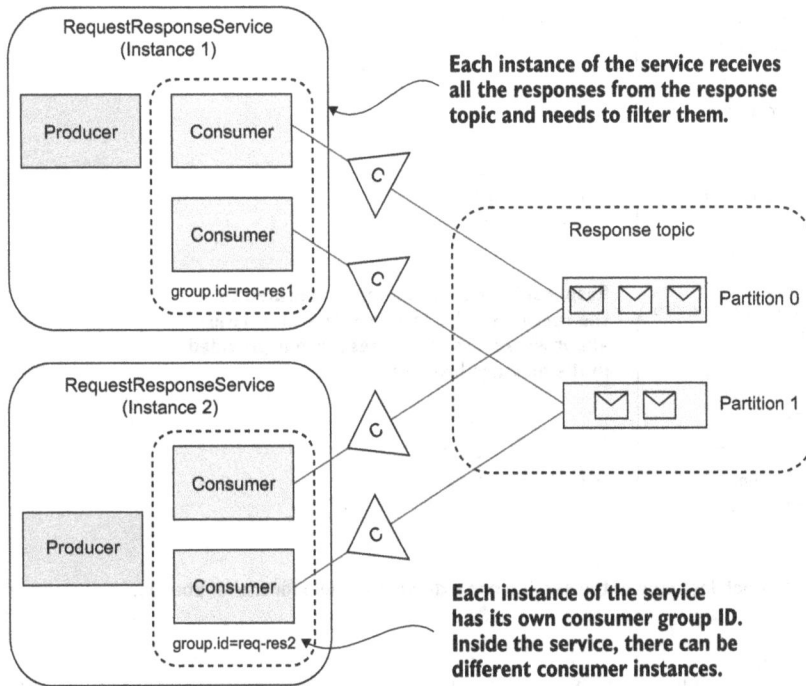

Figure 7.8 Each instance of the service has its own consumer group assigned.

- *Dedicated reply topics for each instance*—In this approach (shown in figure 7.9), a dedicated reply topic is created for each instance of RequestResponseService. When a request is sent, it specifies the dedicated topic for the instance that initiated the request, ensuring the response is delivered only to that instance. This approach provides isolation but can lead to a large number of topics if many service instances are running. Managing these topics becomes a consideration.

All of these implementations must address two key challenges:

- *Recovery when* RequestResponseService *fails*—In the request-response pattern, consumer rebalancing cannot be used across different service instances, so a process for handling recovery is essential. When an instance of the service fails, the request context is lost. This loss must be monitored and reported. One option is to store the request context in external storage, but this obviously impacts performance. The system must ensure that recovery mechanisms are in place for dealing with these failures.

- *Handling unpaired requests*—Special logic is required to handle cases where a request is sent but the response is never received within a specified timeout. For instance, if no response is received, the client may choose to resend the request. Ensuring idempotence is crucial here, to avoid side effects when resending

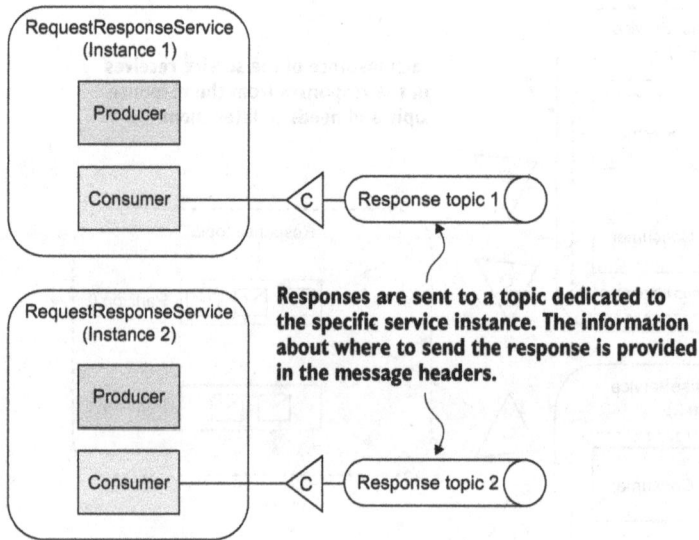

Figure 7.9 Each instance of the service has a dedicated topic for the responses.

requests. Alternatively, unpaired requests can be sent to dead-letter topics, where they can be monitored and investigated.

All in all, implementing this pattern in Kafka introduces complexity and is often regarded as an antipattern. Kafka is optimized for asynchronous, broadcast-style communication, where consumers are decoupled from producers, and messages can be processed independently by multiple consumer groups. Attempting to enforce synchronous request-response behavior in Kafka can lead to several drawbacks:

- Difficulty in handling consumer failures
- The need for complex correlation and context management
- Potential performance drawbacks, especially when external storage is used for context tracking

Whether using manual partition assignment, broadcasting responses to all consumers, or dedicated response topics, all request-response patterns in Kafka share a key limitation: Kafka itself provides no guarantee that the responding service will send a response at all. If the responder crashes, times out, or encounters an error before replying, the requesting client will never receive a response—unless additional logic is implemented. To address this, the client application must handle timeouts, correlation, and potential failure scenarios independently. Kafka's log-based architecture offers durable messaging, but it does not enforce or monitor the completion of response flows, making it essential to build reliability mechanisms into the surrounding application logic.

In many cases, other messaging systems like RabbitMQ or protocols like gRPC, or even simple HTTP—might be better suited for strict request-response interactions, as they are designed to handle synchronous, point-to-point communication natively.

7.1.3 CQRS pattern

In the previous chapters, when we introduced the ProfileService in our examples, we treated it as the microservice responsible for all profile updates: it handled write operations, stored records in its own database, and published events whenever profile data changed. In this architecture, the ProfileService is the single point for updating profile data. But what about reading data? Should the ProfileService expose a synchronous REST service for reading profile information? Or, perhaps that's the responsibility of another microservice? Perhaps any other microservice interested in profile data should simply listen for events and build its own view of profiles, tailored to its needs? What are the criteria for making these decisions?

The pattern where write operations and read queries are separated is known as *Command Query Responsibility Segregation* (CQRS). In this context, a command refers to an operation that changes the state (e.g., creating or updating data), while a query refers to an operation that retrieves data.

This separation is illustrated in figure 7.10 where two different object models exist: one for updating data and one for reading it. These models may differ conceptually

The service uses separate interfaces for writing and querying data. Alternatively, it can be split into two distinct services, each dedicated to either writing or querying.

The command model validates data and updates records.

The databases for updating and querying data can be separated. In this setup, data is asynchronously replicated from the write database to the read database to ensure eventual consistency.

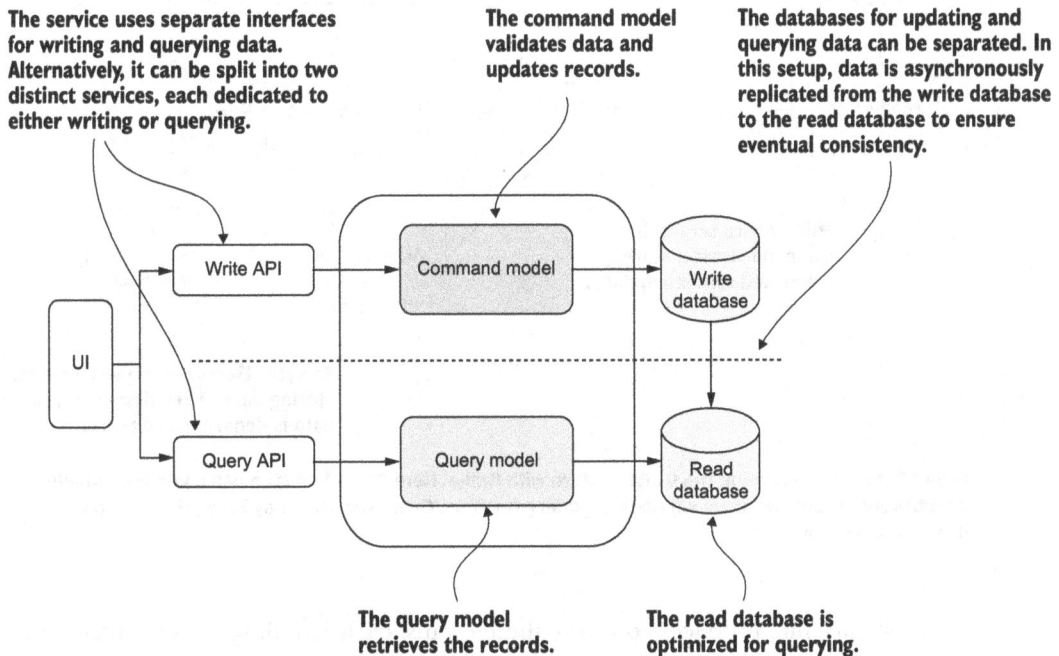

The query model retrieves the records.

The read database is optimized for querying.

Figure 7.10 Different object models are responsible for writing and reading the data.

or physically and may even rely on distinct persistence mechanisms. However, CQRS doesn't necessarily mean that these models must belong to separate microservices. CQRS can be applied at different levels, and whether you need to split a service depends on factors such as the complexity of your application, performance needs, and architectural considerations.

For services that primarily handle CRUD operations, CQRS can introduce unnecessary overhead. In the following scenarios, CQRS can definitely add value:

- When the model for querying is much more complex than the model for updating data
- When read operations are far more frequent than write operations, and the reading logic requires different scaling strategies

The CQRS pattern fits perfectly into the Kafka ecosystem and is often combined with event sourcing. In figure 7.11, you'll see a microservice responsible for command logic writing data into its internal storage and emitting events to Kafka.

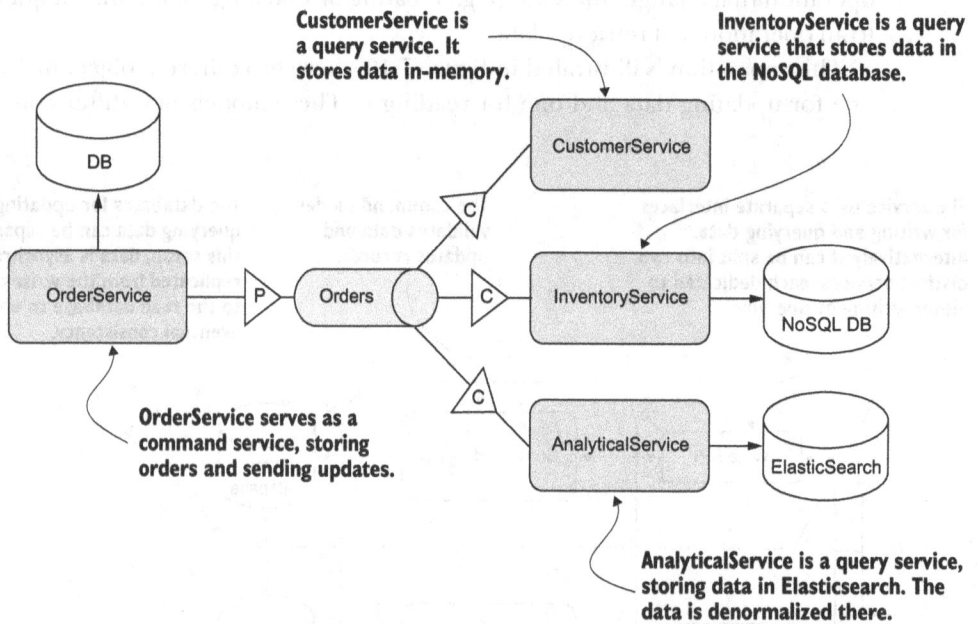

Figure 7.11 Implementing the CQRS pattern with Kafka. Here `OrderService` is a command, which updates orders, and the other services are query services. Query services may have pretransformed denormalized data.

Various other microservices consume these events, each handling data for reading in different ways. Some services may read data directly from Kafka topics and maintain an in-memory image, while others may store the data in their own internal databases, pre-optimized for various types of queries. Implementing the CQRS pattern with Kafka is an excellent choice when you need to maintain a complete history of all data changes.

While CQRS is widely used in event-driven architectures, it does come with certain drawbacks:

- *Eventual consistency*—The data in the read models is not updated transactionally but rather with some delay. This means the read views may not always reflect the most current state at any given time.

- *Data duplication*—To support different models for reading and writing, data is often duplicated, which can lead to increased storage costs.

- *Model synchronization*—When business requirements change, any updates to the system must be applied to both the write model and all corresponding read models, which can increase the complexity of keeping the system synchronized.

7.1.4 Event sourcing with snapshotting

The idea of restoring state from events works conceptually but raises important concerns about performance, particularly when a microservice needs to restore its state during startup. Replaying every event to rebuild the state can be resource-intensive and time-consuming. This challenge is addressed by the pattern known as *event sourcing with snapshotting*. The same concept appears in Kafka's compacted topics, where for each key, only the most recent message is guaranteed to be accessible.

However, if a full log of events is required for auditing or complete history tracking, compacted topics are not suitable. Instead, a process can periodically capture the current state of the system (a snapshot) and store it in a more efficient, external storage. This snapshot can be taken on a regular schedule (e.g., once per day), or after a certain number of events (e.g., every 100,000 events), or it can be triggered by a business event (e.g., "end-of-day" in a banking system).

Figure 7.12 illustrates the general idea, where snapshots are stored in external storage like MongoDB. Along with the snapshot data, we also store the corresponding position in Kafka, identified as <topic, partition, offset>. This enables the system to know exactly where the snapshot was taken within the event stream.

When the consumer microservice starts, it first retrieves the latest snapshot from MongoDB. It then replays only the events that occurred after the snapshot was taken, significantly reducing the time and effort needed to restore the state.

While snapshotting improves performance during state restoration, it comes with certain drawbacks. Snapshot creation adds overhead, as it requires additional processing and storage. Additionally, managing snapshot consistency across distributed systems can be complex, especially if there are concurrent updates or failures during the snapshot process.

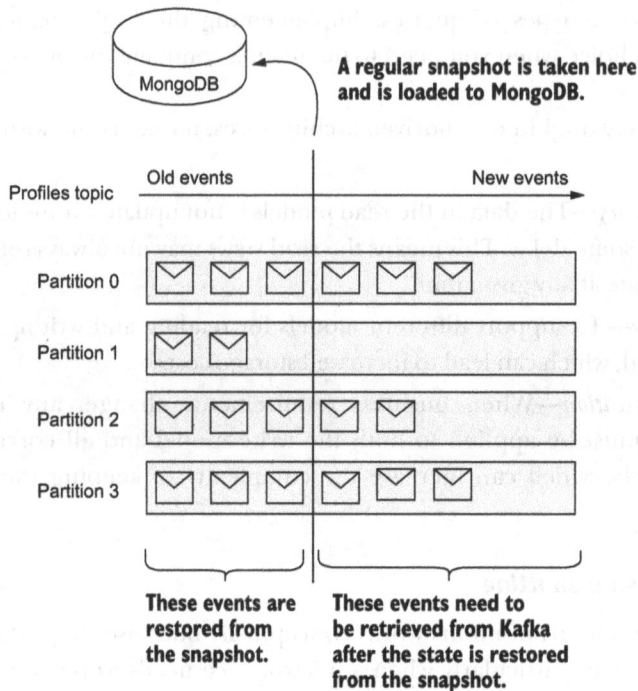

Figure 7.12   The state can be periodically uploaded to the database and then restored from there.

7.1.5   *Having "hot" and "cold" data*

Storing messages on disk can become a challenge when you need to retain a large volume of data for an extended period. Additionally, access patterns vary significantly: recent ("hot") data is accessed much more frequently than older ("cold") data. The concept of *tiered storage* addresses this by segregating hot and cold data into different storage tiers, optimizing both performance and cost. This feature is available in Kafka starting from version 3.6.0.

As illustrated in figure 7.13, hot data resides on the local disks of the Kafka broker, ensuring low-latency access, while cold data is periodically offloaded to cheaper, cloud-based storage. In practice, this allows Kafka to retain data much longer—potentially indefinitely—without being constrained by the size of local disk storage.

The configuration allows you to specify a remote storage location where older, rolled-over segments are moved. Current implementations support Amazon S3, Azure Blob Storage, and Google Cloud Storage, while also offering the flexibility to integrate custom storage solutions, whether in the cloud or on-premises. To enable tiered storage, the `remote.log.storage.system.enable` property must be set to `true` at the cluster level. It is also possible to set it at the topic level by setting the `remote.storage.enable` property.

From a consumer's perspective, access to the data remains completely transparent. Consumers do not need to be aware of whether the data resides on local disk or in

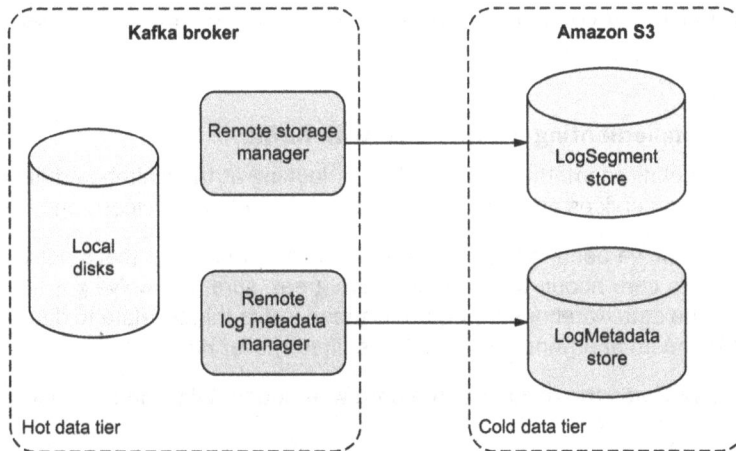

Figure 7.13 When the tiered storage feature is enabled, the cold data is moved periodically to cheaper, cloud-based storage.

remote storage. They can perform normal operations as if all data is local, and operations that do not require access to remote storage will function normally, even if remote storage is temporarily unavailable. In cases where consumers attempt to access data stored remotely and the remote storage is inaccessible, Kafka provides graceful error handling with meaningful error messages.

When data is offloaded to remote storage, not only are the data segments moved, but so is the associated metadata. Kafka does not clean up local logs until these segments are successfully copied to the remote storage, even if their local retention time or size limit has been reached. This ensures consistency between local and remote data storage.

Additionally, tiered storage alters the behavior of follower replicas. Traditionally, followers would continuously copy data from the leader to keep their replicas in sync. With tiered storage enabled, the role of the followers changes:

- Followers need to copy local data from the leader.
- Followers must also copy and maintain remote log metadata from the remote storage manager to construct any auxiliary state they might need for full functionality.

In general, hot storage should retain the actively accessed working set and the window required for recovery and backfills; older data belongs in the cold tier. In Apache Kafka's tiered storage, uploads are not scheduled manually. The Remote Log Manager automatically offloads closed (inactive) segments—including their index files—to remote storage after segment roll; you influence the cadence indirectly via `segment.bytes`, `segment.ms`, and `remote.log.manager.task.interval.ms`. To avoid overloading infrastructure, apply remote-storage quotas (e.g., `remote.log.manager.copy.max.bytes.per.second` and related settings).

If you need tiering for compacted topics, Confluent Tiered Storage supports it, starting with Confluent Platform 7.6.

Field notes: Implementing a data mesh with Kafka

Back in the meeting room, the lead architect is looking at the whiteboard filled with diagrams of microservices and Kafka pipelines, but something is clearly on his mind.

Rob: You know, we've been talking a lot about microservices, but that's not the only thing we need to care about. Microservices are great, sure, but we've got a serious problem with the data warehouse. How do all these Kafka things relate to data analytics? I've never heard of anyone doing analytics directly over Kafka.

Max: Analytics? That's the domain of the data warehouse. Why don't we just leave it there?

Eva: That approach is outdated, Max. Data warehouses want to hoard all the data, but they can't possibly know it all. They try to centralize everything, but it doesn't work in practice anymore.

Max: Well, you're right about one thing—those guys aren't going to want to give up ownership of their data anytime soon.

Rob: They should, though. Their tight grip on the data makes them a bottleneck for the entire organization. We're slowed down whenever we need to get data from them.

Max: Okay, I get it. That's a problem. But we're here to talk about Kafka, right? So how does this relate to Kafka?

Eva: Oh, it's connected to Kafka, too. We need to start thinking about adopting the data mesh paradigm. It deals with analytical data, but the key is that Kafka plays a big role in making it happen.

Rob: Data mesh? I haven't heard of that. Let's hope it's not just another data mess.

7.2 Decentralizing analytical data with a data mesh

So far, we've discussed operational data—generated by microservices through their day-to-day activities, and continuously updated to reflect the current state of the business. However, we haven't addressed analytical data, which is typically derived from operational data and used for long-term analysis. Traditionally, analytical data is aggregated from multiple sources into a central repository. This repository can take the form of a data warehouse, which stores structured data optimized for business intelligence and historical reporting, or a data lake, which stores raw data allowing flexible processing across various formats.

While centralizing data enables comprehensive analysis pipelines across all available data, it also introduces significant challenges. Analytical teams often find it overwhelming to manage and build logic across all domain data, struggling to keep up with evolving application models. Can we apply the same principles of microservice architecture—breaking tasks into smaller, manageable components?

This is where the *data mesh* (www.datamesh-architecture.com) paradigm comes in. Data mesh advocates for decentralizing analytical data based on four core principles:

- *Domain ownership*—Responsibility shifts from a central analytics team to domain teams that have the best understanding of their data.
- *Data as a product*—Data is treated as a product, with clear contracts and a guarantee of quality, making it reliable and consumable by others.
- *Federated governance*—Although it's decentralized, data must still comply with enterprise-wide standards related to business, legal, and security requirements. This is enforced through governance policies applied consistently across all data products.
- *Self-serve platform*—There must be an automated, consistent way to inform data consumers about planned changes and provide them with the tools to access and use data without heavy dependencies on centralized teams.

The data mesh is a conceptual framework and does not prescribe a specific technology for implementation. However, we can explore how it can be effectively implemented using Apache Kafka.

7.2.1 Domain ownership

Exposing data from Kafka aligns strongly with the data mesh principle of domain ownership. As discussed in chapter 6, in event-driven systems, data ownership resides with the producer. The producer holds the domain knowledge necessary to decide what data to expose and how to structure it. When Kafka is used as the integration layer, domain boundaries are naturally established through topics and schemas. It's the producer team that manages the structure, schema, and quality of data they publish, ensuring it aligns with the needs and semantics of their specific domain. Kafka's Schema Registry further supports this by enabling data contracts at the technical level, helping maintain consistency and quality across data consumers.

Challenges arise, however, when use cases require combining data from multiple domains. Meeting such cross-domain requirements calls for well-established collaboration processes between teams to ensure interoperability and alignment without compromising individual domain autonomy.

7.2.2 Data as a product

Treating data as a product means data becomes a first-class citizen, with exposed data meeting the standards of a public interface. Kafka naturally supports this approach, because events are viewed as data products with structures defined by data contracts in clear, understandable formats. Schema Registry plays a key role here, enabling teams to define and manage these contracts. As requirements for data contracts evolve, Kafka's support for schema compatibility allows for a smooth evolution, minimizing disruptions for data consumers.

With data as a product, it's also essential to provide comprehensive documentation and metadata that help consumers understand the data's purpose, structure, and context. However, a gap often exists between analytical models and the technical data contracts maintained in Schema Registry. This gap, as discussed in chapter 6, highlights the need for alignment between business-oriented data definitions and the technical schemas that represent them.

7.2.3   Federated governance

Enabling autonomous data management is valuable, but all data products within an organization must still comply with legal or industry-mandated policies, such as the following:

- *Personal information protection*—Ensuring compliance with data privacy regulations, like GDPR or CCPA, by controlling access and anonymizing sensitive data
- *Standardizing data structures*—Enforcing consistent data formats, such as specifying whether object identifiers must be integers or strings, to improve data compatibility across systems
- *Logging and data profiling*—Defining guidelines for logging and profiling data to detect and address potential errors proactively
- *Data access policies*—Setting rules on who can access specific data products to maintain data security and regulatory compliance

While federated governance is achievable with Kafka as the integration layer, the platform alone provides limited direct support for enforcing these policies. Regular audits and reviews are essential for maintaining compliance without compromising the decentralized model, helping to ensure that each domain meets the organization's governance standards.

7.2.4   Self-serve platform

Allowing domain teams to publish their own data significantly accelerates product delivery. However, for effective cross-team collaboration, a self-serve platform is essential. This platform should provide

- *Capabilities for creating, monitoring, and publishing data products*—Enabling teams to independently manage the full lifecycle of their data products
- *Data product discovery*—Allowing teams to easily locate and understand data products across the organization
- *Processes for requesting data product changes*—Providing a streamlined way for consumers to request modifications, fostering responsiveness and adaptability
- *Automated policy enforcement*—Ensuring that all data products adhere to compliance and governance standards without manual intervention

A platform with these features helps teams work with data products in an automated and consistent manner. Technically, this can be supported through DataOps practices, which are explored further in chapter 10.

It's worth mentioning that while Kafka provides strong alignment with data mesh principles, it doesn't need to serve as the system of record. In practice, the producing system remains the source of truth. Kafka's role is to expose the data produced by these systems through well-defined, governed interfaces—typically in the form of event streams.

7.3 Using Kafka Connect

Kafka Connect is a standalone component designed to simplify the integration of external systems (such as databases, filesystems, cloud services, and business applications) with Kafka, requiring minimal to no coding. The goal is to enable developers to transfer data to or from Kafka via a connector that's configured with a connector configuration file containing all the necessary information for the integration process. In addition to connector configurations, Kafka Connect also relies on plugins—Java libraries that enable specific types of connectors to interact with different technologies.

Kafka Connect offers two types of connector plugins:

- *Source connectors*—These connectors retrieve data from external systems and publish it to Kafka topics.
- *Sink connectors*—These connectors take data from Kafka topics and send it to external systems.

This entire process operates in real time, meaning new data in one system is quickly propagated to the other. The speed of this propagation depends on factors such as the configuration of the connector, the performance of the source or sink system, the network bandwidth, and the processing capacity of the Kafka Connect instance.

Kafka Connect is designed to be modular and pluggable, requiring specific plugins to be installed for integration with external systems (illustrated in figure 7.14). For instance, to connect with a relational database, a developer must:

1 Install a connector plugin for database integration.
2 Configure the connector with mappings between database tables and Kafka topics.

A wide variety of plugins are available, covering most common technologies; some are open source, while others require a commercial license. All plugins are built on the Kafka Connect framework and can be uniformly managed.

Using Kafka Connect offers several key benefits:

- *Ready-to-use connector plugins*—A marketplace of connector plugins enables rapid integration, significantly reducing time to market.
- *Customizable API for new connector plugins*—If a connector plugin does not exist or licensing is a concern, developers can create a new connector plugin using the API and framework provided.
- *Management via REST API*—Kafka Connect includes REST API endpoints for creating, starting, stopping, and managing connectors, offering centralized and streamlined control.

Source and sink connectors operate entirely independently, meaning you can have either a source or a sink without needing both to create a complete pipeline.

A dedicated plugin is required for database integration. This plugin, a Java library, must be added to the classpath to enable connectivity.

Kafka cluster

A dedicated plugin is required for publishing data to Azure Data Lake. Each technology integration requires its own specific plugin.

P   C

Kafka Connect

<<lib>> DB connector plugin   <<json>> DB source connector   <<json>> Azure sink connector   <<lib>> Azure sink connector plugin

A source connector retrieves data from an external system and publishes it to a Kafka topic. In Kafka Connect, the connector's behavior is defined by a configuration file that specifies how the data should be pulled.

Relational DB

Azure Data Lake

A sink connector retrieves data from Kafka and publishes it to Azure Data Lake.

Arrow indicates logical data flow; the connector retrieves data by polling the external system.

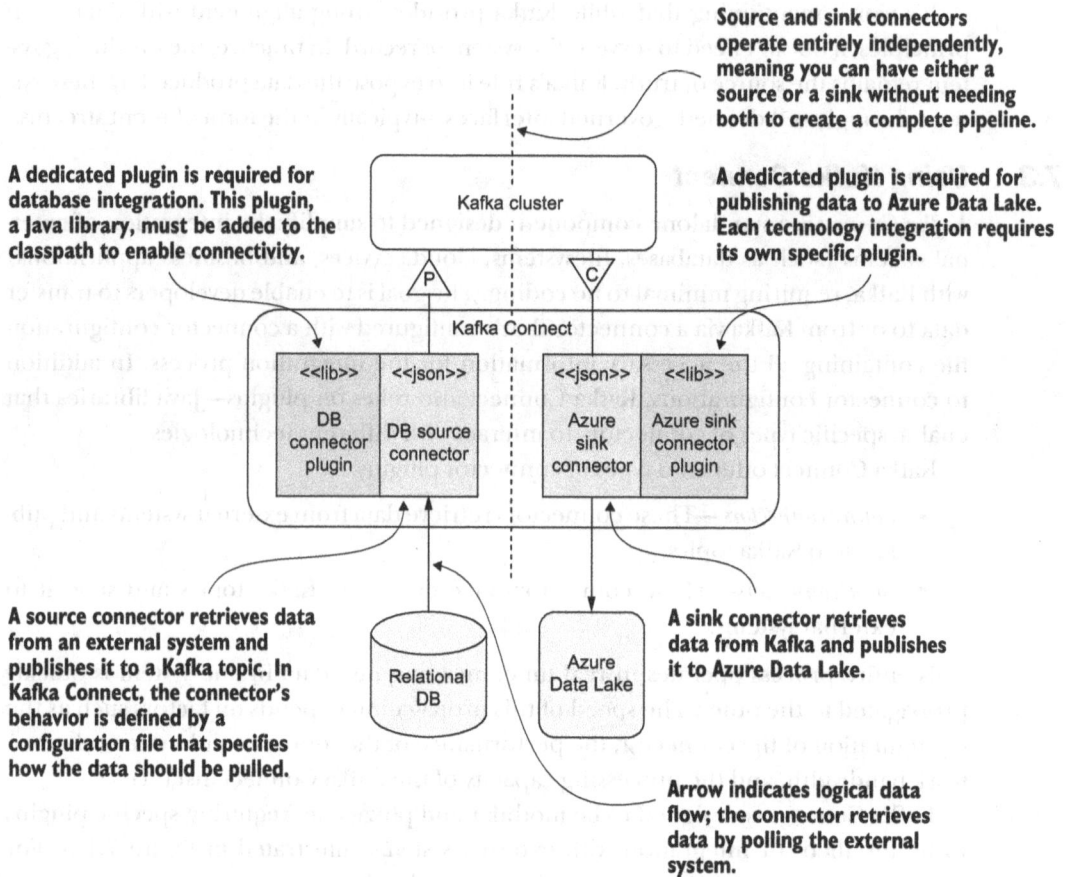

Figure 7.14   Connector plugins must be installed in Kafka Connect to enable specific technologies. Connectors are configured via configuration files that contain instructions on how to pull or push data.

- *Built-in scalability and reliability*—Kafka Connect is designed to be natively scalable, with automatic failover and recovery capabilities, ensuring reliability in production environments.

7.3.1   Kafka Connect at a glance

Figure 7.15 illustrates how Kafka Connect integrates into the Kafka ecosystem.

Suppose we have installed a connector plugin and created a JSON file containing the connector configuration. Next, we can deploy this configuration via the REST API, after which the connector will begin running on the Kafka Connect server. Kafka Connect doesn't require dedicated storage, such as a database; instead, it uses a dedicated Kafka topic (by default, connect-configs) to store configuration data. Connectors themselves function as clients within the Kafka cluster:

Connectors may need to access the Schema Registry to serialize or deserialize messages.

These are internal Kafka Connect topics used for storing configurations, source connector offsets, and status information.

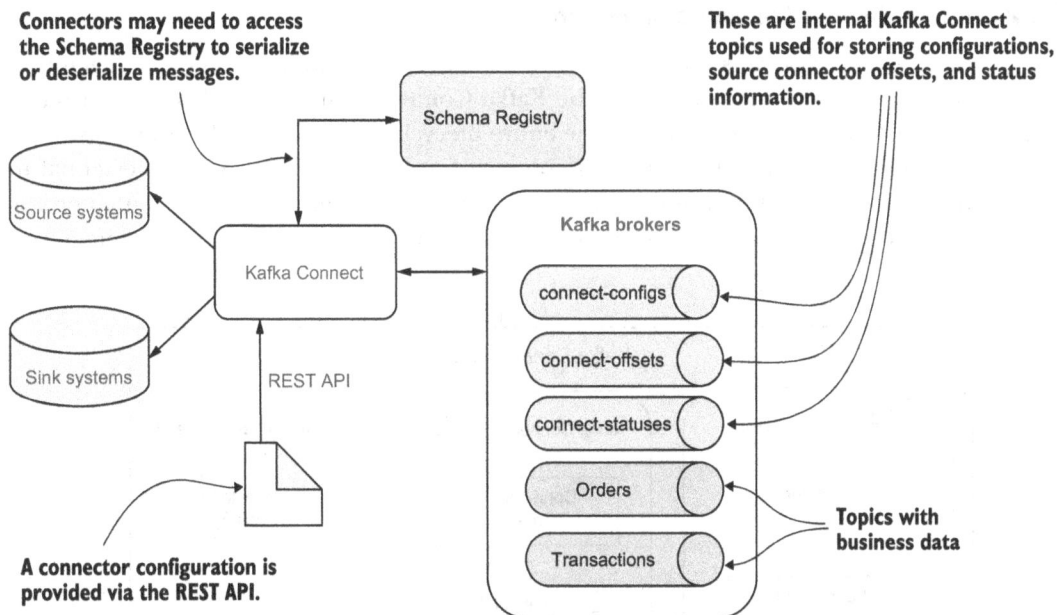

A connector configuration is provided via the REST API.

Topics with business data

Figure 7.15 How Kafka Connect fits into the Kafka ecosystem

- *Source connectors*—These connectors pull data from external systems into Kafka, acting as producers. All producer-specific configuration settings, covered in chapter 3, can be applied to source connectors for customization.

- *Sink connectors*—These connectors pull data from Kafka and send it to external systems, functioning as consumers. They support all standard consumer configuration options for fine-tuning, as discussed in chapter 4. Specifically, each sink connector has its own group.id, which is automatically assigned if not explicitly set, and is used to manage partition assignments and offset tracking like in any Kafka consumer group.

Messages in Kafka are serialized using a chosen format. When connectors read from or write to Kafka, they must perform deserialization or serialization as needed. To facilitate these operations, connectors may require access to the Schema Registry.

Kafka Connect also creates two additional internal topics within Kafka. The first, connect-statuses (the default name), stores status information for running connectors. The second, connect-offsets (default name), which we will explore in section 7.3.5, is used to track offsets for source connectors.

Importantly, Kafka Connect operates within the context of a single Kafka cluster, meaning all connectors and their configurations are tied to that specific cluster. This ensures that the internal topics and connector management are centralized within the same Kafka environment.

7.3.2   Internal Kafka Connect architecture

Kafka Connect servers form a cluster to enable scaling and fault tolerance. Each process that runs connectors within the Kafka Connect framework is known as a Kafka Connect worker. *Workers* manage the entire lifecycle of connectors, handling tasks like starting, stopping, and monitoring connector tasks. This makes workers essential to Kafka Connect's overall operation. When running in containers, each container typically hosts one Kafka Connect worker. Figure 7.16 illustrates its internal architecture.

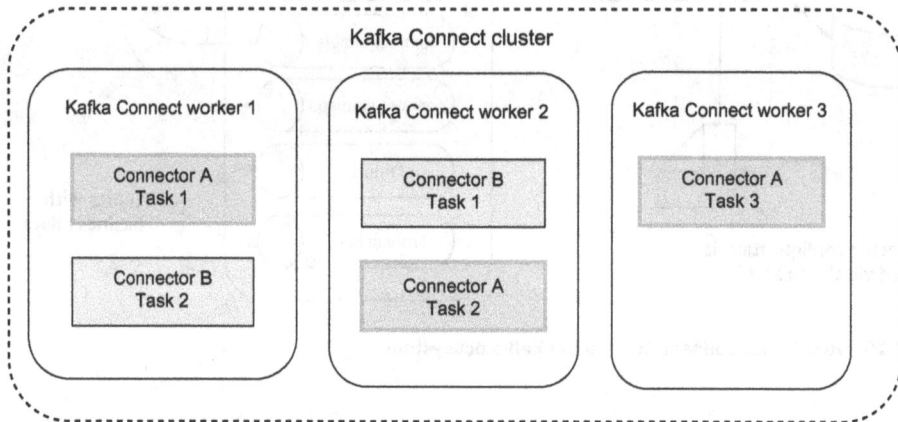

Figure 7.16   Connector tasks are distributed among workers, with each worker receiving its assigned portion.

Within each worker, the logic for copying data to or from Kafka is divided into *tasks*. Tasks run in parallel, and the connector configuration defines the maximum number of tasks allowed to run. Tasks may be configured differently; for example, each task might read data from a different database table. Kafka Connect distributes task configurations across workers, which then instantiate and execute tasks. Each task runs in its own thread to enable efficient parallel processing.

Kafka Connect workers in a cluster share the same group.id, even for source connectors, which act as producers rather than consumers. This shared group.id enables all workers to participate in group coordination. Workers send periodic heartbeats to the group coordinator, signaling that they are active. If a worker fails, it stops sending heartbeats, and the group coordinator detects this failure, redistributing its tasks to the remaining active workers.

It's worth noting that while this shared group.id applies at the Connect worker level, individual connectors—particularly source connectors that internally use a Kafka consumer—may define and use their own group.id as part of their consumer configuration. This group ID governs the behavior of the embedded consumer and is distinct from the Connect worker group coordination.

In some cases, a task may also fail. For instance, if a connector sends data from Kafka to a database and the data violates the database's integrity constraints, an exception is thrown, and the task enters a FAILED state. In this scenario, the task will not restart automatically. Therefore, it is essential to monitor task states closely to detect failures, resolve the root cause, and manually restart the task.

7.3.3   Converters

Different systems store data in their internal formats, and connectors need to understand them to be able to read or write the data. Source connectors read data from external systems and convert them to ConnectRecord, an internal model of Kafka Connect.

The class hierarchy is shown in figure 7.17.

When Kafka Connect is used, we have an external system on one end and Kafka on the other. In the external system, data is stored in its native format, and in Kafka, data is stored in bytes, which can be produced by different serializers. Inside the Kafka Connect framework, the data is represented in the internal format of the Kafka framework. So, inside Kafka connector we have three different data formats:

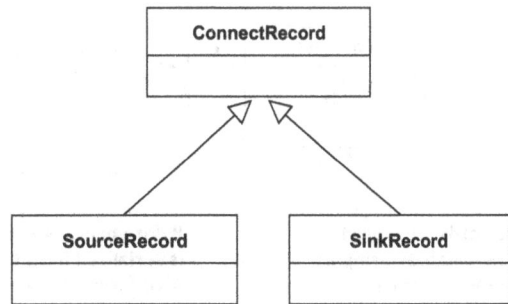

Figure 7.17   ConnectRecord **is the parent class for the** SourceRecord **and** SinkRecord **classes.**

- Data in the external system, such as records in the database
- Data inside Kafka Connect, represented by ConnectRecord objects
- Data stored in Kafka, commonly using the Avro, JSON or Protobuf formats

Converters are responsible for converting data between ConnectRecords and Kafka. Each connector must specify a converter, depending on how data is stored in Kafka. The flow for source connectors is shown in figure 7.18.

Source connectors understand the format of the external system. They read data from those systems and convert it into ConnectRecord. Then the data is passed to the converter, which serializes it for storing in Kafka. Converters are specific to the format. In the example in figure 7.18, AvroConverter is used, which serializes data into Avro.

On the other hand, sink connectors must receive data from Kafka, and again this is the responsibility of the converter. The flow for sink connectors is shown in figure 7.19. Converters convert data from Kafka messages into ConnectRecord, and then sink connectors convert them into the format that the external system understands.

As you can see, converters act as serializers and deserializers translating data between Kafka and ConnectRecords. As they operate only with Kafka and Kafka Connect's format, they do not depend on the external systems and can be reused in different connectors.

The connector retrieves records from the database and converts them into ConnectRecord, Kafka Connect's internal format.

The Avro converter retrieves the schema for the topic from the Schema Registry.

Records are stored in the database using its internal format.

Before being sent to Kafka, the data is serialized from ConnectRecord into Avro format by the Avro converter.

The data is sent to the Kafka topic in Avro format.

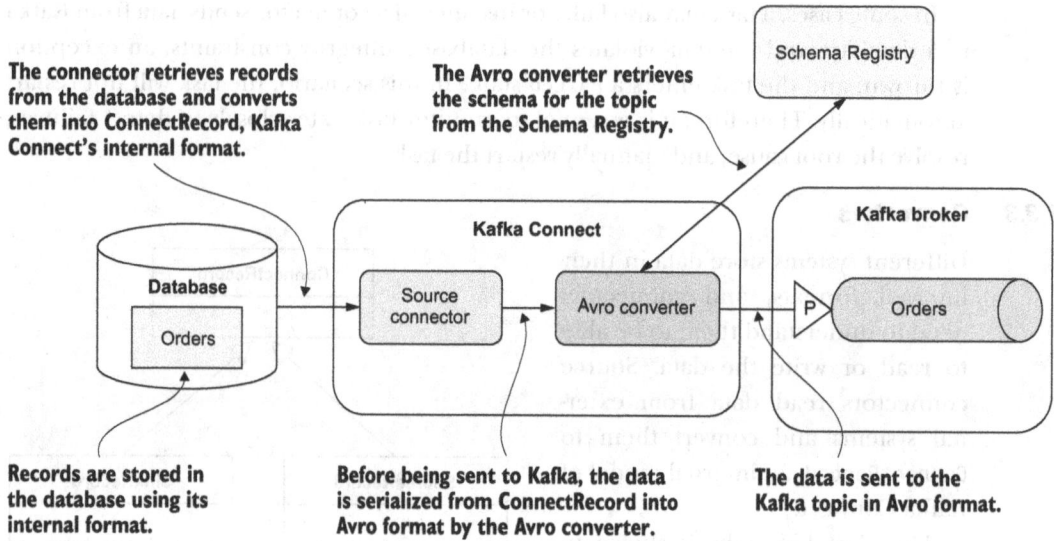

Figure 7.18   How converters are used in the source connector flow

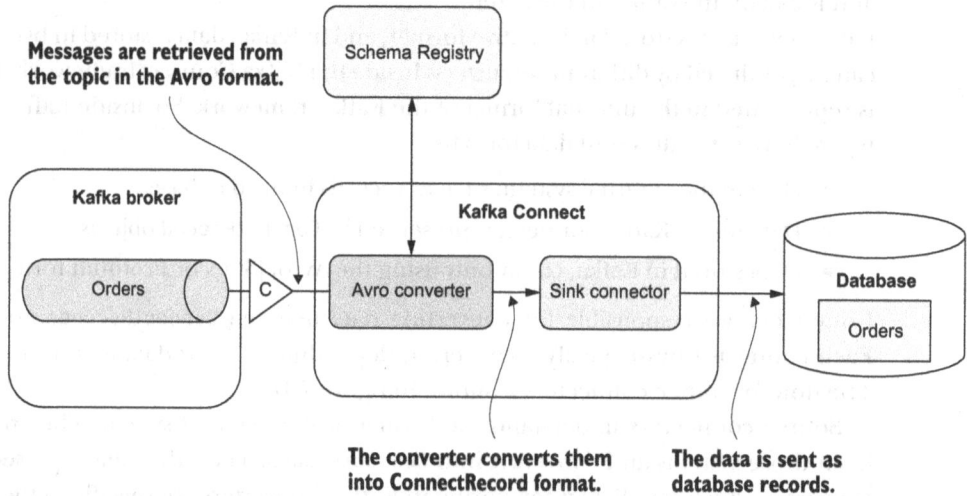

Messages are retrieved from the topic in the Avro format.

The converter converts them into ConnectRecord format.

The data is sent as database records.

Figure 7.19   How converters are used in the sink connector flow

7.3.4   Single message transformations

In many integration scenarios, the goal isn't simply to transfer data between systems one-to-one but to perform various transformations. Common transformations include casting data types, filtering messages, and renaming attributes. Kafka Connect provides several built-in transformations (https://docs.confluent.io/platform/current/connect/transforms/overview.html), but it also allows developers to implement custom transformations in Java by implementing the `org.apache.kafka.connect.transforms.Transformation` interface.

Figure 7.20 illustrates how transformations are integrated into the Kafka Connect framework. These transformations are always stateless, processing one message at a time: a single message is received as input, and at most one modified message is produced as output. Since transformations cannot operate on multiple messages simultaneously, they are often referred to as *Single Message Transformations* (SMTs). The input and output of these transformations use the internal `ConnectRecord` format, making them reusable across different connectors. The transformation chain is static and defined in the connector's configuration, meaning that any modifications require redeploying the connector.

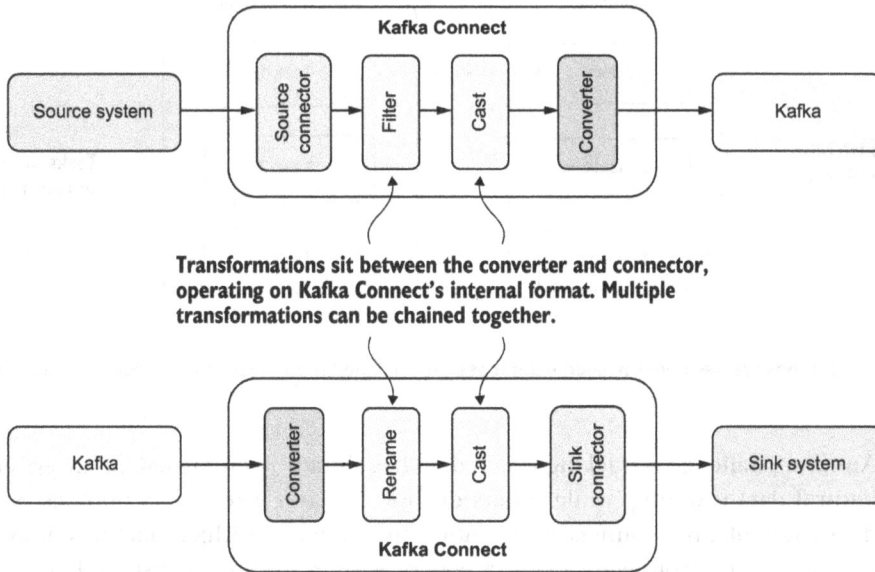

Figure 7.20   Transformations are stateless and can be chained together.

For more complex data transformations, a streaming framework like Kafka Streams or Apache Flink may be more appropriate. We'll explore complex data transformations further in chapter 8.

7.3.5 *Source connectors*

Source connectors pull data from external systems and load it into Kafka topics. They function as clients to these external systems, actively polling for data at regular intervals. For example, a connector may be configured to request data every five seconds.

Source connectors face two main challenges: how to load data in parallel, and how to determine whether data is new (i.e., how to identify data that has not yet been processed by the connector). Both challenges are specific to the external systems in use and typically cannot be solved in a generic way.

In Kafka Connect, the unit of parallelism is the task, with each task being assigned a different portion of work. Tasks are created when the connector starts, and the maximum number of tasks is defined in the connector's configuration. A key responsibility of a source connector is to devise a strategy for parallel data loading. For example, when loading data from CSV files, each file can be assigned to a different task. When loading data from a database, different tables can be assigned to separate tasks, as illustrated in figure 7.21.

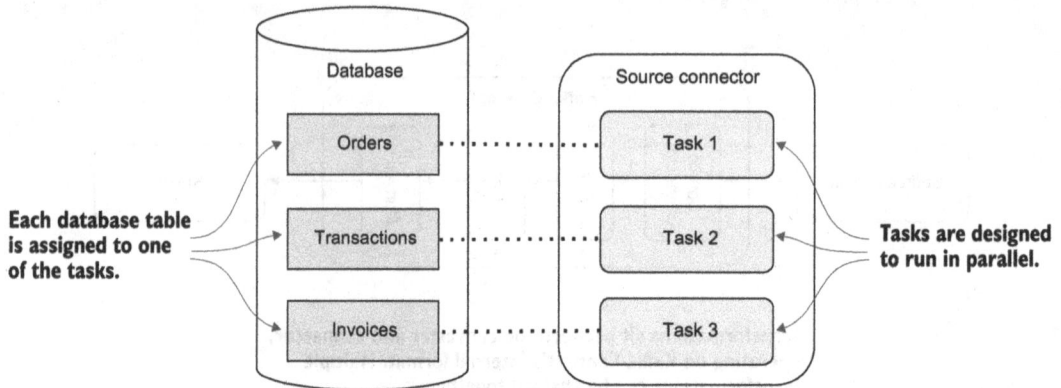

Figure 7.21   Database tables from the source database are assigned to the tasks in the source connector.

Another challenge is tracking which data has already been loaded. Some systems have natural data ordering, while others do not. In cases where data updates occur in a database table, the connector may not inherently know which data was modified. To handle this, the connector needs a type of *offset* in the source system. For example, a database table might include an updated_time column that records the timestamp of the latest data update. This timestamp then serves as an offset for the source connector, which stores it in Kafka's connect-offsets topic. Whenever the source connector loads data, it retrieves records with timestamps newer than the last stored offset. Figure 7.22 shows an example of this approach.

By design, source connectors retrieve data within each task, polling the external system at regular intervals. However, because connectors are Java-based applications, they also have the flexibility to spawn additional threads if more complex data exchange or asynchronous handling with the external system is required. For instance, a connector might launch a background thread to prefetch data, ensuring it is ready to be returned when the poll method is called.

A table of account balances. Each time the balance is updated, the update_time column is set to the current time.

Each time the connector queries the table, it records the maximum update_time as an offset in the connect-offsets topic.

These records were updated after the last stored offset, and they will be returned in the next query.

```
account id  balance   update_time
023544      2178.45   2024-10-05 10:15
003421      2028.45   2024-10-05 10:12
002897      1697.55   2024-10-05 10:09
004563      1497.25   2024-10-05 10:06
001234      1047.25   2024-10-05 10:04
002765      921.50    2024-10-05 10:00
003210      826.50    2024-10-05 09:57
004789      526.25    2024-10-05 09:54
001678      351.25    2024-10-05 09:51
003876      100.50    2024-10-05 09:48
```

```
BalanceConnector {
    update_time: "2024-10-05 10:04"
}
```

BalanceConnector

connect-offsets

balances

The source connector periodically queries for records, selecting rows that were updated after its last stored offset.

```
select * from balances
where update_ time > '2024-10-05 10:04'
```

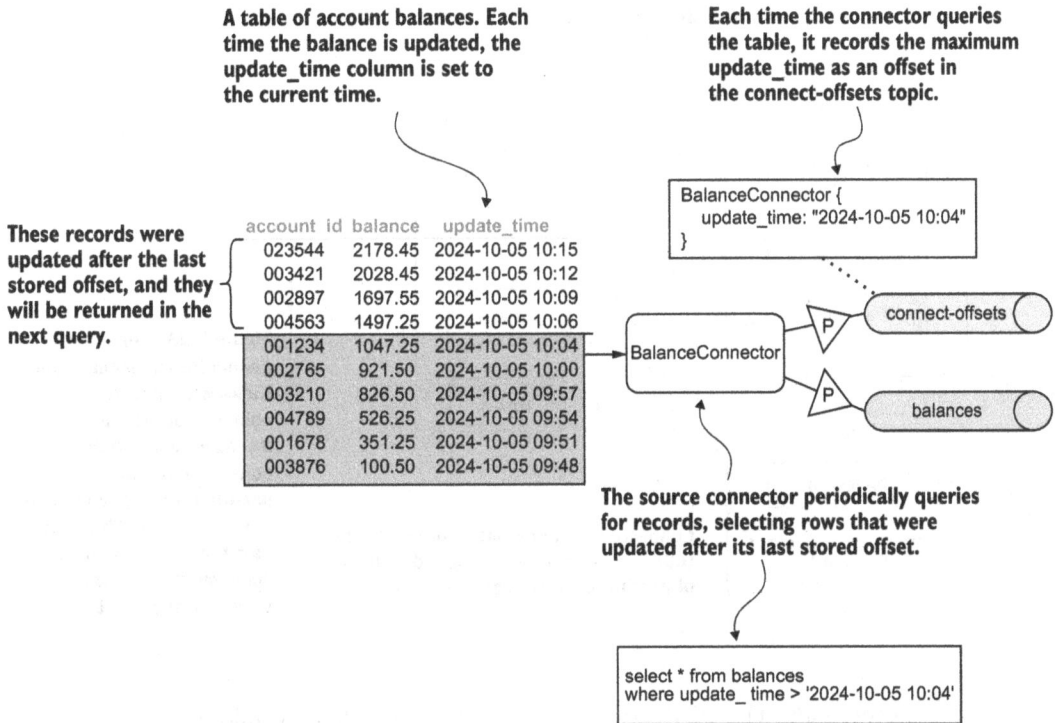

Figure 7.22 Update_time is used as an offset for BalanceConnector. Each time, the connector loads data that was updated after the stored offset.

7.3.6 Sink connectors

Unlike source connectors, sink connectors read data from Kafka, allowing them to utilize Kafka's native partitioning and offset tracking. Acting as Kafka consumers, sink connectors can assign different partitions to separate tasks, and Kafka offsets help determine which data has already been sent to the target system. Sink connectors are illustrated in figure 7.23.

Sink connectors can be configured to handle errors that occur when they cannot push data to an external system. For instance, if a sink connector reads data from Kafka and attempts to insert it into a database, an error might occur if the data violates database integrity constraints. This is considered a non-retriable error, meaning retrying the insertion won't resolve the issue, since the data itself must be corrected. Sink connectors have standard configuration options to manage such cases:

- *Fail the connector*—In this case, an exception is thrown, and the connector stops running. This failure state requires monitoring to address the problem.
- *Send messages to a dead-letter topic (DLT)*—The connector routes problematic messages to a special topic, known as a dead-letter topic, and continues processing

**Partitions are assigned
to the tasks.**

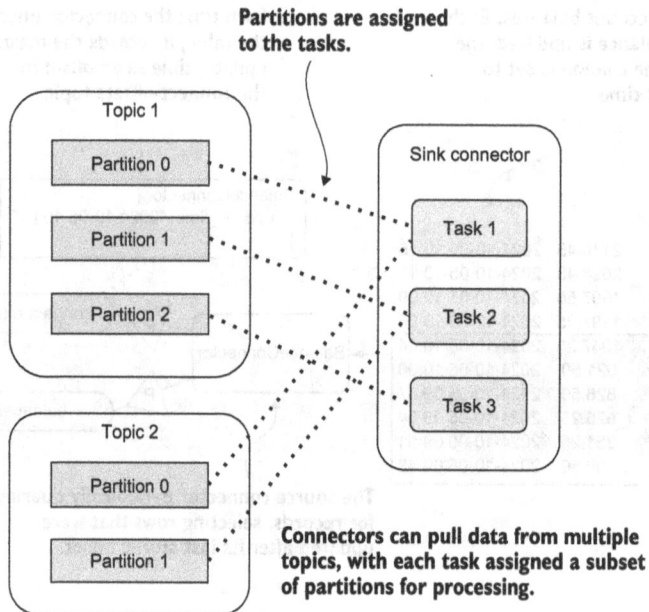

Figure 7.23   **Sink
connectors consume from
Kafka with partitions
balanced across tasks.
Because tasks share a
consumer group, each
partition is assigned to only
one task. Topic 2 has two
partitions, so only two tasks
consume it—task 3 gets no
topic 2 assignment.**

**Connectors can pull data from multiple
topics, with each task assigned a subset
of partitions for processing.**

other data. The DLT should be monitored, and alerts should be set up for when
messages are sent to it.

The typical pattern for sink connectors is to consume data from Kafka and push it to
external systems. However, since sink connectors are Java-based applications, they can
perform additional background tasks as needed.

7.3.7   *Changes in the incoming data structure*

Connectors are designed to be dynamic, adapting to changes in the structure of
incoming data. For instance, when loading database tables into Kafka, a source connector may load all tables from a specified schema. If new tables are added, the source
connector should detect these changes and reconfigure tasks to incorporate the new
tables. Source connectors also specify how to handle schema evolution. When the
input data schema changes (for example, with the addition of a new column in a database table), the auto.register.schemas property controls whether the serializer should
automatically register the new schema, ensuring that compatibility requirements are
maintained.

If changes cannot be handled dynamically, such as when a connector tries to register an incompatible schema, the connector will fail. These errors are challenging to
resolve, as they require stopping the connector, correcting the issue, and potentially
resetting source connector offsets.

For sink connectors, tasks must be prepared to handle changes in partitions and input
topics. Adding partitions to a topic triggers a consumer rebalance, reassigning partitions

to tasks. Adding new topics may require the creation of corresponding resources in the target system, such as additional database tables.

7.3.8 Integrating Kafka and databases

Integrating Kafka with relational databases is one of the most common tasks in enterprise data pipelines. Let's explore how this can be achieved, along with the available options and potential challenges.

One solution is to use JDBC source and sink connectors, which are available under a community license. As their name suggests, these connectors access databases through the JDBC protocol and support various database systems, as long as they are paired with the appropriate JDBC driver.

JDBC SOURCE CONNECTOR

The JDBC source connector loads data from a database into Kafka. It can operate with multiple tasks, assigning each table to a different task, and dynamically adapting to database schema changes (such as added or removed tables). Each table is mapped to a corresponding Kafka topic.

The source connector polls tables to capture updated data, with several options for tracking new records:

- *Bulk*—Periodically loads the entire table. This approach may produce duplicate entries, which consumers must handle. Since it loads the full table, it is unsuitable for large tables.
- *Incrementing*—Uses a column with incrementing values (typically a database sequence, which is used as a primary key) to track new records. This mode only detects inserts, making it ideal for immutable data but unable to track updates.
- *Timestamp*—Uses a timestamp column that updates whenever a row is modified, tracking rows by the last modified time.
- *Incrementing + Timestamp*—Combines incrementing and timestamp columns, identifying rows by both values for more accurate tracking.
- *Query*—Selects data using a custom query instead of polling the entire table. This mode can be used with incrementing or timestamp tracking, or the query itself must manage offset tracking. Additionally, query mode allows developers to join multiple tables directly in the query, enabling more complex data extraction scenarios such as enriching records or consolidating data from related tables.

Most standard data types convert seamlessly to `ConnectRecord`, though custom or database-specific types may require extra handling. The JDBC source connector does not support hard deletes; if a row is deleted from the database, the connector cannot detect this. However, soft deletes are possible by using a special column that flags rows as deleted.

JDBC SINK CONNECTOR

The JDBC sink connector writes data from Kafka into a target database. It can also run multiple tasks, each assigned to a subset of Kafka partitions, allowing for parallel writes. Each Kafka topic maps to a corresponding table in the database.

There are two modes for writing data:

- *Insert*—The connector generates INSERT statements.
- *Upsert*—Performs idempotent writes by either inserting a new row if no matching primary key exists or updating the row if it does.

When the sink connector encounters a tombstone message (a message with a null value), it deletes the record in the database that matches the specified key.

JDBC connectors can be somewhat restrictive, as they require specific table structures, including designated columns for tracking updates, and they do not support hard deletes.

INTEGRATION ALTERNATIVES

An alternative for integrating Kafka with databases is to use connectors that directly access the database's transaction logs, like Debezium (https://debezium.io). Instead of issuing SELECT queries, these connectors capture data directly from the transaction logs, bypassing the need for schema modifications and allowing them to capture all types of database changes, including inserts, updates, and deletes.

A significant drawback, however, is that the transaction log must be exposed to the connector, which can raise security concerns.

7.3.9 *Creating a connector for the Customer 360 ODS*

The idea of integrating data purely through configuration is appealing—it promises a quick setup with minimal development time and is worth experimenting with. For architects, it might be a nostalgic reminder of the days when data transfers were configured with a few well-placed scripts. From the data engineering perspective, however, there may be some concerns about the security of this approach. Working at such a low level may feel like it's exposing the entire database model directly to the integration layer, essentially bypassing data contracts. Isolating the integration work by setting up a separate cluster dedicated to Kafka Connect is a safer option.

Instead of the usual TransactionService, the architects of an ODS project like this may opt to use a source connector to load data directly from the database table into the TRANSACTIONS topic in Kafka. To do this, you'd install Kafka Connect, deploy the JDBC source plugin, and prepare the configuration, as shown in the following listing.

Listing 7.1   Configuration of the JDBC source connector

A short name for the connector class can be specified.

Maximum number of tasks. Here we have only one table, so it is 1.

A prefix for the topic. The whole name of the topic will be this prefix + the name of the table.

```
{ "name": "jdbc-source-transactions",
  "config":
    {"connector.class": "JdbcSource",
     "tasks.max": 1,
     "topic.prefix": "connect-",
     "connection.url": "jdbc:postgresql://postgres:5432/trans_db",
```

Connection to the database URL

```
                                          ┌─ Incrementing      The name of the column
                                          │  mode is used.      for incrementing
    "mode": "incrementing",         ◄─────┘         ┌─────
    "incrementing.column.name":"ID",          ◄─────┘
┌─► "value.converter": "io.confluent.connect.avro.AvroConverter",
│   "value.converter.schema.registry.url":"http://schema-registry:8081", ◄─┐
│   "table.whitelist" : "public.transactions",  ◄────┐                     │
│   "connection.user": "demo",                        │                    │
│   "connection.password" : "demo"                    │             URL for the
│   }                                                 │         Schema Registry
│ }                                   Table to be loaded ┘
│
Messages will be
serialized in Kafka in Avro.
```

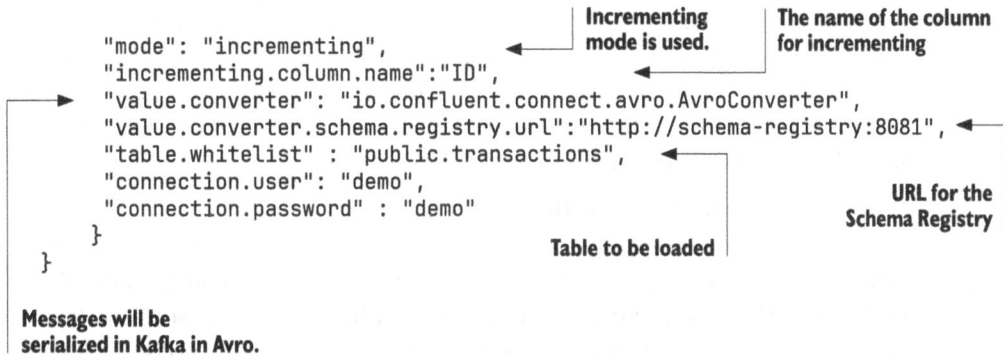

Now you can deploy this configuration to the Kafka Connect server via the REST API, and the connector will immediately begin transferring data from the database into Kafka.

Since transactions are immutable, the design team on this ODS uses an incrementing column, ID, to track and load new records efficiently.

7.3.10 Common Kafka Connect problems

Implementing data integrations with Kafka Connect significantly simplifies development; however, it also comes with certain drawbacks.

DATA TYPE MISMATCHES

Types in external systems often do not map directly to the types supported by Kafka serializers. While connectors attempt to find the best matches, certain types—such as enumerations, geospatial data, and complex structures like arrays or structs—require special handling and cannot be directly mapped. Even Boolean values may vary in representation, appearing as 0/1, Y/N, or true/false. For types without a direct representation in Kafka's supported formats, implementing custom serializers or message transformations is necessary.

DEFINING OFFSETS IN THE SOURCE SYSTEM

Using databases as an example, tracking which data has already been loaded into Kafka can be challenging. Some systems expose only the current state without providing mechanisms to track updated data. In such cases, a full data dump may be necessary, which is resource-intensive and can lead to duplicate records in Kafka.

PARALLELIZING LOADING OF DATA

Loading data in parallel is challenging in systems that lack natural partitioning. If a source system consists of a single large CSV file, splitting it into chunks for parallel loading may require manual processing, as the file itself lacks partitions. In these cases, connectors that cannot parallelize data loading are limited to a single task, which significantly impacts performance by restricting throughput.

IMBALANCE IN TASK DISTRIBUTION

Kafka Connect aims to distribute tasks evenly across workers, but achieving a balanced load is often challenging. For example, when loading database tables, the connector may assign an equal number of tables to each task. However, tables often vary significantly in the number of records or update frequency, leading to imbalanced workloads where some workers are underutilized while others are overloaded. This uneven distribution is a common challenge, especially in systems where data volumes and update rates differ widely across tasks.

CALCULATING MEMORY REQUIREMENTS

Estimating memory requirements for Kafka Connect is tricky, particularly in environments where multiple connectors are running simultaneously, each with unique workloads. Memory usage varies widely depending on factors such as data volume, connector type, task parallelism, and transformation complexity. For example, source connectors handling large batch loads or performing complex transformations may consume significantly more memory than lightweight connectors with minimal processing. Additionally, memory usage can fluctuate based on peak data flows and buffering needs, making it difficult to set precise resource allocations. As a result, memory planning for Kafka Connect often requires careful monitoring, tuning, and scaling to prevent bottlenecks and ensure stable performance across all connectors.

SCHEMA EVOLUTION AND POISON PILL MESSAGES

A serious issue in Kafka Connect is the presence of *poison pill messages*—messages that are corrupted or incompatible with one of the systems involved. For instance, if the schema in the source system changes (such as with the addition of a new column to a table), it may no longer align with the Avro schema expected in Kafka. As a result, attempts to write this message to the topic fail, causing the connector to stop, since source connectors lack dead-letter topic (DLT) support. Such errors require careful monitoring to ensure timely resolution.

For sink connectors, schema incompatibility with the target system is a common cause of failures. In this case, incompatible messages can be redirected to a DLT without interrupting the connector's operation. However, it's crucial to monitor and alert on these events to avoid data loss or processing delays.

This challenge is compounded by the fact that data replication in Kafka Connect operates at a granular level, replicating the data field by field rather than as an abstract service or high-level entity. This fine-grained replication requires precise schema alignment across all participating systems. As a result, coordinating schema changes becomes a significant challenge, as each system must be aware of and prepared for updates as they occur.

MANAGEMENT OF DLT

When a sink connector encounters non-retriable errors, messages may be sent to a DLT. However, Kafka does not provide built-in management for DLTs, so all processes involving this topic require custom implementations. It falls to the operations team to establish monitoring for the DLT and to determine how to handle messages that accumulate there.

Non-retriable errors can stem from various issues. For instance, a message may have an incompatible schema and be redirected to the DLT. Once the target system's schema is updated—often by the team responsible for that system—the messages resume processing successfully. However, messages sent to the DLT are lost from the main flow, creating a partial data loss. This makes it challenging to restore the original event order and reapply messages correctly. In such cases, teams frequently implement reconciliation processes, and in some cases, they may need to reload the entire dataset from scratch.

7.4 Ensuring delivery guarantees

One of the most serious concerns in asynchronous message transfer is the risk of undetected data loss. If there's a suspicion that data has been lost, pinpointing the issue can be challenging. Several scenarios could lead to data loss:

- The message was never sent by the producer system.
- The message was not written to Kafka brokers, and the lack of acknowledgment was not properly handled.
- The message was written to Kafka and acknowledged by the leader, but the leader failed before replicating the message to followers.
- The message was deleted due to the retention policy before it was consumed.
- The message was consumed, the offset was committed, but an exception occurred during processing that was not properly handled.

The common solution is to trace messages throughout the entire pipeline, logging each step. However, tracing a high volume of messages can be resource-intensive.

Another challenge is the potential for duplicates in Kafka. If a batch of messages is published and acknowledged, but the acknowledgment is lost, the producer may resend the batch, which leads to duplicate messages. Duplicates can also occur on the consumer side if the consumer fails before committing offsets of processed data, causing previously processed data to be read again.

Kafka provides certain guarantees to prevent data loss and duplication when specific criteria are met. Let's examine these guarantees in detail.

7.4.1 Producer idempotence

Producer idempotency in Kafka prevents duplicate and out-of-order messages by ensuring that each message is written only once to a partition, even if retries occur. Idempotency addresses several potential problems, such as these:

- *Duplicate messages*—If a batch of messages is sent and acknowledged by the broker, but the acknowledgment is lost, the producer might resend the batch. Without idempotency, this would lead to duplicate messages.
- *Out-of-order messages*—If a producer sends multiple batches to the same partition, batch order can become disrupted if acknowledgments fail. For example,
  a The producer sends batch 1, which fails to acknowledge.
  b The producer then sends batch 2, which is successfully acknowledged.
  c If batch 1 is resent and written after batch 2, the messages are stored out of order in the partition.

In earlier Kafka versions, setting `max.in.flight.requests.per.connection` (number of unacknowledged requests) to 1 helped avoid out-of-order messages by ensuring only one batch could be in flight per partition. However, recent Kafka versions (starting from 0.11.0) have made idempotency simpler and more robust with the default setting of `enable.idempotence=true`. This setting causes Kafka to assign each producer a unique identifier and each batch a monotonically increasing sequence number for each partition. When a broker receives a batch, it expects a specific sequence number:

- If the sequence number matches, the batch is written, and the broker updates the expected sequence.
- If a batch arrives with an out-of-sequence number, the broker detects this and throws a retriable exception, allowing the producer to retry sending the batches in the correct order.

Kafka's idempotency requires a few additional configuration settings:

- `max.in.flight.requests.per.connection`—Set to 5 or fewer to avoid concurrency issues.
- `retries`—Set to a positive number, allowing retries on transient errors.
- `acks`—Set to `all`, ensuring data is acknowledged only after replication across all in-sync replicas.

These configurations ensure that Kafka can maintain a strict order of events in each partition and prevent duplicate messages, providing the highest level of message delivery guarantee. The sequence numbers and producer identifiers operate internally and are not accessible via the Kafka API.

7.4.2   Understanding Kafka transactions

One of the most common questions is whether Kafka supports transactions. Before answering, let's clarify what we mean by a transaction. In databases, *transactions* are processes that adhere to four key properties, known as ACID:

- *Atomicity*—Ensures that all operations within a transaction are completed successfully, or none are. If any part of the transaction fails, the entire transaction is rolled back, preventing partial updates.
- *Consistency*—Ensures that transactions take the system from one valid state to another, maintaining data integrity based on defined rules or constraints.
- *Isolation*—Guarantees that transactions are executed independently, so intermediate states are not visible to other concurrent transactions.
- *Durability*—Ensures that once a transaction is committed, its changes are permanent, even in the event of a system failure.

In Kafka, transactions are slightly different. Kafka's transactions are designed specifically for stream processing applications in a read-process-write pipeline, where an application reads events from a topic, processes them, and produces results to one or more output topics. Kafka transactions guarantee *exactly-once semantics* in this pipeline, meaning each input event is processed exactly once, with outputs produced only once, even in the event of retries or failures.

Figure 7.24 illustrates this with an example. Suppose we have an OrderService that reads data from the ORDERS topic, processes it, and produces events to three output topics: SHIPMENTS, BILLING, and INVENTORY. Enabling exactly-once semantics ensures that for each incoming Order event, the service generates precisely one corresponding Shipment event, one Billing event, and one Inventory event, even in cases of service failure. In this setup, exactly-once processing is essential. Duplicating or skipping any Order event would lead to incorrect downstream data and significant discrepancies.

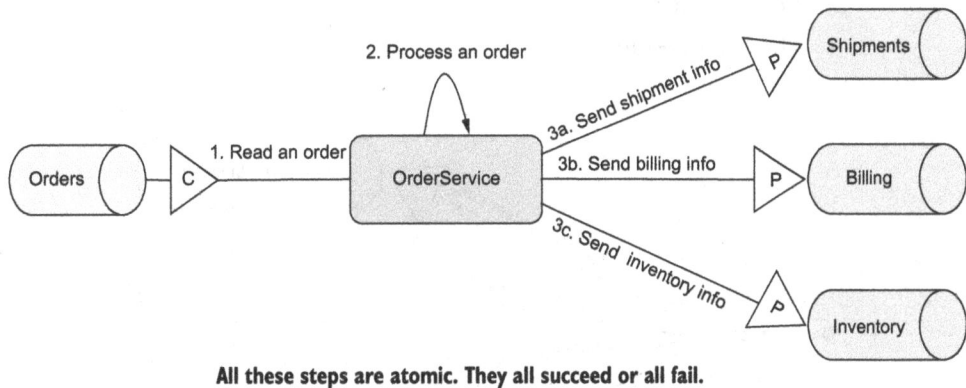

All these steps are atomic. They all succeed or all fail.

Figure 7.24 OrderService reads, processes, and writes each event atomically.

Here's how exactly-once semantics ensures consistency in this scenario:

- *Read*—The service reads order data from the ORDERS topic. Each order event includes details such as product information, quantity, payment amount, and shipping details.
- *Process*—The service processes each order, generating three different events based on the incoming data.
- *Write*—The service then writes three output events:
  - Shipment—Contains information for shipping the order.
  - Billing—Contains information for invoicing the order.
  - Inventory—Contains information for updating inventory levels.

With exactly-once semantics enabled, Kafka guarantees that all three events (Shipment, Billing, and Inventory) appear exactly once per each incoming order, even if retries occur. This transactional setup ensures atomicity for the entire read-process-write cycle, meaning the operation is all or nothing: either all events are successfully processed and written, or none are. If the service fails before commit, none of the outcoming events are visible and the input will be reprocessed.

Kafka ensures this behavior by enabling atomic writes across multiple partitions, as shown in figure 7.25. The process requires atomic confirmation of both reading the input and producing the output. Confirming that data has been read is equivalent to performing a write to the `__consumer_offsets` topic, which marks the offset at which processing occurred. To achieve atomicity, a transaction must perform atomic writes to the following:

- The `__consumer_offsets` topic to confirm the read and processing of the `Order` event
- The `SHIPMENTS` topic
- The `BILLING` topic
- The `INVENTORY` topic

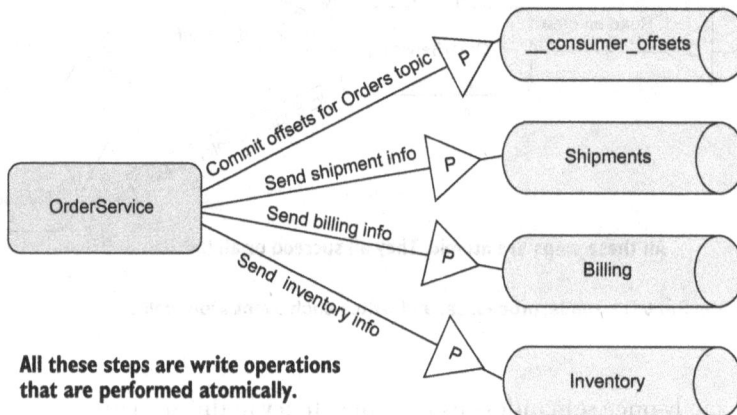

Figure 7.25   A transaction involves writing atomically to all four topics.

All these operations must succeed together or all fail together. Kafka transactions allow these operations to be executed as a single atomic unit, ensuring exactly-once processing throughout the pipeline.

While transactions in Kafka were originally designed for stream-processing frameworks, where they are managed automatically, this feature can also be utilized independently. Any producer application can use Kafka's transaction API to send multiple messages atomically. Using methods such as `beginTransaction`, `commitTransaction`, and `abortTransaction`, producers can group multiple writes into a single atomic operation, as illustrated in figure 7.26. This flexibility makes Kafka transactions a powerful tool for ensuring consistent state changes across multiple topics, even outside the context of stream processing.

Kafka's transaction mechanism seamlessly integrates the process of writing and reading transactional messages. While the producer API enables atomic writes across multiple partitions, the way these messages are consumed depends on the isolation level configured for the consumer. The `isolation.level` consumer property has two possible values:

- `read_committed` (default)—Returns only committed transactional messages, filtering out any aborted messages.
- `read_uncommitted`—Returns all messages, including both committed and aborted transactional messages.

Nontransactional messages are returned in both modes. Figure 7.27 demonstrates the difference between these isolation levels.

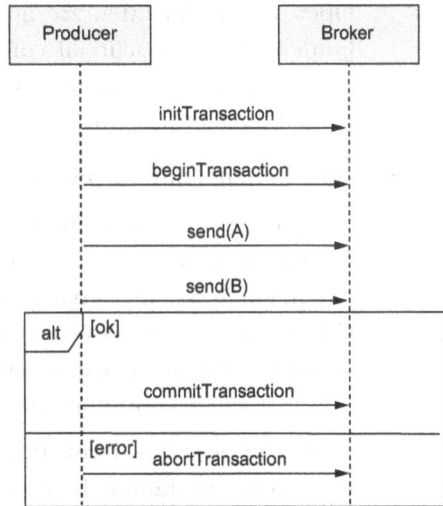

Figure 7.26 Creating a transaction using ClientAPI. Both send operations are part of a single transaction, ensuring that they either both succeed or both fail atomically.

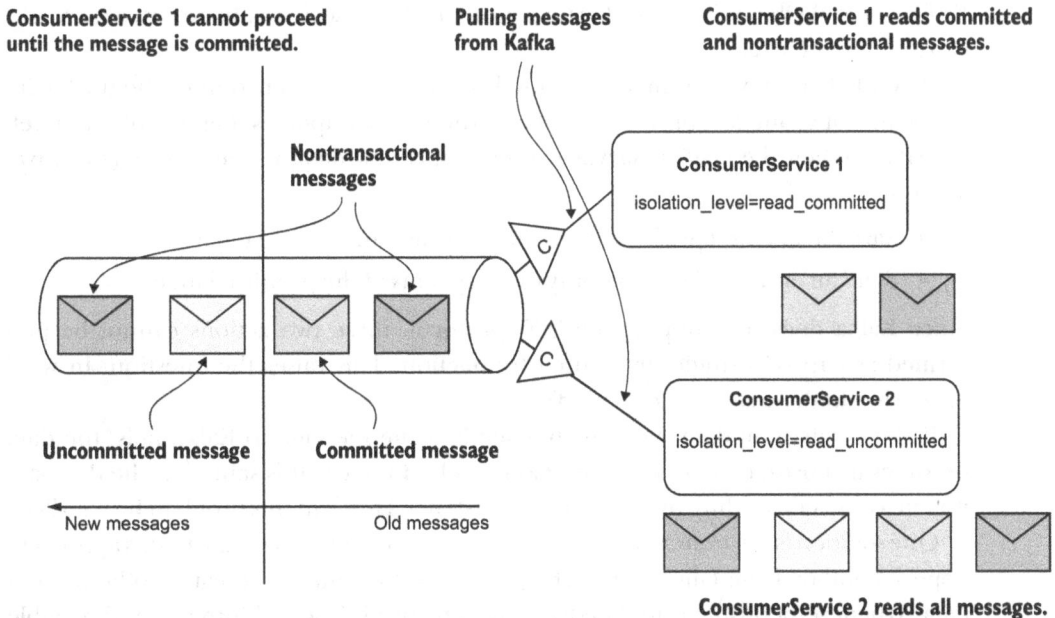

Figure 7.27 Isolation levels determine whether consumers can read uncommitted messages. This figure shows two consumers with different isolation settings.

Open transactions that are neither committed nor aborted can cause performance bottlenecks. Transactional consumers encountering uncommitted messages cannot proceed and must wait until the transaction is completed. If the producer does not commit or abort the transaction, it will eventually be aborted due to a timeout.

7.4.3   *Transactional outbox pattern*

A common question is whether Kafka can participate in distributed transactions that involve multiple systems. *Distributed transactions* are transactions that span multiple independent systems or databases, ensuring that all operations across these systems are either completed successfully or none are, maintaining consistency across the distributed environment. The most widely used protocol for this is the *two-phase commit* (2PC) protocol, which coordinates transactions in two main steps:

- *Prepare*—The transaction manager sends a "prepare" request to each participant, prompting them to complete their part of the transaction. Each participant responds with either a "ready to commit" or a "failure" message.

- *Commit*—If all participants are ready, the transaction manager sends a "commit" request to finalize the transaction. If any participant fails, the transaction manager issues a request to abort the transaction for all participants, ensuring consistency by rolling back.

Currently, Kafka does not support the 2PC protocol. However, support for distributed transactions is proposed in KIP-939 (https://cwiki.apache.org/confluence/display/KAFKA/KIP-939%3A+Support+Participation+in+2PC), which aims to introduce 2PC capabilities in Kafka.

When Kafka is involved in a distributed process, we often encounter the dual-write problem. For example, consider a scenario where a user updates their profile via a web interface. When the ProfileService receives this new data, it needs to perform two actions:

- Save the updated profile data to the internal transactional database.

- Send an event to Kafka to notify other systems of the profile change.

Since Kafka does not support the 2PC protocol, these two actions cannot be performed as part of a single distributed transaction. This raises the question: In what order should these steps be executed?

If the database update succeeds but sending the message to Kafka fails, the data becomes inconsistent across systems. Conversely, if the event is sent first, the database update could fail, leading to a similar inconsistency. How can this problem be handled?

One solution is the *transactional outbox* pattern, shown in figure 7.28. In this approach, a special outbox table (shown as ProfileEvents in the figure) is created to hold event data. Whenever a profile is updated, an event record is inserted into the outbox table within the same database transaction. This ensures that either both steps succeed, or both are rolled back together. A separate process then monitors the outbox table and

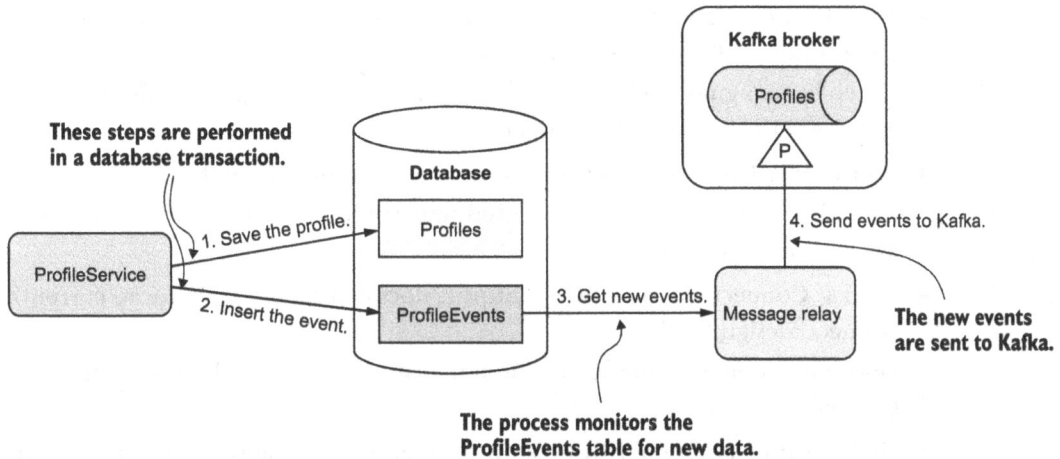

Figure 7.28 When the transactional outbox pattern is used, a separate process (step 4 in the figure) publishes events to Kafka.

sends new events to Kafka, retrying until successful. After sending, it either deletes the successfully published events from the table or tracks the last sent event ID.

In essence, this pattern shifts the dual-write problem to the outbox cleanup process, which lacks an inherent guarantee that event deletion and publishing to Kafka will be atomic. If deletion and publishing are not perfectly synchronized, this could result in duplicate messages in Kafka if messages are resent, or orphaned records in the outbox if cleanup fails.

In cases where cleanup or sending fails, duplicate events may be published, which can be managed by designing consumers to handle idempotent processing. Additionally, many teams implement reconciliation processes or, if necessary, a complete data reload to ensure consistency.

The transactional outbox is often implemented as a separate microservice process. However, with Kafka, it may be beneficial to implement this process as a Kafka connector using Kafka Connect, which can monitor the outbox table and handle event publishing efficiently.

7.5 Online resources

- "What is a Service Mesh?" https://konghq.com/blog/learning-center/what-is-a-service-mesh
  A tutorial-style overview explaining the purpose and core concepts of a service mesh.
- "Kafka Mesh filter": www.envoyproxy.io/docs/envoy/latest/configuration/listeners/network_filters/kafka_mesh_filter
  Documentation describing Envoy's Kafka mesh filter and how to configure it.

- "Synchronous Kafka: Using Spring Request-Reply": https://dzone.com/articles/synchronous-kafka-using-spring-request-reply-1

  A step-by-step guide to building a synchronous request-reply workflow in Kafka with Spring's request-reply template.

- "Discover Kafka: connectors and more": www.confluent.io/hub

  A marketplace of officially supported and community-built Kafka connectors available for download.

- "Kafka Connect Architecture": https://docs.confluent.io/platform/current/connect/design.html

  Documentation explaining the design principles and architecture of Kafka Connect.

- "Kafka Connect Deep Dive—Converters and Serialization Explained": www.confluent.io/blog/kafka-connect-deep-dive-converters-serialization-explained

  A detailed explanation of how converters and serialization work inside Kafka Connect.

- "Transactions in Apache Kafka": www.confluent.io/blog/transactions-apache-kafka

  A guide to Kafka's transactional model, including exactly-once semantics and producer guarantees.

- "KIP-939: Support Participation in 2PC": https://cwiki.apache.org/confluence/display/KAFKA/KIP-939%3A+Support+Participation+in+2PC

  A Kafka Improvement Proposal outlining support for integrating Kafka producers into two-phase commit (2PC) transactions.

Summary

- Kafka is best suited for publish-subscribe, event-driven architectures, rather than traditional request-response models.

- Kafka follows a "smart endpoints, dumb pipes" model, where message processing logic is handled at endpoints, leaving Kafka as a pure transport layer.

- The service mesh does not fully align with Kafka's client libraries; however, experimental solutions, such as Kafka mesh filters, are emerging to bridge this gap.

- Kafka supports CQRS well, separating read and write operations across services and enabling event-driven updates to query models.

- Kafka supports event sourcing, but snapshotting is often necessary to optimize data restoration performance for consumers.

- Kafka can support data mesh architectures by enabling decentralized data ownership, data-as-a-product principles, federated governance, and self-serve data platforms.

- Kafka Connect simplifies data integration with source and sink connectors, though managing schema evolution and handling errors (e.g., poison pill messages) can be challenging.
- Kafka's exactly-once semantics ensures that data is processed exactly once per transaction in a read, process, write pipeline, maintaining atomicity across multipartition writes.
- Kafka does not currently support two-phase commit (2PC) but may offer this in the future (e.g., KIP-939); the transactional outbox pattern is often used as a workaround.

Designing streaming applications

8

This chapter covers

- Real-time processing
- Designing streaming applications
- The architecture of the Kafka Streams framework
- Exploring ksqlDB and Apache Flink for real-time data processing

To implement real-time processing use cases, you need a clear grasp of the underlying building blocks for streaming on Kafka so you can create a plan for transforming and aggregating the system data. In particular, you need to know when, where, and how to transform, join, and aggregate events as they arrive. The big decision to make at this point is whether to use a dedicated stream-processing framework or traditional service code. If you decide to use Kafka Streams, you'll need to understand its processing model, including stateless operators like map and filter as well as stateful capabilities such as joins, windowing, and aggregations. The Processor API is useful when you want to implement custom logic, such as if you want to invoke an external service to detect anomalies in events.

There are, of course, alternatives to Kafka Streams, and we'll also look at when it might make more sense to use ksqlDB, Apache Flink, or managed cloud services.

Field notes: Transforming data in motion

Back at work, the ODS team turns to the question of how to transform and aggregate their data in the Customer 360 project.

Eva: Since we're doing all this research, I think it's worth considering transforming the data not just at the final service but somewhere in the middle. We could use a streaming framework for that.

Max: A streaming framework? What do you mean by that, Eva?

Eva: Let's take our Customer 360 service as an example. Instead of doing the aggregation and joins in the final service that reads from Kafka, we could introduce an intermediate service. This service would join the data—like transactions and customer profiles—and produce an aggregated result back into Kafka. The final service would just read the ready-made aggregated data.

Max: What's the point? I don't see how the intermediate results would be useful to any other service.

Rob: It's not just about the results, Max. The real benefit is in how the joining is done. Frameworks like Kafka Streams make this much easier because they provide tools for joining streaming data, aggregating objects in memory, and backing everything up to Kafka seamlessly. You don't need to reinvent the wheel.

Max: Hmm . . . another service with more Java code, huh? Sounds like we're complicating things again.

Rob: That's the beauty of it, Max. It doesn't have to be Java. You can define transformations in simpler ways, even using SQL-like approaches.

Max: SQL, you say? Well, now you're speaking my language. That does sound more manageable. But we'll need to be sure it's worth the extra step.

Eva: If it makes joining and aggregating easier, then it's worth exploring. Let's give it a try.

8.1 Introducing Kafka Streams

In chapter 5, we discussed when to use real-time data processing. Now let's delve into the technical aspects of these kinds of applications. Figure 8.1 provides a helicopter view of a streaming application, abstracted from any specific implementation framework.

Consider an application that enriches each `Order` with information about the customer who placed it, producing a composite enriched order as its output. This application, which we'll refer to as `OrderEnrichmentService`, processes a stream of incoming `Order` events and `Customer` events to maintain an up-to-date view of customer information.

**OrderEnrichmentService joins incoming Order events
with customer data and produces EnrichedOrder events.**

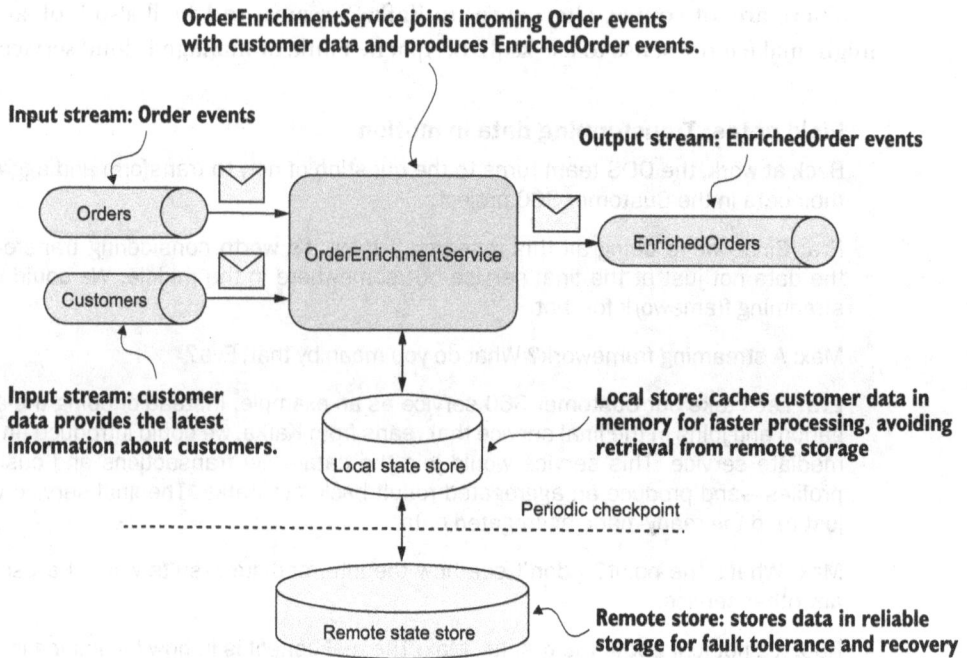

Figure 8.1   Example of a real-time streaming application. OrderEnrichmentService **processes** Order
events by enriching them with customer data, producing EnrichedOrder **events as the output.**

When OrderEnrichmentService receives a new Order event, it extracts the customer
identifier from the event and uses this ID to retrieve the corresponding customer
information from the local state store, which is continuously updated (or fed) by the
Customer data stream. In streaming frameworks, a local state store is a stateful storage mechanism that resides on the same node as the processing logic. It allows for
fast, in-memory lookups, minimizing latency when enriching events. Additionally, this
in-memory data is periodically synchronized with a remote state store for fault tolerance and recovery, ensuring reliability and consistency even in the case of failures.

Stream processing refers to the continuous processing of an unbounded flow of data as
it is generated, enabling real-time or near real-time insights and actions. The idea of such
applications is to process incoming events immediately as they arrive and produce output
results with minimal latency. Different frameworks for real-time processing handle this
scenario in various ways, utilizing diverse sources for incoming events, different technologies for local and remote state stores, and varied mechanisms for emitting output events.

Since this book is dedicated to Kafka, we will focus primarily on the Kafka Streams
framework (https://kafka.apache.org/documentation/streams/), which seamlessly
integrates into the Kafka ecosystem. While this book does not cover all the details of
streaming programming, it aims to provide a clear understanding of the architecture
and key concepts of real-time stream processing.

Before we dive into the architectural details, let's first examine how real-time processing compares to the more familiar batch processing and extract, transform, load (ETL) pipelines.

8.1.1 ETL, ELT, and stream processing

Let's consider three main paradigms for data transformation:

- *Extract, transform, load* (ETL)—Extracts data, transforms it in a staging area, and loads it into the target system
- *Extract, load, transform* (ELT)—Extracts and loads data into a target system, and then transforms it there
- *Stream processing*—Processes data in real time as it arrives

These paradigms represent different approaches within the broader framework of data collection and processing. Their shared objective is to collect data from various sources, perform operations to prepare and transform that data for analysis, and present the results in a form that enables actionable insights or further processing. Figure 8.2 illustrates an example of the ETL process.

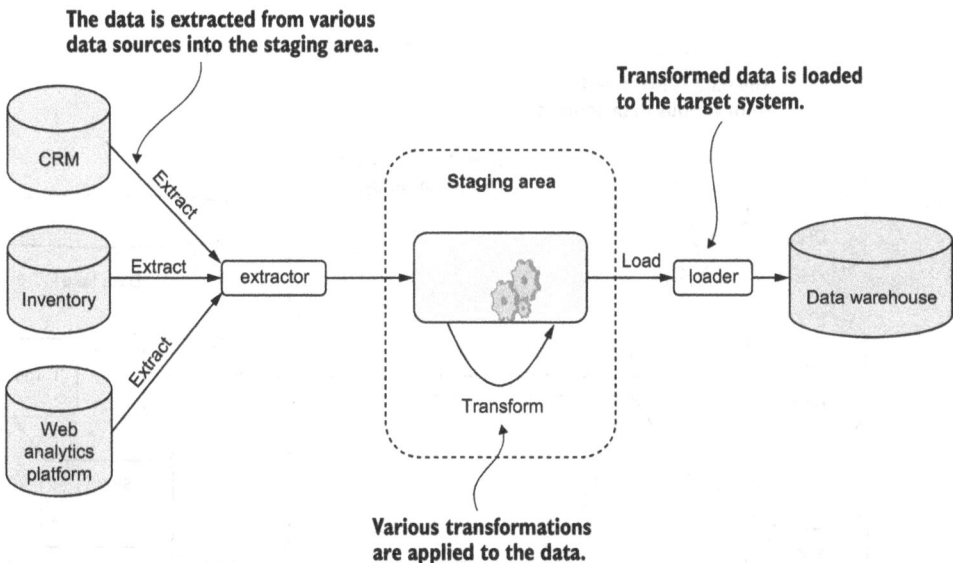

Figure 8.2 An example of the ETL process. Data is loaded from various data sources into the staging area, transformed there, and then loaded into the target system.

In a traditional ETL workflow, data is collected from various data sources and temporarily stored in an intermediate area known as the *staging area*. Within this staging area, multiple transformations can be applied to the data:

- *Data cleansing*—Removing errors, inconsistencies, and inaccuracies
- *Filtering*—Excluding irrelevant or unnecessary records
- *Data aggregation*—Summarizing data for downstream use
- *Format conversion*—Transforming data into a structure compatible with the target system

Once the data has been fully transformed and aligned with the target system's format, it is loaded into the target system for storage and analysis. ETL processes are typically scheduled to run periodically (e.g., daily or hourly) and process data in batches.

There are several common use cases for ETL:

- Loading data into data warehouses
- Performing historical data analysis
- Supporting reporting and business intelligence (BI) needs

With the rise of cloud-based solutions for data lakes, which offer extensive built-in data processing capabilities, ELT (extract, load, transform) solutions have gained significant popularity. In ELT (illustrated in figure 8.3), data is extracted from various data sources and loaded directly into the target system in its raw form. Transformations are then performed within the target system, using its computational power.

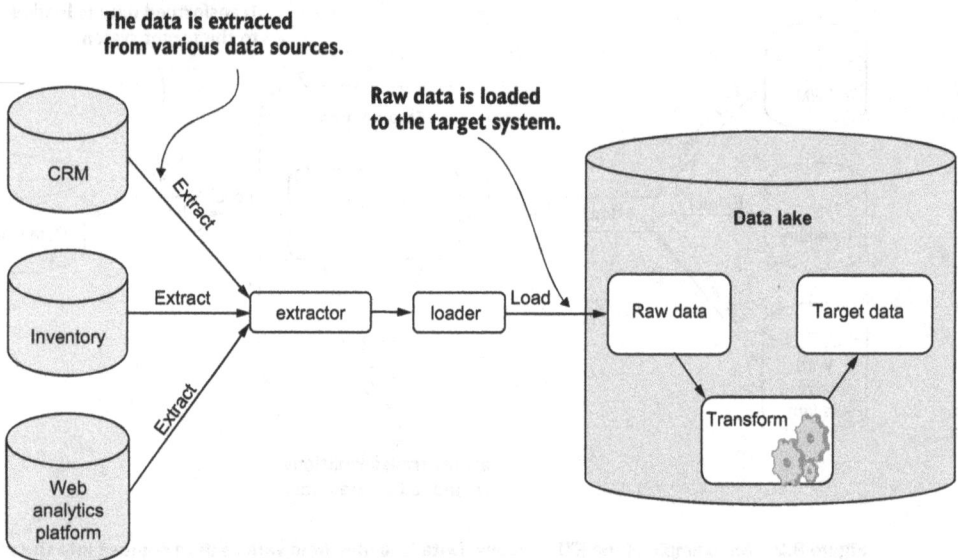

Figure 8.3 In the ELT process, transformation happens on the side of the target system.

The key difference between ETL and ELT lies in the location of the transformation step: in ETL, transformations occur in a transient (or temporary) staging area, whereas in ELT, they happen in the target system. Like ETL, ELT processes are typically scheduled to run periodically. They are highly scalable, capable of handling large datasets, and work effectively with both structured and unstructured data.

With a stream-processing approach, illustrated in figure 8.4, the application captures incoming events, processes them in real time, and produces output events as a result.

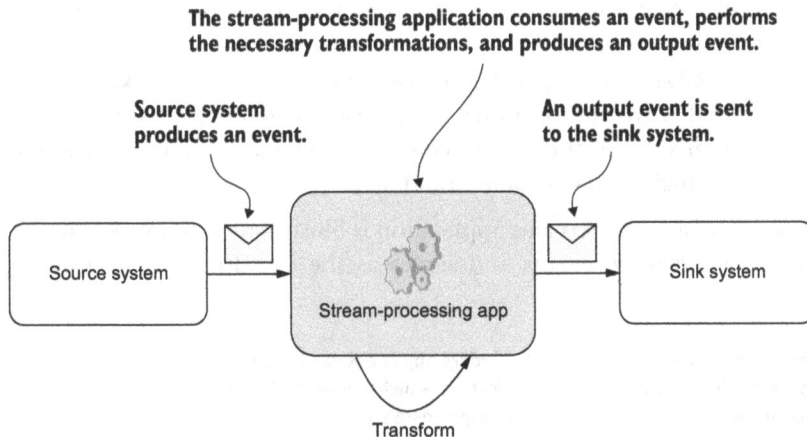

Figure 8.4 An example of a stream-processing application where data is processed event-by-event in real time, rather than being periodically loaded in batches

It is not entirely accurate to consider stream processing as fundamentally different or opposed to ETL, because streaming also follows the same basic steps:

1 *Extract*—Read an event as it arrives from an external source.

2 *Transform*—Process the event, such as filtering, format conversion, or aggregation.

3 *Load*—Send the processed event to an output system.

The primary distinction between stream processing and traditional ETL lies in *latency*. Unlike ETL, where data is processed in periodic batches, stream-processing applications handle data as soon as it becomes available, ensuring low latency and processing in near real-time.

It is also worth noting that stream processing and batch processing are often presented as opposing paradigms. However, under the hood, Kafka still consumes and produces data in batches. The key difference lies in the batch size and how it is managed: in stream processing, these batches are typically small and transparent to the application, which processes data one record at a time, giving the appearance of continuous, event-by-event processing.

Various frameworks are available for stream processing; in this book, we will primarily focus on the Kafka Streams framework, but we will also touch on some alternatives.

8.1.2   *The Kafka Streams framework*

Stream-processing applications built using the Kafka Streams framework have the following key aspects:

- *Server-side application*—These applications are implemented in Java. Frameworks like Spring Boot are commonly used, but other approaches can also be applied based on project requirements.
- *Kafka Streams as a library*—Kafka Streams is a Java library, integrated as a dependency within the application.
- *Event workflows*—The application consumes events from Kafka topics, processes them, and sends the resulting events back to Kafka topics. If events originate from other sources, they must first be sent to Kafka, and the same applies to sink systems, which must consume from Kafka.

The structure of a Kafka Streams application is illustrated in figure 8.5. Kafka is always the source of incoming events and serves as the sink for processed events, so the

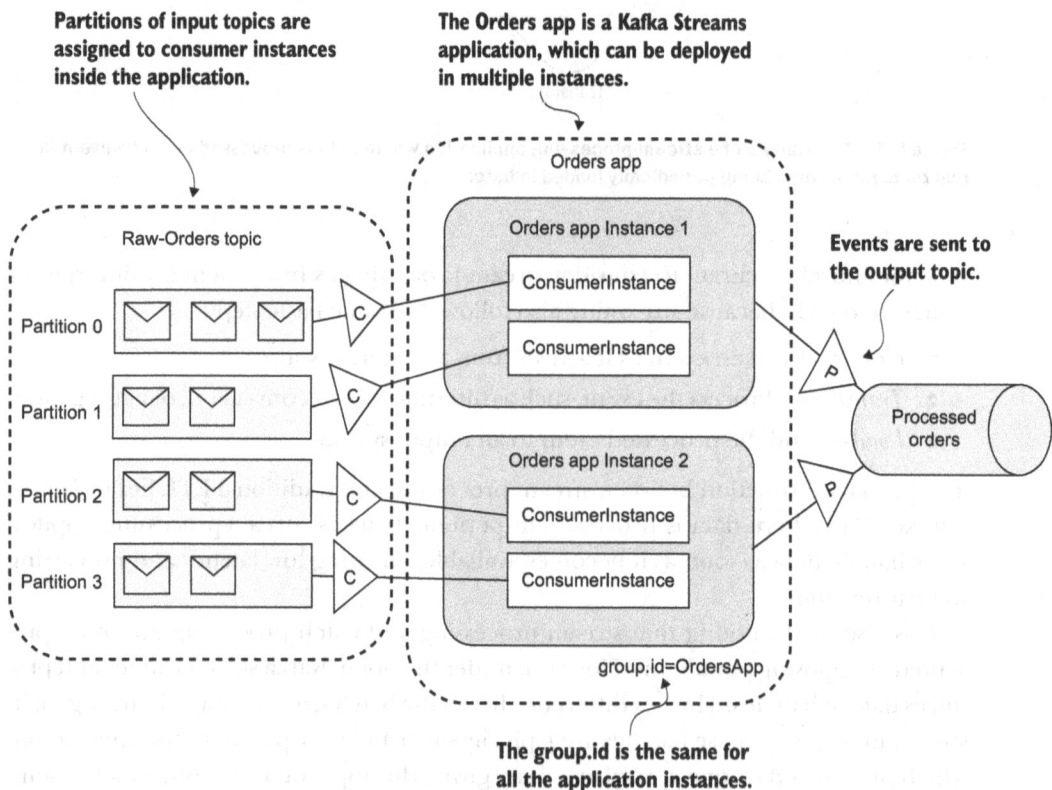

Figure 8.5   The Orders app is a Kafka Streams application that reads raw orders from an input topic, processes them, and sends the processed results to an output topic. It can be deployed in multiple instances, all of which operate as part of a single consumer group.

application functions as both a consumer and a producer. The application can be deployed in multiple instances, all sharing the same group.id. These instances collectively form a consumer group, with each instance assigned one or more partitions from the input topics, using Kafka's natural parallelism for distributed processing.

The instances of the streaming application, shown in figure 8.5, can be added or removed dynamically. However, the true scalability of the application is tied to the number of partitions in the input topics. Since each partition can be processed by only one consumer instance at a time, the total number of parallel processing units across all application instances is limited by the number of partitions.

If an application instance fails, a consumer rebalance is triggered, redistributing the partitions among the remaining active consumers to ensure uninterrupted processing. This resilience and fault-tolerance make Kafka Streams applications an excellent fit for microservice architectures.

8.1.3 Benefits of using Kafka Streams

If a streaming application uses Kafka as the input and output for events, why do we need a framework for this application? Why can't we read events with a usual consumer, process them in Java code, and then write them back with a producer? We could implement it that way, but using Kafka Streams brings several benefits:

- *A domain-specific language* (DSL)—Kafka Streams provides high-level constructs for operations like transforming, filtering, and aggregating data. These constructs allow programs to be implemented without worrying about low-level Kafka details, such as managing offsets or partitions. Kafka Streams provides two core abstractions: KStream, for processing continuous streams of events, and KTable, for managing stateful, table-like views of data that update with incoming events. To get an understanding of what a Kafka Streams program looks like, look at listing 8.1, which shows a program that performs filtering and mapping. Instead of manually creating producers and consumers, we simply specify the condition for filtering and the mapping logic for transforming fields into another object.

- *Powerful stateful processing*—For stateful aggregations, such as counting the number of orders in real time, Kafka Streams offers a transparent way to manage state, automatically persisting it into Kafka topics as fault-tolerant storage. This simplifies development by eliminating the need for custom state management.

- *Feature-rich time-based operations*—In streaming applications, aggregations are often performed over specific time windows rather than the entire stream. For example, when counting orders, we are typically more interested in the number of orders per hour or per day than in the total number of orders from the start of the stream. Kafka Streams provides robust constructs for handling various types of windows, such as tumbling, hopping, and sliding, making time-based aggregations straightforward.

- *Exactly-once semantics* (EoS)—Kafka Streams natively supports exactly-once processing, ensuring that each record is processed exactly once, even in failure scenarios.

This eliminates the need for custom deduplication logic, which can be challenging to implement when working directly with raw Kafka consumers and producers.

Listing 8.1   `OrderApp` performing filtering and mapping of orders

```
public class OrderApp {
    public static void main(String[] args) {
        Properties props = new Properties(); //          ◀── Define Kafka Streams
        ...                                                   properties.

        StreamsBuilder builder = new StreamsBuilder(); //    ◀── Build the topology.

        KStream<String, String> ordersStream = builder.stream("raw-
    orders"); //                                         ◀──
                                                              Read from the
        KStream<String, String> processedOrders = ordersStream    raw-orders topic.
            .filter((key, value) -> {                    ◀──
                Order order = Order.fromJson(value);          Filter orders with total
                return order.getTotalAmount() >= 50;          amount >= 50.
            })
            .mapValues(value -> { //                     ◀──
                Order order = Order.fromJson(value);          Map the order to a
                return String.format("{\"orderId\": \"%s\",   simplified format.
                    \"customerId\": \"%s\"}",
                    order.getOrderId(), order.getCustomerId());
            });                                          ◀──
                                                              Write the results to the
        processedOrders.to("processed-orders"); //       ◀──  processed-orders topic.
        KafkaStreams streams = new KafkaStreams(builder.build(), props);
        streams.start();
        Runtime.getRuntime().addShutdownHook(new Thread(streams::close));
    }
}
```

Next, we'll delve into the various operations commonly used in streaming applications and explore how Kafka Streams supports them from an architectural perspective.

8.2   Sketching out the ODS with Kafka Streams

Back in chapter 2, we saw the first sketch of the updated service design for the ODS example, reproduced here in figure 8.6. As you can see, `Customer360Service` was responsible for aggregating data, storing all results in a relational database, and exposing a REST API for client access.

In the new design, a streaming service called `CustomerJoinService` has been introduced. This service performs real-time joins of customer data and produces enriched, ready-to-use records in the `Customer360-enriched` topic. The updated design, depicted in figure 8.7, shows this new approach.

The `Customer360-enriched` topic is configured to use log compaction, meaning Kafka will retain only the latest message for each customer ID key, discarding older ones over time. This configuration is not automatic—it must be explicitly enabled by setting the topic's `cleanup.policy=compact`. By doing so, Kafka ensures that each customer's latest aggregated state is preserved in the topic.

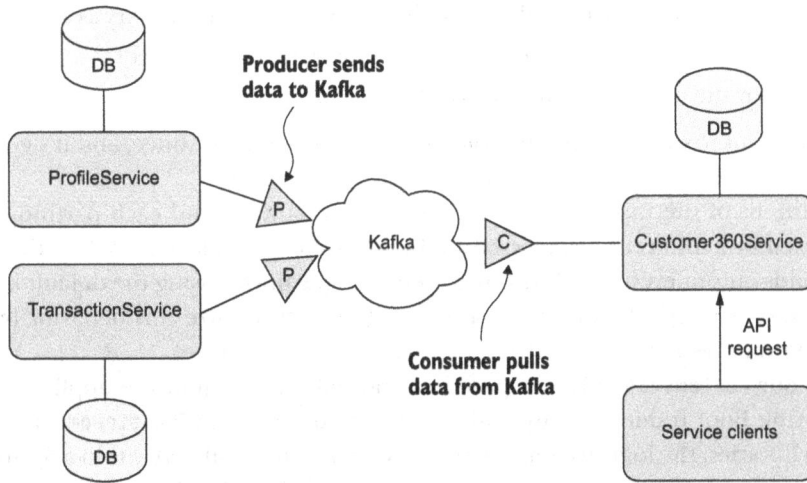

Figure 8.6 The initial sketch of the service design

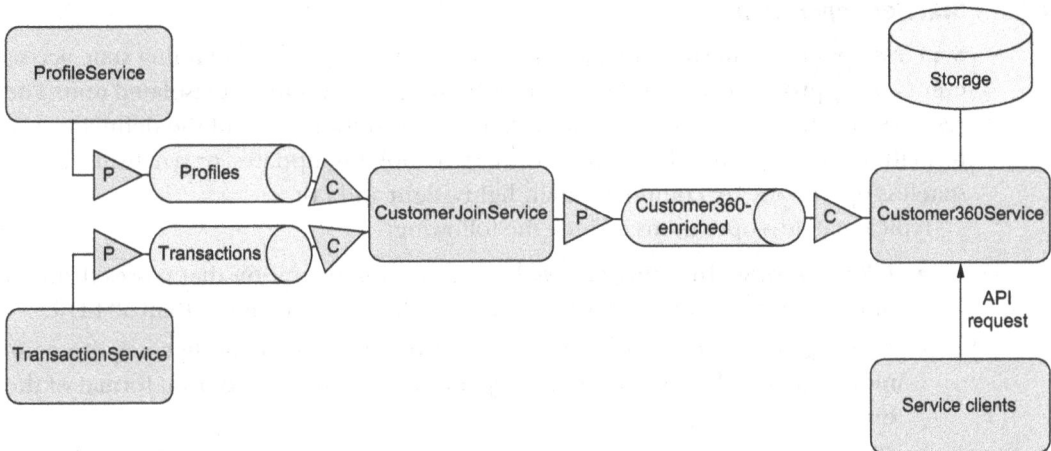

Figure 8.7 In the updated design using a streaming service, joining of different topics is performed in the intermediate CustomerJoinService **service.**

With ready-to-use data now available in Kafka, the team considered replacing the relational database in the Customer360Service with a more lightweight solution, such as Redis or MongoDB, to improve efficiency and simplify storage.

8.3 *Processing data*

Kafka Streams enables developers to create lightweight, standalone applications that act as self-contained microservices without requiring a separate cluster. To implement an application with Kafka Streams, three steps are needed:

1 Create a Java application that includes the Kafka Streams library as a dependency.
2 Implement your application logic using the Kafka Streams API.
3 Deploy the application to your runtime environment.

It's important to note that input topics must be created in advance, and it's good practice to create output topics in advance as well.

Partitions of the input topics are processed in parallel, and each partition may be processed by a different instance of the Kafka Streams application. When the application sends output events, it distributes them into partitions using the default key-based distribution strategy. However, it's also possible to customize this behavior by implementing your own logic using the `StreamPartitioner` interface.

For our `Customer360` ODS, a practical approach is to build the application using the Spring Boot framework. By utilizing the `spring-boot`, `kafka-streams`, and `spring-kafka` libraries, the logic for joining streams can be encapsulated within a Spring Bean. Once implemented, the application can be packaged as a Docker image and deployed to a containerized environment for scalability and ease of management.

Next, let's discuss the features supported in Kafka Streams.

8.3.1 Stateless operations

Stateless operations in streaming applications do not require maintaining state across events. They process events independently, treating each event as an isolated unit. The result of stateless operations depends solely on the input event and the defined transformation logic. Because they don't involve state lookups, updates, or synchronization, stateless operations are computationally lightweight and fast.

Typical stateless operations include the following:

- *Filtering events*—In listing 8.1, we have a filtering operation that passes through only expensive orders and discards orders where the sum is less than 50 EUR.
- *Mapping events*—Converting events from one format to another is quite common. Again, in listing 8.1 the map operation simplifies the output format of the objects.
- *Flat mapping events*—Operation which maps one event into several other events, such as splitting a CSV string into individual tokens.
- *Routing events*—Operation that sends events to different output topics based on their attributes.
- *Changing the key*—Alters the keys of events, which affects how they are distributed across partitions in the output topics.

The complete list of supported operations is available in the official documentation.

8.3.2 Stateful operations

In stateless operations, events are processed in isolation. For operations like filtering or mapping, each event is processed independently, requiring no additional context or history.

However, the situation changes when we talk about stateful operations. For instance, if you need to count the number of orders per country, processing a single incoming event is not enough. With each order, you need to increment a counter for the corresponding country. This introduces two key challenges:

- *Event locality*—Orders from the same region must be processed by the same instance of the application to ensure accurate counting.
- *State storage*—The counters must be stored in a fault-tolerant manner to guarantee durability, while still providing low-latency access for efficient processing.

This scenario is illustrated in figure 8.8. Since incoming events originate from Kafka, we can ensure that orders from the same region are routed to the same application instance. This is achieved by using the region as the key, which guarantees correct distribution to partitions.

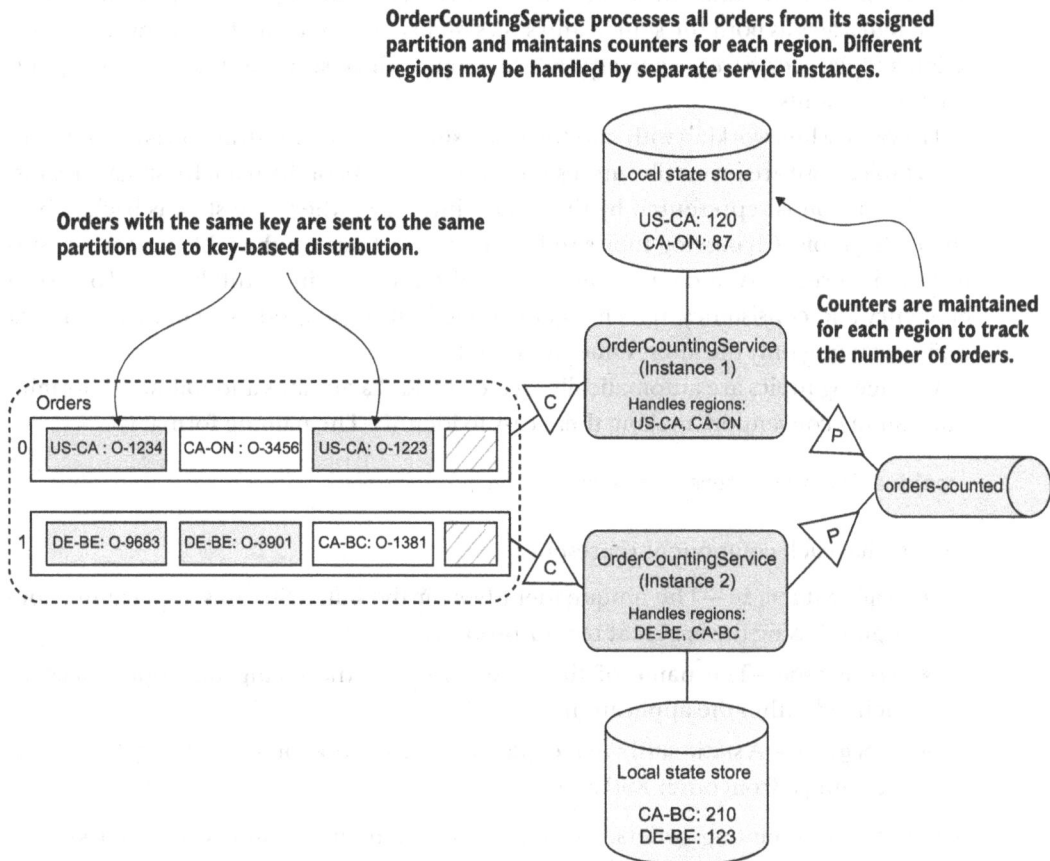

Figure 8.8 `OrderCountingService` **counts orders per region, with each instance maintaining its own set of counters.**

This is the general approach for stateful processing in Kafka Streams. A state store is a key-value storage mechanism that maintains state for each unique key. In our example, the region serves as the key, and the counter represents the value.

The state data is kept in memory, by default using RocksDB (https://rocksdb.org) for persistence. For fault tolerance, Kafka Streams backs up the state to a changelog topic in Kafka. The local state store is automatically synchronized with Kafka. If an application instance fails, the state is seamlessly restored from the changelog topic during recovery.

These operations—storing, backing up, and restoring state—are handled automatically by Kafka Streams, without requiring explicit intervention, as demonstrated in listing 8.1. Since the objects in state stores are persisted to Kafka, they must be serialized and deserialized. Therefore, it is essential to define appropriate serializers and deserializers for the state store objects, as was explained in chapter 3.

In streaming applications, incoming and outgoing events are treated as continuous streams of data. In Kafka, these streams are abstracted through the KStream interface. Since Kafka acts as both the source and sink systems, the concept of a stream aligns with a Kafka topic: every stream corresponds to a topic, which serves as the underlying storage for the events.

However, when working with stateful processing, the native abstraction is not a stream but a table, as we are primarily interested in the final state of the data. In Kafka Streams, this abstraction is represented by the KTable interface, where the state is backed by a changelog topic. Changelog topics reflect the current state of the table or store, ensuring efficient recovery and synchronization without preserving a full history. To ensure efficiency and consistency, the changelog topic is implemented as a compacted Kafka topic, retaining only the latest values for each key.

Changelog topics are automatically created by Kafka Streams and follow a deterministic naming convention, making them easy to identify. The naming format is

```
<application_id>-<store_name>-changelog
```

Here's what each component represents:

- application_id—The unique identifier for the Kafka Streams application, configured using the application.id property
- store_name—The name of the state store that the changelog topic backs, as defined within the application
- changelog—A static suffix that explicitly indicates the topic is a changelog, distinguishing it from other Kafka topics

In the case of counting orders, the state store maintains counters for each key. To emit updates of these counters to an output topic, we can convert the table into a stream using the toStream() method. This allows changes in the state (such as updated counts) to be sent as a continuous stream of updates to the output topic.

8.3.3 *The Processor API*

So far, we have discussed data processing in Kafka Streams using the DSL functions provided by the Kafka Streams library, where predefined methods are chained to perform operations. But what if we need to implement custom processing logic, such as invoking an external service to detect anomalies in events?

Creating a streaming application can be conceptualized as constructing a graph of stream-processing tasks. Each node in the graph represents a processing unit, performing specific operations such as filtering, mapping, joining, or aggregating. For stateful operations, nodes are linked to state stores, which maintain intermediate results for tasks like joins or aggregations. Edges in the graph represent the data flow between these units, which can occur either in-memory or via Kafka topics. This graph is referred to as the *topology*. A topology is a *directed acyclic graph* (DAG) where data flows from source nodes (Kafka topics) to sink nodes (output Kafka topics).

An example of a topology is shown in figure 8.9, which includes the following types of nodes:

- *Source nodes*—Read data from input Kafka topics, serving as entry points for the data stream.
- *Processing nodes*—Contain the actual processing logic, such as filtering, aggregation, and transformation.
- *Sink nodes*—Write the processed events to output Kafka topics.

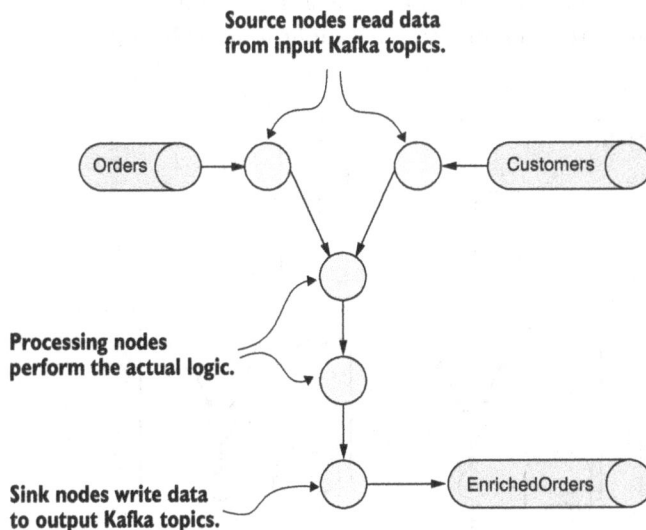

Figure 8.9 Internally, the Kafka Streams application is represented as a graph. Events flow from input topics through source nodes, are processed by processing nodes, and are finally published to output topics via sink nodes.

When we use DSL functions (as demonstrated in listing 8.1), the Kafka Streams library automatically builds this graph for us. However, it is also possible to implement custom processing logic manually in Java. In this case, processing nodes, or processors, are implemented as Java classes that implement the `Processor` interface. These processors can encapsulate custom logic, making them reusable across different applications by organizing them into a shared library. The graph's topology is defined programmatically, allowing developers to explicitly specify the structure of the graph and the connections between processors. Within a custom processor, you can

- Work with state stores for stateful processing.
- Schedule periodic actions, such as triggering logic at regular intervals.
- Access Kafka at a low level, interacting directly with the Kafka client API.

For example, when detecting fraudulent transactions, a custom processor can analyze incoming transactions in real time and compare them against historical patterns stored in state stores to identify anomalies.

8.3.4 *Kafka Streams internal architecture*

Let's take a closer look at the internal architecture of a Kafka Streams application. The parallelism of a Kafka Streams application is determined by the number of partitions in the input topics. If there are multiple input topics, the parallelism is defined by the topic with the maximum number of partitions. This relationship can be expressed as

```
taskCount=max(PartitionCount(Topic1),PartitionCount(Topic2),...,
PartitionCount(TopicN))
```

Here, `taskCount` represents the number of tasks (instances of graph topologies) created per application instance. Each task processes a subset of input partitions.

The internal architecture of a Kafka Streams application is illustrated in figure 8.10.

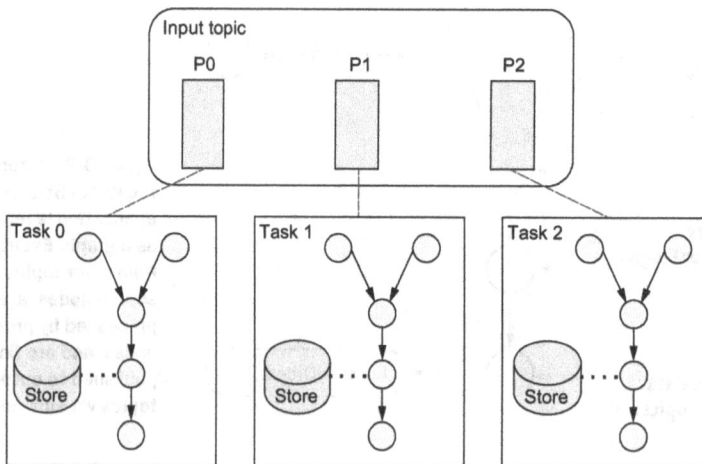

The structure of the task, attached stores, and input partition assignments never change.

Figure 8.10   The internal architecture of a Kafka Streams application: partitions of input topics and state stores are assigned to tasks, and these assignments remain static throughout the application's lifecycle.

The task is a unit of distribution in a Kafka Streams application and it consists of the following:

- The assignment of input partitions
- The state stores used by the task for maintaining intermediate or aggregated results
- An instance of the graph topology responsible for processing the data

These tasks can run independently on different threads within the same application instance or across different application instances. The number of threads is configurable, with a default value of 1. Importantly, tasks are independent and do not rely on colocation with other tasks. This independence ensures that the failure of a single task or instance does not affect others.

Tasks are immutable in terms of their structure. If an application instance fails, the entire unit—comprising the partition assignment, state stores, and graph topology—is reassigned to a different application instance, as shown in figure 8.11. Kafka Streams handles this reassignment seamlessly, ensuring fault tolerance and recovery.

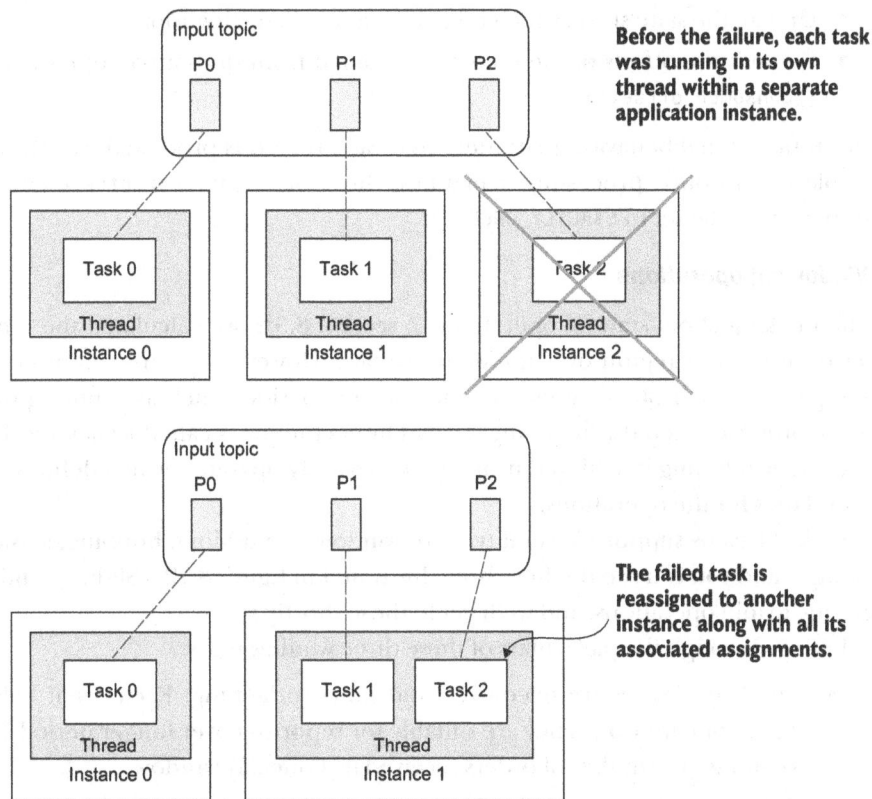

Figure 8.11   In case of failure, tasks are reassigned to one of the healthy instances.

It is important to note that each event consumed from one of the incoming topics traverses the entire processing graph and is emitted to the output topic (unless it is filtered out) before the next event is consumed. This means that Kafka Streams processes events one at a time through the topology.

If multiple events are required for processing—such as in stateful operations like aggregations or joins—these events are not passed directly between tasks. Instead, each task maintains its own local state store, which acts as a persistent layer to store and access intermediate or historical data needed during processing.

The state stores are fault-tolerant with persistence enabled by default (for example, when RocksDB is used as a state store implementation). If an application instance fails (or more specifically, if a task topology crashes, though typically this results in the instance crashing), the state store can be restored from the corresponding changelog topics in Kafka.

Kafka Streams also supports transactions, enabling atomic consume-process-produce operations. Kafka Streams ensures exactly-once processing by executing the following steps in an atomic, all-or-nothing transaction:

1 Produce data to the output topic.
2 Update the state store, which is backed up to changelog topics.
3 Commit the offsets of the records consumed from the source topics (tracked in `__consumer_offsets`).

This transactional behavior guarantees that each record is processed exactly once. To enable exactly-once processing semantics, the `processing.guarantee` configuration property must be set to `EXACTLY_ONCE_V2`.

8.3.5   *Windowing operations*

When talking about stateful operations in section 8.3.2, we calculated the total number of orders per region over the entire stream. However, a more common use case is to perform such calculations over specific time periods, such as counting the number of orders created during a single day. This technique is called *windowing*. In Kafka Streams, windowing is achieved using the `windowedBy` operator, which defines the time boundaries for the operations.

Kafka Streams supports several types of windows—tumbling, hopping, session, and sliding—and you can see the first three illustrated in figure 8.12. (Sliding windows are specific to join operations, and we'll get to those shortly.)

Let's go through the particulars of these three window types:

- *Tumbling windows* are fixed-sized and non-overlapping. Each event belongs to exactly one window. They are suitable for reporting over longer periods, such as counting the number of orders received in a one-day window.
- *Hopping windows* have a fixed size and an advance interval, where the window advances at a specified interval, allowing events to belong to multiple overlapping

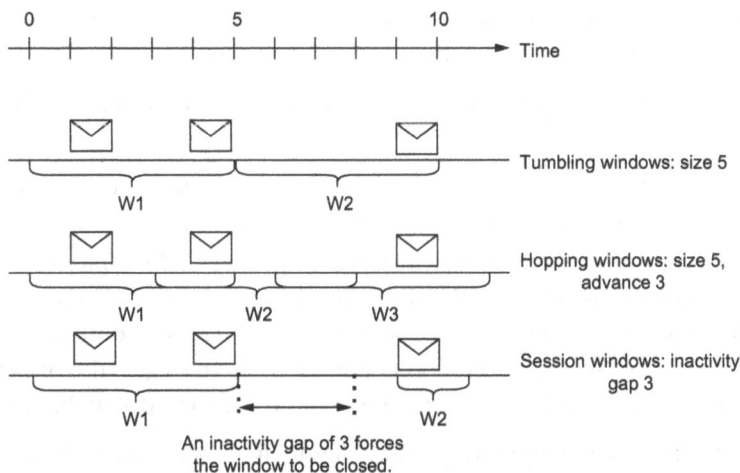

Figure 8.12 Windowing in Kafka Streams. Brackets show window intervals (W1, W2, …) along the time axis; the icons indicate messages that fall within each window.

windows. These are useful for sliding calculations, such as counting the number of logged-in users every five minutes with a one-minute advance interval.

- *Session windows* do not have a fixed size but are determined by periods of activity separated by inactivity gaps. A session window closes after a specified inactivity gap, such as ten minutes without new events. They are ideal for scenarios like user sessions in web applications, where the session closes if no activity occurs for ten minutes.

Kafka Streams determines whether an event belongs to a particular window based on its timestamp. In addition, windows can have a grace period, which specifies how long to wait for late-arriving data. If an event's timestamp is greater than the window end time plus the grace period, it is discarded, even if it would otherwise belong to the window.

Windows are created per key, and windowing logic applies to each key individually. Each key in the stream will have its own set of windows based on the defined time boundaries.

8.3.6 Joining streams

A frequent use case is *event enrichment*, where multiple related events are joined to create a more complete or meaningful object—for instance, combining an order event with its payment event. In databases, this is a join operation, and it is possible to define joins in streams. We define how objects are matched (usually based on attributes with the same value) and output an aggregated object.

Suppose we want to join orders and corresponding payments—we have an incoming order from one stream and want to join it with the payment using the condition `order.id = payment.order_id`. Here we have two questions:

- How can we ensure that the order and its matching payment are processed by the same application instance?

- How can we deal with the fact that the order and payment do not arrive at the same time, and we don't know which one will arrive first?

For the first point, the topics being joined must meet the following copartitioning requirements:

- The number of partitions for the input topics must be the same. All input topics participating in the join must have the same number of partitions.
- The topics must use the same key distribution strategy. The topics must use the same partitioning logic (e.g., the same key and partitioner) to ensure records with the same key are routed to the same partition across all topics. It is important to note that ensuring the correct key distribution strategy is the responsibility of the programmer, as Kafka Streams does not validate or enforce this at runtime.

Figure 8.13 illustrates the join operation. The assignment of partitions to Kafka Streams tasks is done automatically, such that partitions with the same index are assigned to the same task. This is why, if we want to join events from different streams, we must ensure that the events we want to join are sent to partitions with the same index. The easiest way to achieve this is to use the attribute on which the join is performed as the key.

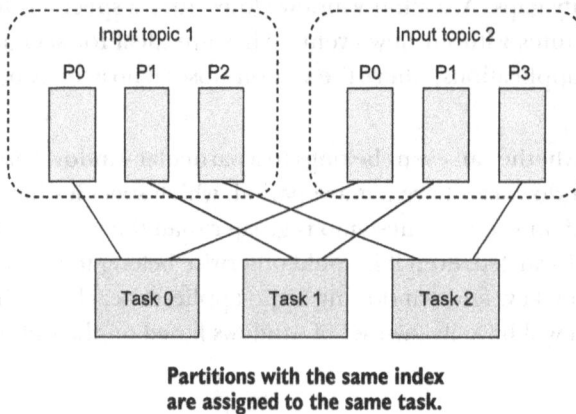

Partitions with the same index
are assigned to the same task.

Figure 8.13 Partitions with the same index are assigned to the same task, and this assignment remains fixed. Elements in input topics that arrive in partitions with the same index will be processed together.

What if the keys in the incoming topics are different? Suppose the key for the Orders topic is orderId, and for the Payments topic it is paymentId. The solution is the same as discussed in chapter 4: the key for the Payments topic must be changed to orderId, which is an attribute of the Payment event. This operation is invoked in Java code using the selectKey method provided by the Kafka Streams API. The selectKey operation sets the new key for each input event and automatically creates an intermediate topic with the new keys, as shown in figure 8.14.

To address the problem of the Order and Payment not arriving at the same time, joins are always performed within windows. Events wait in the state stores for their

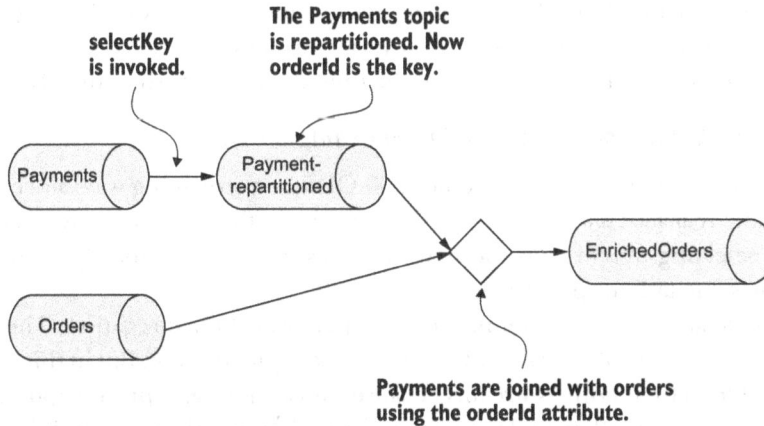

Figure 8.14 When the Payments and Orders topics are joined, they must have the same number of input partitions and the same key (orderId).

matching events until the matching event arrives or the window period expires. For example, if we define a one-day window, it means the payment and order will wait for each other for a one-day period. If a matching event does not arrive within this period, it will be discarded.

These windows are called *sliding windows,* and they are calculated based on the difference in event timestamps. In this example, the order and payment will meet if the difference between their timestamps is less than one day.

Let's consider another use case where we want to join orders with the corresponding customer data. Unlike Payments, which is treated as a stream, Customer data can be treated as a table where we are only interested in the latest value for each customer. This behavior differs slightly from stream-to-stream joins.

When an order arrives, the application checks if there is corresponding customer data in the table:

- If a match is found, an aggregated object is produced.
- If no matching key exists in the table, no output is generated.

It is important to note that a new incoming order triggers the join operation, producing a new result. However, updates to the Customer table do not trigger a reprocessing of the already processed orders.

The copartitioning requirements must also be met when joining streams and tables to ensure that matching keys are processed together. However, there is an alternative for tables where the entire dataset can be broadcast to all tasks. This is achieved by wrapping the table with the GlobalKTable interface. GlobalKTables are immutable and serve as a *read-only* view for the application, ensuring fast lookups without partitioning constraints.

Finally, as databases, Kafka Streams provides the ability to perform left, right, inner, and outer joins. However, these advanced topics are beyond the scope of this book. Consult the corresponding Kafka Streams documentation for further details.

8.3.7   Implementing CustomerJoinService in the example ODS

We've continued to design the Customer 360 ODS in a streaming way. Since we have `Profiles` and `Transactions` topics with different keys, the first step is to rekey transactions by selecting `clientId` as the new key. This ensures that matching events will arrive at the same task for processing.

The next challenge is determining how to perform the aggregation. The natural conclusion is to join the `Profiles` and `Transactions` topics directly. But in this situation, it's not feasible to treat both as streams because transactions and profile updates arrive independently of each other, and there is no way to define a window for joining.

Using `Profiles` as a table (`KTable`) is another seemingly logical approach, because it represents the latest state of each customer. But joining the `Transactions` stream with the `Profiles` table creates a significant limitation: updates to the `Profiles` table will not trigger an output result. This is unacceptable for the ODS project because changes to a customer's profile, such as an updated address, would never be propagated to the aggregated Customer 360 view unless a new transaction happened to arrive. As a result, the aggregated customer record would quickly become stale, violating the requirement that Customer360 always reflects the most current profile data.

After considering these limitations, we can arrive at the design in figure 8.15.

This solution involves four key steps:

- *Select new key*—The `customerId` is chosen as the new key, causing the `Transactions` topic to be repartitioned based on this key.

- *Aggregate transactions*—`Transactions` are first aggregated per customer, retaining only the latest transaction details or summarized data. This aggregated result is then sent to an intermediate topic.

- *Treat aggregated transactions as a table*—The intermediate topic, containing the aggregated transactions, is treated as a table (`KTable`).

- *Table-to-table join*—The aggregated transactions table is joined with the `Profiles` table. Since this is a table-to-table join, it does not require a window, and importantly, updates to either table trigger a new output result.

This design ensures that whenever a transaction is updated or new profile data arrives, the final aggregated view is updated and emitted.

8.3.8   Interactive queries

Suppose we have a streaming application that emits counts to the output topic so that consumers can receive them. However, if these counts are already stored in a key-value state store, is it possible to access them directly without sending the results to Kafka? The answer is yes. Kafka Streams allows querying of state stores that implement the `QueryableStoreType` interface. This feature is known as *interactive queries*.

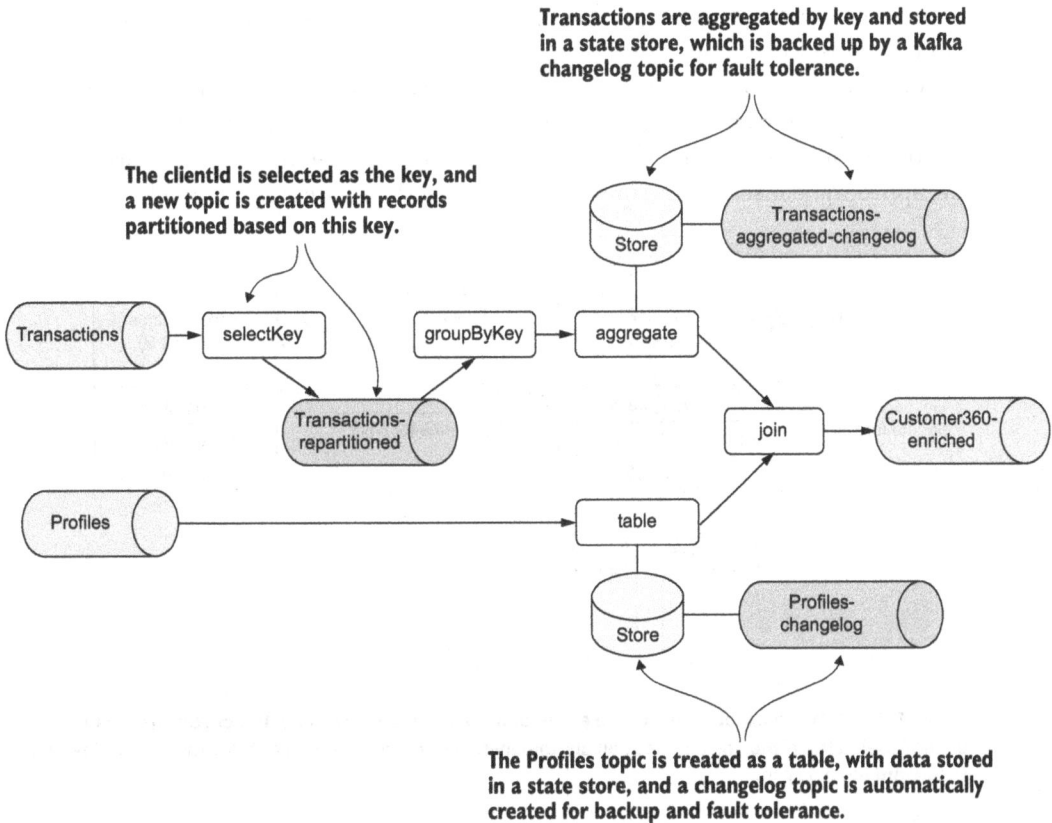

Transactions are aggregated by key and stored in a state store, which is backed up by a Kafka changelog topic for fault tolerance.

The clientId is selected as the key, and a new topic is created with records partitioned based on this key.

The Profiles topic is treated as a table, with data stored in a state store, and a changelog topic is automatically created for backup and fault tolerance.

Figure 8.15   A pipeline design using Kafka Streams. The source topics, `Profiles` and `Transactions`, serve as input streams, while `Customer360-enriched` is the output topic. Kafka Streams automatically creates intermediate topics for operations like repartitioning and changelog management. Both source topics are converted into tables using state stores, and the resulting tables are joined to produce the enriched output.

As discussed in the previous section, a Kafka Streams application typically consists of multiple instances, each running tasks independently. In this model, the state store is local to the task's topology. It is straightforward to query this local state store from within the same application instance using Java code. For example, if we want to retrieve the counts per region (with regions stored as keys in the local state store), we can query the store directly within the program.

However, this approach presents a challenge: What if the data we need is hosted on another instance? And how do we determine which instance contains the key we are looking for? Kafka Streams provides a mechanism to address this challenge. While it is possible to query data across all state stores, Kafka Streams exposes metadata about the key-to-instance distribution. Using this metadata, the application can determine which instance holds the specific key. However, Kafka Streams does not implement the actual remote querying logic. Instead, it is up to the application to implement the necessary layer to access the remote state store.

An example of how to query stores transparently for the client is shown in figure 8.16. Each instance of the Kafka Streams application must expose a host and service endpoint where it runs. The application code can then use the key metadata to locate the appropriate instance and query the corresponding state store remotely.

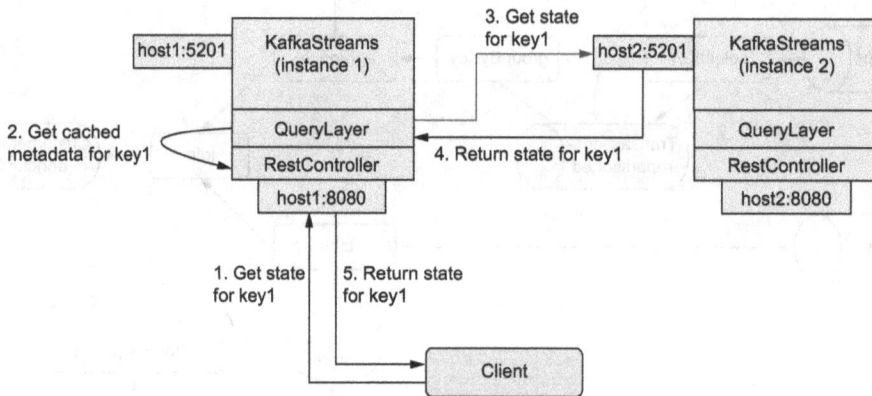

Figure 8.16   When a client requests the state for a given key, the instance first checks its locally cached metadata. If the state resides on another instance, the metadata identifies the correct instance to forward the query to.

8.4   *Alternative solutions*

In the field of stream processing, several solutions compete with Kafka Streams, ranging from lightweight libraries to fully managed cloud-based offerings. In this section, we will briefly explore two notable alternatives: ksqlDB (www.confluent.io/product/ksqldb), which enables stream processing using a SQL-like language and is built on top of Kafka Streams, and Apache Flink (https://flink.apache.org), a powerful stream-processing framework. Additionally, we will touch on managed stream-processing solutions provided by major cloud platforms.

8.4.1   *Confluent ksqlDB*

Kafka Streams allows us to process streaming data by building applications implemented in Java. These applications follow a typical lifecycle: writing code, committing it to a repository, and building and deploying the application. However, in many organizations, creating a new application involves more than just development effort—it often comes with significant administrative overhead. This includes obtaining approvals to create a new application, setting up repositories, configuring continuous integration/continuous deployment (CI/CD) pipelines, and managing other operational tasks.

This raises an important question: Can stream processing be achieved with less coding and fewer administrative steps? Is it possible to deploy processing logic without the need to create a full-fledged application? Ideally, this could be done using a high-level, domain-specific language (DSL) rather than relying on low-level programming code.

Another product from Confluent, ksqlDB, enables event processing through SQL-based queries. These SQL statements are known as KSQL queries—the name reflects Kafka + SQL. KsqlDB allows these KSQL queries to be deployed to a cluster of servers where they run continuously, enabling developers to express stream-processing logic declaratively without extensive programming. Let's explore the architecture of this solution.

KSQL QUERIES

Earlier, when we discussed operations over streams, such as filtering, mapping, and aggregating, it might have sounded like processing data with SQL. In traditional databases, SQL queries typically operate on a static snapshot of data. For example, we might ask, "What is the current address of a specific customer?" However, we rarely deal with the entire history of changes, unless extensions for time-series data are used.

This is where streaming queries differ fundamentally. In stream processing, data arrives continuously, and queries operate on the real-time flow of events. Instead of querying a fixed dataset, streaming systems process and analyze data as it changes, enabling use cases such as tracking events over time or identifying trends in real time.

We previously explored how to process streaming data using Java applications, so let's now focus on how this can be achieved declaratively, with high-level query languages, as shown in the following listing.

Listing 8.2 Selecting high value orders

```
SELECT * FROM Orders
WHERE paid_amount > 100;
```

Imagine we execute the preceding query, which retrieves all orders exceeding 100 EUR from the relational database. At that moment, the query returns a static snapshot of the current data. However, if a new high-value order arrives a few minutes later, this result won't update automatically. The only way to reflect the new data is to rerun the query, as traditional queries are transient—they exist only for the duration of execution and vanish after returning results.

How, then, can we achieve continuously updated results? As demonstrated with Kafka Streams, we treat the data as an ongoing stream of events. For instance, imagine a Kafka topic containing incoming orders. We can create an application that reads from this topic, applies a filtering condition to select orders exceeding 100 EUR, and writes the filtered results to an output topic. Each time a new order arrives, it is processed immediately, and if it matches the condition, a new event is published.

This is precisely what the KSQL language does. Instead of querying a static table, KSQL operates on a stream of events backed by a Kafka topic. In the following listing, we create the stream by specifying its structure and defining a corresponding topic. This works like a create table command in traditional SQL.

```
CREATE STREAM Orders (                    Create the Orders stream.
    order_id BIGINT,
    customer_id STRING,
    amount_paid DOUBLE                    The stream is backed by
) WITH (                                  the corresponding topic.
    KAFKA_TOPIC = 'Orders',
    VALUE_FORMAT = 'JSON',                The format of the data
    PARTITIONS = 8                        in the topic is JSON.
);
                                          The number of partitions
                                          in the topic is 8.
```

Next, we create a continuous query that reads from the previously created stream, applies the filter condition, and writes results to an output stream.

```
CREATE STREAM Expensive_Orders AS
    SELECT *                              Create the output stream.
    FROM Orders
    WHERE amount_paid > 100               The data is selected from
    EMIT CHANGES;                         the Orders stream.

                                          The output results are
                                          updated continuously.
```

Here, the corresponding Expensive_Orders topic will be created automatically, and the EMIT CHANGES clause indicates that the output results are continuously updated in a streaming fashion as new data arrives. Later, we will explore another type of queries that operate on snapshot data, providing results at a specific point in time.

The streaming query runs continuously and acts much like a live application, processing new events as they arrive and publishing updates in real time. The resulting events are written to an output topic, where downstream applications or consumers can subscribe to receive up-to-date results. This approach eliminates the need to rerun queries, enabling real-time, low-latency processing.

In KSQL, you will find many of the familiar constructs supported by traditional SQL. For example, in the next listing, we calculate the total number of orders, grouping the results by the country attribute. Whenever a new order arrives, the count for the corresponding country is updated, and a new result is published.

```
CREATE TABLE Orders_Count_By_Country AS
    SELECT country, COUNT(*) AS total_orders    Count the orders.
    FROM Orders
```

```
GROUP BY country
EMIT CHANGES;
```
◀─── **Group by the country attribute.**

In practice, it is often more useful to compute these aggregations over a window of time rather than for the entire stream. This approach, demonstrated in the following listing, allows us to perform calculations such as counting orders within specific time intervals (e.g., every one hour), enabling more focused and timely insights.

Listing 8.6 Calculating the number of orders by country per hour

```
CREATE TABLE orders_count_by_country AS
    SELECT country,
           COUNT(*) AS total_orders
    FROM orders
    WINDOW TUMBLING (SIZE 1 HOUR)
    GROUP BY country
    EMIT CHANGES;
```
◀─── **Calculate the number of orders in a one-hour window.**

Since defining such queries requires structured data, the events in a Kafka topic must be serialized using formats that ksqlDB understands. This includes primitive data types and more complex formats such as Avro, JSON, or Protobuf, which are typically managed and validated through the Schema Registry.

It's important to note that most of the things you can achieve with Kafka Streams—such as filtering, aggregating, or transforming data—can also be done with ksqlDB. The key difference is that ksqlDB allows you to define and execute stream-processing logic declaratively using SQL-like statements, eliminating the need for extensive Java programming and reducing the operational complexity of stream-processing applications.

KSQLDB ARCHITECTURE

How are ksqlDB queries created, where do they run, and how does this technology fit into the broader Kafka ecosystem? The overall architecture is illustrated in figure 8.17.

KSQL queries run on a ksqlDB server (typically a cluster of servers), which acts as a client to Kafka brokers and the Schema Registry. Queries are created using UI or command-line tools and are submitted to the ksqlDB server via its REST API. These queries are stored in a special Kafka topic, which serves as a centralized mechanism for sharing query commands and metadata across all instances in the ksqlDB cluster, ensuring consistency and fault tolerance.

Figure 8.18 shows a closer look at the ksqlDB server. When the server receives a query, it translates it into an equivalent Kafka Streams application that executes the defined processing logic. Internally, ksqlDB essentially turns SQL queries into a continuously running Java application that performs stream processing. For stateful queries, such as aggregations or joins, RocksDB is used as the local state store, with the state data being backed up in Kafka topics for durability and fault tolerance.

ksqlDB queries are submitted through a REST API to the ksqlDB servers.

KSQL queries are shared through the command topic in Kafka.

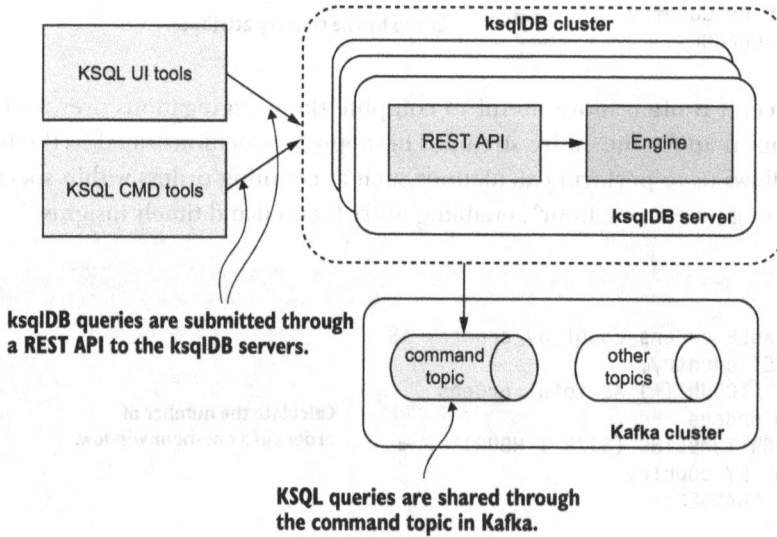

Figure 8.17   KSQL queries are submitted through a REST API and are shared through the command topic.

Within a KSQL cluster, queries are translated into Kafka Streams applications. These applications function as both producers and consumers.

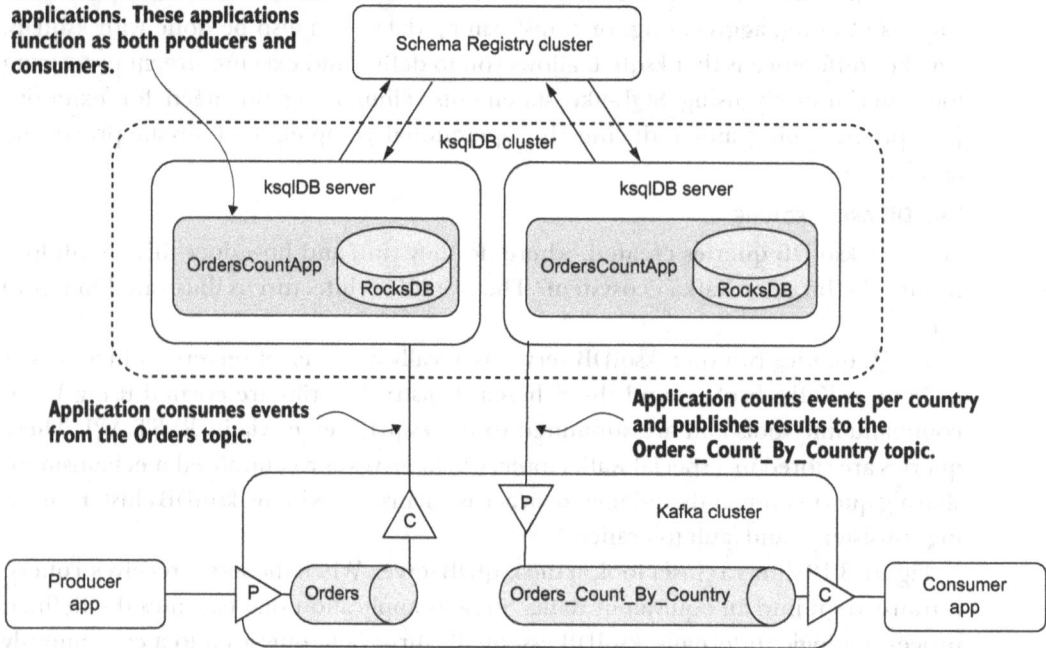

Application consumes events from the Orders topic.

Application counts events per country and publishes results to the Orders_Count_By_Country topic.

Figure 8.18   In the ksqlDB server, the KSQL query is transformed into multiple instances of Kafka Streams applications. These applications consume events from the Orders topic, process the data, and produce the results to the Orders_Count_By_Country topic.

All queries running on the ksqlDB server share the server's available resources, such as memory and CPU, which makes them less isolated compared to standalone Java-based Kafka Streams applications. While this shared resource model simplifies query deployment and management, it may introduce limitations for workloads requiring strong isolation or dedicated resources.

PUSH AND PULL QUERIES

So far, we have discussed queries that operate over an unbounded stream, running continuously and pushing updates each time a new event is processed. These are known as *push queries*. However, ksqlDB also supports *pull queries*, which behave more like traditional database queries by operating over a snapshot of the data.

Pull queries are transient: they run on demand, retrieve the current state of the data, and terminate immediately after delivering the results. For example, if we simply want to ask, "What is the status of the order with ID 123?"—meaning the state at the time of the query—we don't need to create a continuously running application. Instead, a pull query executes, fetches the latest result, and then stops.

Pull queries can operate over

- *Streams or tables*—In this case, the pull query scans the underlying Kafka topic (the changelog or the original stream) to retrieve the latest relevant record at query time. The result reflects the most recent event written for the queried key, based on what is stored in Kafka.

- *Materialized views*—Here, the pull query reads directly from a locally stored, continuously updated view (backed by RocksDB and replicated through Kafka). Because the data is already precomputed and indexed by key, the query can return the current state immediately without scanning a topic.

When a pull query is executed, it finds the most recent record that matches the query condition, delivers the result, and then terminates.

Both push and pull queries can be easily managed and executed via the ksqlDB REST API, providing a consistent interface for interacting with streaming and snapshot queries.

While ksqlDB remains supported and widely used, Confluent has shifted most new stream-processing development toward Apache Flink.

8.4.2 Apache Flink

Among the various frameworks for data processing, Apache Flink stands out for its comprehensive feature set. Compared to Kafka Streams, Apache Flink is more versatile, supporting both batch and streaming modes. Unlike Kafka Streams, which is tightly integrated with Kafka as its primary data source and sink, Apache Flink offers seamless integration with a wide range of external systems, such as files, databases, and other platforms. This flexibility, comparable to the functionality provided by Kafka Connect, makes Flink a powerful choice for managing complex and diverse data processing pipelines.

APACHE FLINK JOBS

Apache Flink introduces the concept of a *job*, which represents the logic or workflow for processing both streaming and batch data. A Flink job is a data processing application that defines how data is ingested, transformed, and output, running efficiently on the Flink runtime.

Data streams in Flink are categorized as unbounded or bounded. *Unbounded streams* consist of events that arrive continuously and are processed as they are ingested, often in their natural order. These streams have no defined start or end, making them ideal for real-time processing. In contrast, *bounded streams* have a clearly defined start and end, meaning all events are ingested first, before computations are applied. This approach allows bounded streams to behave like batch processing, where operations are performed on a complete dataset. This dual capability allows Flink to process data in both streaming and batch modes, providing a unified framework for handling real-time and historical data.

A Flink job begins with a connector that reads data from a source system, processes the incoming events, and ends with a connector that writes data to a sink. Flink supports both bounded sources, such as files or batch database queries, and unbounded sources like Kafka topics. Flink provides a wide range of predefined connectors for common systems, such as files, databases, and messaging systems like Kafka. Users can also implement custom connectors by extending the relevant Java interfaces. While the Kafka ecosystem relies on Kafka Connect, which runs on dedicated clusters for integration with external systems, Flink handles this integration directly within its jobs, embedding connectors as part of the application logic.

Flink jobs can be created programmatically, and data pipelines can also be defined declaratively using Flink SQL or YAML configurations. This flexibility enables users to design, implement, and manage complex data workflows with ease.

USING FLINK FOR THE CUSTOMER 360 ODS

Instead of using Kafka Streams, the Customer 360 project can be implemented with the Flink framework, as illustrated in figure 8.19. The streaming logic can be developed as a Flink program, written in a language like Java utilizing Flink's DSL. Flink also provides built-in support for connector components, enabling seamless reading from Kafka topics and writing back to Kafka topics.

Alternatively, it's possible to implement the Customer 360 ODS without using Kafka at all, as shown in figure 8.20. Flink offers connectors to various external systems, including databases, much like Kafka Connect. In this case, as Kafka is not part of the architecture, there are no Kafka topics that could be reused by other consumers. While this approach eliminates the dependency on Kafka, it also reduces the flexibility of sharing data streams across multiple consumers.

APACHE FLINK ARCHITECTURE

To work effectively with Apache Flink, it is essential to understand its architectural components, as they offer significant opportunities for customization and optimization.

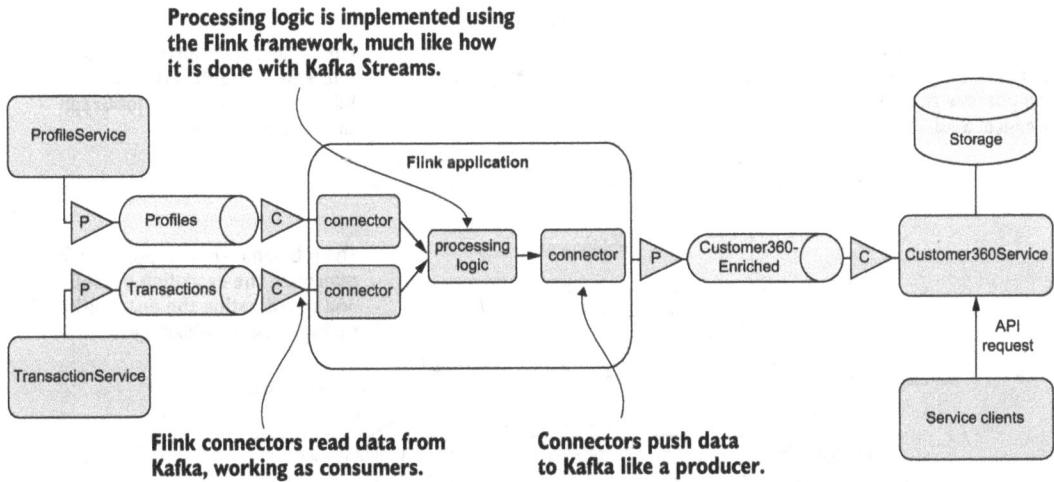

Figure 8.19 Implementing the Customer 360 ODS with Apache Flink

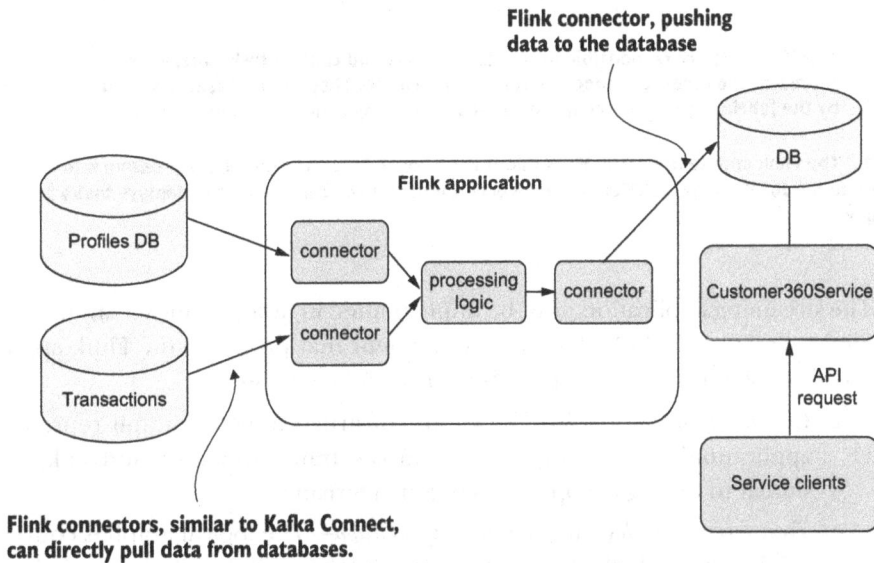

Figure 8.20 Implementing the Customer 360 ODS with Flink but without Kafka

While Kafka Streams is a Java library that runs as part of the streaming application itself, Apache Flink requires a dedicated cluster for operation. Figure 8.21 illustrates the architecture of Apache Flink, highlighting its primary components: the Flink Client, TaskManager, and JobManager.

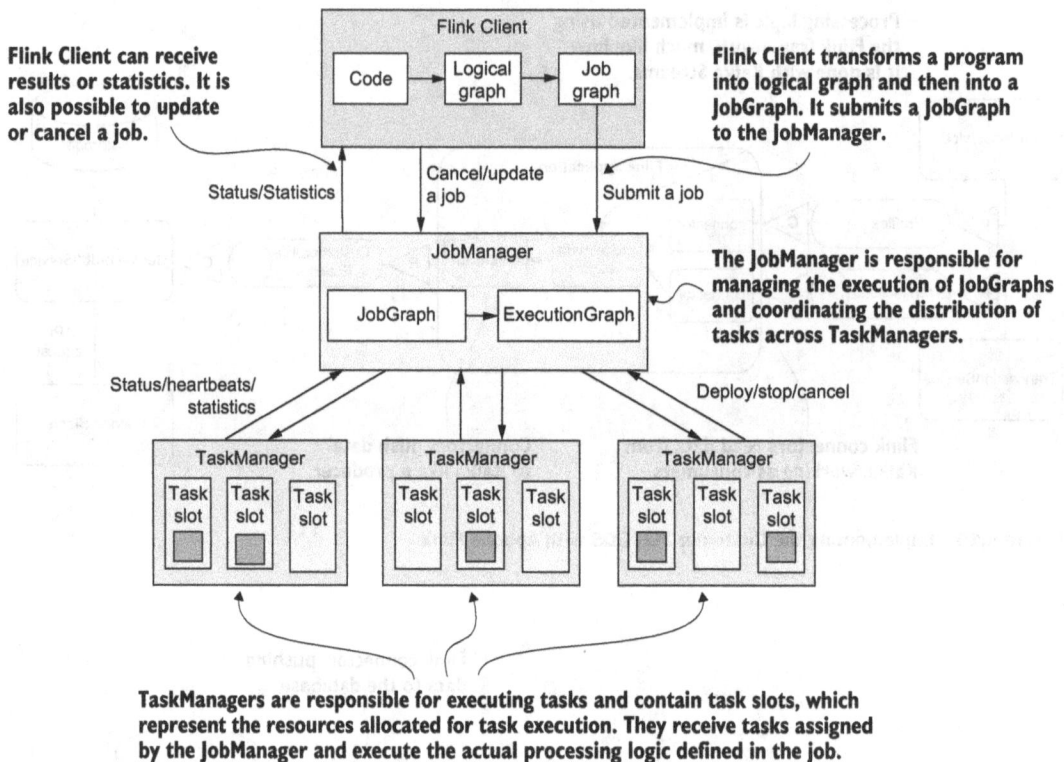

Flink Client can receive results or statistics. It is also possible to update or cancel a job.

Flink Client transforms a program into logical graph and then into a JobGraph. It submits a JobGraph to the JobManager.

The JobManager is responsible for managing the execution of JobGraphs and coordinating the distribution of tasks across TaskManagers.

TaskManagers are responsible for executing tasks and contain task slots, which represent the resources allocated for task execution. They receive tasks assigned by the JobManager and execute the actual processing logic defined in the job.

Figure 8.21   The Flink architecture. The Flink Client is responsible for transforming a program into a graph, which is submitted to the JobManager. JobManager converts it into an ExecutionGraph and deploys tasks to available TaskManagers.

The streaming application must be implemented in Java (the most common choice for Flink), Scala, or Python. The first component that processes the Flink application is the Flink Client, which is responsible for the following steps:

1   *Creating a logical graph*—The client constructs a logical graph representing the application's operations, such as sources, transformations, and sinks. These are similar to the logical operators in Kafka Streams.

2   *Transforming the logical graph into a JobGraph*—The logical graph is converted into a JobGraph, which defines task dependencies and includes optimizations for execution.

3   *Submitting the JobGraph to the JobManager*—Finally, the client submits the JobGraph to the JobManager, which coordinates the execution across the cluster. The job can be submitted through application code or packaged as a Jar and submitted to the cluster via the Flink console (CLI) or REST endpoint.

After the JobManager receives the JobGraph, it transforms it into an ExecutionGraph, a distributed execution representation that defines how the job's tasks will be executed across the cluster. This transformation includes determining task parallelism, dependencies, and resource requirements to optimize execution. The JobManager can operate in different deployment modes:

- *Application mode*—The entire Flink cluster is dedicated to a single application. The JobManager is created specifically for this application and manages all its jobs. Typically, the JobManager and TaskManagers run in separate JVMs but are tied to this single application.
- *Session mode*—A single JobManager instance manages multiple jobs from different applications, all sharing the same cluster resources. This mode facilitates resource reuse across jobs but requires careful resource allocation and management.

The JobManager supports various resource management backends, such as standalone JVM, Kubernetes, or Yarn, to adapt to different deployment environments:

- *Standalone JVM*—Suitable for simple setups or local testing, where the JobManager and TaskManagers run as individual JVM processes.
- *Kubernetes*—This approach is ideal for cloud-native deployments, using Kubernetes for container orchestration, scalability, and fault tolerance. The JobManager runs as a Kubernetes pod and uses Kubernetes' native mechanisms for resource allocation, scaling, and recovery.
- *Yarn*—Common in big data environments, particularly those using Hadoop ecosystems. The JobManager integrates with Yarn to request and allocate resources dynamically, ensuring compatibility with existing Hadoop-based infrastructure.

Once the ExecutionGraph is constructed, the JobManager distributes its tasks to TaskManagers, which execute the individual subtasks. The distribution of the ExecutionGraph's topology to TaskManagers depends on the parallelism configured for each task. Some tasks within a single ExecutionGraph can run in parallel, potentially on different TaskManagers located across multiple machines.

The TaskManagers (also known as *workers*) have the following key features:

- *TaskManager is a process*—Each TaskManager runs as a separate JVM process and can execute multiple tasks concurrently using multiple threads.
- *Task slots for resource allocation*—TaskManagers provide task slots, which represent resources allocated for task execution. The JobManager assigns tasks to these slots, and the TaskManager executes them within the allocated slots.
- *Memory management*—Each task slot reserves a specific amount of memory, which is managed by the TaskManager to ensure efficient execution and isolation.
- *Distributed execution*—Tasks within the same ExecutionGraph can be distributed across multiple TaskManagers. Intermediate results are exchanged over the network, enabling parallel and distributed processing.

You can provide configuration hints to the JobManager, enabling it to construct a more efficient ExecutionGraph tailored to the specific requirements of your application.

In summary, Apache Flink is a more sophisticated solution than Kafka Streams, and it typically requires a steeper learning curve. However, its comprehensive feature set makes it well-suited for handling large-scale, distributed data processing workloads.

STATE MANAGEMENT

In Kafka Streams, stream partitioning is directly tied to the concept of Kafka partitions. When a stream is partitioned by key, it corresponds to the underlying Kafka topic's partitions, where each key in the stream aligns with a Kafka key.

In contrast, Apache Flink does not rely on Kafka for partitioning. In Flink, stream partitioning is a logical concept that governs how data is distributed in memory among the parallel tasks during execution. Flink's partitioning is independent of Kafka or any other external system, offering flexibility to dynamically partition data based on the execution plan and task parallelism.

Stateful operations in streaming often rely on keys, where events are grouped by keys before applying operations such as aggregation. For example, to calculate the number of orders per region, the region acts as the key, and events are grouped accordingly. In Flink, this is managed through *keyed state*, which associates state with specific keys and provides methods to access and update it.

Flink requires a storage mechanism to manage state. During normal execution, state is typically stored in the TaskManagers' memory, enabling fast access. Periodic checkpoints capture the state and are stored in the JobManager's memory. However, these checkpoints are not persisted to durable storage, meaning that while recovery is possible if a TaskManager fails, the state will be lost entirely if the JobManager or the entire cluster fails. This approach is suitable for small-scale jobs or testing but is not reliable for production environments.

For more robust state handling, Flink can use RocksDB, an embedded key-value store that persists state to disk. This setup allows Flink to efficiently handle large state sizes. Like many stream-processing frameworks, Flink supports checkpointing, which periodically saves the application state to external storage systems such as HDFS or S3. In contrast, Kafka Streams uses Kafka itself as the storage layer for changelogs and checkpoints, ensuring durability and fault tolerance. RocksDB, when used as Flink's state backend, is often preferred in production environments due to its ability to handle extensive and long-lived state efficiently while seamlessly integrating with Flink's checkpointing mechanisms.

In addition to keyed state, Flink also supports *operator state*, which is not tied to keys but to individual operator instances. Operator state is typically used in source or sink operators to retain data needed across events, restarts, or failures. For example, a source operator might use operator state to track progress, such as how much data has been read from an input source like Kafka or a file. Similarly, a sink operator might use it to buffer events before committing them to an external system.

Both keyed and operator states are integrated into Flink's checkpointing mechanism. State is persisted during checkpoints and restored upon recovery, ensuring fault tolerance. This flexibility, combined with Flink's scalable and durable state storage options, allows Flink to efficiently handle a wide range of streaming workloads while maintaining consistent and reliable processing.

FLINK CDC

The Flink CDC (change data capture) project facilitates integration with databases by reading database transaction logs to detect insert, update, and delete operations. These captured changes are converted into a stream of Flink records for further processing.

Flink CDC pipelines are defined declaratively in YAML files, similar to Kafka Connect configurations. These YAML definitions include details for sources, sinks, and optional transformations. This declarative approach simplifies setup while enabling real-time streaming of database changes with low latency.

Flink CDC provides a powerful alternative to Kafka Connect for real-time database integration. By embedding CDC logic directly into Flink jobs, it eliminates the need for additional infrastructure like Kafka Connect clusters, offering an integrated, low-latency solution for database change capture and stream processing.

FLINK SQL

Similar to ksqlDB, Apache Flink allows you to define data loading and transformation logic declaratively using Flink SQL. Flink SQL provides an API for executing SQL queries as Flink jobs. These queries are parsed, optimized, and translated into a Flink execution plan, which runs seamlessly on a Flink cluster.

Flink SQL queries can be embedded directly into Flink programs using the Table API or submitted externally through the Flink SQL CLI. Additionally, Flink offers the Flink SQL Gateway, a component that enables submitting SQL queries via REST and other protocols, providing a centralized and flexible way to execute and manage SQL-based Flink jobs.

FLINK ML

Traditionally, machine learning models are trained on a finite dataset in an offline, batch-oriented manner. However, the rise of stream processing has opened new opportunities for online machine learning, where models are incrementally updated as new data arrives. This approach allows models to adapt to evolving data patterns in real time, making them ideal for dynamic and fast-changing environments.

The Flink ML project introduces online machine learning capabilities as part of its broader library for building machine learning pipelines. Flink ML provides a unified API that supports both streaming and batch processing, enabling seamless integration of batch and online learning workflows. This unified approach ensures that the same code can handle offline training on historical data and real-time learning on streaming data.

Flink ML includes several pre-implemented algorithms for common tasks such as regression, classification, clustering, and feature extraction. Additionally, it offers flexible interfaces that allow users to implement custom machine learning algorithms, giving developers the freedom to design solutions tailored to specific use cases.

One of Flink's key strengths is its ability to support the entire machine learning pipeline within a single framework. This includes feature engineering, data preprocessing, model training, and inference stages. Flink's streaming-first architecture makes it particularly well-suited for online feature engineering, enabling real-time transformation and enrichment of raw input data. Once trained, models can be used for low-latency inference to generate predictions on live data streams.

By unifying streaming and batch machine learning under one library, Flink ML competes with other platforms like Apache Spark, offering a powerful and scalable solution for modern machine learning workflows. In contrast, Kafka Streams does not provide an integrated offering for machine learning pipelines. Instead, users must rely on separate projects and libraries, which are not consolidated under a single umbrella like Flink ML. Despite this, Kafka Streams can still be used effectively for certain stages of machine learning workflows, particularly for real-time feature engineering or inference.

Flink ML's online learning capabilities make it especially relevant for applications requiring continuous adaptation, such as fraud detection, real-time recommendation systems, and predictive maintenance.

8.4.3 Solutions from cloud providers

Major cloud providers such as AWS, Azure, and Google Cloud offer fully managed services and libraries for stream processing. While they provide their own proprietary solutions, they also support Apache Flink as a managed service for advanced use cases. Examples include Amazon Kinesis Data Analytics (https://aws.amazon.com/pm/kinesis), Azure Stream Analytics (https://azure.microsoft.com/en-us/products/stream-analytics), and Google Dataflow (https://cloud.google.com/products/dataflow).

These tools simplify real-time data processing by seamlessly integrating with their respective cloud ecosystems. They offer serverless and scalable architectures for handling streaming data at scale. Stream-processing services can ingest and output data to a wide variety of data sources, including messaging systems, databases, and storage services. Additionally, they provide support for defining SQL-like queries to process data declaratively and can integrate with machine learning services to enable real-time predictive analytics on streaming data. This makes them a good fit for building intelligent, real-time applications that combine data transformation with advanced analytics.

8.5   Common streaming application challenges

Troubleshooting streaming applications can be a complex task due to the dynamic and continuous nature of data processing. Challenges can arise at various stages, including data ingestion, transformation, state management, and output delivery. Unlike batch processing, where data is processed as a finite set, streaming applications operate on unbounded data streams, making debugging and diagnosing problems more challenging. Let's take a closer look at challenges with common streaming applications.

8.5.1 Memory and disk capacity planning

In stateful Kafka Streams applications, RocksDB state stores manage data primarily on disk while caching frequently accessed data in memory. Memory usage includes components such as RocksDB's block cache and write buffers, which are used to optimize read and write performance. Additionally, memory is required for buffering records read from input topics during processing. Calculating the required memory for state stores involves considering these factors alongside the application's workload and configuration.

Certain operations, such as repartitioning or state store backups, create additional topics:

- *Repartition topics*—Generated when records are rekeyed or redistributed
- *Changelog topics*—Used to back up state stores for fault tolerance

The disk capacity for these intermediate topics and state store changelog topics must be carefully planned to avoid bottlenecks or running out-of-space, especially as data volume grows.

8.5.2 Incorrect topic partitioning

When events need to be processed together, selecting the correct key for processing is essential. Proper partitioning ensures that records with the same key are sent to the same partition and, consequently, are processed by the same task.

In Kafka Streams, the DSL (e.g., for joins) enforces that the input topics have the same number of partitions. This requirement is enforced at runtime, and if it is not met, the application will throw a runtime error. However, Kafka Streams cannot verify whether the correct keys have been chosen for partitioning. If the keys are not chosen properly, events that logically belong together may end up in different partitions, leading to incorrect or incomplete processing of joins or aggregations.

This problem requires even more attention when using the Processor API or implementing custom partitioning logic. In such cases, the responsibility for ensuring consistent key selection and partition alignment falls entirely on the developer. Poor partitioning choices can lead to unexpected behaviors, such as incorrect joins, aggregations, or data loss in stateful operations.

These are some key considerations:

- Verify that the keys used for partitioning align with the application's business logic.
- Ensure that topics involved in joins or stateful operations have the same partition count and consistent partitioning logic.
- When implementing custom logic with the Processor API, carefully test key distribution to prevent data from being spread across incorrect partitions.

Proper topic partitioning is critical for ensuring the correctness and efficiency of Kafka Streams applications, especially in distributed environments.

8.5.3   *Out-of-order data*

Kafka Streams processes data in the order in which it is stored within partitions, which corresponds to the order of offsets. However, this can lead to out-of-order records under certain circumstances. For example, within a single partition, events with smaller offsets may sometimes have higher timestamps due to delays or clock differences at the producer side. Also, when consuming from multiple topics, events are read from internal buffers. In this case, an event with a higher timestamp from one topic may be processed before an event with a smaller timestamp from another topic.

If the application's logic depends on event time (the time embedded as an attribute in the event itself), Kafka Streams does not automatically use this time. Instead, you must explicitly configure it by implementing the `TimestampExtractor` interface.

8.5.4   *Late-arriving data*

In streaming applications, late-arriving data can occur due to network delays, out-of-order event production, or delays in upstream processing. When records arrive late, they may fall outside the window boundaries and be silently discarded, leading to data loss that is difficult to detect. Unlike typical errors, these issues do not trigger exceptions, making them especially challenging to identify and debug.

To mitigate the risk of silent data loss, it is crucial to configure appropriate grace periods. A *grace period* defines how long the application will wait for late records to arrive before finalizing the results of a windowed operation. In Kafka Streams, you can specify a grace period as part of the time window definition. For instance, setting a grace period of five minutes allows the application to process late records for an additional five minutes before finalizing the results.

8.5.5   *State store initialization*

Applications with stateful operations must rebuild their state stores (e.g., RocksDB) by reprocessing historical events. This can cause several problems:

- *Disk I/O bottlenecks*—Excessive read/write operations during state restoration can overwhelm disk capacity.
- *Memory pressure*—Buffering and state rebuilding consume significant memory resources.
- *Slower application recovery*—The time required to restore state can delay the application's readiness.

Several possible solutions are available:

- Plan carefully the number of partitions to distribute the state restoration load across multiple tasks and instances.
- Optimize RocksDB settings, such as buffer sizes, block cache, and write buffer configuration, to improve performance.
- Use standby tasks to preload state stores on inactive instances, ensuring faster failover by avoiding full state rebuilds.

By addressing these factors, applications can mitigate state restoration bottlenecks and achieve faster, more efficient recovery. This problem is quite common, as it applies to any application that needs to restore its state during startup. A practical recommendation is to perform benchmarks to simulate state restoration under various conditions, such as differing state sizes, partition counts, and RocksDB configurations. These benchmarks will help identify bottlenecks and provide valuable insights for optimizing resource allocation and tuning system performance.

8.5.6 *Monitoring and debugging challenges*

Kafka Streams applications often suffer from a lack of visibility into state stores, lags, and throughput, making it challenging to detect errors and performance bottlenecks. Debugging becomes even more complex when working with chained processors, where the flow of data through multiple processing steps is harder to trace. To address these challenges, it is essential to integrate with monitoring tools to gain insights into application performance, resource usage, and key metrics like lag and throughput.

However, monitoring tools alone may not provide sufficient visibility into the application's behavior. To achieve deeper insight, you can use logging and tracing libraries to trace the data flow through each processor step and identify bottlenecks or errors. One practical solution could be to use distributed tracing tools like OpenTelemetry, Jaeger, or Zipkin to trace data as it flows through your streaming application.

8.6 *Online resources*

- "Kafka Streams": https://kafka.apache.org/documentation/streams/
  This page introduces the Kafka Streams API and explains how to build real-time stream-processing applications directly on Kafka.
- *Kafka Streams in Action, Second Edition*, by William P. Bejeck Jr: www.manning .com/books/kafka-streams-in-action-second-edition
  This book offers a hands-on introduction to designing, building, and deploying stream-processing applications using the Kafka Streams API.
- "Crossing the Streams—Joins in Apache Kafka": www.confluent.io/blog/crossing -streams-joins-apache-kafka
  This article explains how to perform different types of joins in Apache Kafka using Kafka Streams.

Summary

- Real-time processing enables low-latency transformation of data compared to traditional batch-oriented ETL and ELT pipelines. Consider using streaming frameworks when latency is a crucial requirement.
- Kafka Streams integrates seamlessly with Kafka and simplifies operations such as filtering, transformation, aggregation, and joins. This is a good solution for most cases for processing in Java. Applications implemented with Kafka Streams are

fault-tolerant, scalable, and support exactly-once processing semantics (EoS), ensuring reliability.

- Kafka Streams supports stateful operations using state stores backed by RocksDB and changelog topics for fault tolerance. The concept of windows is supported in queries used for time-based aggregations over event streams.

- Alternatives like Apache Flink and ksqlDB offer additional flexibility for stream processing and make it possible to create processing logic declaratively with SQL-like languages.

- Cloud-based solutions such as AWS Kinesis, Azure Stream Analytics, and Google Dataflow provide fully managed options for real-time data pipelines.

Part 3

Delivering projects with Kafka

Architecture sets the vision, but projects succeed only when that vision is delivered in practice. In this part of the book, we'll focus on what it takes to run Kafka in the real world—from deployment to daily operations—and finally, at what the future holds.

In chapter 9, we'll look at deployment choices, metadata management, and security practices that protect Kafka in the enterprise. Chapter 10 turns to project organization: collecting requirements, structuring the cluster, and testing Kafka applications under realistic conditions. Chapter 11 highlights the operational side, exploring maintenance, monitoring, scaling, and the upgrades needed to keep Kafka healthy in production. Finally, chapter 12 looks ahead at emerging trends, showing how Kafka is evolving and what architects should anticipate for the future.

Managing Kafka within the enterprise

This chapter covers

- Handling configuration, leadership assignments, and state coordination
- Exploring Kafka deployment strategies: on-premises, cloud-based, and hybrid solutions
- Best practices for authentication, authorization, encryption, and protecting data

When you get close to launching a prototype into production, it's time to think about the concrete operational details. How will your system manage metadata and coordination so you can size and place controllers, anticipate behavior during incidents, and plan migrations from older architectures (such as ZooKeeper) to KRaft? Here is where another key actor in the Kafka ecosystem, the controller quorum, comes into play. Controllers manage metadata and ensure that clusters remain operational; they use quorum-based decisions to maintain fault tolerance. All of this needs to be configured.

Then there is the question of deployment. On-premises, cloud, and hybrid deployment models are all viable, and it's important to compare them to match latency, cost, and operability.

Finally, you'll want to make security actionable from end to end, including authentication (mTLS/SASL), authorization (ACLs), encryption in transit (TLS), data-at-rest protection, and even optional end-to-end encryption. We'll look at all these operational details in this chapter.

Field notes: From prototype to deployment

Max: Alright, team, how are things going? Don't you think it's time to stop playing around and finally move this prototype into some sort of environment? You know, make it visible, accessible, so other teams can start working with it?

Rob: You're absolutely right, Max. And that's exactly what we want to discuss today. But before we can do that, we need to talk about something important: the budget.

Max: The budget? Didn't we already settle this? Start on-prem, get the brokers running, and keep it simple.

Eva: True, but brokers alone won't be enough. We'll also need a cluster of controllers to manage the metadata.

Max: Metadata? What are you talking about?

Rob: All the topics, configurations, partition details, and other operational data—Kafka needs to store that somewhere, and that's the job of the controller cluster.

Max: Another cluster? Really? Look, databases also manage metadata, but they handle it silently, behind the scenes. Why does Kafka need this extra setup?

Eva: It's more complicated with Kafka. The metadata isn't just static—it's dynamic and needs to be constantly updated and coordinated across the cluster. But don't worry; for development purposes, we can reuse some of the existing hardware to keep things simple.

Max: Alright, but I'm going to need more explanations. Right now, it's not very clear to me why this is necessary.

Eva: Don't worry; we'll explain everything.

9.1   *Managing metadata*

So far, we've discussed Kafka primarily as a cluster of message brokers responsible for transferring messages. However, we haven't yet addressed any operational aspects. Where is the configuration of topics stored? How is it updated? Which process decides where to assign leaders for each partition?

To draw a parallel with cloud infrastructure, we can think of message handling as the data plane, responsible for the actual flow of messages, and the management of cluster configuration as the control plane, overseeing the cluster's metadata and ensuring everything operates smoothly.

The servers participating in the cluster assume one of two primary roles:

- *Broker*—Responsible for processing and storing messages, as well as serving producer and consumer requests
- *Controller*—Responsible for managing metadata updates, communicating changes to brokers, and detecting server failures through heartbeats

It's also possible for a single server to perform both roles simultaneously, depending on the cluster configuration. However, in production environments, it is recommended that you run dedicated controller nodes to minimize latency and reduce the risk of metadata unavailability.

Controllers are responsible for storing and managing metadata, as well as maintaining the cluster's state by detecting failovers. Metadata is stored in a dedicated metadata log called `__cluster_metadata`, which is replicated across all controllers in the quorum to ensure fault tolerance. Controllers operate as a quorum, with one designated as the leader. An example of a Kafka cluster structure is shown in figure 9.1.

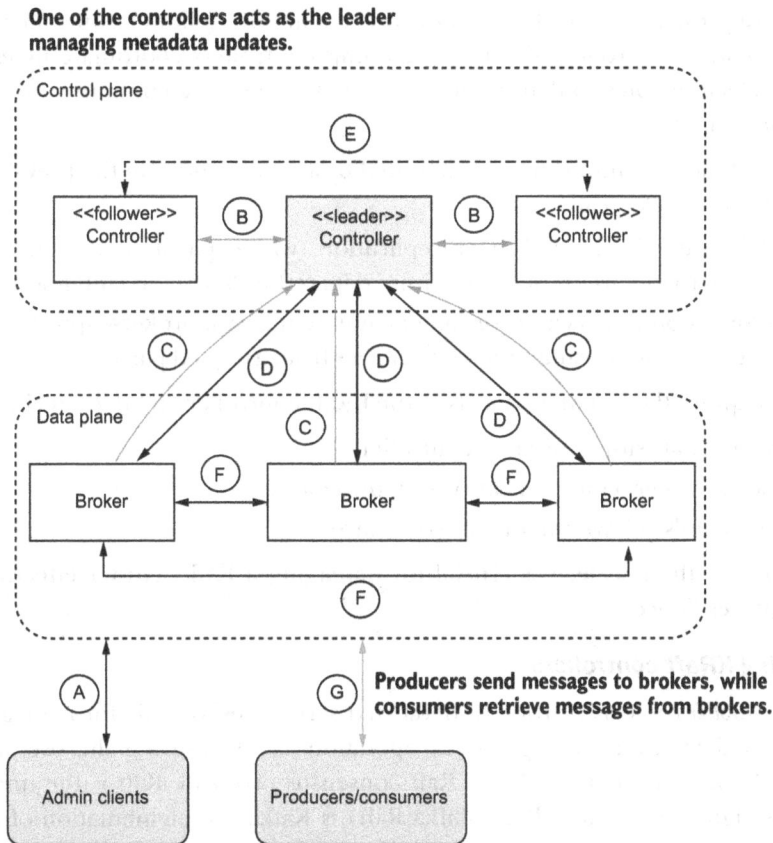

Figure 9.1 Controllers operate as a quorum, responsible for storing metadata and monitoring cluster health.

Let's start with understanding what all the arrows in figure 9.1 indicate:

- *A*—Represents how admin clients send requests to brokers, which then forward relevant metadata operations (such as topic creation or configuration changes) to the leader controller. The controller processes these requests and updates the cluster metadata accordingly.
- *B*—Illustrates the leader-follower communication between controllers. Follower controllers fetch metadata updates from the leader to stay in sync. If a follower does not receive timely responses, it assumes the leader is unavailable and may initiate a new election.
- *C*—Depicts communication between brokers and the controller. Brokers send heartbeats to the leader controller to signal their liveness. If a broker fails to send heartbeats within the expected interval, the leader controller detects the failure and updates the cluster state accordingly.
- *D*—Shows communication where brokers fetch metadata updates from the leader controller to stay synchronized with the cluster state.
- *E*—Represents the leader election process among follower controllers. When the leader controller fails, the remaining controllers coordinate by exchanging election votes to determine a new leader, ensuring continuity in metadata management.

We discussed the communication represented by arrows *F* and *G* in the previous chapters, so here's a quick recap:

- *F*—Illustrates broker-to-broker replication, where partition leaders replicate messages to follower replicas to ensure data redundancy and fault tolerance.
- *G*—Shows producers and consumers interacting with brokers—producers send messages, while consumers fetch messages from assigned partitions.

Now, let's explore the essential aspects of the KRaft controller architecture, including

- The metadata stored in KRaft controllers
- How controllers communicate within the cluster
- The system's behavior in the case of failure

Understanding these aspects is crucial for managing a Kafka cluster effectively and ensuring its resilience.

9.1.1 Introducing KRaft controllers

A *KRaft controller cluster* is a group of dedicated servers responsible for managing and storing metadata, coordinating broker operations, and ensuring the overall stability of the Kafka cluster through the Raft consensus protocol. Raft is the underlying consensus algorithm, while KRaft (Kafka Raft) is Kafka's implementation of Raft for metadata management. In this discussion, we will use the term "Raft protocol" when referring to the consensus mechanism and "KRaft" when specifically discussing Kafka's implementation.

KRAFT CONTROLLER CLUSTER

Controllers are responsible for storing and managing the metadata of a Kafka cluster. Metadata is stored in Raft logs, which are files located on the controller's filesystem. Some sources refer to metadata storage as the `__cluster_metadata` topic with one partition. However, this can be misleading, as it is not a typical Kafka topic stored on brokers. While only controllers participate in the Raft quorum and write to the metadata log, broker nodes may also maintain a local, read-only copy for faster startup and metadata access.

Unlike a normal topic that uses Kafka's replication protocol, this internal log uses a Raft-based replication approach. In Raft replication, the leader controller does not commit an update until a majority of follower controllers acknowledge it, ensuring strong consistency. This differs from broker replication, where consistency is configurable and does not rely on quorum acknowledgment. In such setups, a newly elected broker leader might miss recent messages, especially if they were not fully replicated. In contrast, Raft ensures that a new leader is elected only if it has all committed entries, avoiding the risk of committed data loss.

It is also important to note that regular Kafka clients never interact directly with the metadata log. Instead, brokers retrieve metadata from the controllers and serve it to clients as needed.

The metadata stored in the controllers includes the following elements:

- *Topic metadata*—Topic names, number of partitions, replication factor, and configuration parameters.
- *Runtime partition information*—The leader for each partition, the brokers hosting replicas, and the replicas that are currently in sync.
- *Broker metadata*—Identifiers of brokers, connection details, rack location (if rack awareness is enabled), and broker-level configuration parameters.
- *Controller cluster state*—Information about the roles assigned to controllers.
- *Access control lists (ACLs)*—Authorization rules for accessing cluster resources (discussed later in this chapter).
- *Transaction metadata*—Identifiers of transactional producers and mapping of identifiers to the partitions where transaction state is stored. (Note: The actual transaction data, including which records are in the transaction and whether the transaction is ongoing or completed, lives in the `__transaction_state` topic on the brokers).
- *Consumer group metadata*—Identifiers of consumer groups and their partition assignments. (Note: Committed offsets for consumer groups are stored in the `__consumer_offsets` topic on brokers, not in the Raft log.)
- *Quotas*—Traffic limitations for clients, which are enforced to prevent excessive resource consumption by clients or brokers. These limits help maintain cluster stability by ensuring that no single client or broker overloads the system.

In the KRaft architecture, as shown in figure 9.1, participants are assigned one of two roles:

- *Leader* (also called the *active controller*)—Primary controller responsible for receiving metadata updates and propagating them for replication.
- *Followers*—Participants that act in the quorum by voting on changes. The leader is also a voter and contributes to the quorum.

One of the controllers is elected as the leader, preferring the most up-to-date node, which handles all metadata updates. The election process follows the Raft consensus protocol, details of which can be found in the official Kafka documentation.

Updates originate from clients (e.g., admin clients creating topics or updating configurations) and are sent to brokers, which forward the requests to the leader controller. The leader makes metadata updates available to the followers, as shown in figure 9.2. Followers periodically fetch these updates from the leader and, upon receiving

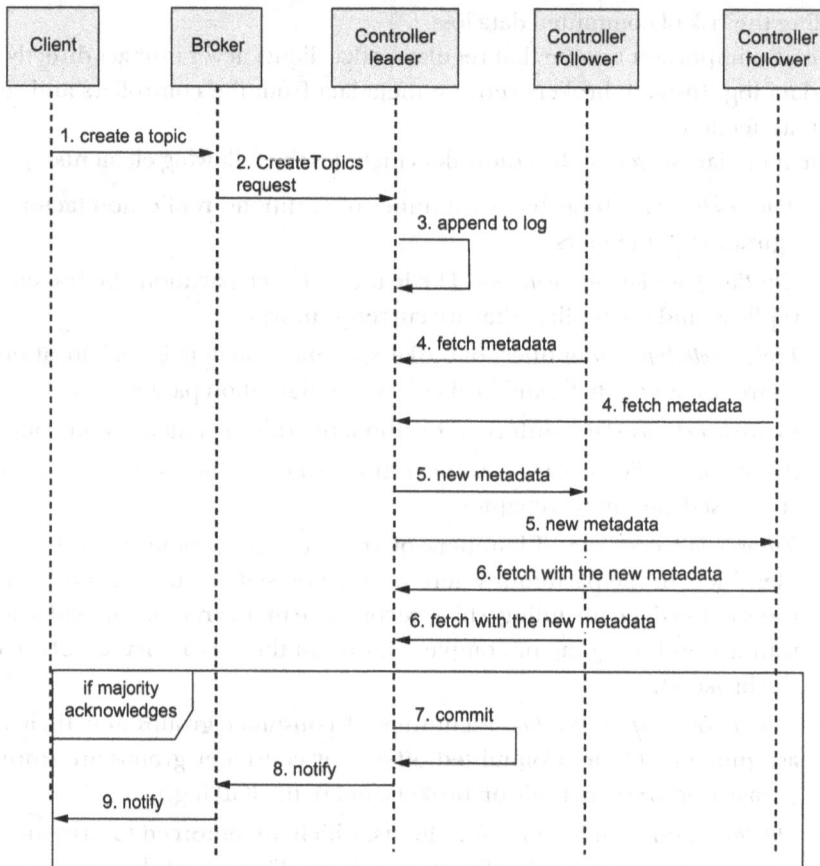

Figure 9.2   Metadata updates are sent to the leader controller, which appends each update to its log. Follower controllers fetch these updates from the leader, and once a majority have replicated the update, it is marked as committed.

them, append the entries to their local metadata log. If the append is successful, the follower includes the log offset in its next fetch request, which the leader interprets as an acknowledgment. To mark an update as committed, the leader must receive acknowledgments from a majority of voters (including itself), ensuring that committed state cannot be lost in the event of a crash. This majority-based decision-making process is what defines the quorum architecture. Once committed, the metadata becomes visible to brokers that request it from the controller.

The requirement for a majority of voters to be operational has significant implications for the architecture. In this context, N represents the number of node failures the cluster should be able to tolerate. To maintain a quorum, more than half of the voters must be available, which is why the voting set is sized to $2N+1$ nodes: even if N nodes fail, the remaining $N+1$ nodes still form a majority and the cluster can still function. To ensure survivability in the event of a complete data center outage, the cluster must span at least three data centers (as shown in figure 9.3).

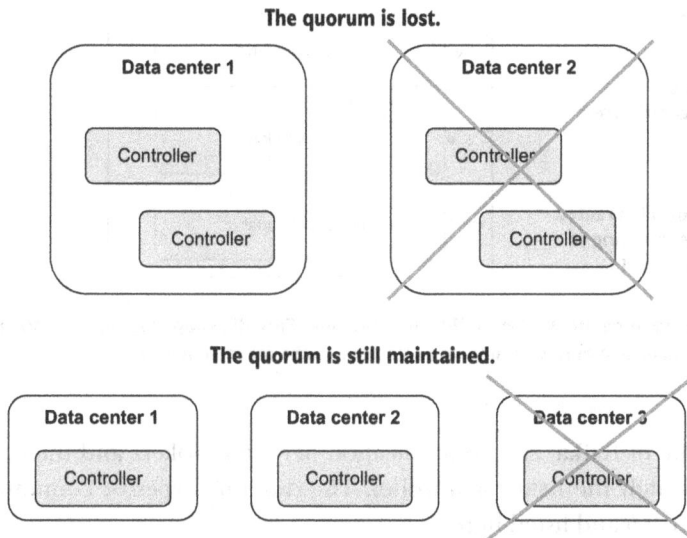

Figure 9.3 In the event of a complete data center outage, losing the majority of controllers causes a loss of quorum if the cluster is distributed across two data centers. However, with three data centers, quorum can still be maintained despite the failure of an entire data center. In this case, $N = 1$, meaning the system can tolerate only one node failure.

This ensures that even if one data center goes offline, the majority of controllers remains available to maintain quorum.

STORING AND DISTRIBUTING METADATA

Controllers maintain the metadata log as files, recording all metadata updates sequentially. To prevent the log from growing indefinitely, the controller periodically creates a snapshot, which retains only the latest metadata state rather than historical data. This process is conceptually similar to compacted topics in Kafka. Snapshots are generated locally by the controller, derived from the current state reconstructed from the Raft log. Once a snapshot is created, older log segments containing updates already reflected in the snapshot can be safely deleted.

During startup or recovery, a controller first loads the latest snapshot and then replays any log entries added after the snapshot was taken to fully restore the cluster state.

In addition to persistent storage, metadata is also cached in memory to enable fast responses to real-time metadata requests. Figure 9.4 illustrates the three locations where metadata is managed: the metadata log, the metadata snapshot, and the in-memory cache.

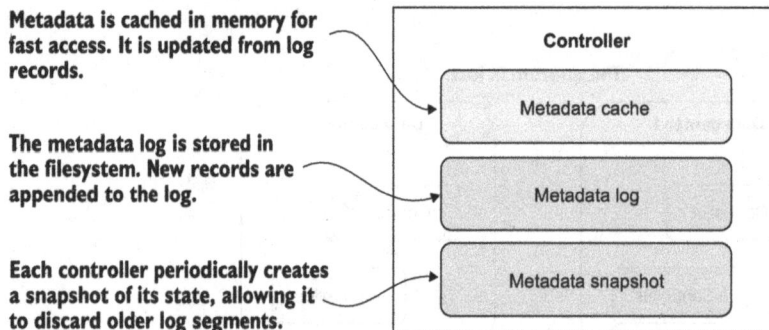

Figure 9.4   Metadata records are written to the metadata log. Periodic snapshots capture the latest committed state, which is also maintained in an in-memory cache for rapid access.

In the current state of Kafka, all communication between brokers and the controller cluster occurs through the leader controller. The different types of communication are shown in figure 9.5 and listed here:

- *Heartbeats*—Brokers send periodic heartbeats to the leader controller to indicate they are alive and functioning. The leader controller uses these heartbeats to track the liveness of brokers.

- *Metadata fetching*—Brokers periodically fetch updated metadata from the leader, ensuring they stay in sync with the current cluster state.

- *Metadata updates*—Brokers forward client-initiated metadata update requests (e.g., topic creation or partition reassignment) to the leader controller, which processes and commits them through the metadata log.

Brokers, as well as controllers, maintain a metadata cache in memory to support faster operations. In KRaft mode—the deployment configuration in which Kafka uses KRaft

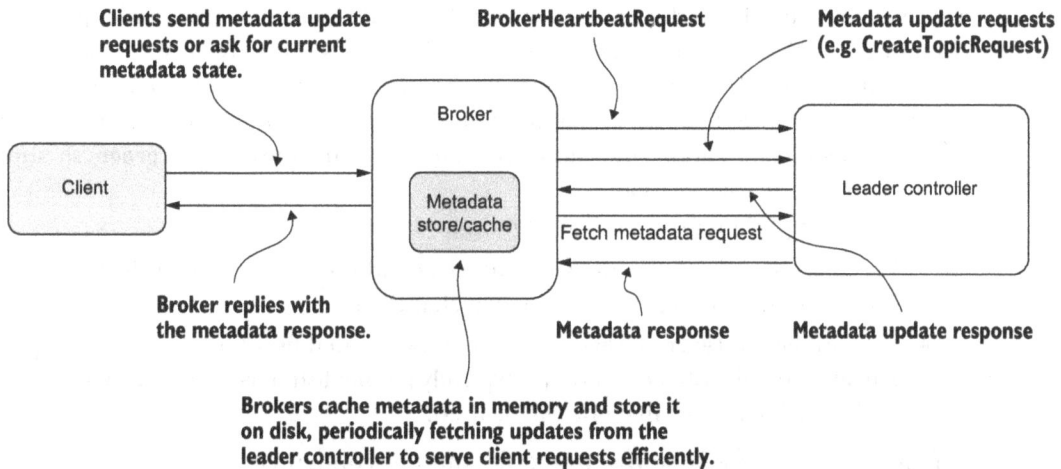

Figure 9.5 Clients send metadata requests to brokers and receive responses containing the current cluster metadata. Brokers forward client-initiated metadata changes to the leader controller and periodically fetch updated metadata. Brokers also send heartbeats to the controller, which uses them to track broker liveness.

controllers to manage metadata—brokers may also persist a local copy of the metadata log on disk, but they do not participate in committing updates. The authoritative source of truth for cluster-wide metadata resides exclusively within the Raft log managed by the controller quorum.

When a broker restarts, it contacts the leader controller to fetch the current metadata. The broker keeps this metadata in memory and continuously updates it as it receives pushed updates from the leader controller.

CONFIGURING CONTROLLERS AND BROKERS

Operating Kafka in KRaft mode requires a specific configuration. First, for each server, we must specify whether it will act as a controller, broker, or operate in a combined mode. This is done by setting the `process.roles` property, where the following values can be used:

- `controller`—The server will operate exclusively as a controller.
- `broker`—The server will operate only as a broker.
- `broker,controller`—The server will operate as both a broker and a controller simultaneously.

If this property is not set, the server is assumed to be running in ZooKeeper mode (discussed later in this chapter).

Another property you must set is `node.id`, which is a unique identifier for the server across all brokers and controllers in a particular cluster.

Controllers need to know about each other, and there are two ways to configure this. The first method is to specify the quorum statically using the `controller.quorum.voters` property. The format for this property is a comma-separated list of controllers, where each controller is defined as `{node_id}@{host}:{port}`. For dynamic quorum configuration, the `controller.quorum.bootstrap.servers` property must be specified. This property should include as many servers as possible, defined as a comma-separated list of `{host}:{port}`. It works much like `bootstrap.servers` in client configurations. New controllers can be added or removed dynamically using the `kafka-storage.sh` and `kafka-metadata-quorum.sh` tools.

Two other important properties are configured on the controller side:

- `listeners`—Defines the network interfaces where a controller will listen for incoming connections (as described in chapter 3).
- `controller.listener.names`—This comma-separated list of listeners is used specifically for controllers. There will typically be one listener—you can specify several listeners, but the first one will be used.

On the broker side, the following properties must be configured:

- `controller.listener.names`—Specifies which listener on the broker should be used for communication with the controller, particularly for receiving metadata updates.
- `controller.quorum.voters`—Defines the list of controller nodes that brokers should connect to for sending heartbeats and metadata change requests.

Additionally, properties such as `listeners`, `advertised.listeners`, and `inter.broker.listener.name` must be set to configure network communication. These were covered in chapter 3.

Other properties, such as those for setting timeouts, can be found in the official documentation.

9.1.2   *Example of cluster configuration*

Listing 9.1 shows the configuration of a KRaft quorum with three controllers. Each server is configured to function exclusively as a controller, as defined by the `process.roles` property, and each node is assigned a unique identifier using the `node.id` property. The configuration also specifies the list of controller nodes that form the quorum (`controller.quorum.voters`) and defines which listener the controller should use for communication (`controller.listener.names`), while the actual listener details are set in the listeners. Additionally, the `listener.security.protocol.map` property maps listeners to their corresponding security protocols. Each controller provides such a configuration with a different `node.id`.

> **Listing 9.1   An example of a KRaft controller's configuration (static quorum)**

```
                    Unique identifier
                    of the node          Role of the server—this          Comma-separated
                                          server serves as a controller    list of controllers:
node.id=1  ◄────                    ┌──                                   {node_id}@{host}:{port}
process.roles=controller  ◄─────────┘
controller.quorum.voters=1@node1:9093,2@node2:9093,3@node3:9093  ◄──
```

```
controller.listener.names=CNTRL
listeners=CNTRL://node1:9093
  listener.security.protocol.map=CNTRL:PLAINTEXT
```

Name of the listener for the controller

List of addresses where the controller listens

Mapping of listeners to protocols

Listing 9.2 shows the configuration for a server that operates exclusively as a broker. It contains settings for communicating with controllers (similar to the controller configuration), the listener used for communication with brokers (inter.broker.listener .name), and additional settings for communicating with clients.

Listing 9.2 An example of a broker's configuration in a KRaft cluster

Unique identifier of the node

Role of the server—this server serves as a broker

Connection to controllers

```
node.id=4
process.roles=broker
controller.quorum.voters=1@node1:9093,2@node2:9093,3@node3:9093
listeners=BROKER://broker1:9092, EXTERNAL://broker1:9095
controller.listener.names=CNTRL
inter.broker.listener.name=BROKER
advertised.listeners=BROKER://broker1:9092,EXTERNAL://broker1:9095
listener.security.protocol.map=CNTRL:PLAINTEXT,BROKER:PLAINTEXT,
 EXTERNAL:SSL
```

Name of the listener for communicating with a controller

Other configuration properties can be found in the official documentation.

9.1.3 *Failover scenarios*

In this section, we'll explore possible scenarios and examine what happens in the event of a controller failure (whether a leader or follower) or a broker failure. Understanding potential failures helps Kafka administrators prevent downtime, optimize failover handling, and maintain data integrity.

FAILURE OF A LEADER CONTROLLER

Follower controllers periodically send fetch requests to the leader controller to retrieve metadata updates. These requests serve a dual purpose: replicating the metadata log and implicitly confirming that the leader is still alive. If a follower does not receive a response within the configured timeout period (controller.quorum.fetch.timeout .ms), it considers the leader unavailable and transitions to the candidate state to initiate a new election. This pull-based heartbeat mechanism is internally managed by Kafka's Raft implementation.

In the candidate state, each candidate sends vote requests to other controllers. These requests include information about the candidate's replicated metadata log. A recipient grants its vote if it hasn't already voted in the current term and the candidate's log is at least as up-to-date as its own. The node that secures a majority of votes becomes the new leader controller.

The newly elected leader does not begin serving immediately. First, it ensures that its local metadata state is consistent by verifying it has all previously committed log entries. If any entries are missing, the leader fetches them from other controllers to achieve a consistent state. Once the leader is fully synchronized, it begins serving metadata requests from brokers and managing metadata updates.

When brokers cannot communicate with the leader, they detect the failure and attempt to locate the new leader controller. Brokers are preconfigured with a list of controllers (`controller.quorum.voters`) and use this list to contact the remaining controllers. A functioning controller responds with the details of the new leader; the broker then establishes communication with the new leader and updates its internal state with the metadata provided by the leader.

FAILURE OF A FOLLOWER CONTROLLER

In KRaft mode, follower controllers periodically send fetch requests to the leader controller to retrieve metadata updates. These fetches also serve as an implicit heartbeat. If a follower fails to send fetches within the specified timeout period, it is considered unavailable and stops participating in the quorum. As long as a majority of controllers remain operational, the cluster continues to function normally. However, if the quorum is lost, no new metadata updates can be committed until it is restored.

Brokers are unaffected by the failure of a follower controller because they communicate exclusively with the leader controller. Metadata updates and failover decisions are managed entirely by the leader and do not depend on any specific follower. Similarly, clients are unaffected because they do not communicate directly with controllers.

When a failed controller comes back online, it identifies the current leader and fetches the latest metadata log entries from it to synchronize its state before rejoining the quorum.

FAILURE OF A BROKER

Brokers send periodic heartbeats (not explicitly configurable) to the leader controller to indicate they are alive and functioning. The leader controller tracks the last heartbeat time for each broker, and if the leader controller does not receive a heartbeat from a broker within the specified timeout period, the broker is marked as failed.

This failure impacts the partitions whose leaders were hosted on the failed broker, as new leaders need to be assigned. For each affected partition, the leader controller selects a candidate from the in-sync replica (ISR) set and assigns it as the new leader. If no ISR is available, the partition becomes under-replicated, and depending on the configuration of `unclean.leader.election.enable`, the partition may either

- Remain offline (if the property is set to `false`, ensuring data consistency)
- Elect an out-of-sync replica as the new leader (if the property is set to `true`, prioritizing availability over consistency)

The controller appends metadata records to the Raft log reflecting the broker failure, new partition leaders, and updated ISR lists. Once committed, these changes become part of the cluster metadata state.

Brokers and clients receive updated metadata through periodic metadata fetches, ensuring that producers and consumers are aware of the new partition leadership. During this transition, clients may encounter transient errors, such as "replica not available," but they automatically reconnect to the new leaders once metadata is refreshed.

When the failed broker recovers, it reconnects to the leader controller and re-registers itself. The leader controller then sends the latest cluster metadata to the broker, enabling it to synchronize its state. The recovering broker must catch up its replicas for any partitions it hosts that became out of sync during the failure. Once a replica is fully caught up, it is restored to the ISR set, and the cluster returns to a fully healthy state.

9.1.4 Using ZooKeeper

KRaft was introduced in Kafka version 2.8.0 as an experimental feature and in version 3.7.0 became the default metadata management system. Older versions of Kafka (which, at the time of writing this book, still represent the majority of systems in production) do not use the KRaft quorum but instead rely on Apache ZooKeeper. In this setup, the architecture is divided into two separate clusters:

- *ZooKeeper cluster*—Handles metadata management and monitors broker liveness.
- *Kafka cluster*—Manages topics, partitions, and client communications. Each node in the Kafka cluster has only one role: a broker.

An example of a Kafka setup with ZooKeeper is shown in figure 9.6. The ZooKeeper cluster consists of multiple servers, one of which acts as the leader (dynamically elected), while the others function as followers. This cluster has two primary responsibilities:

1. Storing metadata:
   a. ZooKeeper stores the same types of metadata now managed by the `__cluster_metadata` log in KRaft.
   b. Metadata updates, such as topic creation or partition assignments, are sent by brokers to the ZooKeeper leader and are replicated to the followers using the ZooKeeper Atomic Broadcast (ZAB) protocol. ZAB also requires a majority to acknowledge changes; however, unlike KRaft, it follows a leader-follower model where changes are committed only after replication, rather than being replicated as uncommitted entries first.
2. Broker liveness:
   a. Brokers send periodic heartbeats to the ZooKeeper cluster.
   b. If a broker fails to send a heartbeat within the configured timeout, ZooKeeper marks the broker as unavailable. The leaders of partitions hosted on the failed broker are reassigned to other brokers.

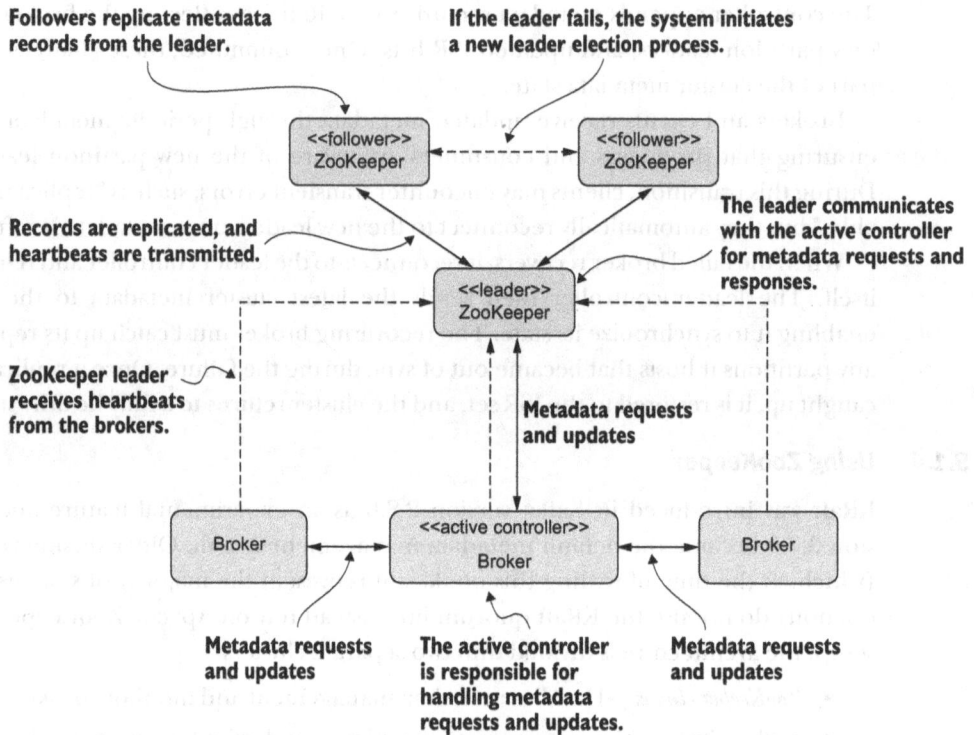

Figure 9.6   Various types of communication within a Kafka cluster using ZooKeeper

When Zookeeper is used for managing metadata, one of the brokers assumes the role of the active controller. This active controller communicates directly with the Zoo-Keeper leader to

- Load metadata updates, which are kept in the active controller's memory.
- Ensure cluster-wide coordination.

Other brokers rely on the active controller for two key operations:

- *Receiving metadata updates*—Brokers receive updates from the active controller to stay in sync with cluster state changes.
- *Initiating metadata updates*—Brokers forward requests initiated by clients (e.g., creating topics or changing configurations) to the active controller, which coordinates these changes with ZooKeeper.

ZooKeeper is a quorum-based system, requiring a majority of servers to function. This follows the $2N+1$ rule, meaning the system can tolerate the failure of up to N servers in a quorum of $2N+1$. ZooKeeper servers maintain liveness through heartbeats. If a server fails to send heartbeats, the cluster structure is updated, and if the leader fails, a new leader is elected from the remaining followers.

In the current versions of Kafka, ZooKeeper is deprecated and will be removed in future releases for a few primary reasons:

- *Simplified operations*—Removing the dependency on an external system like Zoo-Keeper makes Kafka easier to deploy, monitor, and maintain.
- *Improved metadata storage*—The KRaft architecture enables faster metadata restoration using snapshots, which enhances system availability.
- *Efficient metadata propagation*—KRaft's Raft-based protocol provides a more efficient way to deliver metadata updates to brokers, reducing latency and improving scalability. Brokers receive pushed metadata updates from the leader controller instead of pulling it from ZooKeeper.

To sum up, Kafka separates the control and data planes, so a quorum of KRaft controllers owns cluster metadata and coordination, while brokers store and serve records. Controllers replicate metadata via a Raft log, elect a leader, and commit updates only with a majority; they also snapshot the log and keep an in-memory cache. Brokers heartbeat to and fetch metadata from the active controller and forward admin changes. Understanding these flows—and where metadata lives—is key to a secure network layout, to troubleshooting startup and failover behavior, and to capacity and placement planning as Kafka moves beyond ZooKeeper.

> **Field notes: Choosing a deployment solution**
>
> Max: You know, when we first talked about a Kafka cluster with three brokers, it all seemed manageable. But now, things are getting a lot more complicated. We need a separate cluster for metadata, and that's not even counting Schema Registry, Kafka Connect, and who knows what else. I keep thinking—are we really prepared to maintain all of this on-prem without deep operational expertise? And what about the cost? Not just hardware, but also the people needed to run it. Wouldn't moving everything to the cloud be simpler?
>
> Rob: Well, sure, cloud providers make things easier, and you get predictable costs—for now. But what happens if the provider changes something? Pricing models shift, new limitations appear, or support for key features gets discontinued. When you're fully dependent on a cloud provider, changing solutions isn't simple.
>
> Max: Yeah, migrating between cloud providers is never easy. Once you're committed to an ecosystem, everything—from APIs to infrastructure tuning—gets tightly integrated.
>
> Eva: And then there's data gravity. The more services we rely on in the cloud, the harder it becomes to change direction. Even if the provider doesn't force a move, we might end up stuck because everything else depends on it.
>
> Max: So we need to be careful about what we commit to. But what about our current infrastructure? Is it even realistic to run everything on-prem long term?
>
> Rob: That's another big question. A lot of our core systems are still on-prem, and they're going to stay that way for a while. Running all of our integration services in the

(continued)

cloud while keeping the data on-prem doesn't make much sense. That would just add latency and operational complexity.

Eva: True, but we are moving toward cloud-based systems. And don't forget data analytics—most of the advanced tools for that are only available as managed cloud services. Even if our core systems stay on-prem for now, we'll still need to push data to the cloud for analysis.

Max: Alright, but what about disaster recovery? Whether we run Kafka on-prem or in the cloud, we need to think about what happens if something goes wrong.

Rob: That's a fair point. With on-prem, we'd need a dedicated backup strategy and redundant hardware for high availability. The cloud, on the other hand, offers built-in options for disaster recovery, like multi-region replication. But that comes at a cost, too.

Max: So we've got on-prem complexity, cloud lock-in risks, and no clear middle ground. Before we commit to anything, we need to define exactly what should go where— otherwise, we'll be running in circles.

9.2   Choosing a deployment solution

Deploying Kafka is not just about setting up a cluster—it requires careful consideration of operational complexity, scalability, multi-region architecture, and security requirements. Whether they're running Kafka on-premises or in the cloud—or using a hybrid approach—organizations must evaluate their needs and find the solution that best aligns with their use cases, balancing infrastructure management, fault tolerance, and compliance constraints.

9.2.1   Choosing between on-premises and cloud Kafka deployment

Let's start by comparing the on-premises and cloud Kafka deployment approaches.

HANDLING OPERATIONAL COMPLEXITY

If you plan to deploy Kafka in an on-premises environment, one of the biggest obstacles is the steep learning curve. While Kafka excels in handling server-side workloads, it lacks user-friendly operational tools. Managing an on-premises Kafka cluster means handling cluster setup, configuring brokers, securing authentication, monitoring system performance, and ensuring disaster recovery. This involves provisioning servers, setting up authentication mechanisms like SASL or SSL, integrating observability tools such as Prometheus and Grafana, and implementing replication across data centers. All these operational complexities fall on the shoulders of your team, making stability and performance a constant concern.

Opting for Kafka as a managed service shifts many of these responsibilities to the cloud provider. Your team no longer needs to worry about maintaining the hardware, configuring the clusters, monitoring the setup, or patching security. Cloud-managed services handle provisioning and updates, allowing teams to focus on application development rather than infrastructure management. However, this convenience comes with tradeoffs. The ability to fine-tune Kafka's configurations becomes limited, as cloud providers often restrict direct access to broker settings. Users also lose control over version upgrades, meaning they cannot freely upgrade or downgrade Kafka based on their specific needs. Additionally, while managed services reduce operational burden, they often come at a higher cost than running Kafka in-house, especially at scale.

Small companies benefit most from managed Kafka services, as they can focus on application development rather than the complexities of infrastructure management. In contrast, on-premises Kafka is a better fit for large enterprises with dedicated Kafka engineers who can fine-tune performance and optimize costs effectively.

VENDOR LOCK-INS

Another critical factor when choosing a managed Kafka service is the risk of vendor lock-in. Different providers introduce proprietary features and integrations that can make migration to another platform challenging. Confluent Cloud (www.confluent .io/lp/confluent-cloud), for example, offers exclusive capabilities beyond open source Kafka, such as role-based access control (RBAC), enforced data constraints for schemas, and advanced topic mirroring for seamless multicluster replication, among others. Amazon MSK (Amazon's fully managed Kafka service) integrates tightly with AWS services such as IAM, Kinesis, and CloudWatch, making it difficult to migrate workloads outside the AWS ecosystem. Aiven (https://aiven.io) provides multicloud replication capabilities, but its customizations might require adjustments if you're switching to another provider. If Kafka clusters store and replicate large amounts of data, egress fees alone can make switching to a different provider impractical.

That lock-in can be a reasonable trade if your strategy does not include near-term portability and you value seamless integration, reduced operational overhead, and vendor SLAs. The key is to choose intentionally: document exit costs, avoid proprietary features on critical paths, and keep a minimal migration path (e.g., standard serializers and APIs) for future flexibility.

KAFKA MULTI-REGION DEPLOYMENTS

Managing Kafka metadata requires a majority of servers (whether KRaft controllers or ZooKeeper nodes) to remain operational, which introduces significant challenges. As discussed earlier in this chapter, ensuring system availability during a full data center outage requires Kafka clusters to span at least three data centers. This requirement poses a challenge for smaller companies that typically do not have the infrastructure to operate across multiple data centers. However, even without three data centers, Kafka can still function, but with the risk of downtime in the event of a complete data center failure.

When deploying Kafka in the cloud, distributing brokers across multiple regions becomes significantly more feasible. Cloud providers offer built-in infrastructure to support cross-region deployments, reducing the operational burden and improving resilience. Still, multi-region Kafka setups come with their own considerations, including replication latency, networking costs, and data consistency challenges.

SCALABILITY OF KAFKA DEPLOYMENTS

The concept of automatic scaling works well for stateless microservices, where new instances can be launched as demand increases and then shut down when traffic decreases, optimizing resource utilization. This leads many to expect a similar autoscaling behavior for Kafka in the cloud. However, Kafka is fundamentally different because it is stateful, and each broker is responsible for managing a specific set of partitions. Unlike microservices, Kafka does not automatically redistribute partitions when a new broker is added, which makes scaling more complex.

Scaling Kafka is not as simple as just adding a broker. While cloud-based Kafka services promise scalability, the reality is more nuanced. Adding a broker does not automatically balance the workload; partitions and their associated data must be migrated to the new broker, which is a time-consuming and resource-intensive process. Partition movement requires transferring data between brokers and updating partition leadership, which impacts system performance by consuming

- CPU and disk I/O on the source broker
- Network bandwidth, potentially leading to latency spikes
- Time, as rebalancing large partitions can take a significant amount of time

Even though some managed Kafka providers automate parts of the scaling process behind the scenes, they still have to handle partition rebalancing and networking constraints. For example, Confluent Cloud offers autoscaling in some configurations, but many other providers, including Amazon MSK and Aiven, require manual intervention to add brokers and redistribute data.

Scaling down Kafka brokers is harder: partitions must be migrated off a broker before it can be safely removed. If a broker disappears abruptly, the cluster stays up but runs under-replicated and hot while replicas rebuild. Clients with stale metadata keep targeting the dead node until they refresh, causing timeouts and retries. Most cloud providers do not offer built-in broker downscaling, making it difficult to scale clusters dynamically. Although tools like Cruise Control can help with rebalancing, removing brokers is still an operationally intensive process.

Another challenge is storage scalability. Many managed services do not allow storage to scale independently from compute, meaning that if a broker runs out of disk space, the only option is to add an entirely new broker instead of simply expanding storage capacity. Some providers offer tiered storage to mitigate this issue by offloading older data to cloud storage like Amazon S3 or Google Cloud Storage, but this does not eliminate the need for careful storage planning.

In both on-premises and cloud environments, Kafka clusters are typically over-provisioned to avoid the challenges of emergency scaling. Capacity planning—based on expected traffic growth, storage needs, and partition distribution—is often more practical than relying on reactive scaling, given the complexities of partition rebalancing, network constraints, and storage limitations.

SECURITY AND COMPLIANCE

Another serious concern is data location and compliance, particularly for industries subject to strict regulations such as finance, healthcare, and government sectors. Many organizations must adhere to data sovereignty laws, which mandate that certain types of data remain within specific geographic boundaries. Deploying Kafka in the cloud can introduce compliance risks, as cloud providers may store metadata, logs, or even actual data across multiple regions or data centers outside the organization's control.

These concerns make on-premises Kafka or private cloud deployments attractive for certain industries, as they offer full control over data locality and regulatory compliance. However, they also come with the trade-offs of higher operational complexity, infrastructure costs, and lack of elasticity compared to cloud-managed Kafka services. Organizations considering cloud Kafka must thoroughly assess regulatory requirements and, where necessary, choose dedicated region-specific deployments, private cloud setups, or hybrid architectures to maintain compliance while benefit from cloud scalability.

9.2.2 Hybrid approach

The most common real-world scenario is a hybrid architecture, where core operational systems remain on-premises, while services—such as data analytics, machine learning, or business intelligence—run in the cloud. This setup creates a need for seamless communication between on-premises and cloud environments. The key question is: Where does Kafka fit in to ensure both technical efficiency and cost-effectiveness?

USING REPLICATION TOOLS

A widely recommended solution, shown in figure 9.7, and often advocated by data integration experts, involves deploying separate Kafka clusters—one on-premises

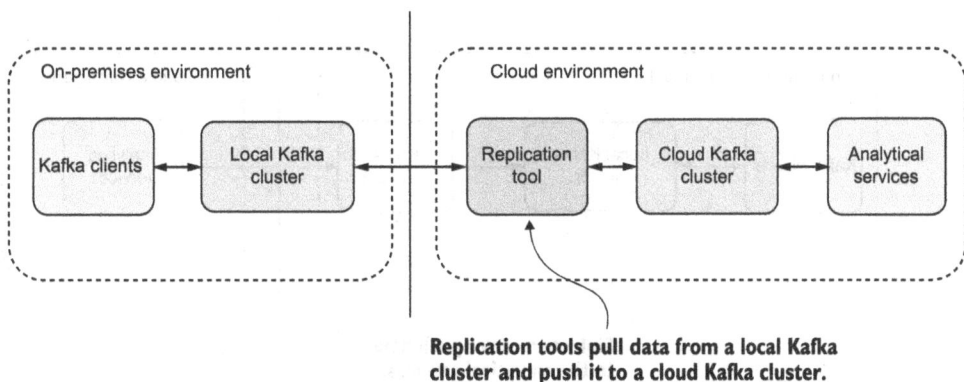

Replication tools pull data from a local Kafka cluster and push it to a cloud Kafka cluster.

Figure 9.7 Replicating data from a local Kafka cluster to a Kafka cluster in the cloud

and another in the cloud. A replication tool, such as Apache MirrorMaker or Confluent Replicator, is then used to synchronize data between these environments. This setup allows organizations to transfer only the necessary data to the cloud, potentially anonymized for analytics or transformed into a format compatible with cloud-native applications.

Replication tools function as both producers and consumers, continuously pulling data from the source Kafka cluster and pushing it to the target cluster. Many of these tools are built on Kafka Connect, enabling additional transformations such as renaming topics, fan in and fan out configurations, and ensuring exactly-once delivery guarantees. Replication tools are often deployed near the target cluster so the replicator's producer writes are local; placement, however, depends on network topology and security constraints. Local writes keep the commit path fast and predictable, with lower round-trip time for acknowledgments and fewer retries, while fetches from the source traverse the WAN and can add replication lag.

Although this dual-cluster architecture is considered a reference model for hybrid Kafka deployments, it frequently raises cost concerns among organizations. Running both an on-premises and a cloud Kafka cluster means paying for infrastructure, storage, and networking in both environments. The operational complexity of managing two clusters also adds to the total cost of ownership. Nevertheless, a hybrid Kafka architecture with replication is a robust solution that combines the low-latency reliability of on-premises Kafka with the scalability and flexibility of cloud Kafka, ensuring high availability, disaster recovery, and seamless data synchronization across environments.

BRINGING ON-PREMISES DATA TO THE CLOUD

Various architectures are available for bringing data to the cloud, and here we will explore a few of them. Figure 9.8 illustrates a scenario where a local Kafka Connect instance bridges the on-premises Kafka cluster with cloud-based services. This architecture provides low latency and reliable processing for on-premises clients while

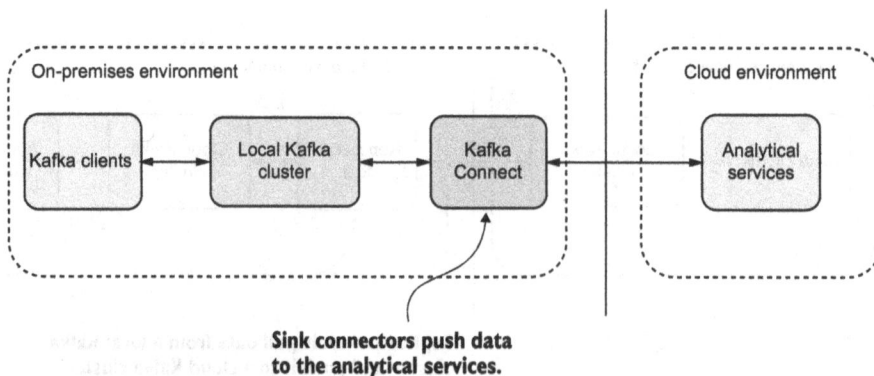

Sink connectors push data
to the analytical services.

Figure 9.8   **Bringing data from local Kafka cluster to the cloud with the help of Kafka Connect**

maintaining control over the location of sensitive or restricted data. Data, which may be transformed or anonymized, is selectively pushed to the cloud for analytics, without requiring a separate cloud Kafka cluster. This reduces the complexity and cost of maintaining a dual-cluster architecture.

However, the absence of a cloud Kafka cluster introduces some limitations. Real-time cloud applications or microservices may experience higher latency when accessing on-premises data, as all interactions must go through Kafka Connect. As cloud workloads grow, this setup may become a bottleneck for high-throughput use cases, where the performance of Kafka Connect could struggle to keep up.

For example, imagine an e-commerce company where the order processing system runs on-premises, sending transactions to an on-premises Kafka cluster, while the fraud detection service operates in the cloud. Pulling data from on-premises Kafka to the cloud via Kafka Connect introduces additional network latency and potential throughput limitations, which become increasingly difficult to manage as the volume of transactions grows.

Figure 9.9 presents another variation, where all Kafka infrastructure, including brokers and topics, resides entirely in the cloud. In this architecture, Kafka Connect is deployed on-premises to push data to the cloud Kafka cluster. Additionally, on-premises clients can directly produce data to the cloud Kafka cluster. This approach allows on-premises systems to both produce and consume data, while seamlessly integrating with cloud analytics. On-premises clients retain access to the cloud Kafka cluster, enabling hybrid use cases without duplicating Kafka infrastructure.

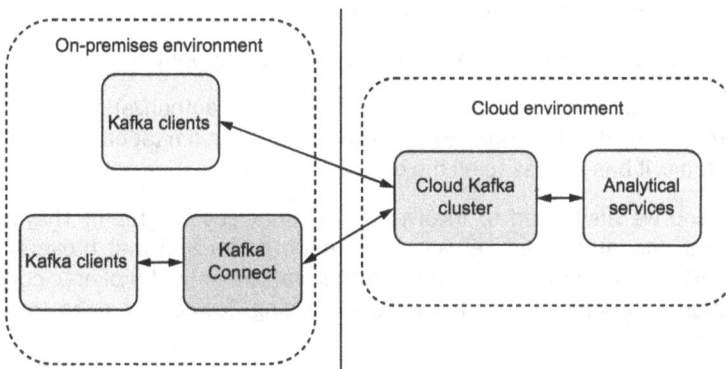

Figure 9.9 Bringing data to the cloud cluster with Kafka Connect or directly

Despite its simplicity, this architecture has drawbacks. On-premises systems become heavily reliant on a stable, high-bandwidth connection to the cloud. Network disruptions can severely impact operations, and data transfer costs can become significant when moving large volumes of data to the cloud, particularly if egress or cross-region charges apply.

This setup is best suited for companies aiming to centralize their infrastructure in the cloud while maintaining minimal on-premises integration. However, organizations must carefully assess network reliability, data transfer costs, and latency requirements to ensure this architecture aligns with their needs.

9.2.3 *Choosing the right deployment for the Customer 360 ODS*

The deployment decision for an ODS like the Customer 360 project is hardly straight-forward. Using all available cloud features may seem appealing, but given the pro and cons, it may be more practical to adopt a hybrid model, with the core systems generating data residing on-premises. This would allow the team to gain a deeper understanding of the technology while maintaining full access to its internals. As you integrate with managed cloud services for analytics, you may need to explore more hybrid deployment options further down the road.

Field notes: Protecting Kafka

At the team meeting, lead architect Rob leans forward, addressing data engineer Eva and account manager Max with even more intensity than usual.

Rob: Guys, this is serious. We keep postponing this, but don't forget—the security team has to approve the entire solution before we can move forward to production. Even for this proof-of-concept, if we don't get the green light, we're going nowhere.

Max: Alright, let's just do it. Is it really that different from other systems? Communication runs over TLS—that should be enough, right?

Eva: Security isn't just about encrypting communication. We also need to control who can access Kafka and what they're allowed to do.

Max: Okay, but isn't that just a matter of setting some config values?

Eva: As always, it's all about configuration. But with Kafka, authorization is tricky. Permissions are managed at the topic level, which is a serious limitation. If a client has access to a topic, it has access to all the data in that topic.

Rob: Right, and we also need to involve the network security team. They'll need to ensure that only authorized services can reach Kafka and that brokers aren't exposed to external clients. What about internal traffic—should broker-to-controller communication be encrypted? And if we're still using ZooKeeper, does that need securing too?

Max: Alright, alright. This is getting more complicated than I thought. What else?

Rob: First, we need to define our security policies—what authentication method we'll use, how we set up ACLs, and whether internal broker communication should be encrypted. Then, we need to engage with the security and network teams to align on the architecture.

Max: Great. Another meeting with the security guys. Can't wait.

9.3 Creating a security solution

Settling on a security strategy is not just about Kafka—it's about ensuring the entire architecture is secure, resilient, and compliant. Doing this means planning ahead so you can get security right from the start.

9.3.1 Kafka security overview

For successful integration, Kafka must comply with the enterprise's security policies. Kafka security is structured around three key aspects:

- *Authentication*—Verifying that participants are who they claim to be
- *Authorization*—Ensuring that a participant has the necessary permissions to access a requested resource
- *Encryption*—Protecting data by converting it into an unreadable format, which can only be decoded using a special key

When discussing security in the Kafka ecosystem, we focus on client-server communications:

- Kafka brokers communicate with controllers to exchange metadata.
- Brokers also communicate with each other during data replication.
- Kafka clients interact with brokers to produce and consume messages.

It's worth noting that Kafka clients include not only producer and consumer microservices but also Kafka Connect, Schema Registry, and other components that integrate with the Kafka ecosystem.

The good news is that Kafka does not introduce any proprietary security mechanisms; instead, it relies on well-established, industry-standard technologies. All security features are configurable and do not require modifications to client application code. Figure 9.10 provides an overview of the security features supported by Kafka.

By default, Kafka is not secured. So far, we have run examples without enabling authentication, authorization, or encryption. To secure Kafka, specific configurations must be added. In this section, we'll cover the key security concepts and how Kafka supports them. Detailed configuration properties and setup instructions are available in the official documentation.

9.3.2 Encrypting using TLS

Kafka allows you to encrypt data using Transport Layer Security (TLS), ensuring that intercepted data remains unreadable to unauthorized parties. The process of configuring TLS communication is well documented and widely available in tutorials across the internet.

Setting up TLS involves creating keys, certificates, and keystores, which can be done using tools provided by the Java Development Kit (JDK) or OpenSSL, among others. The *keystore* contains private and public keys along with their associated certificates, which are used to authenticate and identify the participant. The *truststore* holds public

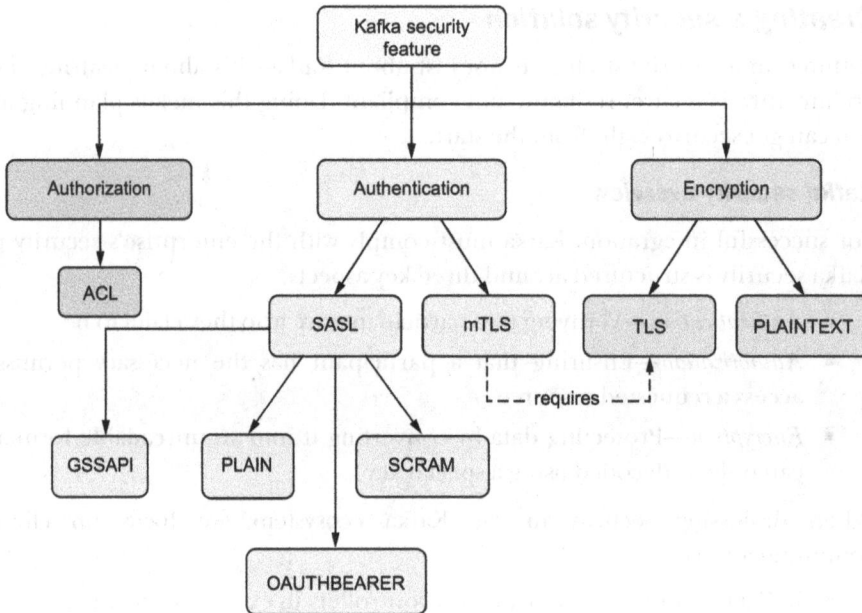

Figure 9.10   Overview of the security features supported in Kafka

key certificates of trusted servers and certificate authorities (CAs), ensuring secure communication by verifying the authenticity of remote entities.

The basic steps for configuring server certificates (illustrated in figure 9.11) are:

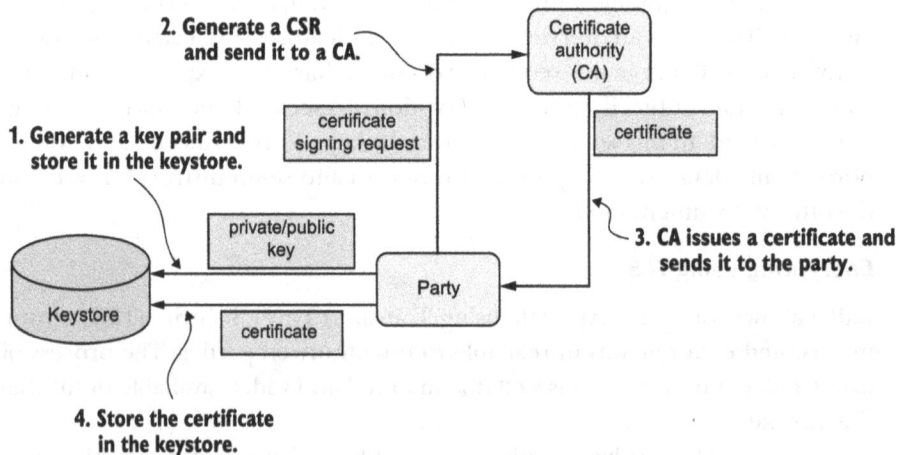

Figure 9.11   Generating keys and receiving a certificate. The Party (client or server) is the entity that generates the key pair and requests a signed certificate from the certificate authority.

1 Generate a private key and create a keystore.
2 Create a certificate signing request (CSR) and submit it to a certificate authority.
3 Once the certificate is received from the CA, import it into the keystore.

After generating the necessary certificates, the keystore properties must be configured on the server side. A key property, `ssl.client.auth`, determines whether client authentication is required. If mutual TLS (mTLS) is enabled, clients must also generate their own keys, obtain certificates, and configure their keystore accordingly.

After preparing the keystores, the next step is to create a truststore for each interested party, which stores the certificates of trusted participants, including the CA certificate and any intermediate CA certificates needed for proper validation.

Once TLS is set up, the keystore and truststore properties must be configured on both the client and server sides. Listing 9.3 provides an example of the required properties for a Kafka broker. Note that Kafka officially supports TLS, but some configuration properties still use the historical term SSL.

Listing 9.3 Server configuration for TLS

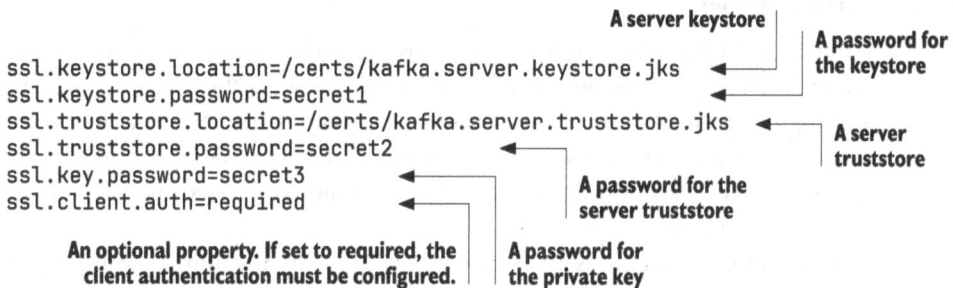

```
ssl.keystore.location=/certs/kafka.server.keystore.jks
ssl.keystore.password=secret1
ssl.truststore.location=/certs/kafka.server.truststore.jks
ssl.truststore.password=secret2
ssl.key.password=secret3
ssl.client.auth=required
```

A server keystore
A password for the keystore
A server truststore
A password for the server truststore
An optional property. If set to required, the client authentication must be configured.
A password for the private key

Listing 9.4 shows the configuration for a Kafka client (producers and consumers).

Listing 9.4 Client configuration for TLS

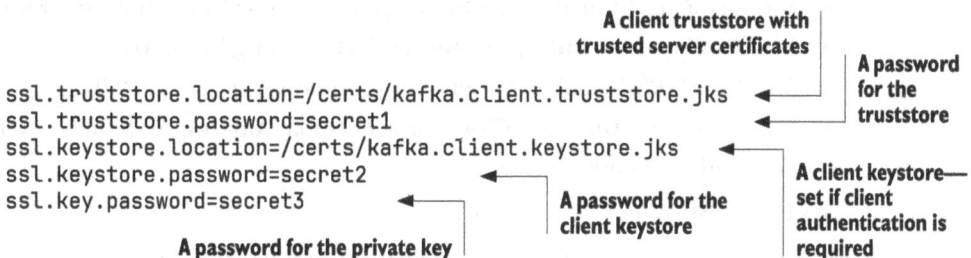

```
ssl.truststore.location=/certs/kafka.client.truststore.jks
ssl.truststore.password=secret1
ssl.keystore.location=/certs/kafka.client.keystore.jks
ssl.keystore.password=secret2
ssl.key.password=secret3
```

A client truststore with trusted server certificates
A password for the truststore
A client keystore—set if client authentication is required
A password for the client keystore
A password for the private key

Configuration for other components, such as Kafka Connect and Schema Registry, may vary, but the underlying principles remain the same: each service must present its own private key and certificate, trust the certificate authority that signs the certificates of its peers, and optionally enforce client authentication.

Storing passwords directly in configuration files is not secure, but more secure alternatives exist:

- *Environment variables*—Instead of hardcoding passwords, use environment variables, such as

```
ssl.truststore.password=${env:KAFKA_SSL_TRUSTSTORE_PASSWORD}
```

- *External secure files*—Store sensitive credentials in a separate, restricted-access file. For example, you can store passwords in /etc/kafka/secret:

```
ssl.keystore.password=${file:/etc/kafka/secret:ssl.keystore.password}
```

- *Secret management vaults*—Use plugins to integrate with secure vault solutions like HashiCorp Vault, AWS Secrets Manager, or Azure Key Vault.

These approaches help protect sensitive credentials, reduce security risks, and improve Kafka's overall security posture.

9.3.3 Authentication

When security is enabled in the Kafka ecosystem, clients must present credentials, and servers must verify their identity. A *principal* represents the authenticated identity of a participant (client or broker) in a secure system. If mTLS is enabled, the principal is typically derived from the TLS certificate. By default, Kafka extracts the full distinguished name (DN), but mapping rules can be applied to extract specific fields, such as the common name (CN).

In addition to mTLS, Kafka supports client authentication via Simple Authentication and Security Layer (SASL), which abstracts authentication from application protocols. SASL can operate over TCP (unencrypted) or TLS (encrypted).

Kafka supports multiple SASL mechanisms for client authentication:

- *PLAIN*—Simple username/password authentication (requires TLS for security)
- *SCRAM (SHA-256/SHA-512)*—Secure password-based authentication with hashing
- *GSSAPI (Kerberos)*—Enterprise authentication using Kerberos
- *OAUTHBEARER*—Token-based authentication (e.g., OAuth 2.0)
- *Cloud-specific mechanisms*—Cloud providers like Amazon AWS offer their proprietary authentication methods

Here's how SASL authentication works:

1 The client initiates authentication using a configured SASL mechanism.
2 The Kafka broker verifies the credentials using an authentication backend (LDAP, Kerberos, password file, etc.).
3 If authentication is successful, the client is allowed to proceed with further actions (such as producing or consuming messages).

The security protocol configured in Kafka is a combination of encryption and authentication methods. Table 9.1 lists all the security protocols supported by Kafka, indicating whether they provide encryption and/or authentication.

Table 9.1   Security protocols supported by Kafka

Security protocol	Encryption	Authentication	Description
PLAINTEXT	No	No	Unencrypted communication with no authentication
SASL_PLAINTEXT	No	Yes (via SASL)	Uses SASL for authentication but does not encrypt data
SSL	Yes (TLS)	Yes (via TLS)	Encrypts communication and supports TLS-based authentication
SASL_SSL	Yes (TLS)	Yes (via SASL)	Uses SASL for authentication and TLS for encryption

To enable authentication, a set of properties must be configured on both the client and the server. Listing 9.5 shows the required properties that must be set on the Kafka broker, where external clients are connected via SASL_SSL (using a password for authentication and TLS for encryption) and communication between brokers uses PLAINTEXT. Some authentication mechanisms may require additional properties, which can be found in the documentation.

Listing 9.5   Configuring authentication on a broker

Mapping of listeners to security protocols

Two listeners: one for external clients and one for inter-broker

Only the listener for external clients is advertised.

```
listeners=EXTERNAL://:9093,BROKER://:9092,CONTROLLER://:9094
advertised.listeners=EXTERNAL://broker:9093
listener.security.protocol.map=EXTERNAL:SASL_SSL, \ CONTROLLER:SASL_
SSL,BROKER:PLAINTEXT
inter.broker.listener.name=BROKER
controller.listener.names=CONTROLLER
sasl.enabled.mechanisms=PLAIN
sasl.jaas.config.file=/etc/kafka/kafka_server_jaas.conf
...
```

Specifies the listener for communication with controllers

Here, properties from listing 9.1 should be set for TLS.

Specifies the JAAS configuration in an external file

Enables SASL for external clients and controllers

Specifies the listener for inter-broker communication

On the client side, specific properties must also be defined. The following listing shows an example configuration for SASL authentication using the PLAIN mechanism.

Listing 9.6   Configuring authentication on a client

Specifies the security protocol
for the communication

SASL mechanism (PLAIN
for username/password
authentication)

```
security.protocol=SASL_SSL
sasl.mechanism=PLAIN
sasl.jaas.config.file=/etc/kafka/kafka_client_jaas.conf
...
```

Specifies the JAAS
configuration in an
external file

Here, properties from
listing 9.2 should be set for TLS.

Finally, the next listing presents an example of the properties required for securing KRaft controllers.

Listing 9.7   Configuring authentication on controllers

```
controller.listener.names=CONTROLLER
listeners=CONTROLLER://:9094
advertised.listeners=CONTROLLER://controller1:9094
listener.security.protocol.map=CONTROLLER:SASL_SSL
sasl.enabled.mechanisms=PLAIN
sasl.mechanism.controller.protocol=PLAIN
sasl.jaas.config.file=/etc/kafka/kafka_controller_jaas.conf
...
```

Here, properties
from listing 9.3
should be set for TLS.

In enterprise integration use cases, Security Assertion Markup Language (SAML) is commonly used for authentication. However, since Kafka does not natively support SAML, organizations must rely on indirect integration methods to enable SAML-based authentication.

The most practical approach is to use an OAuth 2.0 identity provider (IdP) that supports SAML-to-OAuth conversion. Many IdPs, such as Okta, Keycloak, and Azure AD, allow users to authenticate via SAML and then issue an OAuth 2.0 token (JWT), which Kafka can accept via the SASL/OAUTHBEARER mechanism.

Another approach is to use a reverse proxy (e.g., Apache Knox or Envoy) to handle SAML authentication and forward credentials to Kafka using a supported authentication method, such as OAuth 2.0 or mTLS.

For organizations needing deeper customization, Kafka supports custom SASL mechanisms, allowing the development of a SAML-based authentication plugin if necessary.

While multiple solutions exist, integrating Kafka with an OAuth 2.0 IdP remains the most practical and widely supported method for enabling SAML-based authentication.

Security is often postponed until the system moves from the development phase to the testing environment. However, implementing security rules early in development helps detect problems sooner, maintain consistency, protect data, ensure compliance, and enable smoother deployments.

9.3.4 *Authorization*

Generally, *access control lists* (ACLs) define authorization rules in terms of resources and operations. An ACL specifies which principal is granted access to a resource and what operations are allowed or forbidden on that resource.

In Kafka, an ACL statement consists of the following elements:

- *Principal*—The identity received from authentication data. Principals are typically users, but they can also be groups, retrieved from LDAP mappings.
- *Resource type*—This can be one of topic, group (meaning consumer group), cluster, transaction identifiers, delegation tokens, or another user.
- *Resource*—The actual resource of the specified resource type.
- *Pattern type*—Specifies how resources are matched—by the exact name or by a prefix. For example, we can grant access rights to the TRANSACTIONS topic or to all topics whose names start with the "ANALYTICS-*" pattern.
- *Operation*—Defines the allowed action, such as read, write, or describe.
- *Permission type*—Can be allow or deny. Deny rules take precedence over allow rules.
- *Host*—Specifies the IP address from which the operation is allowed.

The ACL statement in Kafka follows this structure:

```
Principal P is [Allowed/Denied] Operation O From Host H On Resource R.
```

In Kafka, the most common use case is restricting access at the topic level, specifying

- Which topics producers can send messages to
- Which topics consumers can read from

However, setting permissions correctly can be tricky. It may seem sufficient to grant the write operation on a topic for producers and the read operation for consumers. But this is not entirely true—consumers also need to do the following:

- Commit offsets (write to the __consumer_offsets topic).
- Operate within their consumer group.
- Access metadata (using the describe operation).

Fortunately, utilities like kafka-acls allow us to define all necessary permissions for producers and consumers in one step, eliminating the need to manually configure low-level permissions. However, for consumers it does not include some advanced access control, such as managing offset deletion, altering consumer groups, or fine-grained administrative operations. Additionally, for producers, the --producer flag does not grant idempotent write permissions (IdempotentWrite) or transactional ID permissions, which are required for exactly-once semantics and transactional message production. Listing 9.8 shows an example of configuring ACL for a producer that sends messages to the TRANSACTIONS topic.

```
kafka-acls.sh --bootstrap-server broker:9092 \        ◄──    List of bootstrap brokers
    --add \
    --allow-principal User:card-service \      ◄──
    --operation Write --operation Create \     ◄──        Adds access rights to card-service
    --resource-pattern-type prefix \                      (this is a principal)
    --topic CARDS          ◄──
                                                          Operations for producer,
              Access rights are given for all topics     typically Write and Create
                  that start with the CARDS prefix.
```

The full list of resources and supported operations can be found in the Kafka documentation.

Kafka's authorization system is pluggable, meaning it can be customized at the broker level by specifying the necessary plugins. However, such customization is not very common. Cloud providers may offer their own access control solutions, where role-based access control (RBAC) provides a more user-friendly alternative.

9.3.5   *Protecting data at rest*

Kafka's native encryption mechanisms only apply to data in motion, ensuring secure communication between clients and brokers. When a client sends encrypted data, the broker decrypts it and stores it in plaintext. The data is then re-encrypted when it's sent to the consumer. However, Kafka does not provide any built-in mechanism to protect data at rest—it is stored unencrypted on the broker's disk. This can be a significant issue for systems that are required to store encrypted data due to regulatory compliance.

One approach to securing data at rest is to use filesystem or disk-level encryption with operating system tools, such as the Linux Unified Key Setup (LUKS). Additionally, cloud providers offer their own managed encryption services for securing stored data.

Another option is to implement end-to-end encryption (E2EE), where producers encrypt the data before sending it to Kafka, and consumers decrypt it after retrieval (illustrated in figure 9.12). Since Kafka brokers do not process the message contents, there is no technical barrier to storing encrypted messages in Kafka and leaving the encryption and decryption entirely to clients. Although KIP-317 proposes adding E2EE support to Kafka, it remains under discussion, meaning that custom implementations are currently required.

This behavior can be implemented within the application logic or integrated into the Kafka client library. Here are a couple of points to consider:

- Avoid encrypting partition keys in Kafka messages to preserve data distribution across partitions, even when encryption keys change.
- Encryption parameters can be passed in the message headers instead of the message payload.

Regardless of the approach, such a solution requires a key management service (KMS) to handle key creation, issuance, and revocation. Common KMS solutions include

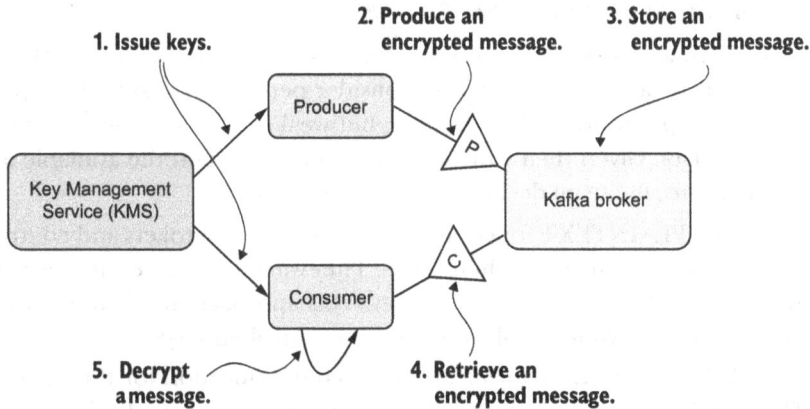

Figure 9.12 Implementing end-to-end encryption with the encryption and decryption of messages done on the clients

AWS Key Management Service (AWS KMS), Google Cloud Key Management (Cloud KMS), Azure Key Vault, and HashiCorp Vault. Most importantly, all participants in the system must support the encryption policy, which can be problematic when working with third-party software that does not allow for such customization.

An alternative approach, illustrated in figure 9.13, involves placing a proxy between clients and brokers to handle encryption and decryption. In this model, clients remain unchanged, and all encryption and decryption operations, as well as key management, are handled at the proxy level.

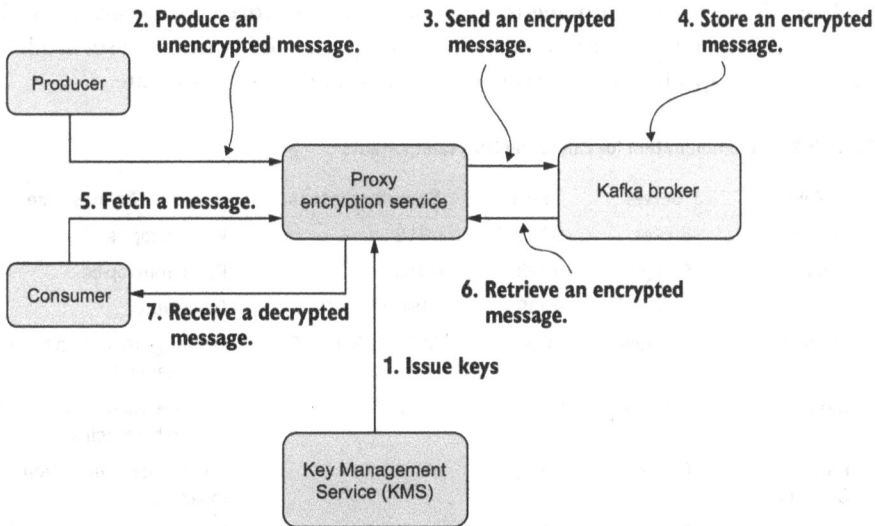

Figure 9.13 Using a proxy for encrypting and decrypting messages

9.3.6   *Enabling security In the Customer 360 ODS*

To come up with a security strategy, the team designing our example ODS needs to study all these rules and approaches and consider performance as well as operational complexity. Encryption does add overhead, but weaker security configurations could expose critical data. Given their infrastructure constraints and the available authentication mechanisms, the team decides on the following plan:

- Use SASL_PLAINTEXT for communication between brokers and controllers, as well as between controllers themselves. They will restrict access to the controllers at the network level to ensure security. This approach avoids the performance overhead of encryption while maintaining controlled access.
- Use SASL_PLAINTEXT for inter-broker communication for the same reasons. The team agreed that encrypting internal traffic between brokers was unnecessary since they could enforce security through network segmentation. This approach kept the setup simpler while still limiting unauthorized access.
- Use mTLS between clients and brokers to ensure secure authentication and encryption. Since client-broker traffic is more exposed, they prioritized strong authentication and data encryption. The team recognized that mTLS adds complexity to certificate management but concluded that its security benefits outweighed the operational effort.

As you can see, the team chose mTLS for client traffic—exposed and cross-boundary—and SASL over plaintext inside the private network to avoid TLS overhead, accepting the risk because the internal fabric is tightly segmented and monitored.

With the help of the infrastructure team, they then generate keys and issue certificates for both clients and servers. Next, they configure ACLs for Kafka Connect and Schema Registry to properly manage authentication and authorization.

The infrastructure team needs to document all network communications within the Kafka ecosystem, to ensure that the necessary ports are opened and secured. Table 9.2 provides a comprehensive overview of all the interactions they create.

Table 9.2   Communication for Customer 360 components

Client	Server	Port	Security protocol	Access type
Producer	Broker	9093	mTLS	Write to topics
Consumer	Broker	9093	mTLS	Read from topics
Broker	Broker	9092	SASL_PLAINTEXT	Replication
Controller	Controller	9094	SASL_PLAINTEXT	Exchange metadata for cluster management
Broker	Controller	9094	SASL_PLAINTEXT	Send metadata updates and leadership election
Kafka Connect	Broker	9093	mTLS	Read/write data to/from connector topics
Schema Registry	Broker	9093	mTLS	Read/write data to/from _schemas topic

Table 9.2 Communication for Customer 360 components (*continued*)

Client	Server	Port	Security protocol	Access type
Producer	Schema Registry	8081	HTTPS	Retrieve schema for serialization
Consumer	Schema Registry	8081	HTTPS	Retrieve schema for deserialization
Kafka Connect	Schema Registry	8081	HTTPS	Retrieve schema for serialization and deserialization

9.4   Online resources

- "How to (actually) Configure a Kafka Cluster in KRaft Mode for Testing & Development": https://medium.com/@hjdjoo/how-to-actually-configure-a-kafka-cluster-in-kraft-mode-for-testing-development-8f90f09e36b1

  An article which provides a practical, step-by-step guide for configuring and running a Kafka cluster in KRaft mode for local testing and development environments.

- "The Apache Kafka Control Plane": https://developer.confluent.io/courses/architecture/control-plane/

  This course explains Kafka's control plane architecture, focusing on how metadata is managed, propagated, and coordinated across the cluster.

- "KRaft Configuration for Confluent Platform": https://docs.confluent.io/platform/current/kafka-metadata/config-kraft.html

  Documentation that outlines how to configure and operate Kafka in KRaft mode, including controller quorum settings, metadata management, and recommended deployment practices.

- "Multi-Cloud Replication in Real-Time with Apache Kafka and Cluster Linking": https://kai-waehner.medium.com/multi-cloud-replication-in-real-time-with-apache-kafka-and-cluster-linking-e02071186b36

  This article explores how to achieve real-time, multi-cloud data replication in Apache Kafka using cluster linking, including architectures, benefits, and practical use cases.

- "Use TLS Authentication in Confluent Platform": https://docs.confluent.io/platform/current/security/authentication/mutual-tls/overview.html

  A page that provides an overview of configuring and using mutual TLS (mTLS) authentication in Confluent Platform to ensure secure, certificate-based identity verification between clients and brokers.

- "Encryption at rest for Apache Kafka": https://developers.redhat.com/articles/2024/06/05/encryption-rest-apache-kafka#implementation_choices

  This article explains how to implement encryption at rest in Apache Kafka, including techniques, configuration options, and the role of the Kroxylicious Kafka proxy in securing data flows.

- "KIP-317: Add end-to-end data encryption functionality to Apache Kafka": https://cwiki.apache.org/confluence/display/KAFKA/KIP-317%3A+Add+end-to-end+data+encryption+functionality+to+Apache+Kafka
This KIP proposes adding end-to-end data encryption to Apache Kafka, outlining the design, goals, and mechanisms for encrypting message payloads from producers to consumers.

Summary

- Kafka clusters consist of brokers (handling message storage and retrieval) and controllers (managing metadata and cluster coordination). This means that brokers are responsible for storing and serving data, while controllers ensure the cluster remains operational by managing leadership elections and metadata updates. Understanding how brokers and controllers work together guides your sizing, HA topology, security rules, monitoring, and incident playbooks.

- Metadata storage is managed in Raft logs (KRaft mode) or via ZooKeeper (legacy mode). So, controllers handle leader elections, partition assignments, ACLs, consumer groups, and transaction states.

- Controllers use quorum-based decision-making, which ensures fault tolerance. To tolerate N controller failures, you run $2N + 1$ controllers so that a majority quorum of $N + 1$ controllers is still available; otherwise, leader elections and metadata changes halt.

- The Kafka ecosystem can be deployed on-premises or in the cloud as a managed service. While on-premises deployments offer full control and compliance, managed services help reduce operational burden but come with the risk of vendor lock-in and limited customization.

- Many organizations operate dual Kafka clusters (on-premises and in the cloud) using MirrorMaker or Kafka Connect for data synchronization. This approach enhances resilience and disaster recovery, while also enabling hybrid architectures, but it introduces additional complexity, potential latency, synchronization overhead, and increased costs.

- Security in Kafka is divided into three key areas: authentication (verifying identities using mTLS or SASL), authorization (enforcing access controls via ACLs), and encryption (secure communication with TLS). Do all three—together—to secure your Kafka deployment.

- Kafka natively encrypts only data in transit, not at rest. Options for protecting stored data are filesystem encryption (Linux LUKS, cloud storage encryption) or end-to-end encryption.

- Permissions in Kafka are enforced at the topic level, which introduces a notable restriction. Once a client is granted access to a topic, it can freely read or write all data within that topic without granular control over specific messages or partitions.

Organizing
a Kafka project

This chapter covers

- Defining project requirements across environment setups, nonfunctional requirements, infrastructure sizing, and resource quotas
- Maintaining Kafka clusters using CLI and UI tools, GitOps, and the Kafka Admin API
- Testing Kafka applications

A successful Kafka adoption depends as much on process as on code. Teams often prototype and size infrastructure yet overlook how Kafka fits the organization's workflow—who owns events, how changes are approved, how reliability is proven. This chapter focuses on that gap. You'll learn how to capture requirements and data contracts, how to maintain the cluster structure across environments, and how to test applications effectively. These practices reduce risk, prevent costly rework, and make performance, cost, and compliance predictable—turning a promising prototype into an operable, supportable system. Without this structure, a promising Kafka platform could quickly spiral into an unmanageable mess.

Field notes: Use-case intake and requirements

Now it's the account manager's turn to shake his head.

Max: Alright, team. Our project is starting to attract a lot of attention. Every time I go for lunch, someone stops me and asks if they can also use Kafka for their use case. It's like we've created a new buzzword in the company.

Rob: Well, before we let everyone jump on board, they need to understand whether Kafka is actually suitable for their use case.

Max: Fair point. But let's say the answer is yes—Kafka is a good fit. Then what?

Rob: Then they need to clearly define their requirements. If we don't collect and structure them properly, we'll end up with a Kafka setup that's as messy as spaghetti code—except it'll be a spaghetti server instead.

Eva: Exactly. Right now, we're just running quick scripts to set things up. But as more teams join in, we need a structured approach. Topics, partitions, schemas, ACLs—everything should be created consistently, not manually hacked together.

Max: What concerns me the most are the nonfunctional requirements. At the end of the day, we're paying for computational resources—storage, CPU, network bandwidth. We need a way to estimate and allocate costs properly before teams start piling on new workloads.

The room went silent for a moment as the challenge of scaling their Kafka project became clear.

Rob: Alright, so we need two things: First, a structured way to evaluate use cases before they jump into Kafka. Second, a process to document and enforce requirements—both functional and nonfunctional—before anything goes live.

Eva: And that includes automation, versioning, and governance over the whole setup.

Max: Sounds like we just gave ourselves even more work.

10.1 Defining Kafka project requirements

Projects start with gathering requirements. What should we analyze to make a Kafka—and event-driven—project successful? Are there Kafka-specific requirements we need to capture?

10.1.1 Identifying event-driven workflows

In Chapter 6, we explored event design and its translation into Kafka artifacts. However, the foundation of a successful event-driven system isn't built on technical details alone—it starts much earlier, at the strategic level. Before they dive into events, schemas, or brokers, teams must first answer a more fundamental question: What business outcomes are we trying to achieve?

Unfortunately, many teams skip this crucial phase. Instead, they jump straight into technical modeling, often driven more by system internals than by real business needs. The problem with this approach is that real-world processes are messy. Designing too early from a purely technical angle can result in an inaccurate model of how things actually work. You may overlook important edge cases (what if the process is cancelled halfway through?), timing constraints (should something happen immediately, or after a delay?), or approval steps (does this happen automatically, or does it require human review?).

To avoid these pitfalls, it's essential to spend time on business discovery. Here are various techniques for collecting business requirements:

- Workshops or whiteboard sessions with stakeholders, often using sticky notes or event storming
- One-on-one interviews with business experts to uncover how processes really work
- Writing user stories that describe interactions from the customer's perspective
- Creating process models using BPMN or simple flow diagrams

Narratives written in business language (not technical jargon) are especially useful. Simple patterns like "When X happens, Y should occur" help frame the conversation around behavior and expectations. For example,

- When a client uploads a document, start the review process.
- When the payment due date approaches, notify the customer.
- When a client pays the debt, the case is closed.

These scenarios help ground your design in real-world expectations—providing a foundation for defining the events that matter.

10.1.2 Turning business workflows into events

At this point, we're still not talking about Kafka or specific technologies, but we're ready to begin transforming business workflows into technical event-driven workflows. The first task is to identify the key events and determine which systems, applications, or services will produce and consume them. These techniques align with *domain-driven design* (DDD), where development is centered on the domain model and bounded contexts, and events express aggregate state changes in the ubiquitous language.

To define events properly, we should look for notifications of state changes in the business process. These notifications must be meaningful to other participants, and they may trigger some downstream actions. For each event, we need to clearly define

- Who emits it (the producer).
- Who is interested in receiving it (the consumer).

These participants may be existing systems or ones we will need to create.

To understand how a proposed event-driven workflow fits into existing business operations, we must analyze the current process landscape. This is where the *event catalogue* becomes essential—a structured view where we map out business processes alongside their event-driven artifacts.

Let's consider a simple example from loan processing. When a customer submits a loan application, the risk team evaluates the financial profile. Once the risk assessment is complete, a compliance check is triggered to ensure legal eligibility. If both checks pass, the approval system finalizes the decision and notifies the applicant.

This process consists of multiple events, each of which can be defined using an event catalogue with the following attributes:

- *Event name*—A clear, past-tense name (e.g., `LoanApplicationSubmitted`, `RiskAssessmentCompleted`)
- *Producer*—The system, service, or actor that emits the event
- *Consumer(s)*—The systems or services that react to the event
- *Business meaning*—A plain-language explanation of what happened
- *Trigger condition*—The condition or action that causes the event to be emitted
- *Expected reaction*—What other participants are expected to do in response
- *Business owner*—The stakeholder responsible for defining and validating the event semantics
- *Event data requirements*—A high-level view of the data that needs to be included in the event

The mapping of the loan processing workflow to the event catalogue is as follows:

- `LoanApplicationSubmitted`
  - *Producer*—Customer Portal Service
  - *Consumers*—Risk Service
  - *Business meaning*—A customer formally applies for a loan
  - *Trigger condition*—Customer submits the application form
  - *Expected reaction*—Initiate risk assessment
  - *Business owner*—Lending product team
  - *Event data requirements*—`applicationId`, `customerId`, `requestedAmount`, `timestamp`
- `RiskAssessmentCompleted`
  - *Producer*—Risk Service
  - *Consumers*—Compliance Service
  - *Business meaning*—Customer's financial profile evaluated
  - *Trigger condition*—Risk scoring is completed
  - *Expected reaction*—Trigger compliance review
  - *Business owner*—Risk department
  - *Event data requirements*—`applicationId`, `riskScore`, `decision`

- `ComplianceCheckCompleted`
  - *Producer*—Compliance Service
  - *Consumers*—Loan Approval Service
  - *Business meaning*—Legal/regulatory review is completed
  - *Trigger condition*—Compliance check finishes
  - *Expected reaction*—Continue to approval decision
  - *Business owner*—Legal Team
  - *Event data requirements*—`applicationId, complianceStatus, checkedAt, reason`
- `LoanApproved`
  - *Producer*—Loan Approval Service
  - *Consumers*—Notification Service
  - *Business meaning*—Application approved after all checks
  - *Trigger condition*—Risk and compliance checks passed
  - *Expected reaction*—Notify customer, create a loan
  - *Business owner*—Credit Approvals
  - *Event data requirements*—`applicationId, approvedAmount, approvalTimestamp`
- `LoanRejected`
  - *Producer*—Loan Approval Service
  - *Consumers*—Notification Service
  - *Business meaning*—Application rejected due to risk/compliance outcome
  - *Trigger condition*—One of the checks fails
  - *Expected reaction*—Notify customer, terminate a loan
  - *Business owner*—Credit Approvals
  - *Event data requirements*—`applicationId, rejectionReason, decisionTimestamp`

These early-stage catalogues are typically modeled by business analysts or solution architects, and serve as a bridge between business understanding and technical implementation. At this stage, it's often better to use general-purpose metadata and catalogue tools like Apache Atlas (https://atlas.apache.org), DataHub (https://datahub .com), or Amundsen (www.amundsen.io), which allow for rich metadata, ownership tagging, and glossary support, rather than developer-oriented tools like AsyncAPI, which are more suitable for documenting APIs and payloads in the implementation phase.

10.1.3 Gathering functional requirements for Kafka topics

Chapter 5 provided an overview of real-world Kafka use cases, along with examples where Kafka might not be the best solution. To decide whether a business process is suitable for Kafka, the next step would be a set of key questions that sit at the intersection of business requirements and technical design.

The following questions help shape the way we model the event-driven workflow and configure Kafka topics and consumers appropriately:

- *Should events be processed in order?*

  This is a fundamental question. Kafka does not support global ordering, only per-partition ordering. If ordering is required, we must consider how to partition the data to preserve it. If ordering is not required, we can use more efficient round-robin strategies for higher throughput.

- *Can we partition events without breaking business logic?*

  If yes, we should identify a suitable message key (e.g., `customerId`, `caseId`) to ensure related events are routed to the same partition, preserving order where it matters.

- *Do we need to retain events permanently?*

  This affects the choice between Kafka's log compaction and delete retention policies. Business rules around auditability, reprocessing, or historical access will guide this decision.

- *Is this critical business data?*

  The importance of the data influences decisions around replication factors, producer acknowledgment settings, and consumer offset-committing strategies to ensure durability and reliability.

- *Does the event contain sensitive data or have regulatory implications?*

  If yes, we may need to implement encryption or field-level masking, or apply strict access controls in accordance with legal and compliance requirements.

- *Are the events idempotent?*

  Kafka does not guarantee exactly-once delivery by default; retries and duplicates can occur under failure conditions. If your consumers are not idempotent, reprocessing the same event may result in data corruption, inconsistent state, or unintended side effects.

- *Do we need to process events in real time or in batches?*

  While real-time processing is often idealized, not all business processes require it. Some workflows, such as nightly reconciliations, reporting, or batch scoring, naturally operate in time-based windows. Understanding the appropriate processing mode helps optimize system design and resource usage.

- *Do we need to correlate multiple events or workflows?*

  Many business processes span several events—like approvals that depend on both risk and compliance checks. In such cases, you need a strategy for event correlation, often via a shared identifier (e.g., `applicationId`, `caseId`). Without correlation, it's difficult to maintain context across distributed events.

- *Do we know the schema of the events? Is this schema fixed or dynamic? Can we define which attributes are optional?*

  Understanding the event schema—whether it's static, evolves over time, or contains optional fields—is crucial for modeling flexibility and avoiding breaking changes.

Once we decide to implement a use case using Kafka, it's time to formally define the functional requirements for the Kafka topics that will support it. These requirements can be captured directly in technical documentation tools such as AsyncAPI, or integrated into existing company-wide systems for managing service and data definitions. Here is a list of key requirements that should be formalized:

- References to the business events defined in the previous step. This ensures continuity between business intents and technical implementations, and helps preserve traceability.

- Producer service identifier. Each producing service or application should be catalogued and have a unique identifier.

- Consumer service identifiers, including expected consumer groups. It's important to document which services will subscribe to the topic and how they will be logically grouped.

- Consumer assignment strategy, if using server-side assignment (introduced in Kafka 3.0 and enabled by default in newer versions). This determines how topic partitions are distributed among consumers in a group.

- Consumption model. Specifies whether a partition can be assigned to only one consumer within a group (the classic approach) or to multiple consumers (using shared consumer groups introduced in Kafka 4.0).

- Topic names that follow your organization's naming conventions.

- Replication factor, to ensure durability and availability.

- Number of partitions. This, along with the replication factor, sits at the intersection of functional and nonfunctional concerns. It may be refined later as more performance or scalability requirements are gathered.

- Retention policy, defining how long messages are kept in the topic.

- Compaction setting, if applicable. Particularly useful for topics that hold the latest state per key.

- Message format—whether the payload is encoded using Avro, JSON, Protobuf, etc.

- Key field, which determines how messages are partitioned.

- Key serializer and the schema used to encode the key.

- Message headers, including which headers are required and their purpose (e.g., correlation ID, versioning).

- Whether null keys are allowed, which may affect compaction or filtering logic.

- Value serializer and the schema used for the message payload.

- Recommended acknowledgment mode for the producer (e.g., `acks=all`).

- Recommended offset commit strategy for consumers (e.g., manual vs. auto-commit).

- Schema evolution compatibility. Defines the compatibility strategy applied to the event schema, such as backward, forward, or full compatibility. This determines whether new schema versions will remain compatible with existing consumers or producers and ensures stability during schema changes.

As you saw in chapter 6, it's often helpful to define a set of event types—reusable patterns that bundle predefined characteristics (such as compaction, retention, and serialization). When a new business event is introduced, you can assign it an appropriate event type from this catalogue rather than define all the characteristics from scratch.

It's also worth noting that not all topics map directly to business events. Some Kafka topics are technical or infrastructure-related. For example, if an event stream is repartitioned by a different key (e.g., for aggregation or joining), an intermediate topic will be created as part of the stream processing pipeline. These topics are typically generated by frameworks like Kafka Streams or Apache Flink and are not tied to a business event as defined in the event catalogue.

However, even though these topics do not correspond to business-level events, they are still part of the data plane and must be included in the event catalogue for purposes of governance, compliance, monitoring, and operational visibility.

10.1.4 *Identifying nonfunctional requirements*

Now that we've defined the functional characteristics of our events and topics, it's time to gather the nonfunctional requirements that will guide the proper configuration of all Kafka participants—producers, brokers, and consumers. Specifically, we need to collect requirements related to message size, latency, and throughput. These parameters directly influence how we configure batching, compression, partitioning, buffer sizes, and memory usage across the system.

DEFINING MESSAGE SIZE REQUIREMENTS

Message size plays a crucial role in the performance and reliability of Kafka-based systems. It affects how events are batched, how memory and network buffers are sized, and how long it takes to serialize, transmit, and process each message. To gather meaningful input for configuration, we should collect the following:

- *Average message size*—Helps determine the typical footprint of a message on the wire and guides decisions on batch sizes, linger time, and compression efficiency.

- *Peak (maximum) message size*—Critical for setting safe limits like `max.message
.bytes` on the broker and `fetch.message.max.bytes` on the consumer side. If messages occasionally exceed these values, they may be rejected or require special handling.

- *Compression strategy*—Compression can significantly reduce the effective size of messages, especially when payloads are text-heavy or repetitive (as in JSON or Avro). Choosing the right compression algorithm (snappy, lz4, zstd, etc.) can improve throughput, disk usage, and network efficiency, but may add CPU overhead. It's useful to evaluate compression ratios and performance trade-offs based on actual message content.

All of these parameters—message size characteristics, batching-related settings, and compression choices—directly impact cloud costs. Many providers bill by throughput, partition count, and retained storage. Smaller, well-compressed messages and sane batch sizing reduce required partitions and storage, often letting you drop to a lower pricing tier.

DEFINING LATENCY REQUIREMENTS

The next nonfunctional requirement to define is *latency*—a measurement of delay within the system. In the context of messaging and distributed systems, latency can refer to different stages of the event flow, depending on where it's measured.

The most common types of latency to consider are shown in table 10.1. End-to-end latency is the most meaningful from a business perspective, but in distributed systems we typically measure and optimize latency for each participant independently—producers, Kafka brokers, and consumers—since each introduces its own variability and tuning parameters.

Table 10.1 Different types of latency

Latency type	Description
Producer latency	Time between calling `send()` and receiving an acknowledgment (`ack()`) from the Kafka broker.
Broker delivery latency	Time the message spends in Kafka before being fetched.
Consumer latency	Time between the message being available in Kafka and the consumer fetching it. This reflects the delivery delay from Kafka.
Processing latency	Time taken by the consumer to process the message after fetching it, including deserialization, validation, enrichment, and DB writes.
End-to-end latency	Time from message production to the final business effect (e.g., from notification sent to decision recorded). This encompasses all of the above stages.

When defining latency requirements, it's best to use percentile-based metrics, as they better represent real-world performance compared to averages. Here are typical latency metrics to collect:

- *P95/P99 latency*—For example, 95% of messages must be processed within 1 second.
- *Maximum latency*—For example, no message should take longer than 3 seconds.
- *Average latency (less common)*—For example, target an average latency under 500 ms. This is less useful on its own, as it can mask spikes and outliers.

DEFINING THROUGHPUT REQUIREMENTS

Another important nonfunctional requirement is *throughput*—the volume of events your system needs to handle over time. Throughput is typically measured in messages per second, per minute, or per hour, and it can vary significantly depending on the nature of the business process.

To define throughput requirements effectively, start by asking these questions:

- How often does this event occur? Is it triggered by regular user actions, background jobs, or integrations?
- Are there peak and off-peak periods? Does traffic spike during business hours, month-end, or during promotional campaigns?
- Is the volume predictable or bursty? Are spikes occasional but massive (e.g., file uploads, batch imports)?
- Is there a pattern to how events are generated? For example, steady real-time streaming, daily batches, or unpredictable bursts?

Based on these insights, you can express throughput requirements using a structured format as shown in table 10.2.

Table 10.2   Defining throughput requirements

Throughput requirement	Example
Expected volume	300,000 messages per day
Peak rate	50 events/sec during business hours; up to 100/sec during bursts
Pattern	Real-time events, with high activity from 9 AM to 5 PM on weekdays
Burst handling	System must buffer and process backlog within 5 minutes during peak load

An essential consideration is to understand how throughput is expected to evolve over time:

- Will the daily volume double in the next year?
- Are there plans to onboard more channels or sources?
- Will future regulations or partnerships introduce more frequent or larger data exchanges?

Understanding the growth trajectory helps ensure that the system is designed for scale, and that partitioning, batching, and resource provisioning can be planned accordingly.

OTHER NONFUNCTIONAL REQUIREMENTS

Other nonfunctional requirements address broader concerns around data integrity, availability, and compliance, which are essential for defining how resilient and trustworthy the system needs to be.

Security policies across the organization typically dictate the requirements for encryption. When defining security-related nonfunctional requirements, consider the following:

- Are messages encrypted in transit (e.g., TLS) and/or at rest (e.g., disk encryption)?
- Are sensitive fields encrypted or masked within the payload (e.g., PII, payment info)?

- Should encryption be handled by the Kafka infrastructure, at the application level, or both?

Another group of requirements relates to data loss tolerance—how critical it is to preserve messages under failure conditions such as broker outages, network partitions, or system crashes. A common classification is as follows:

- *Critical*—No message loss is acceptable. Events must be persisted and fully acknowledged.
- *Important*—Occasional loss is tolerable if fallback mechanisms are in place.
- *Non-critical*—Best-effort delivery is acceptable; message loss has minimal business impact.

And, of course, it is necessary to define dead-letter handling mechanisms—what happens when a message cannot be successfully processed after multiple attempts:

- What should happen to messages that fail repeatedly?
- Should a dead-letter topic (DLT) be configured for inspection and reprocessing?
- Should failures trigger alerts, retries, or escalation workflows?

10.2 Maintaining cluster structure

We've already discussed event governance, emphasizing the importance of publishing event structures, defining schemas, and enforcing compatibility rules to ensure teams understand what events are available. These principles apply not only to events but also to other key artifacts in an event-driven architecture. To design a well-structured Kafka project, we must first gather requirements for event-driven workflows and translate them into technical implementation artifacts, such as Kafka topic configurations, connector settings, and streaming queries.

In the earlier chapters, we explored how AsyncAPI helps document topics, event schemas, and client configurations. Now, we'll examine how such specifications can be used to maintain cluster structure effectively. Specifically, we'll discuss how topics, schemas, and connectors are created, managed, and automated to ensure scalability, consistency, and maintainability.

10.2.1 Using CLI and UI tools

The `auto.create.topics.enable` property (which defaults to `true`) controls whether topics in Kafka are created automatically. If enabled, a topic is created as soon as a producer sends the first message. The topic will be created with default broker-level configuration settings, which may not align with best practices.

Similarly, if Schema Registry is used and the producer-side property `auto.register` `.schemas` is set to `true` (the default), schemas are automatically registered when a producer sends data with a previously unseen schema. In other words, as soon as a message is sent, all required artifacts—topics and schemas—are created automatically.

While this behavior may be useful for development or playground environments, it is unsuitable for production clusters shared across multiple teams. In such cases, both `auto.create.topics.enable` and `auto.register.schemas` should be set to `false` to enforce controlled provisioning.

Different Kafka installations come with command-line tools that allow administrators to perform essential cluster operations, including creating topics, updating configurations, and setting up ACLs. These scripts provide a direct way to manage topics but require familiarity with the command line.

For those less comfortable with CLI tools, various UI-based tools are available, enabling visual management of Kafka topics. However, while they're useful in the early stages of a Kafka project, manual topic management is not a sustainable long-term solution for several reasons:

- Configuration is not formally registered anywhere. The only way to determine what exists in the cluster is by manually inspecting it using tools.

- Cluster structure cannot be easily replicated across environments. There is no seamless way to apply the same topic configurations across development, staging, and production clusters.

- Actions are not audited. No built-in tracking exists of who created artifacts, when they were created, or why they were modified, which leads to governance challenges.

To address these issues, the industry is moving toward a declarative approach, where Kafka configurations are explicitly defined, version-controlled, and automated. This approach minimizes errors, improves maintainability, and ensures consistency across environments.

10.2.2 *Using GitOps for Kafka configurations*

Let's explore how version control can be used to store Kafka's configuration and how it integrates with *continuous integration/continuous deployment* (CI/CD) pipelines to ensure a structured and automated approach to managing Kafka infrastructure.

USING GIT AS A SINGLE SOURCE OF TRUTH

The GitOps approach for Kafka involves defining all Kafka artifacts declaratively and storing them in Git. This method provides numerous benefits:

- *Version control and history*—Git is a well-known system for managing versioned artifacts, offering commits, diffs, and pull request history. With widely adopted tools, it becomes easy to review and collaborate on changes.

- *Full change tracking*—Every modification is logged, so we always know what changed, when, and who made the change.

- *Safe rollbacks*—If a configuration update breaks something, Git allows instant rollbacks to a previous working version.

The most important advantage of GitOps is that it forces us to store the state of our target system. Instead of committing scripts that create Kafka topics, we store the desired final state—a declarative definition of the topic with its full configuration. This concept is illustrated in figure 10.1.

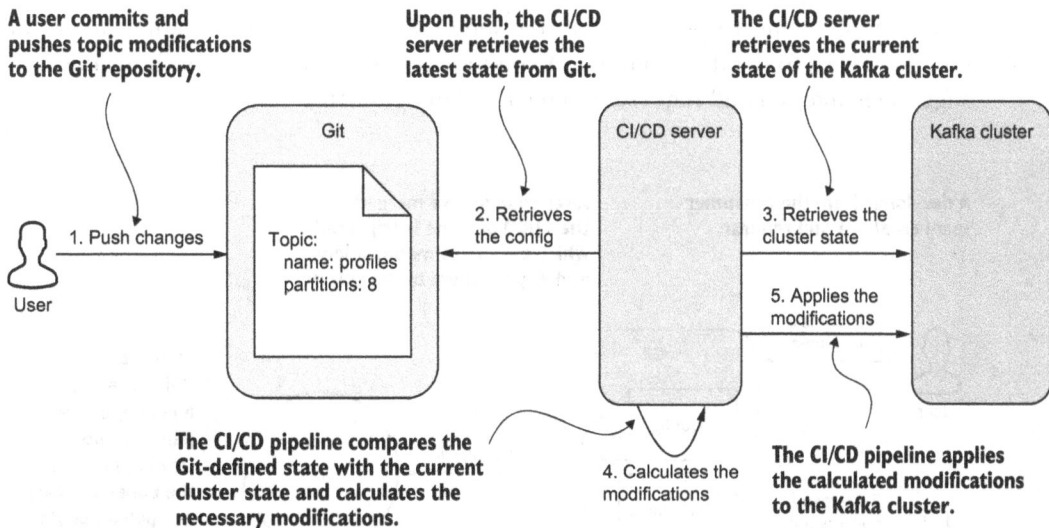

A user commits and pushes topic modifications to the Git repository.

Upon push, the CI/CD server retrieves the latest state from Git.

The CI/CD server retrieves the current state of the Kafka cluster.

Git

CI/CD server

Kafka cluster

1. Push changes

Topic:
name: profiles
partitions: 8

2. Retrieves the config

3. Retrieves the cluster state

5. Applies the modifications

User

The CI/CD pipeline compares the Git-defined state with the current cluster state and calculates the necessary modifications.

4. Calculates the modifications

The CI/CD pipeline applies the calculated modifications to the Kafka cluster.

Figure 10.1 Applying Kafka cluster modifications via GitOps: after the updated Kafka cluster configuration is pushed, the CI/CD pipeline retrieves the current cluster state, calculates the required modifications, and applies them.

Kafka configurations are stored as text-based configuration files (e.g., YAML or JSON). When a change is pushed to Git, a CI/CD pipeline is triggered through webhooks, notifying the CI/CD system to pull the latest changes and start the build process. This pipeline does the following:

- Compares the current state of the Kafka cluster with the configuration declared in Git
- Applies only the necessary changes to bring the Kafka cluster into the desired state

With this approach, Git becomes the single source of truth, always reflecting the actual configuration of the Kafka cluster.

Of course, you cannot technically prevent authorized users from making direct modifications (e.g., creating a new topic via scripts). However, a special validation pipeline running periodically can detect any drift, warn you about discrepancies, and even suggest corrective changes to align the cluster with the desired Git state. This ensures that even if manual changes happen, they are tracked, reviewed, and reconciled to maintain consistency.

USING GIT FOR TEAM COLLABORATION

In chapters 6 and 7, we discussed data ownership, specifically who is responsible for defining Kafka topic structures and data contracts. In the Kafka ecosystem, this responsibility naturally falls on the producer, as it determines the structure of the data being published. Therefore, the producer's team is authorized to maintain all related artifacts, including schemas and topic configurations.

However, teams responsible for consumer services may need adjustments or enhancements to the data contract. A common and structured approach for this is to suggest changes via pull requests, as illustrated in figure 10.2.

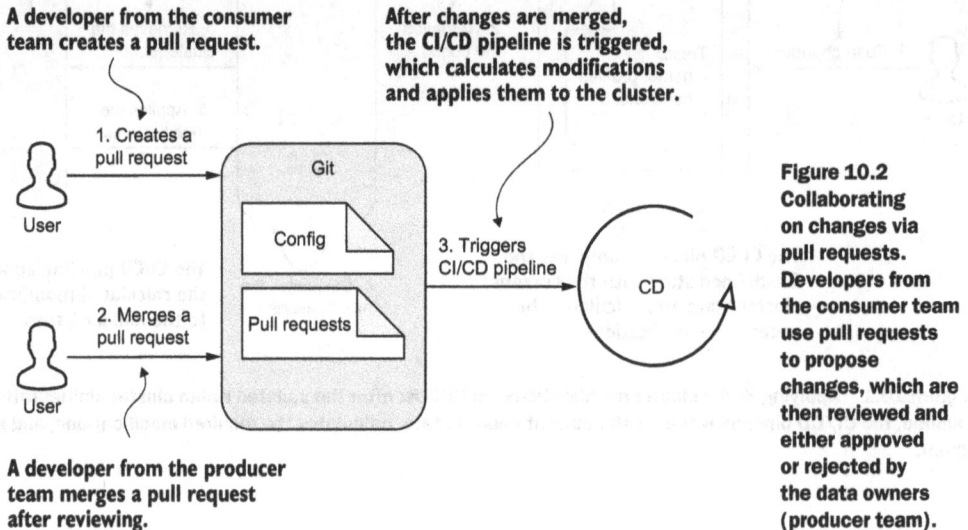

Figure 10.2 Collaborating on changes via pull requests. Developers from the consumer team use pull requests to propose changes, which are then reviewed and either approved or rejected by the data owners (producer team).

When a consumer team requests a change to a configuration or schema, they create a branch, implement the necessary modifications, and submit a pull request. The producer team can then review, approve, and merge the change into the main branch or reject it with feedback, requesting further clarification or adjustments.

This process makes Git a powerful tool for team collaboration, providing transparency, version control, and a structured approval workflow for managing Kafka artifacts.

GITOPS TOOLS

Open source GitOps tools like Kafka-GitOps (https://devshawn.github.io/kafka-gitops) and Jikkou (www.jikkou.io) support custom YAML-based formats for defining Kafka resources. These tools enable teams to build their own CI/CD pipelines to manage Kafka configurations in a structured, automated way.

A typical Kafka GitOps pipeline consists of the following steps:

- *Validation*—Ensures the desired state conforms to defined policy rules, such as minimum partition requirements, naming conventions, and retention policies.
- *Change planning*—Generates a preview of the changes before applying them. Since modifying a Kafka cluster can be potentially destructive, it is common to review proposed changes first, especially in production environments.
- *Applying changes*—Once reviewed and approved, the changes are applied to the Kafka cluster, updating topics, schemas, ACLs, and other resources.

A slightly different approach is used when Kafka runs inside Kubernetes. In this case, GitOps tools like Argo CD (https://argo-cd.readthedocs.io) and Flux (https://fluxcd .io) work alongside Kubernetes operators—custom controllers that extend Kubernetes to manage complex, stateful applications like Kafka—automating tasks such as scaling, self-healing, and rolling updates. This collaboration is illustrated in figure 10.3.

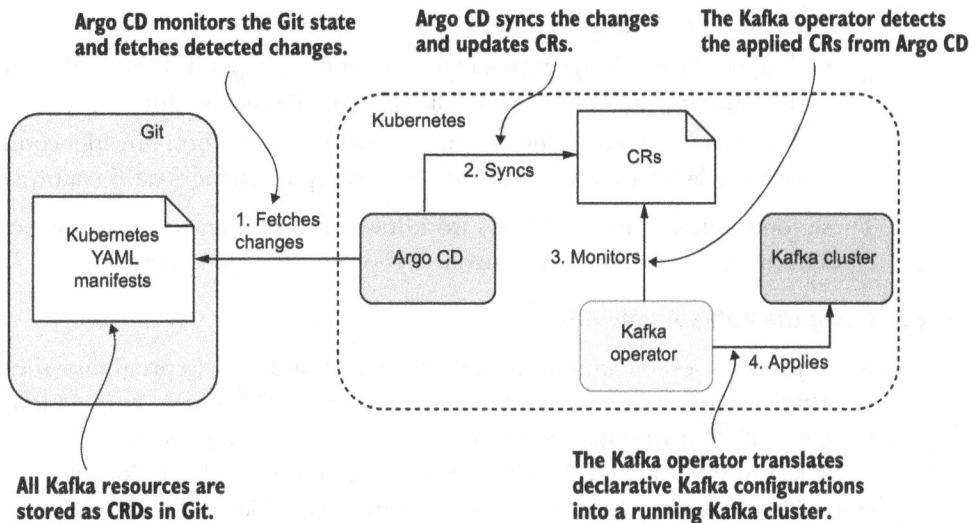

Figure 10.3 Applying changes with a Kubernetes operator. Argo CD synchronizes the desired state from Git with the current state of custom resources in the cluster, and applies the differences automatically.

The key idea is that Kafka artifacts (topics, connectors, ACLs, etc.) can be represented as Kubernetes resources by defining them as *custom resource definitions* (CRDs). A Kubernetes operator is responsible for translating these resource definitions into actual Kafka configurations. The steps are as follows:

1 Kafka resources (CRDs) are defined in YAML and stored in Git.
2 A GitOps tool (e.g., Argo CD or Flux) continuously monitors the repository, following a pull-based approach. This differs from push-based CI/CD, which is

triggered by webhooks. When a change is detected, the GitOps tool calculates the difference between the Git-defined state and the actual system state, and then applies the necessary updates to ensure alignment.

3 The Kubernetes operator receives the updated configuration and creates, updates, or deletes Kafka resources as needed. Several Kubernetes operators are available for managing Kafka, including

– Strimzi (https://strimzi.io)—A popular open source operator for running Kafka on Kubernetes
– Confluent for Kubernetes, commonly referred to as CFK (https://doc .confluent.io/operator/current/overview.html)—A Kubernetes-native operator for managing Confluent Platform deployments.

If the Kafka cluster is not running on Kubernetes, other *infrastructure-as-code* (IaC) solutions can be used instead, such as

- Ansible (https://docs.confluent.io/ansible/current/)—Automates Kafka topic creation and configuration using Ansible playbooks
- Puppet (https://forge.puppet.com/modules/puppet/kafka/)—Manages Kafka infrastructure and ensures consistency using Puppet modules
- Terraform (https://github.com/confluentinc/terraform-provider-confluent)— Defines Kafka resources declaratively and applies changes via Terraform modules

These tools follow a similar GitOps workflow, ensuring that Kafka infrastructure and configurations remain version-controlled, reproducible, and auditable.

10.2.3 Using the Kafka Admin API

Kafka provides several administrative APIs that allow teams to programmatically manage clusters, topics, schemas, and connectors. These APIs enable automation, making them essential for DevOps and GitOps workflows in the Kafka ecosystem.

Kafka's Admin Client API (https://docs.confluent.io/kafka/kafka-apis.html#admin -api) allows you to perform common administrative tasks on a Kafka cluster programmatically, including

- *Topic management*—Create, modify, and delete topics and adjust partitions, replication factors, and retention settings.
- *Broker configuration*—Update broker settings dynamically.
- *Access control*—Manage access control lists (ACLs) to enforce security policies.
- *Consumer group management*—View consumer group offsets and reset offsets.

This API is useful for infrastructure automation tools, ensuring that Kafka resources are managed consistently across environments.

The Schema Registry API provides administrative control over schemas used in Kafka messages. Since Schema Registry communicates via HTTP, it can be accessed through the following:

- *SDKs*—Client libraries that abstract API requests.
- *Direct HTTP requests*—Send API calls using tools like cURL or scripts.

Kafka Connect exposes a REST API for managing connectors programmatically. This API allows

- *CRUD operations*—Create, read, update, and delete connectors.
- *Lifecycle management*—Pause, resume, and restart connectors.
- *Monitoring*—Fetch connector status, task statuses, and error details.

All these APIs can be used for implementing DevOps tasks for Kafka ecosystem servers and achieving fully automated Kafka infrastructure management.

10.2.4 Setting up environments

In software development, it is common to maintain multiple environments to facilitate development, testing, and deployment. At a minimum, three environments are typically required:

- *Development (Dev)*—Used for prototyping, building, and testing new features. This environment contains synthetic data, lacks full integration with external systems, and allows frequent resets.
- *User acceptance testing (UAT)*—A production-like environment used by quality assurance (QA) teams to validate new features. Data in UAT may be synthetic or an anonymized subset of production data.
- *Production (Prod)*—The live environment where end users interact with the system. This environment contains real production data, is subject to service level agreements (SLAs), and requires the highest level of stability and security.

Additional environments may also exist, such as

- *Preproduction (staging)*—A mirror of production used for final validation before deployment.
- *Performance testing*—A dedicated environment for load and stress testing.
- *Production data testing*—An environment containing recent production data, used to reproduce and debug production incidents.

For Kafka, a best practice is to maintain separate clusters for each environment, including all associated components (like brokers, controllers, schema registries, Kafka connect, etc). Each cluster may have different configurations based on the environment's needs. For example, a Dev environment might have fewer brokers and a lower replication factor than production. However, differences in cluster size and setup require careful configuration management. For example, the replication factor in Dev might need to be set lower than in Prod due to fewer brokers being available.

Instead of maintaining separate Kafka clusters, some teams opt to share a single Kafka cluster for Dev, UAT, and other lower environments. This approach reduces infrastructure costs but requires the following:

- Topic name prefixes to distinguish between environments, such as
  - DEV.transactions (for Dev).
  - UAT.transactions (for UAT).
- Separate Schema Registries for each environment to avoid schema conflicts.
- Strict authentication and access control, including
  - Unique credentials per environment.
  - ACLs to prevent cross-environment access.
- Environment-based configuration using variables, such as defining the topic prefix dynamically.
- Quota enforcement to prevent resource overuse in lower environments. This approach requires careful governance to prevent accidental access between environments.

In some cases, UAT requires access to production data for realistic testing. However, copying data in real-time is not recommended for a couple of reasons:

- *Schema evolution differences*—UAT may use newer schema versions than production.
- *Sensitive data exposure*—Production data may contain personally identifiable information (PII) or confidential business data.

Instead, a controlled migration pipeline should be established:

1 Mask and anonymize sensitive fields before transferring data.
2 Transform records to match the UAT schema version.
3 Schedule periodic updates instead of real-time replication.

This approach ensures safe and compliant data usage in testing environments.

10.2.5 *Choosing a solution for the Customer 360 ODS*

Getting back to our example ODS, let's say the team unanimously decides to adopt the GitOps approach for managing their Kafka cluster. They have already created AsyncAPI specifications and plan to use them as the single source of truth for defining their cluster's state. But this choice means they cannot directly use tools that rely on their own proprietary formats for Kafka resources. Also, since they are not running Kubernetes, they can't rely on Kubernetes operators for automation.

To maintain an abstract, technology-agnostic event-driven architecture, they can continue using AsyncAPI files for documentation. But to bridge the gap between design and implementation, they will build a CI/CD pipeline integrating AsyncAPI generators. The pipeline would work as follows:

1 Convert AsyncAPI definitions into Kafka-compatible configurations using AsyncAPI generators.
2 Generate Kafka resources in a format that GitOps tools can process.

3 Commit the generated Kafka resources back to Git, ensuring version control and traceability.

4 Synchronize the Kafka cluster with the latest state stored in Git, keeping the system aligned with the declared architecture.

This approach allows the team to maintain a clear separation between architecture definition (AsyncAPI) and operational implementation (Kafka resources) while ensuring a fully automated, GitOps-driven deployment process.

10.3 Testing Kafka applications

Different types of tests are used to ensure the overall quality of an application. We can test the functionality of components in isolation, verifying that each behaves according to the specified requirements. It's also important to test the integration between components, ensuring they understand each other's contracts and can communicate correctly through the agreed upon protocols. Additionally, performance testing is needed to confirm that our components can handle the expected load reliably. Let's look at how unit tests, integration tests, and performance tests can verify the quality of the components that interact with Kafka.

10.3.1 Unit testing

Unit testing verifies that a single component behaves correctly in isolation. Although developers understand the implementation, effective unit tests assert public, observable behavior. Dependencies are isolated with mocks or fakes; private methods are not tested directly. If important logic sits behind a private method, refactor—extract a helper or expose a minimal API—so tests remain stable under refactoring.

That said, unit tests come with development overhead. Writing and maintaining them takes time, and in many cases, developers estimate that the effort required to cover code with meaningful tests can equal the time needed for the initial implementation. Sometimes tests fail not because the code is wrong, but because the test was written incorrectly—especially if it's too dependent on the internal details of the code.

In contrast, integration testing focuses on verifying how components interact with each other—ensuring they respect defined contracts and communicate correctly. When testing components that interact with Kafka, the line between unit and integration testing becomes more blurred. For example, testing a service that includes a Kafka producer or consumer often involves validating message flow, which inherently crosses component boundaries.

In this context, we define unit testing as the verification that a component (e.g., a service) behaves correctly in response to input—such as passing the right data to a Kafka producer or handling an incoming Kafka message. But testing whether the service actually produces correctly to Kafka or consumes correctly from a Kafka topic falls under *integration testing*, as it involves interacting with external infrastructure. While unit tests may inspect how Kafka-related logic is invoked (e.g., checking method calls and configurations via mocks), the actual end-to-end Kafka behavior is best validated through integration tests.

TESTING PRODUCERS AND CONSUMERS

Let's consider testing the `ProfileService` from our Customer 360 ODS, as illustrated in figure 10.4. This service is responsible for updating user profiles and producing a message to Kafka to reflect the change. In this case, we're not focusing on the actual Kafka communication, but rather on verifying the internal implementation logic of the service.

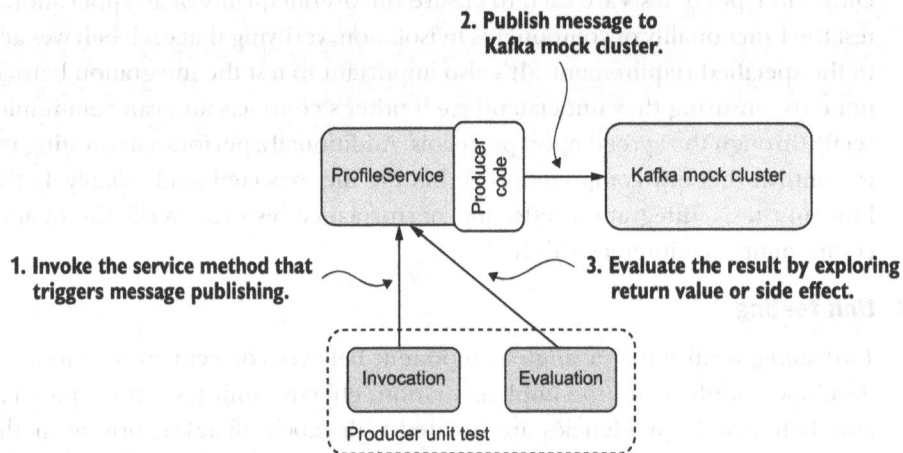

Figure 10.4   Unit testing of the `ProfileService` component. The test invokes the service with test input and verifies its behavior without involving a Kafka cluster. Evaluation is done by inspecting the return value or verifying that the producer was called as expected.

Our unit test will directly invoke the service with a controlled input and then evaluate its behavior by checking either the returned value or a side effect, such as confirming that the Kafka producer was called with the correct arguments.

Testing the `Customer360Service`, which consumes Kafka messages and builds aggregated objects, is more challenging than testing a typical service. This component is not invoked directly in a production environment—it listens to messages from the Kafka cluster, meaning its entry point is tied to Kafka's infrastructure.

However, since we're not focusing on integration in this case, we can test the functional behavior of the service in isolation by invoking the consumer code directly. We can simulate the consumption of a Kafka message by passing a deserialized message to the consumer method, as if it had just arrived from Kafka.

The test then evaluates the behavior of the service by inspecting its side effects—such as whether the expected data was passed to downstream components or persisted. An example of this kind of unit test is shown in figure 10.5.

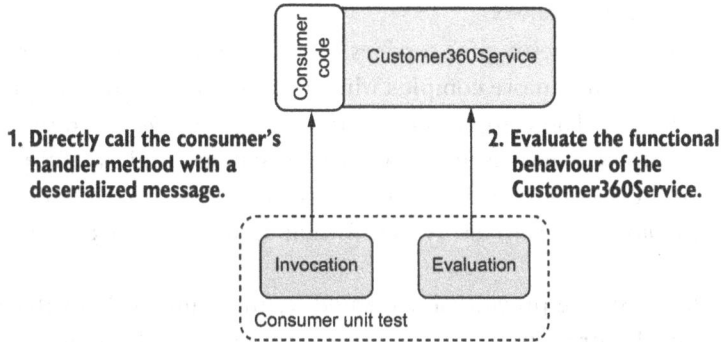

Figure 10.5 Unit testing the `Customer360Service` component. The test directly invokes the consumer's handler method with a deserialized Kafka message, simulating message delivery without involving a Kafka cluster. The test then evaluates the service's behavior by inspecting its side effects, such as interactions with downstream components or state changes.

The actual implementations of our services is designed to communicate with a real Kafka cluster. They load configuration, establish network connections, and send or receive data through Kafka clients. However, to create a lightweight unit test, we need to avoid these external dependencies.

One common approach is shown in figure 10.6. Instead of using the real components from the Kafka client library, we replace the producer and consumer implementations with mocked versions that simulate their behavior. In the Java ecosystem, this is typically done using tools like Mockito (https://site.mockito.org), which allow you to substitute real dependencies with dummy objects during testing. These mocks behave like the real Kafka clients from the perspective of the service code, but without performing any actual network operations.

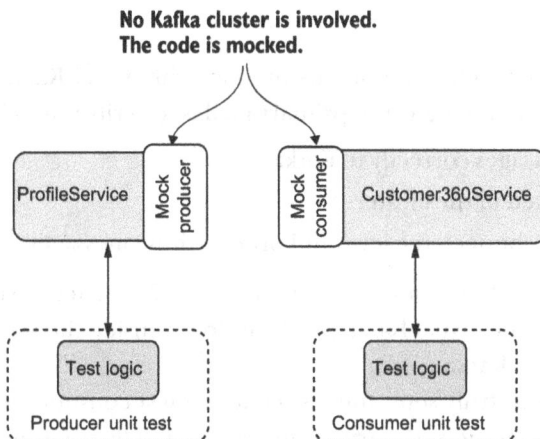

Figure 10.6   Unit testing Kafka components using mock implementations. The services are tested in isolation by replacing the actual Kafka producer and consumer with mocks. This allows the test logic to focus on verifying functional behavior without involving a Kafka cluster or real network communication.

TESTING KAFKA STREAMS APPLICATIONS

So far, we've discussed unit testing for services by mocking Kafka producers and consumers. But testing becomes more complex when dealing with streaming applications built with Kafka Streams. These applications often define a *topology*—a directed graph of interconnected topics, where events flow through stateless and stateful processing nodes. Events are transformed, enriched, or stored as they pass through this graph. Testing the full topology to ensure every transformation behaves as expected is a challenging task.

Fortunately, *Kafka Streams* provides a dedicated testing framework for this purpose (https://kafka.apache.org/40/documentation/streams/developer-guide/testing .html). The core of this framework is the `TopologyTestDriver` class, which enables you to test the entire topology without requiring a running Kafka cluster. You don't even need to create mock producers and consumers. Instead, you define `TestInputTopic` and `TestOutputTopic` objects by specifying the topic name and the serializers/deserializers for keys and values.

These test topics simulate real Kafka topics—messages are serialized and deserialized to and from byte arrays, just like in production. You can pipe records into the input topics and verify the output from the output topics. The framework also provides powerful capabilities for simulating time progression and examining intermediate state, which is especially valuable when testing stateful stream processing.

The tests discussed so far have focused on verifying component behavior without involving a real Kafka cluster. These unit tests isolate business logic and use mocks to simulate Kafka interactions. However, to validate that the communication layer—including serialization, topic configuration, and broker connectivity—is implemented correctly, we need to move beyond isolation.

In the next section, we'll explore how to design integration tests that include real interactions with Kafka, providing greater confidence that the application communicates with Kafka as expected.

10.3.2 *Integration testing*

At this stage, we want to test how our components interact with a real Kafka cluster. Since the focus is now on integration logic, the primary goal is to verify the following:

- The producer sends messages correctly to Kafka.
- The messages are persisted in the cluster.
- The consumer is able to connect, retrieve, and process those messages.

An example of a producer integration test is shown in figure 10.7. The test invokes the `ProfileService`, which triggers the actual Kafka producer logic. Inside the service, the producer publishes a message to Kafka.

To verify that the message was truly sent, the test creates a test consumer that subscribes to the appropriate Kafka topic and retrieves messages directly from the cluster.

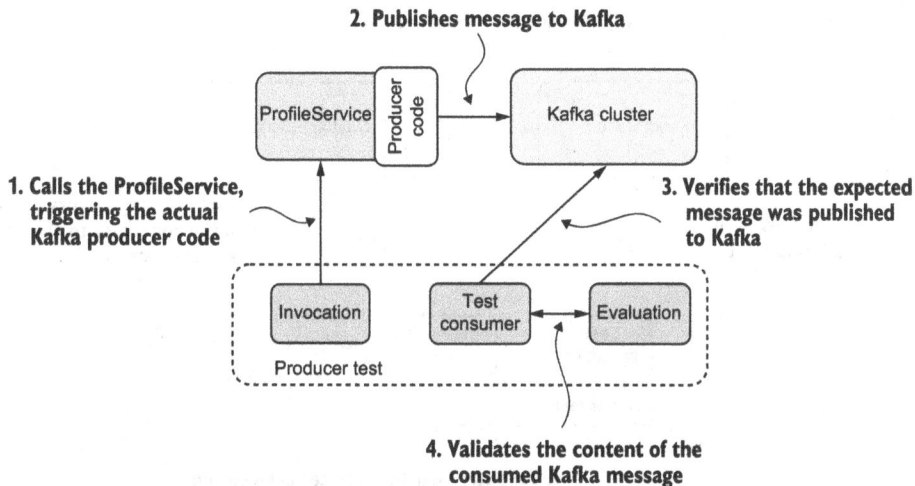

Figure 10.7 Integration testing of the ProfileService producer. The test invokes the service, triggering the actual producer code that sends a message to Kafka. A test consumer subscribes to the topic and receives the message from the Kafka cluster. The test then evaluates the content and metadata of the received message to verify correct delivery and structure.

If the message is successfully received, the test can evaluate its content as well as any relevant metadata, such as partition, offset, or headers.

Testing the consumer side is, as usual, a bit more involved. In this test, we begin by sending a message to a real Kafka cluster using a dedicated test producer component. Once the message is published, we expect our consumer component to receive and process it.

To verify that this happened correctly, we can use the argument-capturing technique. A utility called ArgumentCaptor (provided by the Mockito framework) allows us to inspect the arguments which were passed to the service method invoked by the consumer. By capturing these arguments, we can verify that the consumer was triggered as expected and with the correct data, providing confidence in the integration between Kafka and the consumer logic. An example of such a test setup is shown in figure 10.8.

This raises an important question: We've already discussed environments for development, user acceptance testing (UAT), and production, so do we also need a dedicated environment for integration testing? Or are there other options for running these tests reliably without introducing additional infrastructure overhead?

USING A DEDICATED CLUSTER

While it's technically possible to use a dedicated Kafka cluster for running integration tests, this approach comes with several significant drawbacks.

First, working with a real Kafka environment typically involves more than just the brokers—it also requires a supporting ecosystem that includes Kafka controllers, Schema Registry, and potentially Kafka Connect. Setting up and maintaining this full

2. Consumes message from Kafka

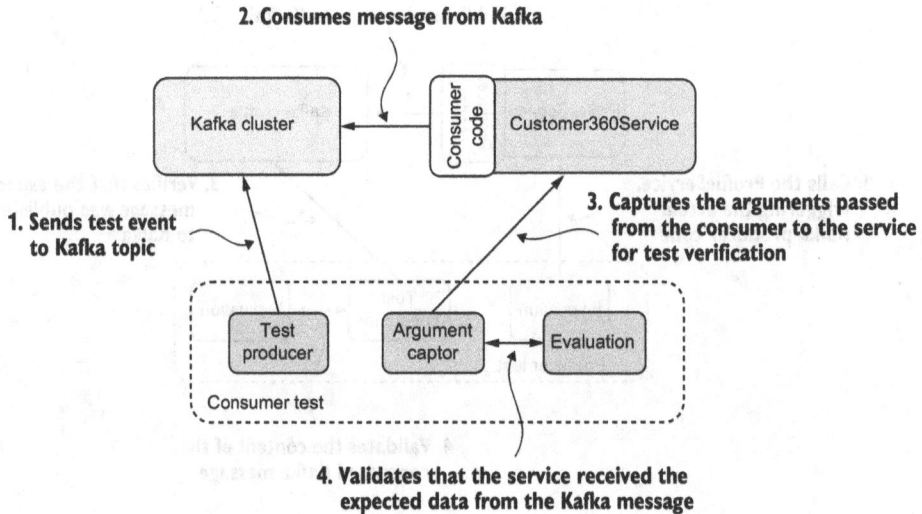

Figure 10.8   Integration testing of the consumer component in `Customer360Service`. The test sends a message to the Kafka cluster using a test producer. When the message is consumed, `ArgumentCaptor` is used to capture the parameters passed to the service logic. The test then evaluates the captured data to verify that the consumer received and handled the message correctly.

stack introduces substantial hardware overhead and increases the operational burden for the infrastructure team.

Second, if the cluster is shared among multiple development teams, coordination becomes a challenge. Teams need to collaborate to avoid topic name collisions, manage consumer group offsets, and prevent test interference, which can quickly become a bottleneck in active development environments.

Even more critically, reliable testing requires that each test starts from a clean state. This means test frameworks must create and delete topics, reset consumer groups, and clean up any test data. In a shared environment, this adds risk and complexity. On top of that, network latency and performance can fluctuate based on the load on the cluster, making test results inconsistent and harder to interpret.

All in all, relying on a full-scale Kafka cluster for testing introduces too much complexity. We need a more lightweight, reliable option that still allows us to verify integration without the operational overhead.

USING EMBEDDEDKAFKA

For Spring-based applications, a better option is to use the `EmbeddedKafkaBroker`—a component provided by the spring-kafka (https://spring.io/projects/spring-kafka) project. This component spins up an in-memory Kafka broker, which isn't a real Kafka cluster, but behaves like one for testing purposes. The broker is automatically started with the test and shuts down when the test completes, making it lightweight and easy to manage.

An example of an integration test using this setup is shown in figure 10.9. In this test, `ProfileService` sends data to the in-memory embedded broker. The test code invokes the service, which internally publishes a Kafka message. Once the message is published, the result can be evaluated similarly as in the unit test shown in figure 10.7, such as by creating a test consumer and checking the message contents.

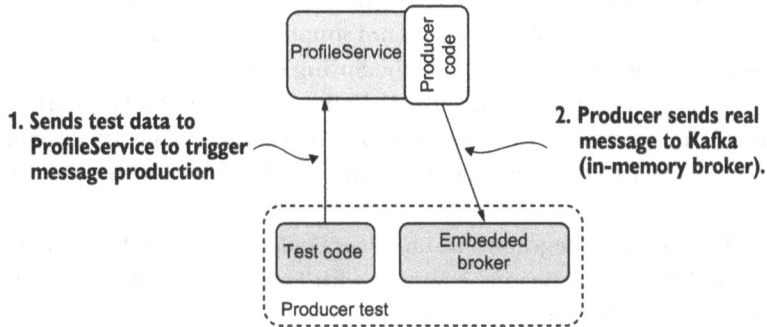

Figure 10.9 Integration testing using an embedded Kafka broker. `ProfileService` **sends a message to an in-memory Kafka instance provided by the** `EmbeddedKafkaBroker` **component. The test code verifies the message by consuming it from the embedded broker and evaluating its content and metadata.**

The situation is similar on the consumer side. Instead of using a real Kafka cluster, we once again use an `EmbeddedKafkaBroker` that runs entirely in memory. An example of such a test is shown in figure 10.10, where the consumer receives messages from an in-memory Kafka broker.

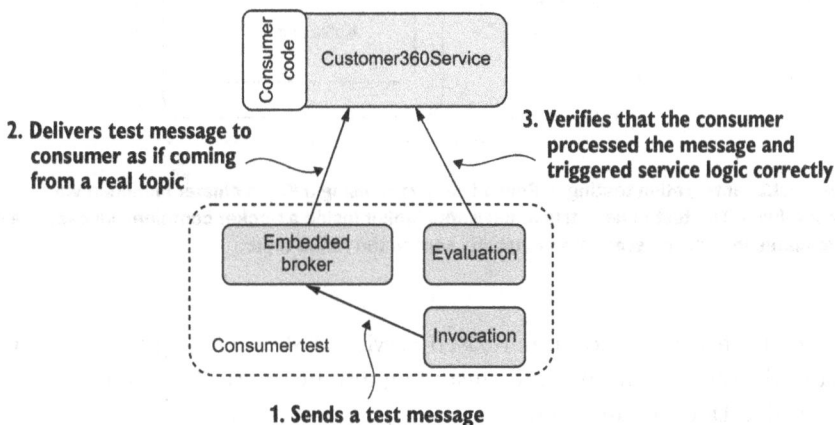

Figure 10.10 Integration testing of the consumer logic using an embedded Kafka broker. A test message is sent to the in-memory broker, which is consumed by `Customer360Service`**. The test verifies that the consumer processes the message correctly, without requiring an external Kafka cluster.**

Using `EmbeddedKafkaBroker` offers several advantages: it provides a clean state for each test run, requires no additional infrastructure, and doesn't require any changes to the component code. The substitution of the real Kafka broker with the in-memory one is handled entirely through test configuration, keeping the application logic untouched.

USING TESTCONTAINERS

While `EmbeddedKafkaBroker` is an excellent option for integration tests in Spring-based applications, it has some limitations. It may not support every Kafka feature—especially edge cases—and it's not available outside the Spring ecosystem.

An alternative approach is to run a real Kafka cluster in Docker during the test lifecycle using Testcontainers (https://testcontainers.com). This allows you to spin up an actual broker dynamically at test runtime, without relying on preprovisioned infrastructure.

Figure 10.11 shows an integration test for `ProfileService` using Testcontainers. The structure is similar to the previous example with `EmbeddedKafkaBroker`, but here we launch a Dockerized Kafka cluster for the test.

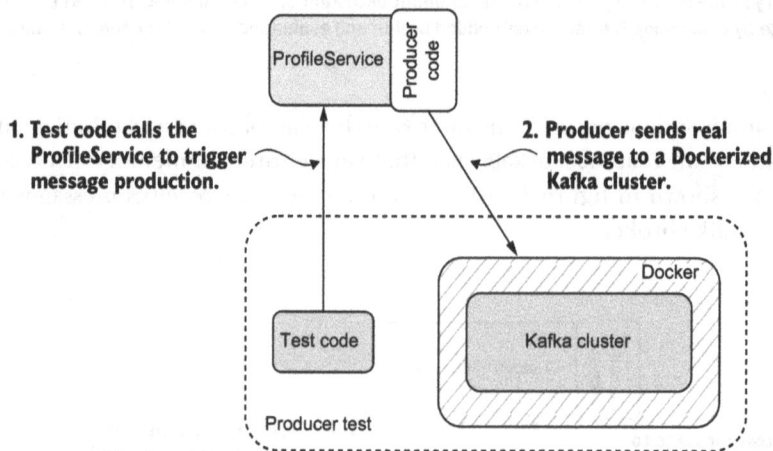

Figure 10.11 Integration testing of `ProfileService` using a Kafka cluster launched via Testcontainers. The test code starts a real Kafka broker inside a Docker container, invokes the service, and validates that the message was correctly sent to the Kafka topic.

A matching test for a consumer-based service is shown in figure 10.12. The logic remains the same—sending and consuming test messages—but the Kafka cluster now runs inside a Docker container.

Testcontainers are a powerful and flexible solution for integration testing, and they're supported across multiple programming languages. The main drawback is the need to run Docker, which can increase resource usage and test execution time

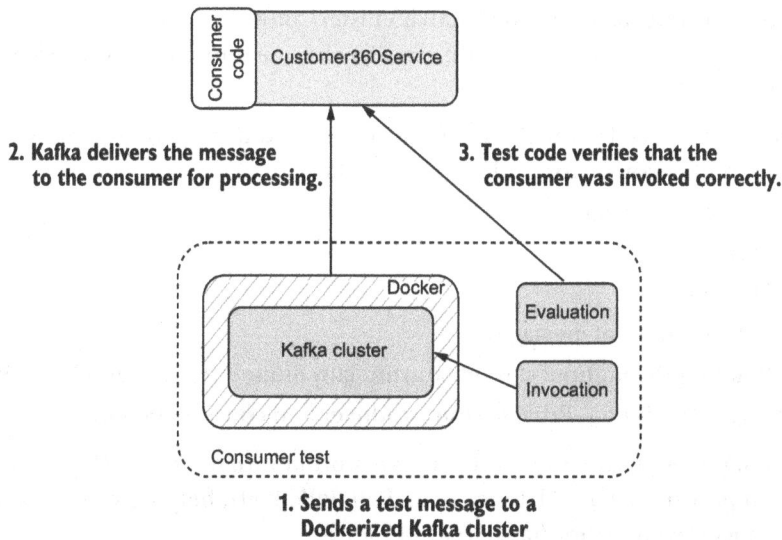

Figure 10.12 Integration testing of the `Customer360Service` using a Dockerized Kafka cluster. A test message is sent to the cluster, and the consumer processes it as it would in production. The test verifies the consumer's behavior by evaluating the resulting side effects or service invocations.

compared to embedded or mock-based approaches. However, the trade-off is higher confidence: tests exercise real network, protocol, and persistence paths (e.g., TLS/SASL, ACLs, Schema Registry compatibility, offsets/rebalances, transactions), avoiding false positives from misconfigured mocks. Use Testcontainers for critical integration paths; keep unit tests for fast, isolated logic.

10.3.3 *Performance tests*

Once integration tests confirm that services work correctly together, performance testing evaluates whether they meet the previously defined nonfunctional requirements. This involves simulating load with different parameters and measuring the resulting performance.

Several tools can help simulate Kafka load and measure key metrics like throughput and latency. The simplest and most accessible tests can be run using command-line utilities that come bundled with the Kafka distribution:

- `kafka-producer-perf-test.sh`—Measures the performance of producers using a given configuration (e.g., batch size, linger time, compression)
- `kafka-consumer-perf-test.sh`—Measures the performance of consumers consuming from specified topics
- `kafka.tools.EndToEndLatency`—A class you can run with `kafka-run-class.sh` to measure end-to-end latency, from production to consumption

These tools run tests against a real Kafka cluster, allowing you to benchmark actual performance under controlled conditions. To run meaningful tests, you need to do the following:

- *Create test topics*—Define them with the desired configurations—number of partitions, replication factor, and retention policy.
- *Define the load*—Specify
  - Message size
  - Message rate
  - Total number of messages
  - Whether throughput should be artificially limited (e.g., to simulate throttling)
- *Configure test clients*—Provide your producer and consumer configurations.

After running the tests, the tools will generate output with metrics such as throughput, latency, and percentile-based latency (e.g., P50, P95, P99), helping you assess whether the system meets your performance requirements.

In addition to the built-in command-line utilities, there are specialized tools for performance and load testing that offer more flexibility and control. Tools like JMeter (https://jmeter.apache.org), Gatling (https://gatling.io) and K6 (https://github.com/grafana/k6) provide Kafka-specific plugins that allow you to simulate realistic load patterns and test how your producers and consumers behave under varying conditions. These tools are often used to design repeatable test scenarios and support parameterization, and they can be integrated into CI pipelines for automated performance regression testing.

Kafka also includes the *Trogdor* framework—a more advanced tool designed for benchmarking and fault injection. Trogdor can simulate various load patterns across producers and consumers and can also introduce faults (such as broker failures or network partitions) to evaluate the system's resilience and recovery behavior under stress.

Once nonfunctional requirements are defined, they serve as input for deriving Kafka configurations that guide an optimal deployment. Performance tuning may be required to meet these requirements, and we'll consider performance optimization—including specific Kafka configurations and the trade-offs involved—in chapter 11.

10.4 Online resources

- "AsyncAPI Generator": https://github.com/asyncapi/generator
  Documentation and reference tooling explaining how to generate code and documentation from AsyncAPI definitions.
- "Automate the deployment of Apache Kafka on any platform": www.confluent.io/product/confluent-platform/flexible-devops-automation/
  Documentation for the tools and APIs for automating the deployment, configuration, and operation of Confluent Platform across different environments.

- "Testing Kafka Streams": https://kafka.apache.org/40/documentation/streams/developer-guide/testing.html
  Official documentation describing how to test Kafka Streams applications, including unit testing, topology testing, and integration testing approaches.

Summary

- Business-first event modeling is essential. Start by identifying meaningful state changes and who needs to react. Don't just jump ahead to topic design.

- Event catalogues bridge business and tech. Capture each event's purpose, producer, consumer, and data long before thinking about serializers or wire formats.

- Functional requirements help validate Kafka as the right fit. They also guide topic design, including ordering, partitioning, retention, and data sensitivity.

- Nonfunctional requirements shape cluster sizing and tuning. Collect data on latency, throughput, and message size to configure producers, consumers, and brokers effectively.

- Declarative GitOps workflows promote consistency. Using tools like Kafka-GitOps or Terraform helps maintain reliable, version-controlled topic and schema definitions.

- Unit and integration testing are critical for Kafka clients. Frameworks like Mockito exist to simulate producers, consumers, and end-to-end flows in automated tests.

- Performance testing reveals real-world behavior. Use tools like JMeter and Trogdor to experiment with different configurations and validate how they impact throughput and latency under load.

Operating Kafka

11

This chapter covers

- The evolution of Kafka clusters
- Monitoring for maintaining cluster health
- Performance tuning strategies
- Disaster recovery and backup considerations

When Kafka is used as a managed service in the cloud, many operational concerns are abstracted away. Tasks like upgrades, monitoring, and broker management are handled by the provider, allowing teams to focus on building applications. But running Kafka on-premises is a different story. It demands deep operational expertise, ranging from performing safe software upgrades to carefully tuning configurations and continuously monitoring cluster health.

In this chapter, we'll explore what it takes to maintain a robust, self-managed Kafka cluster. You'll learn how to

- Safely perform hardware and software updates.
- Add brokers to or remove them from the cluster.
- Modify configurations at the broker, topic, and partition level.

Understanding these maintenance tasks is essential for keeping your Kafka deployment resilient, efficient, and ready to scale.

This chapter is not a complete operational guide. Operational practices and tooling evolve rapidly and are often tightly coupled with specific environments and monitoring stacks. Instead, we'll focus on foundational principles and best practices that apply across most Kafka deployments.

11.1 Cluster evolution and upgrades

Several important reasons exist for upgrading the software of a Kafka cluster:

- To apply critical bug fixes
- To take advantage of new features
- To benefit from performance and stability improvements

While many upgrades are relatively straightforward, requiring only a new software package and minimal configuration changes, others involve significant architectural changes. For example, upgrading to version 4.0 introduces the new KRaft mode and requires fully removing ZooKeeper from the cluster, fundamentally transforming how Kafka's metadata is managed.

One of the challenges with upgrading Kafka is the complexity of the ecosystem. Kafka is rarely deployed in isolation—it typically includes additional components like Kafka Connect, Schema Registry, and client libraries. These components must remain compatible with each other throughout the upgrade process.

Because of this interdependency, upgrades are often approached with caution. While carefully staging an upgrade is a prudent approach, delaying upgrades for too long can be harmful. Clusters that fall behind may miss critical security patches, remain vulnerable to known bugs, or lack performance improvements which could enhance reliability and efficiency. Over time, the gap between versions increases the risk and effort involved in catching up, making future upgrades more error-prone and disruptive.

Before performing any software upgrade in a Kafka cluster, it's essential to verify the compatibility of all underlying components to avoid unexpected failures or inconsistencies. Specifically, you should confirm the compatibility of the following components:

- *Operating system (OS)*—Ensure that the OS version used on your hosts supports the new Kafka release, especially if there are dependencies on system libraries or kernel features.
- *Java runtime environment (JRE)*—Kafka relies heavily on the JVM. Verify that your Kafka version supports the Java version installed on your servers. New Kafka versions may drop support for older JDKs.
- *Kafka broker and ecosystem versions*—This includes not only the broker itself but also supporting services like Kafka Connect, Schema Registry, and REST Proxy.

Consult Kafka's compatibility matrix (https://kafka.apache.org/40/documentation/compatibility.html) to validate that your version combinations are officially supported.

Pay close attention to details like `inter.broker.protocol.version`, message format changes, and client compatibility.

The upgrade procedure can vary depending on the combination of your current and target versions—you should always refer to the specific migration guide for each release to understand the changes and recommended flow. In production environments, it's highly recommended that you automate the upgrade process using tools like Ansible (http://ansible.com) or Terraform (http://terraform.io). These tools help ensure consistency across nodes, reduce the risk of human error, and make it easier to roll out updates incrementally or across multiple environments.

Before starting the upgrade, it's critical to prepare your environment to reduce the risk of failure and ensure a smooth transition. The first step is to back up all configuration files—both for Kafka and ZooKeeper (or KRaft controllers, if applicable). Even small configuration changes introduced in a new version can lead to unexpected behavior, so having a reliable backup allows you to quickly revert if necessary.

Kafka is designed to support rolling upgrades, meaning you can upgrade one node at a time without bringing down the entire cluster. This is a very important operational advantage, but to do this effectively, you need a well-defined plan and careful sequencing.

If possible, always begin by validating the upgrade in a staging or development environment. This helps identify compatibility problems early, such as deprecated settings, behavioral changes, or performance regressions. Your test environment should mirror production as closely as possible to be meaningful.

Upgrading components in the correct order is critical for ensuring stability and minimizing compatibility issues. The typical sequence is as follows:

1 Upgrade the KRaft controllers (or ZooKeeper nodes, if using the legacy mode).
2 Upgrade the Kafka brokers.
3 Upgrade supporting components, such as Kafka Connect, Schema Registry, and REST Proxy.

Each step should be validated before proceeding to the next, particularly in large or production clusters.

11.1.1 Adding brokers and distributing the load

At some point, you may decide to expand a cluster by adding new brokers. To do this, you need to provide a configuration for the new broker that includes a unique broker ID. The configurations of existing brokers do not need to be modified. In most cases, it is sufficient to simply start the new broker—as long as all necessary configurations are correct, including cluster metadata, security settings, and network access. If these prerequisites are met, the broker will automatically join the cluster by contacting the controller quorum.

After adding a new broker, it is also a good practice to include its address in the `bootstrap.servers` configuration used by Kafka clients. This improves fault tolerance and load distribution, ensuring that clients can connect to more brokers and have more options during metadata retrieval.

Pay attention to the following behavior after adding a new broker:

- When a new topic is created, the new broker may be assigned partitions for that topic.
- Existing partitions from previously created topics will not be automatically moved to the new broker. To take advantage of the new capacity, you must manually redistribute partitions.

This redistribution is handled by the partition reassignment tool (`kafka-reassign -partitions.sh`), which is included in the Kafka distribution. This tool can perform the following operations:

- Accept a list of topics and generate a partition distribution plan across the available brokers. The output is a JSON file that specifies the new assignments for each partition.
- Take a JSON file—either generated in the previous step or crafted manually— and execute the actual reassignment of partitions according to the defined plan.
- Check and report the current status of a reassignment in progress.

Additionally, this tool can be used to change the replication factor of topics, modify the preferred replica assignments, or move partition data to a different log directory on the same broker.

11.1.2 Removing a broker from the cluster

At first glance, removing a broker from a cluster may seem like a simple task—just shut it down and move on. However, if it's not handled carefully, this can lead to under-replicated partitions, especially when there are not enough in-sync replicas to maintain the desired replication factor. To ensure a smooth and safe broker removal, the following steps should be followed:

1 *Reassign partition leadership to other brokers*—Use the partition reassignment tool to transfer leadership away from the broker being decommissioned. Note that this tool does not automatically generate a new distribution plan for this scenario. You must manually create a reassignment JSON file that excludes the broker to be removed, and pass it to the tool to execute the reassignment.

2 *Shut down the broker*—Once leadership and replicas have been migrated, gracefully stop the broker. This prevents unnecessary controller activity or leadership flapping during shutdown.

3 *Clean up metadata*—After the broker has been shut down, you should remove its metadata from the controller quorum (in KRaft mode) or from ZooKeeper (in legacy mode). Additionally, update client configurations such as `bootstrap .servers` to exclude the removed broker, ensuring that clients do not attempt to connect to a broker that no longer exists.

For more advanced or automated cluster operations, you can also consider using Cruise Control (https://github.com/linkedin/cruise-control)—an open source tool developed by LinkedIn for Kafka cluster optimization. Cruise Control can automate tasks such as adding or removing brokers, rebalancing partition distribution, and handling broker decommissioning. While it adds some operational complexity, it significantly reduces manual effort and helps maintain a well-balanced and efficient cluster over time.

11.1.3 Upgrading clients

Apache Kafka is well known for its strong bidirectional compatibility, which means that

- Old clients can communicate with newer brokers.
- New clients can also interact with older brokers.

This flexibility makes upgrades safer and less disruptive. However, it often leads to a false sense of safety, where client upgrades are indefinitely postponed. As a result, many applications continue using outdated client libraries—missing out on new features, critical security patches, and performance improvements introduced in newer versions.

Upgrading Kafka clients typically requires rebuilding and redeploying the application with the updated library version. While this adds some effort, it is essential for maintaining long-term stability, compatibility, and access to recent enhancements in the Kafka ecosystem.

11.1.4 Data mobility

Kafka does not include a built-in backup mechanism. Instead, it relies on data replication as its primary strategy for fault tolerance. The idea is simple: if you have multiple replicas of a partition distributed across different brokers, the likelihood of losing all copies of the data is extremely low. This approach becomes even more resilient when the cluster spans multiple geographical locations, making it robust against the failure of an entire data center.

To maintain snapshots of data, organizations often implement additional measures to create secondary copies of Kafka data, such as these:

- Copying data to external storage systems like Azure Blob Storage, AWS S3, or Google Cloud Storage using Kafka Connect and appropriate sink connectors
- Passively replicating data to another Kafka cluster (a topic covered later in this chapter)
- Backing up Kafka data at the filesystem level, typically using storage snapshots or custom scripts

However, none of these approaches offers a true point-in-time snapshot with a clearly defined and foolproof restore path. For example, in the case of human error—such as incorrect data being sent to a topic, a topic being deleted, or retention being accidentally lowered—these methods might still result in irrecoverable data loss.

To address this, some vendors, such as Kannika Armory (www.kannika.io), offer commercial Kafka backup solutions that can create consistent snapshots and store them in cold storage. An effective Kafka backup solution should provide

- Reliable data protection
- Simple and verifiable restoration
- Cost efficiency

No matter which solution you adopt, always ensure you have a tested and documented restore process. Backups are only as valuable as your ability to recover from them when it matters.

11.2 Monitoring a Kafka cluster

Once our applications are successfully deployed, it becomes critical to ensure that they continue to operate reliably and efficiently. This means not only confirming that they run without errors, but also monitoring how effectively they utilize system resources such as CPU, memory, disk, and network.

To achieve this, we must continuously collect technical parameters that reflect the current state of the application. These parameters—commonly referred to as *metrics*—provide insights into the health and performance of the system. By analyzing these metrics, we can determine whether the application is behaving as expected or if performance degradation is emerging.

When something goes wrong, whether it's a service failure, resource exhaustion, or unexpected behavior, the monitoring system should generate an alert. These alerts must be immediately sent to the operations or DevOps team so that they can quickly diagnose the root cause and implement corrective actions. Fast and accurate alerts are key to minimizing downtime and maintaining service level objectives (SLOs).

Monitoring is not just a tool for troubleshooting—it is a foundational pillar of running production-grade systems, enabling proactive maintenance, better performance tuning, and higher overall system reliability.

11.2.1 Types of metrics in monitoring

When we talk about monitoring in distributed systems such as Kafka-based applications, we primarily refer to *technical metrics*. These provide insights into system behavior, performance, and health, and are crucial for enabling engineers to detect problems, resolve failures, and tune performance:

- *Error metrics*—Indicate failures or malfunctions in the system and typically require immediate attention.
  - *Broker-side examples*—Leader election failures, offline partitions, and out-of-sync replicas
  - *Client-side examples*—Serialization/deserialization errors, message send timeouts, and commit failures

- *Saturation metrics*—Measure how close the system is to hitting its capacity limits. Examples include high network I/O throughput relative to available bandwidth, long poll durations, message buffer exhaustion, or low compression efficiency under load.

- *Resource utilization metrics*—Provide a view into how system resources are being consumed. Common examples include CPU usage, disk I/O, memory consumption, and the number of active/open connections.

- *Performance metrics*—Reflect how well the system is performing. Examples include message processing latency, incoming/outgoing byte rates, average batch sizes, and throughput per topic or consumer group.

These metrics are typically exposed through tools like JMX, Prometheus, or custom instrumentation, and they're used by site reliability engineers (SREs), DevOps, and backend developers for operations and performance tuning.

While technical metrics are essential for maintaining system health, *business metrics* focus on understanding the application's behavior from a product or operational perspective. These often require custom instrumentation and are not available out of the box. Examples include

- Volume of domain-specific messages per message type in a given time window (e.g., number of payment requests per minute)

- Message quality indicators such as the number of dropped, delayed, or duplicated messages

- Enrichment or correlation success rates, such as the number of events that were not matched or joined during processing

These metrics are crucial for enabling product teams, analysts, and business stakeholders to evaluate system correctness, SLAs, and user experience impacts. Since they are application-specific, they often require additional development work, such as adding interceptors, custom logs, or Kafka Streams aggregations.

11.2.2 Kafka monitoring objects

Technical metrics in distributed systems can be analyzed across several layers of the stack. In the context of Apache Kafka and its surrounding ecosystem, it is useful to classify these metrics according to the layer or object they are associated with. This section distinguishes three primary categories of monitoring objects: host-level metrics, JVM-level metrics, and Kafka-specific metrics.

HOST-LEVEL METRICS

In environments where Kafka is deployed on bare metal or virtual machines, *host-level metrics* provide fundamental insights into the performance and resource availability of the system. These metrics include, but are not limited to,

- Free disk space
- Disk I/O throughput and latency

- CPU utilization (overall and per core)
- Network traffic (incoming and outgoing byte rates)
- Page cache hit ratio

Among these, free disk space is arguably the most critical metric. Kafka stores all incoming messages as immutable log files on disk, and insufficient disk capacity can lead to complete broker failure. Ensuring that disk usage remains within safe thresholds, and setting alerts for critical thresholds (e.g., <15% remaining), is a fundamental part of Kafka operations.

Monitoring these metrics is essential for detecting saturation conditions, diagnosing hardware bottlenecks, and understanding the baseline system load that Kafka shares with other processes.

JVM-LEVEL METRICS

As Kafka and its core ecosystem components—including Kafka brokers, Connect workers, and Kafka Streams applications—are implemented in Java, *JVM-level metrics* play a critical role in performance observability. Relevant metrics include

- Garbage collection (GC) frequency and pause duration
- Heap and non-heap memory usage
- Number of active threads
- Class loading and unloading statistics

Among all JVM-level metrics, GC activity—particularly pause duration—is the most critical to monitor in Kafka applications. Pauses in GC activity directly affect responsiveness, and long pauses can lead to cascading failures, such as producer timeouts, ISR shrinkage, and consumer lag.

KAFKA-SPECIFIC METRICS

Kafka-specific metrics provide visibility into the internal behavior of Kafka brokers, producers, consumers, and Kafka Streams applications. These metrics are essential for ensuring system correctness, availability, and throughput. Examples include

- Number of under-replicated or offline partitions
- Request latencies (produce, fetch, and metadata APIs)
- Consumer lag, both at group and partition levels
- Leader election rates and controller activity
- Throughput metrics, such as bytes in/out per topic or broker
- Batch sizes, compression ratios, and record rates for producers

Certain metrics stand out in their operational impact. At the broker level, under-replicated partitions and offline partitions are key indicators of replication health and data durability risk. For producers and consumers, request latencies and consumer lag offer early signs of system overload or application inefficiency. In Kafka Connect, task failure counts and task state transitions (e.g., from RUNNING to FAILED) are essential for tracking data pipeline reliability.

These metrics form the foundation for detecting imbalances in partition leadership, network saturation, data skew, and consumer backpressure.

MONITORING OF DEAD-LETTER TOPICS

If the *dead-letter topic* (DLT) pattern is used—where messages that cannot be processed by a consumer are redirected to a special topic, allowing the consumer to continue processing other messages—it becomes essential to monitor this topic closely. The presence of messages in the DLT typically indicates processing failures due to factors such as deserialization errors, business rule violations, or downstream system unavailability.

To ensure timely resolution, an alert or notification should be triggered immediately when a message is written to the dead-letter topic. This allows operational or development teams to investigate and fix the root cause before message accumulation leads to backlog or data integrity issues.

Failure to monitor the DLT may result in silent message loss, as unprocessed events could be indefinitely deferred or forgotten, especially if the topic is not regularly reviewed.

11.2.3 *Ownership of monitoring responsibilities*

In practice, the responsibility for configuring and maintaining monitoring varies across organizations. Developers building Kafka client applications often assume that operational concerns fall within the domain of the DevOps or platform engineering teams. Conversely, DevOps engineers may treat Kafka clients as generic Java applications, focusing on standard JVM health indicators without instrumenting Kafka-specific behavior.

This division of labor can result in critical monitoring gaps. For example, if consumer lag metrics are not exposed or tracked, a Kafka application might continue to operate while silently falling behind, ultimately leading to data processing delays or SLA violations.

To avoid such blind spots, it is imperative that both development and operations teams engage collaboratively in defining and maintaining an appropriate observability strategy. Kafka-specific metrics, in particular, must not be overlooked or left uninstrumented.

In cloud-native deployments, many infrastructure-level metrics—including host and JVM metrics—are automatically collected by the cloud provider's monitoring stack. Platforms such as Amazon Web Services (AWS), Google Cloud Platform (GCP), and Microsoft Azure integrate deeply with container orchestration systems and runtime environments, offering built-in support for CPU, memory, disk, and network monitoring, as well as JVM-level insights through managed services.

This default integration reduces the burden on application teams, who are no longer required to manually collect low-level metrics. Instead, they can focus on instrumenting

Kafka-specific and business-level metrics that are more tightly coupled to the functional requirements of the application.

11.2.4 Monitoring stacks and tools

A variety of monitoring stacks—both open source and commercial—are available for observing and managing Apache Kafka deployments. One of the most widely adopted open source solutions is the Prometheus, Grafana, and Alertmanager stack, which provides comprehensive support for metrics collection, visualization, and alerting:

- Prometheus is responsible for collecting metrics and storing them as time-series data.
- Grafana is used to build dashboards and visualize the metrics collected by Prometheus.
- Alertmanager handles alert routing and notification delivery via email, Slack, PagerDuty, or other communication channels.

Kafka brokers, Kafka Connect workers, and Java-based Kafka clients expose runtime metrics via Java Management Extensions (JMX) by default. No special configuration is needed to enable JMX in Kafka components, but Prometheus does not natively understand the JMX format. To bridge this gap, a JMX exporter (a lightweight Java agent) must be used. This exporter acts as a sidecar or embedded agent that translates JMX metrics into the Prometheus exposition format.

This integration is illustrated in figure 11.1. Prometheus acts as a pull-based client, periodically scraping metrics from the JMX exporter over HTTP. Once collected, these

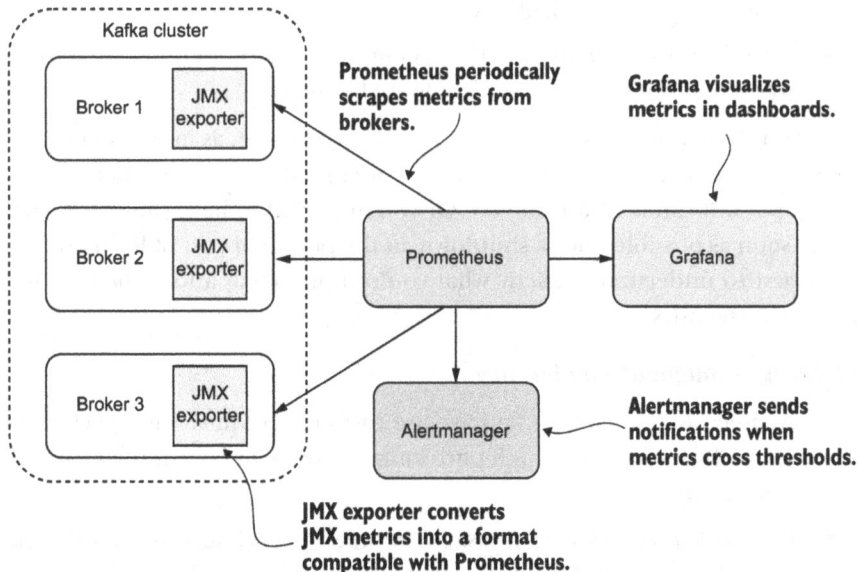

Figure 11.1 Exporting metrics in the Prometheus-Grafana monitoring stack

metrics are stored in Prometheus's time-series database. From there, they can be queried using the PromQL query language and visualized in Grafana dashboards.

In addition to visualization, Prometheus supports rule-based alerting. When a specific metric exceeds a defined threshold, such as a spike in the number of messages in a dead-letter topic, Prometheus triggers an alert. This alert is passed to Alertmanager, which then routes the notification to the appropriate operational team or escalation channel.

This stack is widely used in both on-premises and Kubernetes-based Kafka deployments due to its flexibility, extensibility, and strong ecosystem support.

11.3 *Performance tuning clinic*

Kafka is highly scalable and fault-tolerant, but it is not optimized for your specific workloads. You may want to tune its performance in running systems, adjusting settings and addressing existing pain points, or you may want to conduct a performance evaluation before deployment to estimate hardware sizing or determine the resources needed in a cloud deployment.

You may have several goals in tuning:

- *Meet SLAs*—Ensure your system can handle peak loads and avoid bottlenecks.
- *Improve latency*—Achieve faster data delivery to consumers.
- *Maximize throughput*—Increase how much data can flow through Kafka per second.
- *Reduce resource usage*—Use disk, CPU, and memory more efficiently.
- *Minimize downtime in the case of a crash*—Tune for resilience so that failures have minimal impact on availability.
- *Avoid data loss*—Ensure that the system is robust enough to maintain data integrity even under heavy load or hardware failures.

It's a good strategy to know what you are trying to achieve, as improving one characteristic may degrade another. For example, sending data in bigger batches may improve throughput but can increase latency. Or you may want to have the system up and running as soon as possible after a shutdown, at the potential cost of losing some data. It's always best to understand exactly what you're optimizing and to be able to measure those characteristics.

11.3.1 *Balancing throughput and latency*

We say we need Kafka because we have use cases that require high-performance message delivery. But what does "high-performance" actually mean? Typically, we want to achieve one of two things:

- *Minimal latency*—Deliver messages between participants in as little time as possible. Here, we might talk about the latency between producers and brokers, brokers and consumers, or the end-to-end latency between producers and consumers. A typical use case for this is communication between microservices, where we want notifications to arrive as soon as possible.

- *Maximal throughput*—Maximize the message processing rate (number of messages or bytes per unit of time). This is important for use cases like log collection, where processing as much data as possible is the priority.

By default, Kafka's configurations—both for clients and brokers—are optimized for low latency. Let's explore how we can adjust these settings to improve either latency or throughput.

Two fundamental strategies for increasing throughput are

- Make more partitions to process data in parallel.
- Use bigger batches of data by waiting for more messages to arrive and applying compression to reduce network and disk usage.

Correspondingly, the strategies for decreasing latency are

- Send batches as soon as they are ready, to avoid waiting for more messages.
- Avoid additional manipulations (like compression) that can consume time during processing.

Sometimes, increasing throughput can also increase latency. While parallel processing (using more partitions and consumers) can deliver data faster and reduce per-message latency, batching (sending larger batches or waiting for a batch to fill) can add extra delay before sending messages. Depending on the tuning strategy, higher throughput might mean lower latency (due to faster pipelines) or higher latency (due to waiting for larger batches to fill).

Table 11.1 summarizes the main settings that can be tuned to either improve throughput or latency in Kafka.

Table 11.1 Balancing latency and throughput

Configuration setting	Improve latency	Improve throughput	Comments	Setting type
`batch.size`	Use smaller batches	Use larger batches	Batching improves throughput but can delay individual messages	Producer
`linger.ms`	Set to 0 to send immediately	Increase to wait for more messages	`linger.me` defines how long to wait for more data before sending	Producer
`acks`	Use `acks=1` for faster response	Use `acks=1` or 0 to wait for fewer acknowledgments	`acks=all` ensures data durability, `acks=1` or 0 reduces latency	Producer
`compression.type`	Disable compression for lower CPU overhead	Enable compression to reduce network usage	Compression saves bandwidth but adds CPU cost	Producer

Table 11.1   Balancing latency and throughput (*continued*)

Configuration setting	Improve latency	Improve throughput	Comments	Setting type
`buffer.memory`	Ensure sufficient memory for faster processing	Increase to buffer more data before sending	Buffer memory size limits data waiting to be sent	Producer
`fetch.max.wait.ms`	Reduce to fetch data faster	Increase to allow more data per fetch	Controls how long the broker waits to fill fetch requests	Consumer
`fetch.min.bytes`	Reduce to avoid waiting for more data	Increase to fetch larger batches	Controls the minimum amount of data to fetch	Consumer
`enable.auto.commit`	Set to `false` for faster offset updates after processing	Set to `true` to avoid explicit commit overhead	Controls whether offsets are committed automatically; manual commits give more control but require more coordination	Consumer
`max.poll.records`	Reduce to process smaller batches faster	Increase to fetch and process larger batches	Controls the maximum number of records per poll; smaller values reduce latency, whereas larger values improve throughput but setting too high may overload the consumer and cause long processing cycles	Consumer
`max.poll.interval.ms`	Reduce to detect slow consumers faster	Increase to allow longer processing for large batches	Controls the maximum delay between poll calls; reducing it can force rebalancing if a consumer is too slow, whereas increasing it allows more time for large batch processing but can increase recovery time after failure	Consumer
`num.io.threads`	Tune for optimal load; more threads may reduce bottlenecks	Increase to handle more I/O operations in parallel	More replicas improve durability but add load	Broker
`num.replica.fetchers`	Not directly related to latency	Increase to replicate data faster	Controls the parallelism of replication tasks	Broker
`num.partitions`	More partitions reduce latency (by allowing more concurrent reads/writes)	Increase to allow more parallel processing	More partitions increase parallelism but add coordination cost	Broker

Table 11.1 Balancing latency and throughput (*continued*)

Configuration setting	Improve latency	Improve throughput	Comments	Setting type
replication.factor	Reduce replication factor (may reduce durability)	Not directly related to throughput	More replicas improve durability, but this impacts latency	Broker
socket.send.buffer.bytes	Increase for faster data transmission	Increase to support higher throughput (larger data frames)	Larger buffers allow more data to be queued before transmission, improving throughput	Broker
socket.receive.buffer.bytes	Increase for faster data reception	Increase to support higher throughput (larger data frames)	Larger buffers allow more incoming data to be received without backpressure	Broker
num.network.threads	Tune for optimal load; more threads may reduce bottlenecks	Increase to handle more network requests in parallel	More threads allow more requests to be processed in parallel	Broker

11.3.2 Balancing data safety and uptime

When some brokers are down and we don't have enough in-sync replicas (ISRs), the partition goes offline. This means that producers can't send data to that partition, and the system experiences downtime. This behavior is correct for most use cases, because we don't want to risk losing or corrupting data.

However, what if having the system always available is more important than always having perfect data consistency? This is the classic trade-off between durability and availability:

- *Durability-focused systems (e.g., financial transactions, payment processing)*—Data correctness is critical; downtime is better than risking data loss.
- *Availability-focused systems (e.g., log collection, real-time analytics dashboards)*—Keeping the system online is more important than a small amount of lost data.

We can choose different configuration settings depending on what we want to optimize:

- *Durability*—Avoid data loss and ensure data consistency, even if it means some downtime.
- *Availability*—Minimize system downtime, even if it means potentially losing some messages.

Optimizing durability means ensuring that multiple replicas of the data are created and that data is fully committed before moving on. This involves keeping several ISRs for each partition, waiting for acknowledgments from all replicas to confirm that the data has been safely stored, and committing offsets manually only after the data has been fully processed.

Optimizing availability means recovering the fastest way possible after a failure, even if it means that some data may be lost in the process. The settings are summarized in table 11.2.

Table 11.2   Balancing durability and availability

Configuration setting	Improve durability	Improve availability	Setting type
acks	Use acks=all to ensure data is written to all in-sync replicas	With acks=1 or 0 the producer can continue sending data even if some replicas are temporarily unavailable	Producer
enable.idempotence	Enable to avoid duplicate messages and improve reliability	Enable to avoid duplicate messages and retries in the producer	Producer
enable.auto.commit	Disable and manually commit offsets after processing to avoid data loss	Consumer progresses without waiting for manual commit logic to complete	Consumer
isolation.level	Set to read_committed to read only committed data	Set to read_uncommitted to allow faster reads of all data	Consumer
max.poll.records	Smaller batches reduce memory pressure and risk of data loss during failure	Larger batches improve consumer throughput and avoid stalling (but may risk larger reprocesses)	Consumer
max.poll.interval.ms	Reduce to catch slow consumers faster and avoid stale offsets	Increase to allow slower consumers to stay in group longer	Consumer
session.timeout.ms	Reduce to detect dead consumers quickly and maintain ISRs	May be increased to avoid unnecessary rebalances, but for detecting dead consumers it can be decreased	Consumer
replication.factor	Use a higher replication factor for better data redundancy	A lower replication factor can speed up recovery but risks data loss	Broker
min.insync.replicas	Set higher to ensure more replicas are in sync before committing data	Set lower to allow writes even with fewer in-sync replicas	Broker
unclean.leader .election.enable	Disable to avoid data loss with unclean leader election	Enable to allow faster leader election even if some data is lost	Broker
broker.rack	Distribute replicas across racks to avoid rack failures causing data loss	Ensure rack awareness for faster recovery if a rack fails	Broker
log.flush.interval .messages	Reduce to flush data more frequently to disk, minimizing potential data loss	Increase to flush data less frequently for faster throughput	Broker
log.flush.interval.ms	Reduce to flush data to disk more frequently	Increase to flush less often and improve broker throughput	Broker

Table 11.2   Balancing durability and availability (*continued*)

Configuration setting	Improve durability	Improve availability	Setting type
`num.recovery.threads` `.per.data.dir`	Increase to reduce the window in which durability is weakened	Increase to speed up broker recovery after a crash	Broker
`num.standby` `.replicas`	Increase to reduce the risk of data loss during failover	Increase to maintain availability during maintenance or failures	Broker
`replica.lag.time` `.max.ms`	Reduce to quickly detect lagging replicas and exclude them from ISRs for consistency	Increase to tolerate more lag and avoid unnecessary ISR changes that can affect availability	Broker
`auto.leader` `.rebalance.enable`	Disable to keep leaders stable, avoiding leader changes that can affect data consistency	Enable to allow automatic rebalancing of leaders, improving availability during broker failures	Broker

Ultimately, balancing durability and availability requires careful consideration of your application's requirements. Whether you prioritize data safety or minimizing downtime, tuning these settings lets you achieve the right trade-off for your specific use case.

11.4   Disaster recovery and failover

When Kafka is deployed on-premises, disaster recovery becomes the responsibility of the operational team. A lot can go wrong, so it's essential to have a disaster recovery plan that provides clear guidance on what to do if disaster strikes.

Replication is built into Kafka's architecture, and the high availability of a Kafka cluster relies on having multiple copies of each data partition across brokers. While temporarily losing a broker or controller is a common scenario that Kafka can handle seamlessly, the stakes are much higher in the event of a natural disaster—like a fire, flood, or even a terrorist attack. What happens if the entire data center goes down?

The answer may be that one data center is not enough. Whether you need multisite replication depends on your requirements and the cost you're willing to carry for extra infrastructure and operational complexity. To truly survive a disaster, it's essential to distribute data across multiple data centers. By replicating Kafka data to other locations, you ensure that even if an entire data center is lost, your data and services can continue running in a different location, maintaining both availability and durability.

11.4.1   RTO/RPO engineering

The goal of disaster recovery is to minimize the impact of a failure. We typically measure this with two key metrics:

- *Recovery Time Objective (RTO)*—Measures the period that the service is unavailable after a failure, and the goal is to recover as soon as possible.
- *Recovery Point Objective (RPO)*—Indicates how much data might be lost after a failure, and the goal is to lose as little data as possible.

So far, we've talked about Kafka brokers without mentioning their physical location. To survive a disaster, brokers should be placed in different data centers. This configuration is called a *stretched cluster*. The example in figure 11.2 shows three data centers, each with two brokers and one KRaft controller. Because data is replicated between multiple locations, this setup introduces additional latency requirements to ensure data consistency.

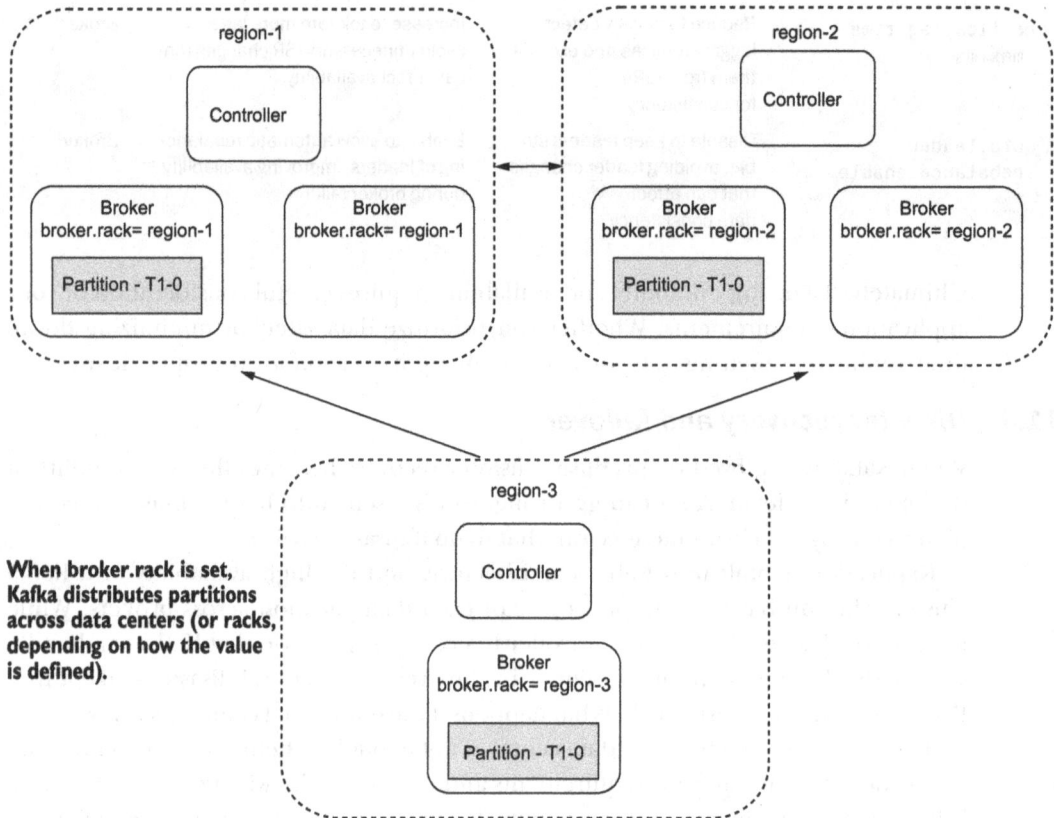

When broker.rack is set, Kafka distributes partitions across data centers (or racks, depending on how the value is defined).

Figure 11.2   Deploying a stretched cluster across three data centers

Another important consideration is to avoid placing all replicas of a partition in the same data center. For each broker, you can configure the broker.rack property. While this was originally designed for identifying racks within a data center, it can also specify logical groups of servers across data centers. When this property is set, Kafka ensures that replicas of a partition are distributed across different racks (or data centers).

Since the KRaft quorum requires a majority of controllers to be operational, you need at least three data centers to achieve true high availability. In general, using a stretched cluster provides the best disaster recovery metrics: RTO = 0 and RPO = 0.

Another common scenario for disaster recovery is the well-known *active-passive configuration*. In this setup, only two data centers are required. One data center handles all producers and consumers, while data is mirrored asynchronously to a passive cluster in the second data center. Figure 11.3 shows this configuration.

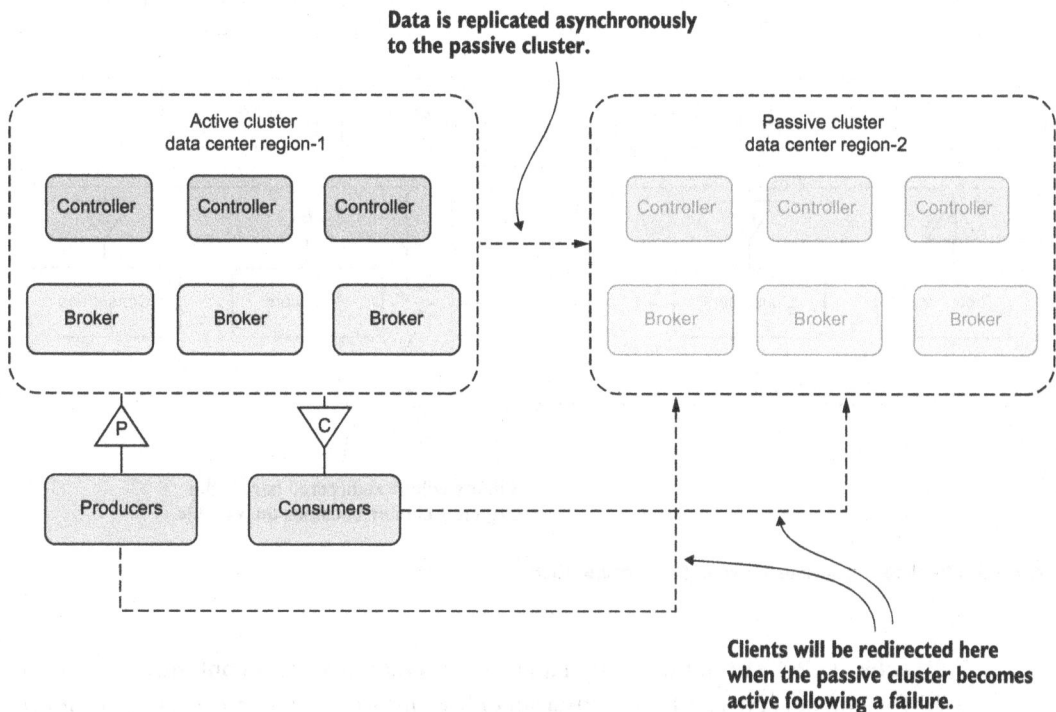

Figure 11.3 Replicating data in active-passive configuration

In the event of a data center failure, producers and consumers will switch to the passive cluster. Because replication is asynchronous, there can be some data loss (RPO > 0). Additionally, because switching clients to the new cluster takes time, there will be some downtime (RTO > 0).

Another disaster recovery architecture is the *active-active configuration* (figure 11.4). In this setup, both data centers are fully operational at the same time, handling producers and consumers simultaneously. This architecture is often implemented using cross-cluster replication to keep data synchronized between the two locations.

Because both data centers are active, there is no need for failover—if clients can be redirected automatically, they can continue working with either data center at any time. This leads to zero downtime (RTO = 0) in that scenario. However, because replication is asynchronous and both sites can accept writes, there is a possibility of data conflicts

**Each cluster contains the same data,
which is replicated asynchronously.**

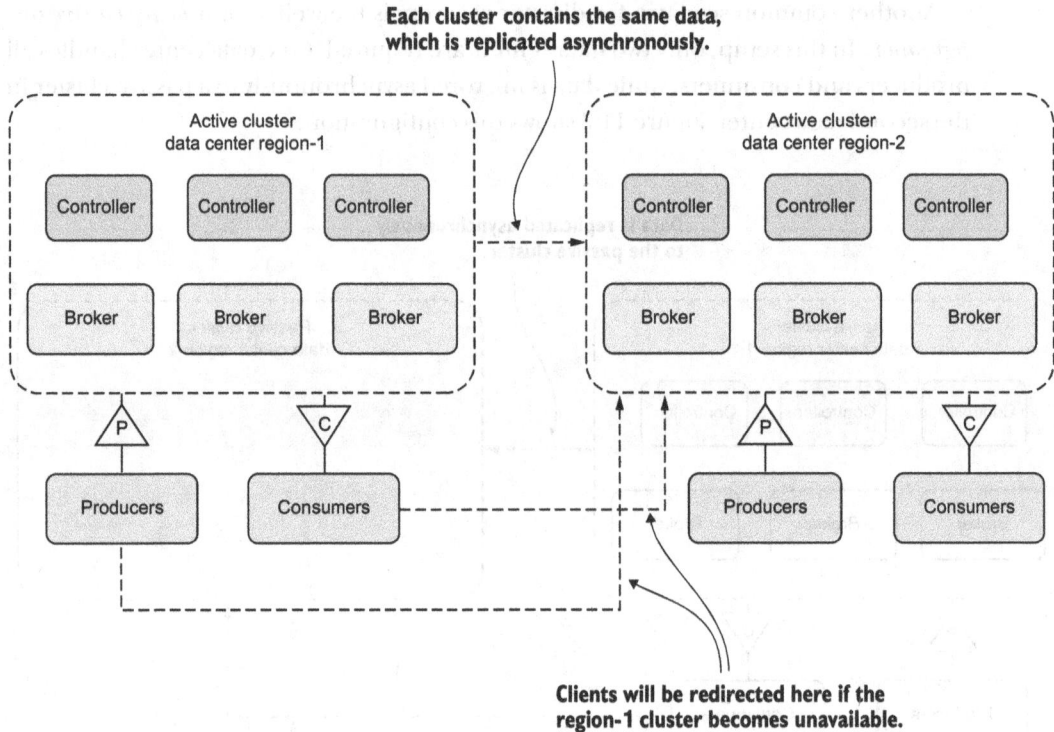

Figure 11.4 Replicating data in active-active configuration

or data loss (RPO > 0) in the event of an unplanned outage. This configuration is often used for global services where high availability and low latency for users in different regions are crucial.

11.5   *Online resources*

- "Monitoring Distributed Systems": https://sre.google/sre-book/monitoring -distributed-systems/
  This chapter from the Google SRE book explains best practices for monitoring distributed systems.

- JMX Monitoring Stacks: https://github.com/confluentinc/jmx-monitoring-stacks
  A Confluent open source repository providing ready-to-run JMX monitoring stacks for Kafka.

- "Upgrading Kafka": https://kafka.apache.org/documentation/#upgrade
  A section of the official Apache Kafka documentation that provides guidance on upgrading Kafka.

- "Supported Versions and Interoperability for Confluent Platform": https://docs .confluent.io/platform/current/installation/versions-interoperability.html

A Confluent documentation page that explains version compatibility and interoperability between different Confluent Platform components.

Summary

- Upgrades are critical for security, stability, and new features. Interdependencies between Kafka brokers, Kafka Connect, Schema Registry, and client libraries must be carefully managed.

- After adding brokers, the partition reassignment tool should be used to balance load. Removing brokers requires carefully reassigning leadership and removing metadata.

- Kafka's strong backward/forward compatibility helps, but delaying upgrades leaves clients vulnerable to bugs and misses out on improvements.

- Monitoring ensures that Kafka remains reliable and efficient, providing visibility into system performance, resource usage, and potential failures.

- Performance tuning involves carefully adjusting Kafka settings to meet workload demands, balancing factors like throughput, latency, and resource utilization.

- Disaster recovery strategies, such as replication and cross-datacenter deployments, protect against catastrophic failures and data loss by ensuring data availability and system continuity.

What's next for Kafka 12

In the late 2000s, LinkedIn was facing a data integration crisis as it transitioned from a traditional web application into a distributed platform. The systems behind the platform were generating enormous volumes of data—user profiles, page views, messages—and LinkedIn's users expected all this information to be fresh and up-to-date with minimal delay.

However, the integration approaches used at the time weren't designed for this kind of scale or responsiveness. The dominant pattern was batch data movement, which introduced unacceptable delays and complexity. These pipelines weren't suited for high-volume, low-latency ingestion, and they made it difficult to reuse or reprocess data across different teams and applications.

A clear need for a new kind of messaging system appeared—one that would

- Handle massive volumes of events per second.
- Support low-latency processing for real-time responsiveness.
- Provide durable storage, so consumers could recover data even after downtime.

Kafka was designed to meet this challenge. Built around the concept of a distributed commit log and inspired by the idea of "smart endpoints and dumb pipes," Kafka shifted the integration model from point-to-point data movement to a central, durable, replayable stream of events.

Since then, Kafka has come a long way—evolving into a full-featured platform for real-time event processing. In this book, we've explored Kafka's core design principles, real-world use cases, and the rich ecosystem of tools that surround it, including the Schema Registry, Kafka Connect, and Kafka Streams. We've seen how Kafka powers modern architectures today, but what lies ahead? What comes next? Where will we find Kafka in the future?

12.1 Kafka as an orchestration platform

When we look at Kafka from the perspective of a client application developer, a clear pattern emerges. While Kafka provides a powerful foundation, most implementations today feel highly handcrafted. Application developers often find themselves dealing with low-level APIs, manual wiring, and repeated custom solutions.

This approach offers flexibility but also results in slow delivery cycles, high complexity, and fragile integrations. Every new application feels like a bespoke project. Developers must reimplement message consumption, correlation, retries, error handling, and schema management—often from scratch. Building on Kafka becomes expensive, time-consuming, and operationally risky.

What we need is a shift. Application developers must be able to move faster, but without losing control. Since the early days of programming, there has been a continuous effort to simplify development by raising the level of abstraction. However, abstraction can take different forms. We do not necessarily need visual tools or complex modeling environments. What we need is a way to apply established patterns, use standardized tools, and build on ready-to-use orchestration frameworks. Kafka must offer a foundation where developers can stay on track and keep moving forward, focusing their efforts on business logic rather than on technical plumbing.

Several projects aim to provide *low-code platforms* accompanied by tools for building streaming services. These platforms enable users with domain expertise to configure and deploy streaming applications without requiring deep technical knowledge. Typically, they include visual design tools that allow users to model scenarios graphically, as well as support declarative configuration, such as through YAML files. They offer a set of predefined constructs for common operations, they and expose customization points where developers can extend functionality using programming code when needed. Figure 12.1 shows an abstract example of such a platform, where tools like Kafka and Apache Flink (discussed in chapter 8) are used for data ingestion, transformation, and processing.

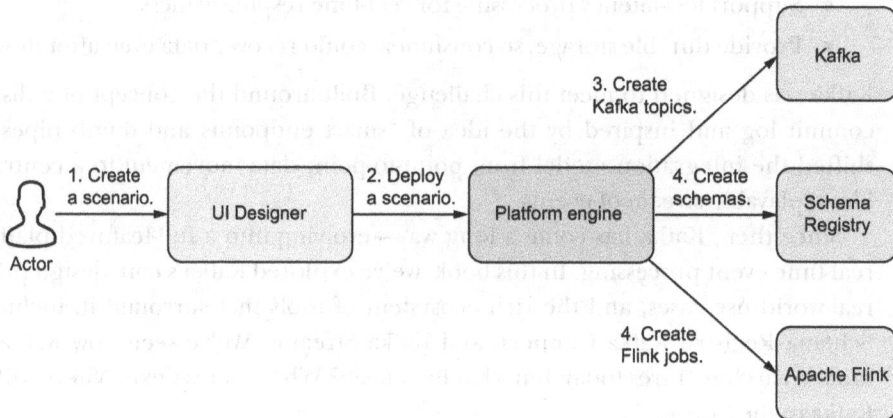

Figure 12.1   Creating a streaming workflow. The user defines a workflow using a visual or declarative tool, and then deploys it to a streaming platform. As part of the deployment process, all necessary artifacts, such as Kafka topics, schema definitions, and Apache Flink jobs, are automatically generated and provisioned.

Some platforms, such as Nussknacker (https://nussknacker.io) and Quix (https://quix.io), use Kafka as the underlying integration backbone. Others, like Apache StreamPipes (https://streampipes.apache.org), support integration with a variety of messaging systems through plugin architectures. These systems are usually composed of multiple microservices communicating over the messaging layer. The typical workflow follows this pattern:

1 Develop a microservice implementing the desired algorithm, either visually or by defining logic through configuration files, using predefined constructs and libraries.

2 Deploy the scenario using platform tools, which package the application automatically, deploy it as a container, and create the necessary artifacts—such as Kafka topics—without requiring manual intervention.

The general trend is clear: integration with Kafka is moving to a higher level of abstraction. Instead of treating Kafka purely as a low-level messaging system, modern platforms increasingly position it as a technical backbone—a foundation for building and orchestrating distributed services. The focus is shifting from managing individual topics and messages toward modeling business processes, automating deployments, and accelerating delivery. As these tools mature, Kafka will not only power event-driven architectures behind the scenes, but will also become a central component of declarative, developer-friendly platforms designed to simplify the creation of complex, real-time applications.

12.2 Integration with new runtimes

So far, we've discussed Kafka primarily in the context of traditional architectures, where applications are deployed as microservices and Kafka serves as the messaging layer for integration. This model has become a standard approach in many modern systems. However, the computing landscape is evolving. New runtimes, such as serverless environments, WebAssembly (WASM) execution, and edge computing platforms, are reshaping how applications are built and deployed. The question arises: How does Kafka fit into these emerging paradigms?

12.2.1 Kafka with WebAssembly

Today, most web application frontends are built using frameworks based on languages such as JavaScript or TypeScript. These frameworks offer flexibility and ease of development, but what happens when their performance is not sufficient? This is where WebAssembly (WASM) enters the picture (https://webassembly.org).

The concept of running code inside the browser is not new. One of the early attempts was the creation of Java applets—small Java programs loaded into browsers to add interactivity to web pages. However, this approach has never been widely adopted. Applets suffered from significant security concerns, required the presence of a Java Runtime Environment on the client side, and depended on browser plugins, making them cumbersome and fragile.

Today, the idea has been reborn in the form of WebAssembly. WASM enables developers to write code in languages like C, C++, or Rust, and compile it into a compact, binary format that can be executed by most modern browsers. *WebAssembly* offers near-native performance and eliminates many obstacles that limited earlier approaches. It allows developers to run complex logic in the browser as efficiently as if it were installed locally (figure 12.2).

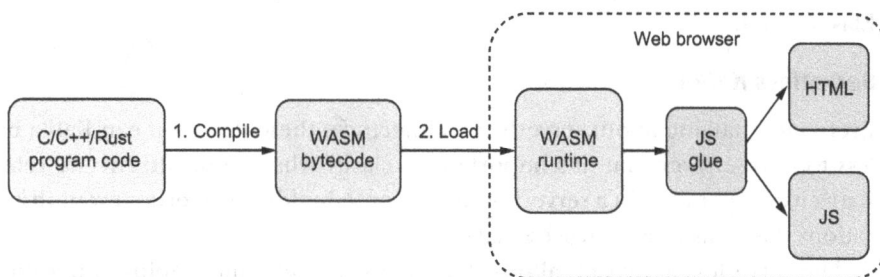

Figure 12.2 WASM programs are compiled into a lightweight runtime that executes alongside JavaScript in the browser. WASM interacts with HTML indirectly by invoking JavaScript functions to access the DOM or browser APIs.

This raises an exciting question: If we can run high-performance code in the browser, can we also connect directly to Kafka?

At first glance, the answer seems promising. However, Kafka communicates over its own binary protocol on the TCP layer, and browsers inherently do not support raw TCP connections—they are limited to HTTP and WebSocket protocols. Simply compiling an existing Kafka client library into WASM is not enough to bridge this gap.

It is worth noting that it is possible to communicate with Kafka through the REST Proxy, which exposes an HTTP-based interface. However, this approach is not without its own considerations and may not be suitable for all use cases.

The integration of Kafka with WebAssembly is still in its early stages. While no mainstream Kafka features are built on WASM today, the idea is gaining significant attention across the community. Several experiments and prototype projects are exploring how WebAssembly could extend and enhance Kafka-based architectures.

One area of exploration is broker-side processing. Projects like Redpanda's Data Transforms (www.redpanda.com/blog/wasm-architecture) demonstrate how lightweight, secure event transformations can be performed directly inside the broker using uploaded WASM modules. Similar concepts could eventually be applied to Kafka itself, enabling filtering, enrichment, or routing logic to run closer to the data, safely and without modifying core broker behavior.

Another active discussion centers on browser-side applications. With WASM enabling high-performance code execution in browsers, there is growing interest in allowing frontend applications, compiled to WASM, to interact directly with Kafka. Experiments using WebSocket-based Kafka proxies have shown that browser-based clients can send and receive Kafka events, overcoming the limitations of native TCP protocols.

Outside of core Kafka, WASM is increasingly being explored as a way to embed custom logic into data pipelines. Its sandboxed execution model and cross-language support make it a compelling option for extending real-time stream processing systems in a safe and portable manner.

While these approaches remain largely experimental, they open new possibilities: enabling frontend applications and distributed components to interact with Kafka directly, without requiring intermediate storage systems such as databases or Elasticsearch.

12.2.2 Serverless Kafka

Everyone is talking about serverless architectures these days, but can Kafka be serverless too? To answer that, it's important to clarify what we mean: Are we referring to Kafka itself operating in a serverless model, or to building serverless event-driven applications that consume or process Kafka data?

The serverless approach allows developers to build and deploy applications without managing the underlying infrastructure. In earlier chapters, we discussed running Kafka as a managed cloud service. With most cloud providers, this means you're freed from hardware maintenance and broker patching, but you still need to provision brokers, create topics, and configure partitions. You pay for a dedicated cluster, even if it's not fully utilized.

Serverless Kafka takes this abstraction one step further. While you still define topics—typically just by name and with a few basic settings—you no longer need to worry about brokers, partitions, or capacity planning. The platform automatically handles scaling, failover, and throughput optimization. Most importantly, billing is based on actual usage, such as volume of data processed, rather than on preallocated infrastructure like VMs or broker instances. For steady, high-throughput workloads, provisioned clusters are usually cheaper; for bursty workloads or many small workloads, serverless can be more cost-effective.

Crucially, behind the scenes, it's still Kafka—the same protocol, the same topics, the same semantics. You're not using some Kafka-compatible layer or different product; you're using real Kafka, just delivered in a way that aligns with the principles of serverless computing.

Another important aspect is serverless event processing. Traditionally, data processing applications are long-running services that continuously poll for new data and apply processing logic whenever an event arrives. However, stream-processing code itself can also be made serverless.

In a serverless model, *function-as-a-service* (FaaS) platforms, such as AWS Lambda, allow you to run small, self-contained units of code that are triggered by events. The function starts when an event occurs, it processes the event, optionally produces a result (or sends it downstream), and then shuts down. Developers can focus purely on writing the processing logic, without worrying about provisioning, scaling, or maintaining the runtime infrastructure.

Figure 12.3 illustrates one of the common patterns in which HTTP requests are transformed and published to Kafka. This approach is especially well-suited for stateless processing, where each event can be handled independently without maintaining context across invocations.

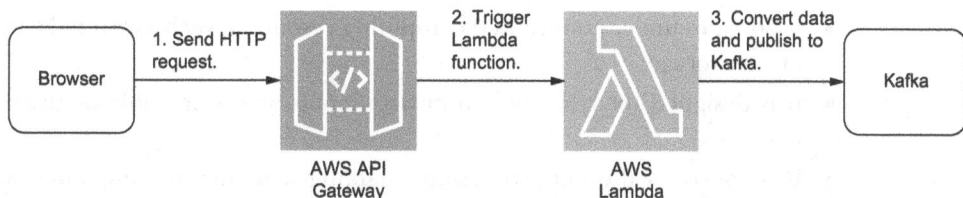

Figure 12.3   Using Lambda functions to publish events. When an HTTP request is received, it triggers a Lambda function that processes the request and publishes the resulting data to a Kafka topic.

While serverless event processing offers simplicity and elastic scalability, it also introduces several important limitations. One common drawback is cold start latency—serverless functions may take time to initialize if they haven't been invoked recently, which can delay event processing.

More critically, Kafka's internal model is built around long-lived consumers that maintain partition ownership and manage offsets. Serverless functions, being short-lived and stateless, are not well suited for this model. Frequent instantiations or rebalancing can lead to performance degradation and coordination overhead.

When dealing with stateful processing, where the logic depends on maintaining context across events, serverless functions require integration with external state stores (e.g., Redis, DynamoDB). This adds complexity and can introduce latency and consistency challenges.

Serverless is generally unsuitable for core Kafka consumption, where you need steady partition ownership, low latency, stateful joins and aggregates, or exactly-once semantics. These workloads are better handled by traditional long-running services or dedicated stream processing frameworks such as Kafka Streams or Apache Flink.

12.2.3 *Kafka at the edge*

In the previous chapters, we explored various options for running Kafka both on-premises and in the cloud. However, these two deployment models—on-premises, where Kafka is managed within a private data center, and in the cloud, where Kafka is provided as a managed service—both typically involve centralized infrastructure. Some use cases demand that Kafka be deployed even closer to the source of events, such as when low latency is critical, when data must be processed locally due to security or compliance concerns, or when the connection to the central data center is intermittent or unreliable.

Technically, this often means deploying a small Kafka cluster directly on-site—whether that's in a factory, a vehicle, a retail location, or an industrial gateway. This deployment model is commonly referred to as *Kafka at the edge*, and it has several defining characteristics:

- It is deployed outside centralized infrastructure, typically close to sensors or devices.
- It operates under constrained computing resources, such as limited CPU, memory, or storage.
- It is designed for resilience in environments with unreliable or disconnected networks.
- It supports local event processing, enabling real-time filtering, enrichment, or alerting at the edge.
- It can forward data to a central Kafka cluster in the cloud or data center when connectivity becomes available.

The architecture is shown in figure 12.4.

To integrate edge deployments with centralized systems, common patterns include using MirrorMaker or Cluster Linking to replicate data from edge Kafka clusters to

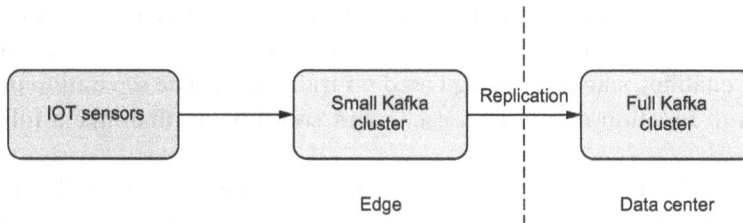

Figure 12.4 The data is replicated from the small cluster at the edge to the full cluster in the data center.

central ones. MirrorMaker is an open source Kafka tool that replicates topics between clusters by consuming from one and producing to another, offering basic cross-cluster replication. Cluster Linking, available in Confluent Platform, provides a more integrated and real-time replication mechanism by linking clusters directly at the broker level without requiring consumers or producers. These tools enable local processing at the edge while ensuring that critical data is eventually available in the cloud or data center for aggregation, analytics, and long-term storage.

12.3 Diskless Kafka: Decoupling storage from brokers

In Kafka's traditional architecture, the broker is stateful—it encompasses both the server process and the local data storage. While this design offers performance and simplicity, it raises several concerns, particularly in cloud environments:

- Disks are expensive, especially when used for high-throughput storage.
- Cross-zone replication in cloud environments incurs significant ingress and egress costs, as Kafka replicates data between brokers.

In chapter 5, we examined the architecture of Apache Pulsar, which separates message serving from long-term storage. This decoupled model enables better elasticity and cost optimization. In cloud-native infrastructure, where object storage (such as Amazon S3 or Google Cloud Storage) is significantly cheaper than attached disks, the same separation is being considered for Kafka.

This direction is formalized in KIP-1150 (https://cwiki.apache.org/confluence/display/KAFKA/KIP-1150%3A+Diskless+Topics), which, at the time of writing, is still under discussion. The proposal introduces the concept of diskless topics, where data is stored exclusively in remote object storage rather than on the broker's local disk. Crucially, the Kafka client API remains unchanged, so producers and consumers interact with diskless topics exactly as they would with traditional ones.

Initially, diskless topics will come with certain limitations:

- Log compaction will not be supported.
- Transactional writes will be disabled.

However, these constraints are expected to be temporary, as ongoing work is under way to address them in future iterations of the design.

Despite these early limitations, the architecture offers compelling benefits. When brokers are freed from maintaining persistent local state, they can be spun up or down dynamically, enabling stateless scaling based on traffic load. The separation of storage allows Kafka to function more like a cache and coordinator, than like a full stateful server.

When a broker receives a batch of records from a producer, it writes the data to remote storage. Since storage is now shared and accessible, any broker can serve read requests, eliminating the need for partition leaders. Kafka's traditional replication layer is no longer needed, as durability and availability are now handled by the object storage itself.

But if Kafka no longer maintains a local sequential log, how is message ordering preserved? In this model, ordering is maintained through metadata. A new component called the *batch coordinator* tracks where each batch is stored and assigns offsets. Brokers report batch metadata to the batch coordinator, which builds a consistent offset stream. When a consumer fetches data, it first contacts the batch coordinator to resolve the correct batch locations. An example of a producer path is shown in figure 12.5.

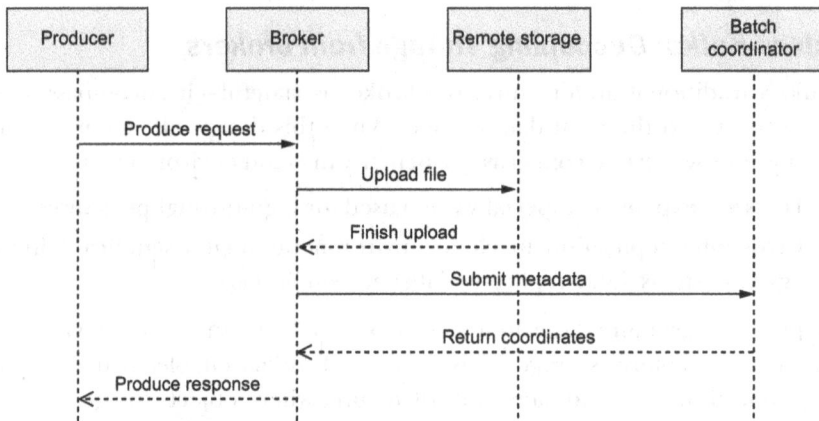

Figure 12.5   Producer path in diskless Kafka

This shift in architecture brings a trade-off: reduced storage costs and improved elasticity at the cost of increased read latency, since data must be fetched from remote storage rather than from a local disk. Still, for many cloud-native workloads, this trade-off is acceptable, especially when throughput, scale-out, and cost-efficiency are top priorities.

12.4   *Kafka in AI/ML world*

Traditionally, machine learning systems were built on batch data. Models were trained on historical datasets, updated periodically, and deployed into production with static feature sets. This approach was effective when the cost of delay was low—when decisions could tolerate being hours or days out of date.

Today, that assumption no longer holds. Businesses increasingly demand real-time insights, low-latency decisions, and continuous adaptation. Whether it's fraud detection, personalized recommendations, or anomaly monitoring, the value of machine learning now depends on how quickly it can react to fresh data.

This is where Kafka enters the picture. With its ability to capture and distribute streams of events in real time, Kafka forms the backbone of modern architectures that support live model inference, incremental learning, and feedback-driven optimization.

12.4.1 Incremental learning

The most widely used approach to creating a machine learning (ML) model is to train it on previously collected (historical) data. This process generally follows these steps:

1 *Clean and normalize static data*—Raw data often contains missing values, errors, or inconsistencies. Cleaning ensures the data is accurate and complete. Normalization scales values into a standard range, which helps algorithms learn effectively.

2 *Define input features and the target variable (learning class)*—The data includes multiple columns (features). One of them is selected as the target—the value the model is supposed to predict, such as predicting whether a user will click on an ad.

3 *Split the data into training and test subsets*—The dataset is divided into two parts:

   a Training data is used to teach the model patterns in the data.

   b Test data is used to evaluate how well the model performs on unseen examples.

4 *Build a model*—Involves choosing a machine learning algorithm (like decision trees, neural networks, etc.) and configuring it.

5 *Train and evaluate the model*—The algorithm learns from the training data. Then it's tested on the test data to measure accuracy, precision, and other performance metrics.

Once these steps are complete, the trained model is ready to make predictions on new, unseen data.

Model training is typically separated from model deployment. When a model is integrated with streaming data, it refers to a real-time setup, like this:

- The model is trained and saved ahead of time.
- It is then deployed to a model server—a dedicated service that hosts the model and handles prediction requests.
- When a new event (data record) arrives from a real-time source (like Kafka), the application
  - Extracts relevant data from the event.
  - Sends it to the model server.
  - Receives a prediction in response.

Modern ML frameworks such as TensorFlow Serving (www.tensorflow.org), MLflow (https://mlflow.org), or Seldon (www.seldon.io) support native Kafka integration.

They can consume events directly from Kafka topics, process them, and publish the prediction results to another topic. This process is shown in figure 12.6.

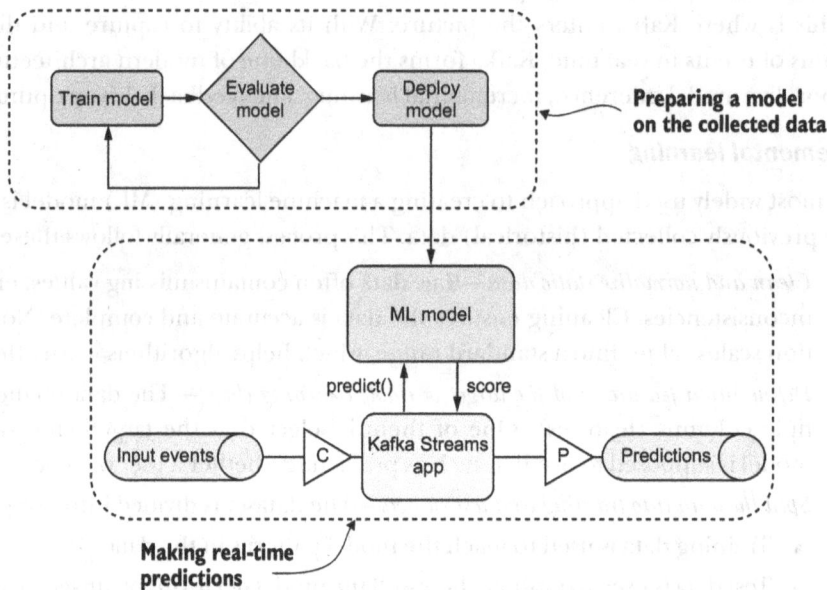

Figure 12.6   The ML model is deployed in advance and is used by the Kafka Streams application for predictions.

In some cases, Kafka is used not just for real-time predictions, but also to feed training data into the model-building pipeline. That is, a separate system reads data from a Kafka topic and uses it to generate datasets for training. While technically different, this method still follows the same basic approach: data is collected, stored, and then used for training a model in batch.

Incremental (or online) learning represents a powerful shift in how machine learning models evolve within real-time systems. Unlike traditional approaches that rely on static datasets and periodic retraining, *incremental learning* allows a model to adapt continuously, updating its parameters as new data arrives, typically in small, manageable batches.

This process is illustrated in figure 12.7, where the model is directly connected to a Kafka topic and receives a stream of events. A Kafka consumer reads these events in small batches and feeds them into the model. The model then updates itself using each batch, so it gradually learns from new information as it becomes available.

Such an architecture is especially well-suited for applications like fraud detection, real-time personalization, or operational monitoring, where things can change quickly and the model needs to keep up with those changes. Instead of waiting for scheduled

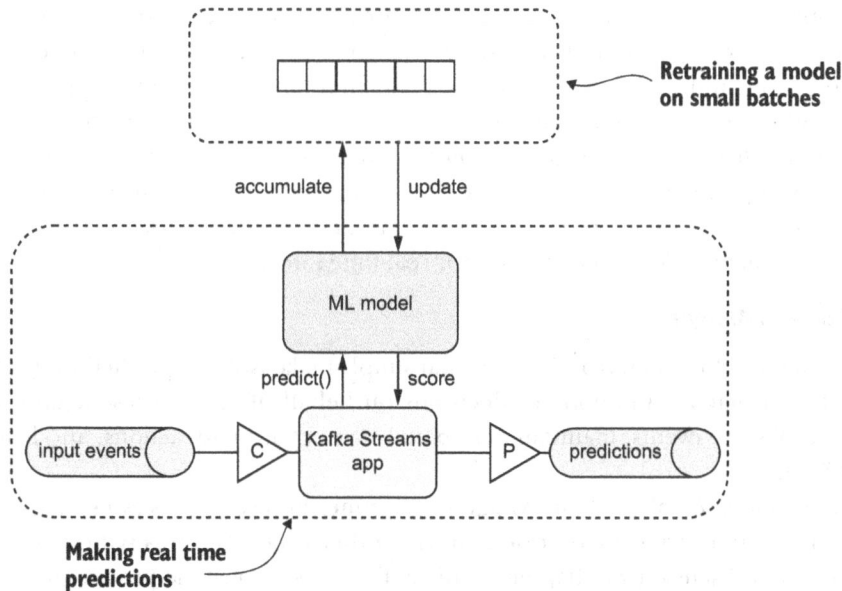

Figure 12.7 Retraining a machine learning model incrementally

retraining sessions, the model learns continuously, which helps it stay accurate and useful as new data flows in.

Incremental learning also brings practical benefits. Since it doesn't require storing vast historical datasets, it can reduce infrastructure costs and simplify compliance with data retention policies. The model learns from what's arriving now—and once data has been consumed, it can be discarded.

Naturally, this approach introduces some trade-offs. The system must be designed carefully to guard against concept drift and the accumulation of bias or noise. Moreover, because training happens over streaming data, it may be more difficult to audit or reproduce specific model decisions, especially if the consumed data isn't archived.

Still, when properly designed and monitored, incremental learning offers a compelling architecture for adaptive, long-running applications, combining scalability, relevance, and efficiency in one continuous learning cycle.

12.4.2 Feature engineering in motion

In machine learning, features represent the relevant characteristics of data used to train predictive models. In traditional datasets, features typically correspond to columns and are defined statically. For example, when building a model to predict customer churn, useful features might include the number of logins, average session duration, or time since last login.

However, in event-driven systems, the raw data arrives as a stream of discrete events. Transforming these events into meaningful features often requires streaming computation techniques. For instance, features like clicks per session or average order value over the last 10 minutes must be calculated continuously, using time-windowed aggregations and session-based grouping—techniques discussed in chapter 8.

Another practical use of Kafka in the ML workflow is to act as a feature store. Once computed, feature values can be published to a Kafka topic, where they are available for consumption by downstream systems. Compacted topics, in particular, can serve as a reliable and up-to-date repository of the latest feature values keyed by entity (such as user ID), enabling low-latency access for real-time inference.

12.4.3 Kafka and AI agents

We've come a long way, from systems that simply make isolated predictions to *AI agents* capable of making autonomous decisions on behalf of users. These agents must be able to observe events, maintain contextual state, coordinate actions, and learn from feedback.

At a fundamental level, an AI agent consumes an event, processes it, and emits a resulting action, typically represented as another event. But this pattern should feel familiar. As discussed in chapter 8, this is the classic consume-process-produce flow that underpins streaming applications. In this sense, an AI agent fits naturally into the stream-aware paradigm:

1 It subscribes to Kafka topics to receive observations or signals.
2 It maintains internal state by continuously processing event streams.
3 It emits new events representing decisions or actions, which may trigger downstream responses.

The second point is especially critical: maintaining context. Agents must make decisions based not only on the current event, but also on a continuously evolving understanding of the world. This is where Kafka plays a crucial role. By subscribing to relevant event streams, an agent can keep its state up to date with minimal latency, enabling real-time decision-making.

Kafka thus becomes the shared memory and coordination layer for distributed agents, allowing them to operate independently, interact asynchronously, and scale without tight coupling or centralized orchestration.

Summary

- Kafka's role has expanded far beyond messaging infrastructure, evolving into a central platform for event-driven architecture and modern system design.
- Kafka can serve as a foundation for orchestration, enabling developers to model workflows and business logic with greater speed and abstraction, often supported by low-code and declarative tooling.
- Kafka is adapting to emerging runtimes, such as WebAssembly, serverless environments, and edge computing platforms, showing its flexibility in supporting next-generation deployment models.

- The proposal for diskless Kafka marks a significant architectural shift, enabling Kafka to decouple compute from storage, reduce cloud costs, and scale more efficiently in dynamic environments.
- Kafka is ready to play a critical role in machine learning systems, acting as the backbone for real-time inference pipelines, incremental learning processes, and continuous feature delivery.
- Kafka enables the construction of distributed AI agents, serving as a coordination layer that allows agents to observe, decide, and act autonomously through streams of events.
- Together, these trends point to a future where Kafka is not just a log, but the nervous system of intelligent, reactive systems that can adapt, respond, and evolve in real time.

index